LETTERS FROM CALIFORNIA

LETTERS
from
CALIFORNIA

or

He Married Me for My Drapes

Norma E. Davidson

CR **PANY**

"My True Love Drove Me Nuts in 12 Days"
by Gary Bogue used by permission of
Contra Costa Newspapers, Walnut Creek, CA 94598

For Information contact:
Creative Arts Book Company
833 Bancroft Way
Berkeley, California 94710

ISBN 0-88739-113-3
Library of Congress Catalog Number 96-71030

Printed in the United States of America

For Gene,
both husband and son-in-law,
par excellence

Dis cue ca !

Note from the Author

These letters were all actually sent to friends and relatives. Nothing is fictional. However, in order to protect the privacy and sensitivity of some individuals, I have changed first names and omitted last names.

Acknowledgments

Publishing a book is sort of like having a baby.

Firstly it takes two — mother, the author and father, the publisher. Prior to this there is the courtship and this corresponds to all those letters of query and letters with sample pages of the book. These are the blind dates when suitors either don't show up (literary agents who don't respond even when stamped self addressed envelopes are included) or suitors bluntly reject or a very few suitors who gently say the subject isn't in their field but urge you to keep writing. The latter are like a couple who enjoy each others company but there is no spark. Sometimes this takes years and in my case it took two years before I realized that literary agents were a dead end for me and I decided courtship was futile and resigned myself to being an old maid with no baby, (translate book).

Then one day while at the library I consulted the San Francisco and Berkeley phone books for names of small press publishers and I wrote a few of them. To my delight one responded and asked me to come for an interview with no promise of publishing my manuscript. Finally I had found a father for my book (baby). Donald Ellis of Creative Arts Book Company. Actual incubation of the book takes almost the same time as a pregnancy. Don's helpful assistance, direction, and collaboration have made this an interesting task. I thank Don Ellis for believing in me and taking a chance with a first time writer.

Along the way there have been others who tried to be helpful, like the lab technicians and nurses in a doctor's office. I really wanted a piece of my drapery material to display and wrote Weekly Home Fashion Newspaper to see if they knew the manufacturer of my material. Jeff put a notice in their publication and I had telephone calls from HFN staff, Donna Boyle Schwartz and Jeff, - Covington Fabrics, -Abby Gilmore, Dean Rorvig, Brenda Arrington - Kravet Fabrics, Cary Kravet and readers Maurey Lauren, Irvin Levine, Larry Pearsons and Barry Simon.

Locally, interior decorators, Russ Simoni, Bill Quataroli and the owner and staff of Fretwells Ethan Allen Furniture store tried to be helpful. Alas. all to no avail. Nobody seems to have this discontinued, long ago made fabric.

Lastly, I want to thank my husband, Gene, who believed in me, encouraged me and put up with my lack of companionship as I sat constantly before a computer.

On May 15, 1997 Norma Davidson and her cooperative husband, Gene, announce the birth of LETTERS FROM CALIFORNIA OR HE MARRIED ME FOR MY DRAPES.

"One of the pleasures of reading old letters is the knowledge that they need no answer."

LORD BYRON

Table of Contents

Featuring, Among Other Things:

FOREWORD He married me for my drapes xv

The 1970's

Easter lilies 1
    Easter egg accident,
    Ann Arbor,
    Move to California
Drought 10
    Bedroom power shortage,
    Pier 39,
    Bechtel

The 1980's

Eugene O'Neill's Tao House 16
    Japanese consul General's house
Woody Hayes 22
    Streaker,
    Ant invasion
California virus 32
    Queen of England's visit
Breadbaking 40
    Earthquakes,
    Preparing for Africa,
    Yakoff Smirnof
21st anniversary 56
    Unplanned African sojourn
Mother's fracture 70
    Retirement,
    Bridge party in the dark
Beach Blanket Babylon 75
    Earthquake,
    Emergency hospitalization
A baby for us! 86
    Luggage tags
Nurses week 93
    Gold sweater,
    A unique Christmas present

Chez Panisse.. 102
    Mother's 93rd birthday
Return of baby 107
    Garage sale,
    Wong disappearance
Accident in France.. 112
    Party in England,
    What's new in honeymoons
Toby hospitalized 118
    Roger and black dog
Toby and classic thunderbird 124
    Heard, Hurd, Herod,
    Baking for a dog
Our baby returns 144
    Persian rug,
    Garage doors up and down on own
Flour catastrophe 155
    The BIG ONE ?
    Kate again
Santa and chimney 166
    My True Love Drove Me Nuts in 12 Days

The 1990's

Valentine 177
    A sewerage plant named Trojan 2000
4 water bills for same period.. 179
    Wedding and baseball game
Leon's sitting duck accident 190
    Hal's safe deposit story
What happened to lost and found 206
    Diane's art museum wedding
Molly's 3rd birthday party.. 216
    $1000 yard material
A Chinese funeral 221
    Little lost girls,
    Flying saucer hits Gene
Medical diagnosis 785.5 239
    Molly's kisses,
    PSA and tears,
    California marriages dangerous to your health
Nitty gritty of Gene's surgery 250
    Kate and tooth fairy,
    Interior decoration

Mother dies.. 263
Balloons at California memorial service
Kay does a Mary Poppins 277
Hing to Kaiser,
Best compliment
Betty Beale's book 287
Red Eggs and Ginger party
Neva and children in Italy... 301
Molly and tooth fairy,
Gene a father ??
Vacation back East.. 305
Hospital stay in California,
O.J. verdict

Foreword

He Married Me for my Drapes

Never in my life did I ever want, hope or plan to live in California.
A Christmas card did it, changed my life completely.

In December of 1963 I decided to weed out my Christmas card list. Over the years acquaintances with whom I had lost personal contact sent cards and I returned cards. This year I determined to send only to friends and acquaintances with whom I had contact , either occasionally or regularly.

One name on the list was a former boyfriend, Eugene Davidson, whom I met in the fall of 1954 and dated till the end of June, 1955 when I returned home to Geneva, N.Y. for the summer. I would not have been surprised to receive a proposal on our last date. Nothing happened and Gene refused my invitation to visit me at my parents' home. He didn't phone or write. I didn't understand this at that time. I felt ten months was long enough for a courtship. Upon my return to Niagara Falls in the fall, I immediately met other fellows and Gene and I were never a twosome again, although we were often in the same group, going square dancing, camping and attending club meetings. Gene changed jobs and moved to Clarence where he bought a house. I bought a house in Niagara Falls where I was a school librarian. For most of the nine years our only contact was this yearly Christmas card.

When I came to Gene's name, I decided to send one last card and on it I wrote that this would be my last Christmas card to him since we no longer had any contact.

Home I went for Christmas vacation and upon my return there was a one sentence "letter" from Gene, asking to see me as soon as possible. I was surprised but I responded that not till the end of January would I be free because I was going home each weekend to help a widowed friend, with children, who was hospitalized. Back came another "one sentence letter" saying Gene would come and take me to dinner on a certain date. The day arrived and we did have a lovley dinner and caught up on each others news. Gene's father had died and his mother, ill and frail, was living with him. At the conclusion of this date Gene made another date. After this I invited him to have dinner with me at my house. That night, he asked me to come, as a favor, to visit his mother who knew not a person in Clarence. Frankly, I was curious about Gene's house. I never attended any of the parties Gene had for the club to which we both belonged, but which I now seldom attended. Friends described Gene's house as nice, furniture attractive but not homelike. Something was lacking.

So the first Saturday in February I drove over. My visit lasted about an hour and then I left and on my way back I stopped at a couple malls. Several stores really interested me. One carried shoes in my narrow width.

On February 13th , 1964 Gene again took me to dinner and when we returned to my house, Gene proposed. I didn't say yes and I didn't say no. I said I wanted time to think about this, maybe even a month. Gene took his diamond back home with him. Before he left, I asked him to come on Sunday and have dinner with my parents and me at a favorite Niagara Falls Inn. It was my mother's birthday and my parents were visiting me for the weekend.

Nine years ago after a courtship of nine months, Gene wasn't ready for marriage and now after 5 dates in 4 weeks, he was. But was I ready for marriage ? I liked my job, my house and my life style. Marriage is always a gamble, especially for two never before married , older people. On February 14th I borrowed books from the library on marriage, not sex. I learned that there were three things that might cause our marriage to fail, so this possible marriage had three strikes against it before it even began. I had to weigh this against Gene's character which was kind, dependable, trustworthy and admirable.

As soon as my parents arrived on Saturday, I told them of the proposal They had met Gene nine years ago but knew nothing of the reunion. They had liked Gene but they were hesitant, as was I.

Sunday was a terrible day. It was snowing and the wind was blowing hard. The snow plows could only keep the main arteries plowed. Gene was supposed to arrive at noon, but he did not appear. Gene is an on time person. I wondered out loud why he didn't appear. My father suggested that maybe he had changed his mind and wouldn't appear. Until that moment, I still didn't know whether I was going to accept or decline his proposal. Suddenly I knew I wanted to marry Gene. Our relationship resumed as if those nine intervening years had never been.

After my parents left, I told Gene I accepted his proposal. We set the date for the wedding, June 27, 1964. We chose the Washington birthday holiday to select the setting for the diamond. Gene said I had to give up my job and move into his house. He wanted only the drapes in my living room and dining room and my refrigerator, which was newer than his. I wanted my furniture. I was adamant about my furniture and it almost canceled the marriage. Gene suggested a marriage counselor but I said I was not entering a marriage where every time a problem came up, we had to see a marriage counselor. Gene gave in.

From June 1964 till September 1972 we were happy in Gene's house. In fact, I wanted never to move from that house but Westinghouse began downsizing some departments and Gene had to search for other employment. He finally was hired by Bechtel and we moved to Ann Arbor, Michigan where a new office for power plant design and construction was being established. Suddenly in 1974 power companies canceled their power plant orders. Gene was transferred to the San Francisco office.

Gene came in December of 1974 but I waited to sell our house in Ann Arbor. This wasn't easy because 1000 Bechtel employees moved from Ann Arbor, so approximately 1000 houses went on sale at the same time. Competition was fierce. Without a sale of the Ann Arbor house, we decided I would move to California. We had purchased a house in Concord, California. The day before the movers came, the house sold. My mother and I arrived March 13th by plane. Gene greeted us with the news that it had snowed that day. SNOW ! So unusual was this that the headline in the newspaper and all the first page was devoted to a description of this snow that fell and melted within minutes.

Having been married thirty-three years, I now understand my husband better than during our courtship. I know why he didn't write me during the summer of 1955. He NEVER writes a letter. Why didn't he call? He is silent, quiet, deliberate, thoughtful and he uses no excess words. Gene doesn't initiate conversation and he is not a phone talking person.

We compliment each other. I talk and I write letters. This collection of letters over the past twenty years tells of a happy marriage , in spite of obstacles and circumstances that have befallen us. Both of us are glad we married each other and the only regret we have is that we let the nine years intervene between courtship and marriage.

Maybe I should have weeded out my Christmas card list earlier.

LETTERS FROM CALIFORNIA

The 1970's

Easter Lilies

Easter Egg Accident, Ann Arbor, Move to California

Dear Isabel,

Never have I had such an Easter!

I was asked to arrange the Easter lilies at the nearby Presbyterian Church, which I joined when we moved to Ann Arbor. I said yes.

So Saturday afternoon Gene and I went over to the church and the janitor let us in. It is a sad fact that churches have to be locked when there is no activity in the church.

We took with us some corrugated cylinders that Gene has been bringing home from Bechtel this past year. They appeared daily in the trash. Paper comes rolled up on these cylinders. They are so strong you can stand on them and they won't break. Gene asked if I could do anything with them and I didn't know at the time but we had lots of storage space in the cellar so I said to bring them home. Now I had a use for them.

Both of us were dumfounded when we saw those many, many pots of lilies, all with unopened blossoms. The janitor said the florist explained that this had been a really cold spring and the hot houses didn't warm up enough for the blossoms to open in time for Easter. What to do? Nothing we could do so we set to work and arranged one row along the front of the altar. Behind and between those we positioned the cylinders and placed a pot on each. In this way the lilies of each pot would show individually and what a spectacle it would be had they all been open. Our job done we, rather disappointedly, went home.

Easter we three went to church and three or four buds had opened. During the service lots of buds opened. Nobody looked at the minister. They may have heard the sermon but all eyes were on those lilies as they slowly burst open.

After the service people congregated in the lobby and one person after another came up to me and this is what they said.

"Norma, how clever you are to arrange for the lilies to open during the service."

"Norma, I couldn't keep my eyes off those lilies. How appropriate to the occasion."

"Norma, you are the first person to arrange such a spectacle"

I'm sure I don't have to tell you any more. You get the drift. I was being congratulated for the lilies performance during the service. It wasn't I who should have been complimented. It was the janitor. When he saw the condition of the lilies, he decided to turn on the heat and leave it on the rest of the day and all night, about 20 hours.

So a calamity turned into a success.

I hope I'm not asked to arrange the lilies next year because I can't reproduce this. What can the arranger next year do to top this?

Mid-westerners are extremely friendly and in the short time we have lived here, I've made many friends. Now people who haven't known me will remember me, all because of those Easter lilies.

MAY 25, 1973

Dear Phyllis,

You haven't heard from me in some time and here is the reason.

On the 26th of April I decided to put away our Easter egg collection. Gene left for Bechtel at 7:50 and I went down cellar to get the boxes we store the eggs in.

Since most of you haven't visited us in Ann Arbor, you don't know the layout of our house. We have an open stairway down to a recreation room which the former owner made into something resembling an out-door cafe with a colored window and door that goes into the other half of our eighty foot cellar. We have some of my mother's furniture down there and a sofa bed and a nice thick rug we brought from our former house. At the far wall in front of the window Gene has his telescope which is stored in two seven feet long wooden boxes. I have a throw over them and it sort of looks like a bleacher.

Last week I went down to the recreation room and I smelled wet wool. I put my hand on the rug and it was sopping wet. I told Gene about this and over the weekend he went down. He didn't know where the water was coming from. This is a new house so no pipes should have broken. He took off part of the paneling on the front side of the house and found that the cellar wall had a crack from top to bottom and the water was coming in this crack. He moved his telescope to in front of the door to the cellar. I had not been down cellar and didn't know this.

So when going for the egg boxes, I went down cellar without turning on the light and walked across the recreation room and fell over the boxed telescope.

I was knocked out. When I came to, my left arm hurt terribly. My nose seemed to be running but it was sticky. I didn't have a cold. I managed to get upstairs and into my mother's bedroom. I shook her bed with my knee because I didn't seem to be able to talk. She woke and saw me standing there with blood coming from my nose and from my forehead. "Call Gene," is all I could get out. She was excited and nervous and had quite some time. Gene had just entered his office and somebody else had taken his call. Without taking off his coat, Gene left for home.

I had been going to an orthopedist so Gene called his office. He was told the doctor was at St. Joseph's Hospital and to take me there. In my nightie and robe we went. I had a broken elbow. I had a big gash on my forehead and my eye was swollen. Next day I had a black eye and cheek. The doctor thought I might also have a concussion. My elbow was put in a partial cast, which the doctor called a cradle. I was cleaned up and sent home.

By afternoon we knew I had had a concussion. My seventy nine year old mother had never seen me in such a state and she watched me every moment. I lay on the sofa in the living room all the rest of the day.

Somehow the minister heard of my mishap and the next morning the doorbell rang and it was the minister. What a sight he saw! A face he couldn't recognize., arm in cast and body stretched out on the sofa.

Saturday Gene took my picture. We had to preserve this.

So I haven't been writing letters, driving the car or doing much on my own. People have been kind and have taken me to AAUW, Bible study, book group, ikebana, garden club and church functions.

We had planned a weekend in Holland, Michigan to see the tulip festival and we decided to do this. Gene took Friday off and we drove to Holland. We watched the parade on Saturday and drove around to see the tulips and came back on Sunday. My left arm was still in the partial cast.

The doctor said he wanted protection but some movement so that is why he had me in a half cast. With a full cast, I might not be able to use my elbow when the cast came off.

Yesterday I saw the orthopedist again and I'm not wearing the partial cast, just the sling. I have to be careful but I must move the elbow a bit.

We sent my picture to Gene's sister and his lawyer brother-in-law said that if ever I wanted a divorce, he could get me one based upon that picture. All he had to say was that Gene did this to me. In a way, that is right but I really did it to myself by not turning on the light. Darn that telescope!

NOV. 8, 1973

Dear Raedina and Milton,

We have lived in Ann Arbor for 13 full months. In that time I've made some observations which I'll pass on. Michigan is known as the MOTOR STATE and you had better believe it. The roads are crowded with cars, parking lots are filled with late model cars. In fact, our Pontiac is probably the cheapest car in most places where I park. Lincoln Continentals and Cadillacs abound. Part of the reason for this is that the automobile workers can lease cars at very low prices and all expenses, even insurance, but not gasoline, are paid. So for the automobile workers it is probably cheaper to lease and get a new car every year than to buy. Leasing from a car dealer by other than auto workers is much more expensive.

The first question I'm asked when I'm introduced is, "Does your husband work for the University?" The University dominates Ann Arbor and all kinds of cultural advantages result. We take advantage of the Michigan League which is an hotel on campus. It has a lovely cafeteria that serves good food at very reasonable prices, a complete meal is not more than $3.00. Thursday nights are International night and each Thursday the food of a foreign country is featured. Customers are faculty and townspeople and not many students because casual attire and casual manners are forbidden. You would pay at least $8.00 at any other restaurant for the kind of meal you get at the Michigan League. We even take guests there.

This fall I was asked to help with the foreign students. One day in August I was on duty to welcome and answer questions of newly arrived students. We answer all questions, help them shop, help them find places to live, show them how to use the bus system and take care of any emergencies. The international student building has a lovely lounge which is being modernized. All the chairs and sofas are being removed and thick red carpets are being installed in alcoves with big pillows strewn around. So I guess from now on students will sit on the floor. An AAUW fellowship grantee from behind the Iron Curtain was amazed at our volunteer service. She said NEVER would this be offered in her country. She used our service and came back several times to observe us. A Mrs. Tefft was in charge for the two weeks. I could tell immediately that she was both educated and cultured, but I learned later that she was wealthy. She mentioned that she had been asked to write a biography of her father-in-law. I learned that he started Consumers Power which is a very large electric company. I was scanning a book and came upon a biography of Mrs. Teffts. She has apparently been an author for many years. When she speaks of herself, she says she is a farmer's wife. Some farmer's wife!

Gene and I are a host family for a Japanese family, husband, wife, a two year old child and a 13 month child, both girls. The two year old is beautiful with the biggest black eyes I've ever seen. Yesterday when I was with the children they brought me books in Japanese to read to them. I did recognize SNOW WHITE but I was at loss for the other stories. We went through an alphabet book and I learned that dogs do not say bow wow in Japan and neither do cats, cows, sheep, etc. make the same noises we associate with these animals. When I questioned as to what each picture was, I sometimes got an English answer and sometimes a Japanese. I'm ashamed to say I think the children learned the English words but I didn't learn one Japanese word. It was queer to have talking toys speaking Japanese.

Michigan is an integrated state. It doesn't matter whether you buy a $50,000 house or a $100,000 plus house, you will have black neighbors. The new city manager of Ann Arbor just moved into the second house from us. I. will say they wear the most vivid colors, these neighbors of ours. Detroit just selected a black mayor. The state has many officials who are black, secretary of state., state education superintendent, judges, you name it. The University Housing is like the United Nations and this tendency fans out through the whole city.

I'm very impressed with the friendliness of the people I meet. This spring a dentist wife, who is also a dentist, told me to come over one morning and she would give me some plants. She had about 75 iris and she told me to look around and select anything else and she would dig it up for me. I had just mentioned we bought a new house and were having landscaping done. By the way this family bought the Robert Mac Namara house when he went to Washington. This fall a lawyer's wife in Detroit said she was thinning out her garden and I could have some perennials and shrubs. When we went to select our new car, we stopped to pick up the things and we had our whole car trunk filled with plants. She kept bringing things to ikebana and I kept asking names and admiring so that is why she thought to give to me. I've never before known such generosity. The lawyer's wife had purchased all her thing from Wayside Nursery so I really have some lovely things from her. I do think Wayside is one of the best nurseries in the U.S.

Gene is happy in his work. Bechtel was named the foremost engineering company in 1972 and we think it is a feather in Gene's cap to be working for such a company. At present Bechtel is quartered in five buildings in Ann Arbor, but they are erecting a 10 story building here in Ann Arbor. Gene has joined the Professional Engineers Society of Michigan. It was guest night last month and we went for the first time. Guest night means you can bring your wife. It turned out that they decided to allow all new registrants in Michigan to be guests so both our dinners were paid for us. There were more new members than regulars. The dinner was excellent.

I've never been so busy. I've joined so many clubs I hardly have time to clean house. Gene says he is getting used to the dirt! I'm having to refuse offices offered to me. I just don't have the time. I've started doing a little substitute work but I've had to refuse all but three assignments. The last was in Saline and the school library was the most beautiful and best planned I've ever been in. The school itself is sumptuous and is spread over acres. I've been lost every time I went there. In spite of the grandeur, I am told the students have little respect for the property. At least, some don't, but the faculty and administration do. A pretty penny was spent on that one school. I'm anxious to get into the other two in this small community.

This was a very busy summer for Gene. The former owner-builder of our home had landscaped the grounds with STONES. We were a couple months digging up stones. Gene spread 22 square yards of top soil over where the stones were. Then he laid sod on top. We had a landscaper plan our front yard and then we planted the shrubs. After this we painted the house. One side had not been properly prepared and the paint was peeling. We changed the color from a mustard to a pretty yellow. Neighbors and walkers stopped and remarked at how hard Gene had worked. He was usually in the yard by six and worked till dark. This past week the city came and planted three trees in front on Tudor and one on the side on Eton Court. A new house requires a great deal of work.

My mother spent five weeks in Geneva this summer and she loved it. It was so wonderful to see old friends. She has adjusted well to Ann Arbor and made some new friends here.

It seems queer to be writing a Christmas letter because just three days ago, November 5th, we had our first killing frost and until then we had marigolds, dahlias and other annuals in full bloom. It wasn't like this in N.Y. state. Suddenly it has turned cold and we know winter is on the way.

With thoughts of the coming holiday season, I say
MERRY CHRISTMAS AND HAPPY 1974

DECEMBER 5, 1974

Dear Ingrid and Jan,

Things have been happening fast and furiously to the Davidsons. Gene was told on the 13th of November that he is being transferred to the main office at San Francisco. We called a realtor on that night and he came the next day. On the 17th we signed with the realtor. We had open house for realtors on the 21st and the 25th. Gene and I left for California on Thanksgiving morning at 7.

We arrived at 10:19 AM and immediately drove to Walnut Creek, about 25 miles outside San Francisco in the East Bay. We spent the next few days house hunting. AND IT WAS SICKENING! WOW! Prices are terrific. Gene felt he couldn't accept the transfer but would have to find another job, but finally he came to accept the idea that we would have to take a big mortgage in order to get the kind of home we now have. This is distressing, I know, because we almost have this house paid for. We have been looking forward to no mortgage but I guess a job with a big mortgage is better than no job with a small mortgage.

I'm sure you are all aware of the economy. That is why Gene is being transferred. Bechtel had contracts with Detroit Edison and Consumers Power to build 9 power plants. All but two have been cancelled. Seven of the nine are just postponed indefinitely but who knows when they will get around to going full blast again on these plants. So Bechtel has been reducing the number of employees to be kept here in Ann Arbor. I think they had almost twelve hundred before the crisis and they will end up with not more than three hundred employees.

We looked and looked at homes. Anything we could afford was either in such bad shape or so small we wouldn't fit in or else on a main thoroughfare. We looked with a realtor and without and once we found a house we both loved from the outside. We got inside and said this is for us but we soon changed our minds when the price was twice what we were going to sell our house for.

Houses in California do not have cellars or attics. We have so much to store, all my flower arranging stuff, Gene's telescope and all the photographic equipment. We have too many irons in the fire so we have to have room. We finally settled on a new house, five bedrooms, three baths, living room, dining room, family room, kitchen. It is a big house for three persons but at least we will have room for our stuff. My mother will have one bedroom for sleeping and the other for her desk, record player, typewriter and a sofa.

Gene told the realtor that distance would probably prohibit us from having much company, but the realtor said it is amazing how many people come to California and end up as guests. We hope this is true and that we'll have lots of company to fill those five bedrooms.

Our house is two miles from BART and Gene will ride it each day to work. It takes almost an hour to get from Concord to S.F. but BART has a station right near Bechtel.

Our new address will be 2155 Brittany Court, Concord, Ca 94518.

Gene will report for work on January 2nd. I won't be able to leave till the house is sold and I hope this is soon, but houses don't sell well in December. People are too busy with Christmas. Competition will be fierce since almost a thousand houses are going up for sale at the same time. We shall see what happens.

This letter may be a bit disjointed. We have only been back four hours. I have a million things to do and much to think about but I want to get Christmas cards sent so I can concentrate on throwing stuff away, packing and generally getting ready to move.

Have a most happy Christmas and start planning a trip to California.

OCTOBER 29, 1975

Dear Lydia,

Never did either Gene or I plan to live in California, yet here we are doing just that. We have learned considerable with this move and I invite you to bear with me while I give you my impressions and conclusions.

Regarding the people—Californians—are not as friendly as Michiganders. New York Staters rank between the two. Even if you are a stranger, you will find a Michigander opening a conversation, helping you or giving you advice. In the grocery stores one customer tells another not to buy an item because it is cheaper in a nearby store or they will point out a good buy in that store. One day my mother was waiting on the corner for me and along came a young man who thought this old lady needed help crossing the street so she was helped across, even though she didn't want to cross. Neighbors in Ann Arbor were like none I've ever known before, giving physical labor, such as shoveling your walk, fixing a TV, driving you someplace. It was fantastic the help neighbors were to each other.

Regarding privacy—Lawns were open in New York and Michigan, except when swimming pools, dogs, or children needed to be fenced and these fences were usually chain link fences you could see through. Here everyone has an unpainted, high., wooden fence over which you cannot see. They start at the front of the house and go to the lot line in the back and join the back fence. There will also be a fence from each side of the house to the side fence. The very first thing a person does when he buys a new house is erect a fence. This tends to perpetuate the reserve one neighbor has toward the other. We think the fences are ugly and we aren't erecting one, but still we have them because both neighbors put one up. We are planting shrubs all along the back and against the fences. In this way we'll have something attractive to look at, not an ugly fence. Of course, it will take years for the shrubs to hide fences.

Regarding grocery stores—Check out is fast here and quite efficient. The checkout person states the cost of each item as it is run up. It is easy to keep track of prices and catch mistakes. Some items we get back East and in the Midwest are not available here, whip and chill, rubber scrubbers for pots and pans, good apples. It sometimes takes two years for items introduced back East to be sold here. Never have I known such a long strawberry season.

Regarding plants—They sunburn out here. Never had this problem before. Now we have to shade some shrubs or cover them.

Regarding weather—Concord's weather is very different from San Francisco's. It gets hot here, over 100 in the summer, but S.F. stays cool and is often 50 or 60 when we are 100. When you go to S.F, you wear a long sleeved dress and coat or jacket. You roast till you get on air conditioned BART. When you return from S.F., you almost think the heat of fire is striking your body. Nights cool off and again there can be 50 degrees difference between night and day. You go to sleep with a sheet or nothing on you and then you wake up and pull up a blanket and maybe a second blanket toward morning. Winters there isn't this difference.

Regarding rain—Rain here is such an unusual thing in the summer that there will a headline and article on the front page of the newspaper. One morning this summer it did rain a little and a person under an umbrella was pictured on the front page and there was an article telling how many decades it has been since there was rain on that day. Yes, I said decades. From April on, no rain usually. About November the rain starts again. When there is no rain, you turn on your lawn sprinklers. The lawns are green but everything else is brown and that is why California is called the Golden State.

Regarding hospitals—We have only had experience with one but it seemed efficient, modern and the emergency room service is quick and thorough. We disliked the big, old University Hospital in Ann Arbor and disliked being put in a ward with 22 beds and one bathroom. It is a teaching hospital. Doctors have to learn but I'd rather they not learn on me.

Regarding divorce—I had never seen ads in the newspaper about divorce but they appear in ours. Cost $70, plus filing fees. Divorce is common out here. When buying a house, you may come upon an unclean, messy, unoccupied house and usually this belongs to a divorcing couple and neither cares how it looks for sale. Sometimes one of the marriage team will be there and will be unfriendly. Realtors tell you that there may be trouble if you make an offer while the house is still owned by the divorcing couple. If the divorce has taken place and the property settlement made, you are O.K. Otherwise beware.

Regarding housing—Houses should be cheaper since they don't have cellars. They don't even sit on concrete slabs. They sit on concrete pillars so they can sway with the earthquakes. Land is extremely expensive here. Lots are tiny. Our whole lot could sit in the back yard of our house in Clarence and we would have room left over. Houses also aren't well built, less and sometimes no insulation. So you have higher heating and air conditioning bills.

Regarding food—It should be cheaper because a lot of it is grown here so there isn't the shipping costs. Not so. Almost everything is more expensive. If you ever harbored the idea that you would retire to California where living is cheaper, forget it! T'ain't so! Houses, cars, clothes, food, all are more expensive. For example, the same amount and brand of typing paper was $1.14 or $1.20 in Ann Arbor and the same brand and amount out here is $2.18.

Even though houses are close together, we have mailboxes at the curb just as farms in the country back East and in the Midwest do. We also have private garbage collection for which we pay extra. In Geneva, Niagara Falls, and Ann Arbor garbage service was paid for in your taxes. Don't think Concord is unusual. All Bay area cities have private garbage collection.

Drought

Bedroom power shortage, Pier 39, Bechtel

AUGUST 15, 1977

Dear Bonna and Wayne,

We have lived here for two years and five months and in that time I can count on the fingers of one hand the number of times it has rained. I have five fingers.

How bad is the situation? We use 600 gallons of water a month. We are now rationed and in June and July we were allowed 431 gallons, August and September 418, and October November 293, and December January 228. Not all of this is for personal use. We have to water the lawn, shrubs, plants and wash clothes and dishes. No car washing is allowed. Our tap water is salty because the sea has come far inland in the bay and river, further east than Concord, and this is where our water comes from.

We aren't as bad off as Marin country where they get 42 gallons a day. This means no baths, washing clothes or watering the lawn. When people in Marin county want to have a party, they rent portable johns because they don't have enough water for the guests to flush toilets. They just put a pipe across the San Raefel bridge so Marin County will get a little more water.

Not only homes are affected. Gasoline stations lock their restrooms and put up a sign, out of order. In buildings hot water is shut off because people let faucets run till hot water comes.

Some faucets are fixed so only a trickle will come. Some restaurants don't serve water with a meal and some charge for a glass of water.

The situation is bad and we are told it will get worse.

Reservoirs are more than 100 feet below normal. The ground is dry and water won't sink in. We are told to expect flooding and fires.

This is my first experience with a drought.

We are told if it rains every day from November thru March, we will still be in serious trouble. Normally this area has lots of rain November thru March which is saved and which we use in the summer.

From your letters I know you don't really understand the climate here. I report what a hot day it is and you tell me you heard differently on TV. You heard what it is in S.F. Today it will be in the 60s in S.F. In Concord today it will be in the 90's. San Francisco is west of the mountains and is cooled by the ocean. We are east of the mountains and in a valley with no ocean breeze. The distance between San Francisco and Concord is only 25 miles, yet the climate is very different. Believe me!

JANUARY 7. 1978

Dear Phyllis and Jay,

For the second time in six months my mother has packed her valuables in preparation for evacuation. The first time was this summer when Mt. Diablo was on fire. Last night at 9:15 Mother was in bed looking at TV when suddenly the lights in her room and the TV went black. She, with her flashlight, came hastily out to the family room where Gene and I were looking at TV, with all the lights on. We checked her room and what she said was true. We also discovered we had no lights in the kitchen, living room, hall, outdoors, garage, laundry room, one bath and three bedrooms. However, the family room, two bedrooms and two baths were O.K. The oven light just barely glowed. The furnace was off but both the freezer and the refrigerator seemed to be on. Gene checked the circuit breaker in the garage and all seemed to be O.K. Then he went outdoors and checked the main fuse box. O.K., too. So what was the matter?

We decided to call P.G.&E. Gene told our tale and was told a man would be here in a little while. Now I know what a little while means. Three hours! We stayed in the darkened living room so we could flag the P.G.&E. man because our house was so dark in front. This didn't seem like an unusual occurrence, according to the P.G.&E. man. We didn't have one phase because there was trouble underground, somewhere between our main and the street. The truck did not have the equipment to fix it temporarily so the man left to get it. Concord had so many of these occurrences that they had used all their jumpers and he had to borrow from Walnut Creek. He was back at 12:30 AM and he jumpered our main to our neighbor's and then we had electricity again and the house began to warm up. This arrangement will remain in use for about a week, until P.G.&E. has time to come and dig up our front yard and replace whatever is wrong. Can you picture my mother seeking out her money, rings and other valuables while holding a flashlight. She didn't get dressed but sat in the family room for sometime till I assured her that we were not leaving and all she was accomplishing was getting cold. This house isn't even three years old so shouldn't the electrical installations last longer than that?

DEC. 30, 1978

Dear Colette and Jean,

From now on, I can take guests into San Francisco and show them something they have never seen, Pier 39, which opened a couple months ago. Having heard about it, I wanted to see it. Today Gene and I acted like tourists at Pier 39.

We took BART and got off at Embarcadero station. As we left the train, we heard lots of noise. When we got to the street, we saw thousands of Iranians, marching and chanting, "DOWN WITH THE MONARCHY and KILL THE SHAH". The mob took up one whole block of Market Street. We walked next to the curb and in the opposite direction from the mob. Adjacent to the curb were seven police cars, manned by two policemen, and two motorcycle cops. What an impact this had on me! I had seen them marching before but not like this. They were militant.

We boarded bus 32, and got off at Pier 39. Pier 39 looks old and weathered and just fits into the harbor in an attractive way. It is a combination of Fisherman's Wharf and Ghiradelli Square. It has slews of restaurants and many interesting little shops. There are steps going from one level to another and lots of corners to go around. In some of the open spots are platforms and performers are doing their thing. We saw the French fry and baked potato stand that Dan White, who killed the mayor and supervisor, ran. I checked the restaurants and found one that had a seafood platter that sounded wonderful and was only $5.00. We bought little, although I saw things that interested me. After we had thoroughly explored, we tried to find the restaurant with the cheap seafood platter. We didn't find it so settled for Yet Wah, a mandarin restaurant. The food was good and the view excellent. We were not disappointed. We bused back to the Embarcadero.

Now all the Iranians were milling around the plaza outside the Hyatt Regency. Through chanting, they were now socializing.

We visited Design Research because it was selling out and I thought I might find a bargain. Almost nothing was left. We headed back to BART.

For the first time I saw S.F. on the last day of the year when office people throw from windows their calendars, IBM cards and other small sheets of paper. It was a mess. After New Year's it will be cleaned up at quite an expense to the city of S.F. The building Gene works in can't follow this custom because none of the windows open.

We waited for the train with lots of Iranians who were headed back to Berkeley. One girl tried to enlist us in the cause. We got home at 4:40, having had a happy day.

Gene would probably have looked at football had he been home. He does love it. I'll let him enjoy football all Sunday and Monday. Last night I was in bed before Gene and the last thing he told me before we went to sleep was that Woody Hayes lost the game for Ohio State. He was penalized for his behavior. I'm not a football fan but I do know Woody Hayes because he was a dirty word in Ann Arbor when we lived there. There is a great rivalry between Ohio State and the University of Michigan. When we lived there cars sported bumper stickers which said BURN WOODY. The local TV station and the Detroit stations were always talking about Woody Hayes. I don't think Woody had a friend in Ann Arbor. This morning when Gene came for breakfast, the first thing he told me was that Woody Hayes had been fired after 28 years with Ohio State. I couldn't believe it but it is true.

How my horizons have been enlarged since we left New York state. Who would have thought I would be interested in this football news. Not I.

MAY 15, 1979

Dear Marge and Roy,

First it was the fire in the tube that disrupted Gene's transportation to work. Now BART is back to normal and along comes the gas shortage. After BART reopened, fewer people rode BART because they were afraid of being trapped under the bay. The gas shortage has removed that fear and now BART is more crowded than before. In addition, some trains have been taken off our line and sent to Richmond. For the last two weeks Gene hasn't been able to get a seat, even at 6:30 AM. He stands both ways and it is crowded. Sort of like riding in Japan where the people are pushed on and then the door is shut.

Disgusted, Gene decided to look into van riding. He called two van drivers but there was no opening on either. The third one had a temporary place. One of the regular riders travels a lot and when he is absent Gene can have his seat. Van riding is cheaper than Bart. Gene walks 4 blocks to Oak Grove to get the van, which holds fifteen persons. I asked Gene about the men who rode the van and he said there were only four. I was amazed and asked how they could pay for the van with so few. It seems all the rest are women. A woman is driving when Gene gets on. After two blocks the regular van driver gets on and drives into San Francisco and two blocks from Bechtel this male driver gets off and the woman again takes over. She parks directly across the street from where Gene works. It is most convenient at the San Francisco end but not at this end.

Did you know that the supervisors in San Francisco voted to charge $2.00 for each half hour in a city parking lot? This is to discourage people from driving into the city. If you park in a lot for eight hours while working, you could pay $32 per day in a downtown lot. The minimum fee is $10. This would certainly discourage me from driving into San Francisco.

How about you?

We didn't get any gas over the weekend. I wanted some today but our license ends in an even number and this is an odd day so I'll have to wait till tomorrow. The station opens at 7 PM, but I won't be there till 9 AM and it will already have been closed for an hour by this time. I'll have to go to a station that is more expensive and wait in a long line and hope the station hasn't run out of gas. This gas shortage is a real pain. When you come to a stop light, it is unwise to get in the right hand lane because if there is a gasoline station, you are in the waiting line. The first time this happened, I wondered why so much traffic at that hour but I soon figured it out and got in the middle lane.

Over the weekend we were so hot that we had to have the air-conditioning on and one night it didn't even cool down all night. Today we have an artic breeze. What a change. The hot weather is normal, but not this artic breeze.

We celebrated Mother's day on Saturday by going out for lunch. Gene and I were going out in the evening. Sunday is really Mother's Day but the crowds that day are terrible and the service slow. We went to the Railroad Station, so named because it formerly was a railroad station. It has atmosphere, and charm and the food is good. My mother loves their Coquilles St.Jacques which is served as an entree. She ordered it and was told that the last two servings had just been given to other patrons. In this restaurant it contains, lobster, crab, shrimp, and scallops and is in a cheese sauce. The waitress suggested a fish entree which she thought might be similar. It turned out to be hot, and what my mother thought was pimento was hot, hot peppers. Her mouth burned for hours. I was sorry she was disappointed. Sunday I made a special dinner and had her favorite angel food cake.

Gene has been out watering the lawn. He just came in and said he was going to call Gordon Cooper. I could see no reason to call our insurance man. For a whole week Gene has been hearing a rattle in his car so he unlocked the trunk and discovered that somebody had stolen the spare tire and left the nuts to rattle around. How do you like that? In broad daylight in the BART parking lot. That is the only place the car has been. They must have picked the lock. Maybe it was the same people who tried to steal the car a year ago. Anyway he has no spare tire.

I never thought sitting at a desk and using paper and pencil would be a high risk job but now I'm not so sure. Friday, Oct. 19, Gene left work at 4:30, as usual, arrived home at 5:30 and on the six o'clock news we saw his 17 floor office building on fire. Monday morning he saw the top ten floor all boarded up. A few days later there was a second arson fire. Somebody wiped a door with lighter fluid and then set fire to the carpet underneath. Bechtel called meetings on each floor. They reported a third arson fire. Security has been beefed up. Since then the alarm went off again but it was late Friday afternoon and it was a prank to get everybody off work early. Gene had eleven flights of stairs to descend because the elevators cannot be used in case of fire.

Windows are built in permanently in this energy saving building. If a fire is on a lower floor, everybody could be trapped.

Everybody who works in Gene's building is working on nuclear power plants. It is believed the anti nuke people are the arsonists. Jane Fonda was in town last week and she made rabble rousing speeches against nuclear power. See what she caused.

So far the Bechtel buildings on Beale and Fremont have not been tampered with. Bechtel also rents several floors in the Metropolitan building and at One California. Not all nuclear power work is done at 221 Main. Frankly, I'm scared. Some crack pot is willing to sacrifice lots of lives just to delay the building of nuclear power plants.

After the Dan White decision people were really mad that Dan White got only four to seven years for killing Mayor Muscone and Supervisor Milk. The jury foreman was a Bechtel man and so crack pots tried to punish Bechtel because a Bechtel man performed his civic duty. Bechtel received several bomb threats. Bechtel took these seriously and sealed off floors and initiated double security. Time consuming. Imagine threatening to bomb a building for a thing like this. San Francisco sure has a lot of kooks.

NOVEMBER 21, 1979

Dear Halys and Gordon,

It is almost five o'clock on the eve of Thanksgiving and I'm sitting down for the first time today. I'm tired.

Three weeks ago I asked Gene to turn our mattress from top to bottom. He rejected my help. A mattress is clumsy and it got in an upside down U shape while being turned. As the days passed, I noticed a wave in the mattress and then a real pain in my back. Long ago I fractured two vertebrae and I wondered if these were causing me trouble. I've slept with a board all these years and been fine. Last Thursday I was in such pain that I lay in the middle of the living room floor. A tear escaped now and then. Gene kept checking on me and I finally had him press on the vertebrae and we located two painful spots. I suggested we change mattresses from the front bedroom to ours. All alone Gene wrestled the mattresses back and forth. The next morning BOTH of us noticed a difference. I was all for buying a new mattress but Gene said I must see the orthopedist first. This I did on Monday. X-rays showed bones O.K. and no arthritis of the spine. The doctor said he thought I had sprained my back. Ho ho!

Put two and two together and you have a faulty mattress as the culprit.

Monday and Tuesday my mother and I were mattress and springs shopping. Today we had delivered the hardest mattress that is made. We have thirty days to decide if we can live with this mattress. Our bed was firm before so I think we will like it. We slept well on a futon on the floor in Japan. I'm telling you this so you can profit from our mistake. Lesson no. 1. Turning a mattress improperly can cost money. Lesson no 2. Don't sleep on a wavy mattress. The orthopedist told me he had just returned from a trip to India and the seat on the plane didn't fit his body. He sprained his back and had been away from the office for a couple of days because of this. He probably isn't more than forty. He says this is a common occurrence.

Next day

Sleeping on our new mattress and springs is utter bliss.

My mother just came in the kitchen singing " It's beginning to smell a lot like eating." Let me tell you she is no Bing Crosby. I'm making lemon bread and the odor is tantalizing. One of my students has a lemon tree and she brought a dozen lemons. I'll freeze some loaves, give some away and we'll eat a loaf.

Gene's group at work ate lunch out today. They celebrate anything with going out to lunch. I think they are celebrating having a few days off. Bechtel had a Thanksgiving meal at the cafeteria last week and turkey and the whole works was only $2.75. Gene went but so did thousands of others. Gene's lunch period was from 11:30 till 12:15. Gene stood in line till 12:10. When he did get a plate, it was skimpy. Either they were unprepared for such a crowd or it was planned this way.

The 1980's

Eugene O'Neill's Tao House
Japanese Consul General's house

NOVEMBER 24, 1980

Dear Ella,

I've just had a most interesting afternoon. I arranged for our book group to visit Tao House, the home of Eugene O'Neill, which is now a National Historic Site. Ever since we moved to California, I have been reading about Tao House. The state bought it and gave it to the U.S. government. The government accepted it on the condition they would not have to restore it. A group established the Eugene O'Neill Foundation and they are searching for the furnishings of the house. The house isn't open to the public yet and it may be years before it is because part way up the small hill are some lovely houses. The owners of these houses like the private, narrow one car road and don't want traffic in front of their houses. Now the National Park Service must build other roads to this house and it isn't easy to acquire land.

The house is isolated. From it you have an unobstructed view of Mt. Diablo, far distant mountains, a stretch of Carquinez Strait with oil tanks nearby and the San Ramon Valley.

I knew someone on the Foundation and she arranged a private tour for ten people in two cars. No more. I explained this carefully and had a sign up list. When we gathered to car pool, there were sixteen. Six didn't belong to our book group. Some people have lots of nerve. We piled into three cars. I had some explaining and apologizing to do but the hostess of the day was understanding.

Built in 1937 for $40,000 from the proceeds of his 1936 Nobel Prize, the house is a white, California hacienda type, two stories with a court-yard in front. The front is covered with white wisteria that Eugene O'Neill planted. We were allowed to pick oranges from trees planted by O'Neill's own hands. The living room and many of the rooms had white walls but the living room had an almost navy blue ceiling. In other spots in the house Chinese red was used. His wife liked oriental things and so the original furnishings were oriental. The floors downstairs were red tile and the living room had a beautiful oriental rug. We saw pictures. The foundation took pictures of the furnishings to stores and tried to locate where they were purchased so they could get duplicates. They are also trying to track down the original furnishings.

Although O'Neill only lived in this house seven years, all his greatest works were written here. I've never been a lover of O'Neill. Depressing and sad are the words I would use to describe his plays. The people aren't normal or at least the kind of people I think are normal. Our guide said you either liked O'Neill or you hated him. He was a Nobel Prize winner so somebody must have thought him a great writer.

When living in Poughkeepsie, I went to N.Y. to see THE ICEMAN COMETH. It had just opened and was very long. As I remember we went at 4 PM, had a break for dinner and came back afterwards to see the rest of the play. Shortly after that it was cut to normal length.

O'Neill became ill while living here and his hands shook so he could-n't write. He couldn't dictate so after that he never wrote another play. Plays he had half completed, he destroyed because he wouldn't accept help. O'Neill was forced to leave this house a few years before his death because it was so isolated. The war was on and when the chauffeur went in the service O'Neill and his wife moved near Oakland. It was there he died.

We all felt so smug to have seen this house since it is almost impossi-ble to do so.

DECEMBER 10, 1980

Dear Millie and Jim,

The headline in our newspaper Dec. 7th was HOUSING SHORTAGE AT CRISIS LEVEL. DRIVING OUT MAJOR COMPANIES.

Quotes from the article 1. Easier to find job than a place to live in Bay area. 2. Many major companies may move. 3. Most expensive housing in nation. 4. Can't fill positions because employees can't find affordable housing. 5. Figures for middle class Americans. 6. Today's modest home in near future predicted to cost four times today's price, example a $100,000 home would become $400,000. My question is where would you find a $100,000 house here?

It is now Dec 9th and I took BART into S.F. and took care of some business. On my way back to BART, I stopped to look at Gump's windows. Gump's is to the west coast what Tiffany's is to the east coast. This year the windows featured the NUTCRACKER SUITE. Each window had a curtain that went up and down on scenes from this ballet. Puppets were doing the dancing. Crowds covered the windows. I had to look between heads. Then I went on to I. Magnim's. Here the windows were scenes from Victorian times with thirty inch animated dolls performing such Christmas deeds, as wrapping presents and decorating a tree. These windows were lovely, but Gump's were exquisite. Maiden Lane was lined with five foot Christmas trees, bedecked with red bows. Simple but very effective. I didn't have time to look at anything else.

December I0th, I, as a member of IIkebana International, was invited to tea at the new residence of the Japanese Consul General. The mansion, built in 1918, has just been renovated, inside and out. It is a gorgeous home, built of marble, and it commands a corner and from windows on one side of the house you see the Bay and Golden Gate Bridges. The interior is pastel in color, very subdued, but oh so rich. A large formal, living room. beautifully furnished. Ceilings are hand carved and highlighted with gold leaf. The entry hall was as big as some homes. Marble floor. Stained glass window on the circular stairs. The Japanese had a rug made to order for the hall because none already made were big enough. A very large dining room. A good sized breakfast room which in any other house would be the dining room, plus the kitchen made up the ground floor. Below were two other floors. Above were two more floors. The second floor was the living room and bedrooms for the Consul General and his family and his office. The third floor had more rooms which at present are not being used. The food was excellent. I felt privileged to be a guest there. Mrs. Kitamura was most gracious and spoke English very well. Wives of other men in the consulate helped serve and mingled with the guests. Mrs. Kitamura said there was no other house the Japanese government was interested in buying. A widower in his 80s lived there and the house had been in his family for years. He had moved to a small apartment. The Japanese Consul General invited this old man to his first official dinner in this house. The old man was pleased to see how it had been restored. Actually the house wasn't in bad condition. It just hadn't received the loving care a woman would give it. Now this house really glows and shines.

CHRISTMAS 1980

Dear Vi and Bill,

The Christmas presents have been opened, dinner eaten and Gene and I took a walk. It has been a quiet but most pleasant day with just the three of us celebrating the holiday. Mother started a large jig saw puzzle and she just can't keep away from it. Now we are relaxing.

This past week we were thrilled to receive a card from a Japanese boy we entertained when we lived in Ann Arbor. He was there for a few months to improve his English and came to visit us a few times. We saw him when we were in Japan in 1976. Last year he sent a picture of his bride and him and said in December he expected to be a father. This Christmas card was a photo card of a beautiful baby boy whose name is Eugene Imagine a Japanese baby named for Gene. What an honor! He probably will be the only Eugene Nakanori in Japan. I wonder how you write Eugene in Japanese. I put the picture in the glass door of our china cabinet and I look at it frequently. This is a beautiful baby with a lovely smile. You can bet we sent a gift.

DECEMBER 30, 1980

I'm trying to kill time till Gene comes home and we pick up our new car. When the dealer called this morning and said the car was ready, I decided to let Gene have the thrill of driving our new car home. So I have the dinner in the oven and the minute Gene walks in the door we are off. It may be a bit inconvenient for the salesman because he will have to stay an hour longer tonight but I think Gene's thrill comes before a salesman's inconvenience. We don't buy a car every day.

This afternoon I took the ornaments off the Christmas tree. Gene will remove the lights tonight and tomorrow the tree will be put out for the garbage man to take. I like a tree before Christmas but afterwards I think a tree is passé.

JANUARY 17, 1981

Dear Chet and Bess,

Our new car, a cutlass Oldsmobile, suits me fine. Gene finds some things he wants investigated, though. The second day we had it, I backed out of the drive and the computer came on and said check engine. It stayed on so I gave up my grocery shopping and went to the car agency. They said it wasn't serious and I could drive that day and bring it in another day to have an adjustment made. No trouble since.

One day last week I spent at our nicest department store doing inventory work. AAUW could earn $1300 if we members volunteered our time. Another member and I were assigned to the men's department. It isn't usual for the store to do this. It seems a water pipe broke on the top floor and water came thru all the floors. They moved all the men's things to a stock room and they did not get wet but it was done hurriedly and piled hit or miss in the stock room. So we sorted and moved it back. The clothes were heavy. We were on our feet every minute so I was very tired when I got home. It was interesting, though. I discovered men's pajamas could cost $85. They were velour. It would have been easier to have been assigned to some other department, maybe stationery.

Monday I'm entertaining book group. Next month I give the review. Gene just shampooed the rug in the kitchen. It had to be done before we entertain.

Next weekend we have reservations for a boat trip on Half Moon Bay to observe the gray whales that are migrating from Alaska to Southern California. I hope the weather is good enough for the boat to sail and that we see some whales.

The following weekend we are having a dinner party, probably fourteen persons. Our first big dinner party since we came to California. We had to build up a circle of friends.

One day last week a TV station in San Francisco sent a reporter to various restaurants in San Francisco to see which was the most expensive. He told each waiter that he wanted the most expensive items and in each case the entree was lamb. Two restaurants were rejected because they weren't expensive enough but Ernie's was accepted and the price of a meal, with wine, for that one reporter, was $199.00 Anyone for Ernie's?

FEBRUARY 7, 1981

Dear Helen and Herb,

It has been a long time since I've written any letters. Too busy.

At the moment we have two Bird of Paradise blossoms. My mother loves to watch them. There are probably eight birds in one blossom. One bird can take a day to pop out. My mother says it is like watching a baby being born. They are right next to the house in front of the living room window so we have a ringside seat.

Later today Gene will so some dormant spraying and fertilize the lawn and then we hope it rains. We have had such a little bit of rain. For the first time this winter there was enough snow in the mountains for skiing.

Last Saturday we had a dinner party for twelve. Usually for this number I serve on trays but I read that no dinner party can be successful when people have to eat on trays. We moved all the furniture from the family room and put up card tables. Husbands and wives were assigned different tables. We had some mixer games. In one we had teams. Each team was given a word and had to make up a meaning. The other had to guess who gave the correct meaning. I spent hours looking up obsolete words, jectigation, emberlucock, angard, relue, hairester, bohea, yataghan, checm, dinkum, dornik, esparto and rubiginous. Do you know any of them? I didn't. We also had interviews between males and females. Nobody was a Barbara Walters. By the time we finished this, everyone was talking to former perfect strangers.

I was busy for a week planning and preparing food. We had a spinach salad and I knew something was missing when I ate it, but almost everybody had seconds. I had forgotten the dressing! The bacon, cheese and sesame seeds gave the flavor.

Thursday I went into San Francisco to a Bechtel Wives luncheon at the Sheraton Palace. I thought it was expensive for what we had, bean soup, chicken salad, a roll and chocolate mousse. I went because Donald Kennedy, president of Stanford, was going to give a speech on GENETIC RESEARCH, WHERE WE ARE GOING AND WHAT WE ARE GOING TO D0 ABOUT IT. He spoke on INDUSTRY AND SCIENCE and it was very general. I was terribly disappointed.

I've been looking for a new bedspread for our bed. Can't find anything ready made so I'm looking at materials and shall have one made. I brought home samples and Gene thought they were all too expensive. Poor Gene. He is thinking of prices twenty years ago. He is going to have to revise his ideas of what we shall have to pay.

My mother hasn't been feeling up to par this past week. No aches and pains but she spent much time in bed and ate little. I called the doctor but she refused to go. She misses her friend, Millie, who died

Christmas day. There really is something wrong with my mother but I don't know what.

Monday I give my book review. LOVE IS NOT FOR COWARDS by Shirly Dyckes Kelly, wife of Clarence Kelly of the F.B.I. of a few years back. Shirly was a nun for fifteen years. Mostly the book is about her search for a husband, although I'm putting this crudely. Kelly is a generation older than Shirly and one year older than her mother. She never should have been a nun. She was always "falling in love ". She thought a priest would leave and marry her but he didn't. She taught school after leaving the convent. Eventually she moved into Watergate and there she was exposed to the type of man she was looking for, position and money. Her family is moderately wealthy, she says, and I believe her. She is used to upper class living. Why she thought she could be happy as a nun, I'll never know. Not a great book, but interesting.

Woody Hayes
Streaker, Ant invasion

JUNE 10, 1981

Dear Connie and Herb,

Life in California! Here is how it goes:

No 1. Snow hasn't melted much in the mountains of Washington, Oregon and northern California so rivers are not flowing strongly to the delta which is where our water comes from. This means that the sea has invaded the bays and delta and consequently salt water comes from our faucets. Not too salty but enough so we are warned to drink bottled water.

No 2. This week there was a cable car accident, nothing unusual, but this time nineteen were hurt, none seriously. Some taxi turned in front of the cable car and when the cable car operator tried to stop, all the people on the cable car were tossed around. Cable cars just can't stop like normal cars but this doesn't make much difference to some car drivers. There was a bunch of kids on the cable car. Good thing it was kids and not old people. There would have been many more broken bones. Everybody loves cable cars. They are fun but not too safe.

No 3. We are in the midst of the Mediterranean fruit fly controversy. Somebody brought in infected fruit and the fly was found in the back yard of a house in Santa Clara. Everybody in the county had to strip fruit trees and the fruit had to be destroyed. This was supposed to control the infestation but it didn't. Next the state got in the act. They were going to spray the whole area by planes so houses, cars, lawns, everything would be sprayed. Next the governor stepped in and they were only going to spray from the ground. So all fruit had to be destroyed. The U.S. government finally decided that that unless California sprayed the whole area by plane, the whole state would be quarantined. No fruit or vegetables sold outside the state. 80 % of all fruit and vegetables grown in California is shipped out of state. I imagine the governor will have to go along with the airplane spraying even though the people object strongly. Farmers whose whole income is based on fruit and vegetables could end up with an income of zero if we are quarantined. This isn't fair to the farmers.

Late news bulletin—The U.S. government says California gets sprayed by plane or else. So Monday night of next week the Santa Clara area will be sprayed by plane from midnight to six in the morning and each Monday night thereafter for six weeks. We hope this eliminates the Med. Fruit Fly.

No 4. We are having a baseball strike in the U.S. and life at 2155 is different. Gene usually watches baseball games on weekends and gets little done. Last weekend I went shopping with Isabel, our guest, and in 3 hours Gene took off the old faucets in the kitchen sink and installed new faucets and a spray. He also installed a fluorescent light in the garage. Three hours! With baseball games on, it would have taken three days to get this done. Hurrah for the baseball strike!. I'm no longer a baseball TV widow.

No 5. Medical care in the state of California costs more than in any other state of the U.S. Believe you me, Gene and I know it. I broke my navicular bone recently and it looks to me that we paid three times for x-ray diagnosis. We paid the doctor, the hospital and a radiology group. The doctor used the x-rays. Whether any doctor in the hospital looked at the x-rays, I don't know. The hospital sends all x-rays to the radiology group. When I showed all the charges to the doctor, he also thought we paid three times for the same thing. I sent off some letters about this and got polite answers in return but we still had to pay. In N.Y. and Michigan we paid a lump sum so we don't know what it all was for but out here they itemize everything and it adds up. I broke this bone on April 5th. It is June 10th and the doctor says it won't be completely healed till September. I'm using my hand normally but I don't lift heavy things with that hand. From this experience I say don't get sick on Sunday in California and preferably don't get sick in California.

No 6. All day a fire has been raging in San Francisco. It started at 2 AM in a gay bath house in downtown San Francisco. Twenty five buildings have burned. This is the biggest fire in San Francisco since the 1906 earthquake. The buildings were old but in the heart of San Francisco. A lot of homosexuals will be out of homes because they lived in apartments in some of these buildings.

No 7. The newspaper today told of a two year old streaker. Her mother put her out to play with her brother. It got hot so she took off her

clothes and ran thru the sprinkler. Her mother put on her bathing suit
and the child took that off too. The man next door called the police and
wanted them to arrest this two year old for indecent exposure. The police
talked to the mother but did not arrest the child. This happened in
Concord.

Life at 2155

Last summer was the coolest summer we had had in several years
and certainly the coolest since we have been in California. Of course, by
cool this means California standards. This year the month of June was
the hottest ever recorded. We have been comfortable, though, because of
the air conditioning. However, our attic fan didn't work. Today I got a
new thermostat which Gene will install this weekend. It won't make us
any cooler but it should keep the air conditioner from working so much
and thereby reduce our electric bill.

DECEMBER 23, 1981

Dear Kathryn.

On our trip to New Mexico, Gene and I bought 5 little wooden
angels, made in Europe, in a Christmas shop in Albuquerque. In March
we saw more of these angels in a store in Solvang but we didn't buy
because we couldn't remember which ones we had. All are playing different instruments. We planned to return in June but my broken bones in
my hand precluded that. Two weeks ago I found two in Lafayette. One
angel had a broken wing. I bought one. The clerk said the broken wing
angel was not salable so if I wanted it, she would give it to me. Gene tried
to make a wing but his first broke. He is still trying.

We want the whole collection so on the 15th I took some friends and
my mother to Sausalito, a little town at the far side of the Golden Gate
Bridge. Many interesting tourist shops here. I found two more angels.
Now we have ten angels. We all enjoyed the outing, even I who unintentionally drove thru San Francisco to get there.

I had planned a trip to San Francisco with two purposes, to view the
Christmas windows and to pick up my watch which was being repaired.
When I bought this Swiss Movado watch years ago, it was supposed to
last a lifetime. I've been having trouble with it so I took it to the Movado
representative in San Francisco for repair. He called recently and said it
was ready but that he had moved his place of business to San Rafael in
Marin County. He offered to send the watch but it is too delicate and far
too expensive to go thru the mail so I said I would come for it. Monday
my mother and I set out. We found his office without any trouble. I
wanted to see the attractive little shops in San Raefel, but with bumper to
bumper traffic and no parking spots, I gave up. I'll go another day, not at

the Christmas season.

We returned to the East Bay via the Richmond Bridge and made a stop at Larkspur Ferry Landing where there are some exclusive little shops. My mother said there was nothing to buy in the shops. What she meant was that nothing was within her price range. Marin County is reputed to be the wealthiest county in the U.S. Also the place where there are the most divorces per capita. On our way back, I decided to stop at Hilltop Mall outside Richmond. Richmond is almost 100 % Black. The contrast between Marin County and Richmond is like black and white, literally and figuratively. At Hilltop Mall the merchandise is ordinary but there are lots of stores. There is a restaurant next to a glassed skating rink and we had lunch and looked at the black skaters.

I didn't see the Christmas windows in San Francisco this year because my days were booked but next year I'll make time for that.

In Danville, before Thanksgiving I saw a wooden egg from Poland which had four bunnies inside it. It was very shopworn so I didn't buy it. I told Gene about it and he determined to find one. He went to a Polish store in San Francisco but it had gone out of business. Consulting the phone book, he found other stores. During his lunch time, he sought them out. He found some interesting places. He even took a bus to a section of San Francisco that scared him. He didn't look around but got in another bus and came back to the financial district. He said that area was just too tough for him. Gosh, I merely mentioned this egg to Gene. I didn't ask for it. Mention of the egg was just part of my telling him what I did that day.

1981 XMAS SEASON

Dear Allene and Ted,

As I sit writing this letter at eight in the morning on a beautiful sunny day in October (letter to be sent with Christmas cards) it might be assumed that we have no winter here but such is not the case. Winter has come early to California this year. In the middle of October there was enough snow in the Sierras so that the ski resorts opened. Concord has had some real rains which are premature. Usually they come middle or late November. The swallows have left San Juan Capistrano, not to return till March 19th or thereabouts.

I read that the swallows return on March 19th to Capistrano, which is about four hundred miles away, near San Clemente. Gene thinks we should go see them this year but when? Native Californians say the swallows can come a week early or a week late. I want to see the twenty three missions in California and there is one a Capistrano. My mother has two records she plays which I love, THE SERENADE OF THE BELLS and

WHEN THE SWALLOW COME BACK TO CAPISTRANO. This phenomenon is similar to the butterflies which come to Pacific Grove each year. We visited there but not at the time the butterflies returned or left. California has so much to offer. We have only touched the tip of the iceberg since we have lived here.

When we moved to California and started to landscape our yard, I knew I wanted some bird of paradise plants, strelitzia.

We bought 6 small plants and placed them in the bed directly under our living room picture window. They were small plants because bigger ones are too expensive. Better it would be to have bought big ones because the plants must have ten healthy leaves before they bloom. They grow slowly. Last year we had a few blossoms, one at a time from different plants. This winter we have had as many as 8 blossoms all at once. They are fascinating flowers. First comes a long, fat, green bud. Then you see an edge of orange, then a bigger edge and finally a petal emerges. You can sit for an hour and watch this petal emerge. It might take a whole day for the first blossom to get out of the bud. In a few days the same thing will happen from the same bud and so you have two blossoms from one bud. There can be five or six "birds" from each bud. My mother says it is like seeing a baby born. Sometimes I go out and help by gently releasing a petal. These are magnificent, dramatic flowers and wonderful in flower arrangements but as yet I can't bear to cut any of ours for this purpose. "Birds" are all over the warm parts of California, but they are native to South Africa. They are perennials and bloom intermittently throughout the year. To an Easterner who never before saw a "bird" grow, it is a real treat to see eight "birds" at once.

JANUARY 6, 1982

Dear Mary and Dave,

Thank you so very much for your phone calls last night. It's not the rain in Spain, but rather the rain in California, that makes friends think of us. We appreciate your concern.

Where to begin? it has rained so long and so hard that I can't remember which day it began and just what happened on each day. I'll start with Saturday. I believe I wrote that Mt Diablo, 3800 feet high, was topped with snow. Not only that, it got down to 2000 feet. It was beautiful. Gene and I went out to buy Gene shoes and it started to rain and continued for the rest of the day. I don't remember whether it was Saturday or Sunday night when we had a bad thunder and lightning storm. This is unusual for this area. We seldom have thunder and lightning, sometimes not even once a year.

Monday was so dark we needed lights on all day. You couldn't see across the road from the rain. I had to take Gene to and from his van ride. He was very late in coming home.

Sunday morning my mother knocked on our bedroom door and woke us up. She said we had millions of ants on the kitchen counter. She wasn't lying as to amount. Gene and I looked and went back to bed. So what, only another million could come in the next 15 minutes. When we did get up, I got out a sponge and ammonia and wiped the counter. Gene came and wanted me to stop so he could study the traffic pattern of the ants. There wasn't any pattern. It was a massive traffic jam, with one ant trying to get around another or over another or aimlessly trying to get someplace. Next I washed the counter with detergent. Gene wiped outside insecticide on the area. We had ant traps out but they were jam packed full of ants. All day we kept wiping up ants and crushing them with paper towels. It was extremely difficult to prepare meals.

Monday I did errands in the morning. My mother stayed home. In the afternoon I was sewing by hand some Christmas felt stockings. As I sat in the family room on the love seat, ants crawled over me. I got up and went into the living room. No sooner had I done this when ants were all over me and the chair. Gene came home, late, and we searched the areas and found the ants coming through the baseboards. I went to the main bathroom and that counter was also covered with ants. I noticed a place by the tub black with ants. Gene and I sat on the sofa after dinner and I felt an ant on my neck. Gene looked and took it away. My mother was in bed, dressed in a long sleeved robe and covered with blankets and ants ran over her hands. We decided this problem was beyond our capabilities to solve. Tomorrow I would call the pest control man.

At 7:30 AM on Tuesday I did call and the man had just arrived at his place of business. When I said we had ants, he said, "You, too!" He got here at 8:45 AM. He said that the water in the ground drove the ants from their nests. They go under the house and then they come inside. We have openings to the crawl space under our house in some closets. The pest control man opened these and we had a couple inches of water under the house so the ants had been driven up on the beams. Those beams were black with ants. The pest control man sprayed all the rooms inside of the house and then he put his hoses under the house and sprayed there. Next he sprayed the yard. It was raining heavily. He said it wouldn't do much good in the rain but he would make the spray double in strength. The job is guaranteed and if this doesn't do it, he will be back and respray. He sprayed the garage and it was as though a hose had been used in our garage. For an hour my mother and I sat in the car in the street while the inside of the house was sprayed. I returned to the garage to lock the kitchen door before my mother and I left for three hours. We shopped and had lunch out. When we returned the house smelled terrible and the spray hurt my throat. When Gene came home, he turned on the furnace fan full force and opened the windows. The windows remained open till we went to bed. So this is what the storm did to us, but others fared much worse,

Our spray man reported that his mother lived in Benicia and that Monday night the disaster people called him and said that his mother had been rescued by boat from her house. We have heard nothing about the damage in Benicia.

Many people at Bechtel who live in Marin County could not go home. Hotels offered lower rates. Gene said lots of Marin County people did not come to work on Tuesday. Monday there was a landslide on the east bound lanes of rt 24 and this is our only direct way to San Francisco. I heard on TV about the landslide but not the word eastbound. I called Gene at work and he made it because he was westbound. Coming home they had cleared away part of the landslide but he was late and traffic was stalled from the bridge to Orinda.

It was either Saturday or Sunday when we heard that campers and small cars were not allowed on the Oakland bridge. The rain and wind were so bad that these vehicles were lifted from one lane to another. After this happened to one car, they made this decision.

Yesterday the only way to get to San Francisco was by the Oakland bridge. There were landslides near the Golden Gate bridge so cars couldn't get to the bridge. The same was true of the Richmond bridge. Route 101 was closed so it wasn't possible to cross the Dumbarton bridge. Today buses from Marin County will go east over the Richmond bridge and then west back over the Oakland bridge to get to San Francisco. This is a long way to get to San Francisco. Ferries are running, though. At 5:5O AM the radio reported that if you weren't already on your way to San Francisco you wouldn't get there by 8 AM. Gene was still in bed. He left at 6:30 so I expect his van will be very late.

You have seen lots on TV and in the papers about this area and the result of the rain. I can only give you some personal comments.

Our neighbor had to drain water from his pool so it wouldn't overflow. Pool water will kill vegetation.

An artificial lake in a residential section of Concord overflowed into roads and houses.

The land under a building in downtown Walnut Creek washed out and the building may fall into the creek at any moment. Ordinarily this creek is either almost dry or dry.

Before Christmas a young girl in ikebana offered me some holly from her yard. She lives on Canyon Road in Orinda. This road is narrow and winds around a mountain. I have never driven up such a steep place. The paper today showed a hole in the road bigger than a car. All that dirt went down the bank.

Another friend in Lafayette lost part of her front yard. All that dirt went down on the neighbor's property below.

These last two houses are on mountains and have beautiful views but they do have problems when it rains.

Route 80 to Reno has been in the news. It is the main route East and it is closed. This happens every year. We traveled this super highway last summer and it is hard for us to fathom this. Lovelock, Nevada was -13 today. We stayed overnight there last summer and it was HOT.

It seems like old times in New York state when we used to hear about school closings. I remember listening to learn if my school would be closed. Here they close schools by county and don't give individual names of communities.

I haven't seen one ant this morning so maybe it was $66 well spent. However this spray job will only last 3 months so we may have to do this again.

It is sunny but cold. We had a frost last night. No rain.

I'm writing this letter when I should be making out my shopping list and preparing to go shopping.

NOVEMBER 10, 1982

Dear Ivy and Hubert.

My feet are tired so before I plunge into my next project, I'm going to sit awhile and write this letter.

The past six days have been filled to overflowing. Saturday we had our first slide show of this vacation and I had twelve people invited. I made a triple chocolate delight that was supposed to feed 16. It looked too small so I made an oatmeal cake which nobody thinks is made with oatmeal. Usually they think it is a date cake. This chocolate delight is very rich and like candy. You need only a sliver. It took a couple days to make because things have to set. There was some left over on Sunday so I suggested we invite the Gordons for supper. I served a tuna, avocado, orange salad, banana bread and the two desserts. We had a busy weekend.

Monday at 9 AM I went to UPS to mail our Christmas gifts that Gene packed over the weekend. I returned home and picked up my mother and took her to a church group luncheon. Then on to Lafayette to see the newly opened Christmas display at a nursery. Last year this nursery had some of our wooden angels from Germany. I asked about them and they said they sent them to their other store which is a year around gift shop. I went there and they had three we didn't have so I bought them and left my name in case any more turned up in the unpacking. When I returned home, I checked ours and found we didn't have one I thought we had so I called and asked to have them put it aside for me. While doing this, they found another. When I picked up my mother, I drove back to Lafayette and bought these two. We now have fifteen and I think there are only 16. I left an order for that, should it show up. Did I say all these little angels are playing an instrument?

Tuesday afternoon I had an Ikenobo lesson. Afterwards I took my mother out while I did some errands.

This morning was my weekly shopping so we left at 9 AM and got home at 12:30. The bank sent a letter saying a transaction we had in motion was now ready so after lunch we went to the bank and I took care of that. Then I did some further shopping for Gruyere cheese. None of the big grocery stores had it. I went to two delicatessens and the second one had some. I think the threatened butchers strike has depleted the shelves of lots of things. The strike was settled last night, before it really started, but on Sunday the stores were overflowing with people hoarding up all kinds of food.

As soon as I finish this letter, I'm going to make walnut bread. Tomorrow night we are having our Swiss friends to dinner and I want to make ahead anything I can. Lotti is a cook, par excellence. Whether it is vegetables, meat, fish or dessert, Lotti's cooking is always something special and European. I aim to come up to Lotti's standards but I can't. She serves beautifully too. Without being asked, her seventh grade son will place plates which are picture perfect in front of us. He will clear the table too. I think European children usually are better mannered than American but this boy is even better.

I've thought carefully about what to serve. I want pretty food and good food. So I'm serving a salad whose color scheme is orange and green. Green avocados and Kiwi fruit with orange slices and Fuyu persimmons. Fuyu persimmons aren't the usual persimmons. They are hard like an apple and sweet. We never had them till we came to California. The main course is Chicken Delancey. Broccoli is wrapped with either chicken or turkey. Ham encircles this. A sauce of sherry and parmesean cheese is poured over this and it is baked. I'm serving spinach in shells. Spinach is mixed with dry onion soup, sour cream and topped with mushrooms, tomato and Gruyere cheese and then baked. For dessert we are having blueberry pie and ice cream. I should do a fancy dessert but I won't have time so I'll just take a pie out of the freezer.

NOVEMBER 29, 1982

Dear Jennie and Harry,

Our Thanksgiving paper was fat with ads. All three of us read it and Friday morning all three left home about 10 AM to take advantage of some of the sales.

The first stop was Flairs where a $12 ham, with coupon, was selling for $9. I forgot to clip the coupon so we couldn't buy the ham with $3 off. Wasted trip. Later I went back and bought the ham.

Next we went to K Mart where they had Whitman candy for $2.99 and it is regularly $4.95. My mother wanted 3 boxes. We were ready about nine but we delayed our trip till ten when K Mart opens. When we arrived at K Mart, there were just a few boxes left and nobody was buying. In small print the ad said the candy was this price only between 8- 10 AM on Friday. We had the right day but not the right time. Gene and I think we can read but I guess this proves we aren't as smart as we thought.

Our third errand was to buy a new TV set for my mother. Some were $100 off but my mother needs remote control and these sets had only $30 off. All stores seemed to have the same price, except one. The price in this store was $70 more than any other store. They had $100 off. So actually they were only $30 off. If you didn't know the regular price, you might think you were getting a bargain. We didn't buy in the morning. Mother and I went out in the afternoon and picked up a TV and Gene installed it and now Mother is happy again.

Traffic was terrible on Friday. Even with CHP directing traffic at the Mall, it was impossible and there was no place to park. I'm glad I have most of my Christmas shopping done.

I've been telling you about the new Neiman Marcus store in S.F. They lock the doors to keep people out of the store. This weekend they let 2000 people in the store each hour. Lines of people waiting to get in extended for blocks. Everything is very expensive, Texas size. Thursday I plan to go into San Francisco to see the store window displays and I want to see Neiman Marcus but I won't wait in line. Gene will meet me after work and we'll have dinner before coming home.

Saturday we entertained at bridge. It was a busy day for me. I had to clean house, make hors d' oeuvres and dessert. I also had to make flower arrangements. Florists sold out before Thanksgiving and they got nothing new on Friday. What was left was sad. I had to pick carefully but I did have some pretty arrangements.

My Christmas table arrangement is 16 little wooden angels from Germany around a Swedish Christmas tree on a tray with cotton puffs. It looks as though the tree and angels are on a cloud. The guests asked to see the arrangement before we played bridge. Gene won first prize, not unusual for him, and I won second, astounding for me! I'm not a good bridge player.

California virus
Queen of England's visit

JANUARY 29, 1983

Dear Shizuko, Kaoru, Sahoko and Tae,

Here is why you haven't heard from me.

Raedina and Milton arrived on Wednesday, the 12th, and we had a busy, happy week. One day we went to Sacramento to see the renovated capitol of California. It cost 67 1/2 million and it is beautiful. My mother went along for the ride. We discovered they had a restaurant in the capitol so we lunched there. With the aid of a borrowed wheel chair, we got my mother in the capitol. She no longer can walk more than one hundred feet at a time. The lunch was excellent. Over the weekend we went to Carmel and that is always an interesting place. Their last day we planned to go to Point Reyes to watch the whales migrating. It wasn't a good day so we changed our minds a couple of times but eventually we went. We should have had our heads examined. Gene said I should have known it would be worse on the coast. We went through San Francisco, over the Golden Gate Bridge and up highway 1. Highway 1 may not mean much to you. It is twisty and curvy with spectular views. Really scary because of the heights and the very narrow road. It rained. No, it poured. I don't know how to describe how hard. Suffice to say, the windshield wiper, even on high, couldn't keep the glass clear. We drove through Stinson Beach and I wish I had driven the one hundred feet to the shore because this week fifty homes have been damaged or washed away and the road we drove on has been flooded. When we got to Reyes Point, the road was closed to the Point due to weather. It is a lovely view on a good day. Oh, well, we had a ride and Raedina and Milton saw what a storm here is like.

They left for Las Vegas and their daughter, Ann, on Wednesday the 19th. After taking them to the airport Mother and I came back to Walnut Creek, had lunch with friends and entertained them here at our house. Thursday I shopped all day, going from store to store, mall to mall and finally ended up with three presents, a velour shirt for Gene and a top for me. Some of our bridge friends do not keep their homes as warm as we and Gene had one warm shirt that he wore whenever we played bridge. Now he has a change.

Friday I went to San Francisco. During the night my throat became raspy and a bit sore. My voice changed its tone. That night it worsened and I began to cough. The coughs came from my toes and almost shook our house. Worse., I was incontinent all day Saturday. I protected the furniture and took measures to keep dry but they were insufficient. Early Sunday morning after a sleepless night for both Gene and me, Gene went to the drug store and bought paper diapers., the size for 24 pound babies. Naturally they didn't fit but I wore tight panties. Now as to those diapers—Luvs. They are the greatest.

Sunday Audrey, my neighbor. called to tell me her husband was in Venezuela. She is a nurse and when she heard me trying to talk, she got me to promise I would go to the doctor Monday. Monday I was so sick I didn't feel like getting dressed and driving there. Gene also urged me to see the doctor. I said maybe Tuesday but Tuesday I didn't have the energy to get off the sofa. Thursday night Audrey called and she insisted I get an appointment with the doctor during her lunch hour. She will leave work and take me to the doctor. That night Gene decided the hospital emergency room was the solution so I dressed and we went. The emergency doctor said I had one of the viruses going around. My lung and nasal passages were clear but my throat and neck were a mess. I coughed and nothing came up but you can hear the congestion moving around. I developed pink eye that afternoon and I was having trouble seeing because of the matter in my left eye. The doctor gave me a cough syrup with codeine and a Vaseline like thing for my eye.

Gene did the weekly grocery shopping Wednesday night. Thursday my mother went out with Audrey to get what Gene didn't. Friday my mother refused to go to her Senior Citizen meeting. I canceled Mary's ikebana lesson.

My mother tried to tell me Friday that she had never seen me so lifeless for so long. She choked up. She couldn't eat her lunch because she was choking back tears. I told my mother to read the jokes to the Reader's Digest and she would feel better. My mother believes in always being on the offensive. She said she would feel better if I didn't nag her. I haven't been able to speak in a more than a week and just wrote notes to my mother in answer to her questions. I had so little voice she couldn't hear me. How could I nag her? My days since the medicine have been spent sleeping. I take the medicine, sleep three or four hours, take the medicine and sleep some more. Thus go the days. Nights are different! I take the medicine and cough, cough, cough and keep both Gene and me awake.

Now it is Saturday night. I didn't take the medicine after supper so I'm awake and sitting wrapped in a blanket writing this letter so Gene can take it for xeroxing on Monday. Right now I'm perspiring. I think I'll take a bath and get out of this damp nightgown.

I must look a mess with my eyes all swollen. At night I wake and can't get my eyes open till I peel away the crust that has formed on my eyelids.

My mother has been coming to view me every fifteen minutes as I'm stretched out on the sofa. Today Gene took over that department. Such a view. My medicine will run out this weekend so I think I'll see my own doctor on Monday, if I can.

I can't see TV because my eyes are so fogged with matter. One day I saw our fireplace on the ceiling, not once but many times and yet the fireplace never moved.

I forgot to tell you the worst symptom. I suppose from the cough I hurt under my rib cage. Not just hurt. but pained. Now this pain has gone to my back and I can't bend over, lie down or get up without great pain. My gosh. Norma is a big girl and easily seen and this darn virus is so small the naked eye can't see it but it seems to have felled Norma. Like the mouse and the elephant!

TUESDAY, FEBRUARY 1, 1983

Gene went to work today. He didn't go yesterday because it was obvious I couldn't get myself to the doctor.

Saturday and Sunday, because of the terrible pain in my lower left back near my hip, it was necessary for Gene to put his arms around my shoulders and lift me to a sitting position. Then with my arms around his neck and he supporting my back, I could get to a standing position. The same in reverse when I had to lie down.

Monday we were at the doctor's office before he opened at 9 AM. There were several things that might be the matter and he checked out what he could in his office and then sent me to the radiology lab across from the hospital. They did one set of x -rays, then another. Lungs clear, no slipped disc, no broken ribs. It was concluded that the coughing had torn the ligaments in my lower back. The next stop was at the drug store where Gene bought forty pills for $1.02 each. The doctor said I must take all forty pills even if I feel better. I also got pills to depress my cough and they really worked. So today I'm toilet trained and not wearing a diaper. The doctor said it is not unusual to be incontinent when coughing is so severe. My voice is still nil. The doctor thought it might return in a week. That will be about eighteen days I will have been silent.

My mother made a packaged cake for Gene's birthday. I tried to sing happy birthday but nothing came out so Gene joined my mother and sang happy birthday to himself. Fortunately I had purchased Gene's present just prior to getting sick and I even had the store wrap it. It wasn't a pleasant birthday for Gene but we did celebrate it.

If I have one thing to be thankful for, it is my super husband. He put my slippers on me because I couldn't bend over to do so. If something fell on the floor, there it stayed. Gene didn't complain about helping me in any way. He put up with sleepless nights. I wanted to sleep in one of the spare rooms but he would have none of it. He couldn't hear me in another room. Of course, I couldn't call. I did have a bell but neither Gene nor my mother, both deaf, heard the bell. In the same bed he is aware of every move and breath.

The doctor called me at 4 PM yesterday. Between two and four I had taken two pills. The doctor asked how I felt. Exactly the same. He said I was a tough cookie. It wasn't till 6 PM that the medicine took effect and the limp feeling came. I didn't know what effect the medicine was to have but I certainly do now.

As I write this, it is 11 AM. I've had a bath and a long sleep on the sofa. I can get up and down today on the sofa because I can grab the back and pull myself upright. I'm ready now to go back to the sofa.

Boy, I'm one useless person. It is a good thing my mother is here to do the cooking. She is a bit rusty in this department but we are getting along

MARCH 8, 1983

Dear Jennie and Harry,

The Queen of England is in San Francisco. Some of her activities are on national TV but I think some of what we saw locally hasn't gone that far. The other morning we awoke to hear the local news man on radio tell about the Queen's trip to the Reagan ranch. This was off and on for several hours and then they decided to do it in jeeps because the limousines might not be able to make it through the water. He said there were seven streams overflowing the road and they have to forge them. The commentator said the Queen was a good sport and seemed to enjoy the outing to the ranch, in spite of the drenching rain and danger. The Reagans served tacos which I don't like. I wonder how the Queen liked their ranch house. It is only 1500 sq. feet. Had she ever been in such a small place?

In spite of the trip being planned to the last detail, there were surprises. Because of the rough weather, she couldn't sail up the coast from Los Angeles to San Francisco. She flew into San Francisco and the landing was far away from the terminal, at the emergency hospital. The young man in charge of the empty hospital was astounded when the advance men descended upon him. He refused to let them do anything until he called his boss and got permission.

The Queen disembarked and at the bottom step she spontaneously and naturally shook her index finger at some woman, I think the U.S. protocol person. Usually we see her with a tight lipped smile. I think there weren't even twenty people to meet her. Nancy Reagan followed immediately behind and then Prince Philip. Originally she would have stayed on her yacht but without it, they had to scurry around and provide other accommodations. The St. Francis Hotel on Union Square seemed the most secure because there was an underground parking garage with an elevator directly to the top floor. Apparently it is a rarity for the Queen to stay in an hotel. What could they do? The royal yacht couldn't come up the coast in that terrible storm. She arrived a day early and people were evicted from the rooms she and her entourage were to occupy. She got the presidential suite and the Reagans had the London suite. For dinner they took her to Trader Vic's. Gene and I went there on our first visit to San Francisco years ago. It is a tourist restaurant just as the St. Francis is a tourist hotel. Lots of conventions meet at the St. Francis and tourists often go to Trader Vic's. We expected she would stay at the Fairmont, Stanford Arms, the Huntington or some other exclusive hotel. At least we expected her to be on Nob Hill and not in a place where the general public congregates.

A few minutes ago a local reporter interviewed the chief chef at the St. Francis. This hotel will provide the food for the banquet at the de Young Museum tonight. The first course is lobster mousse. We read in the newspaper that the Queen would not eat shell fish. This is shell fish. Accompanying it seemed to be a flower made of the skin of the tomato which had been circularly pared and rolled to resemble petals. Dessert seemed to be some kind of puff with fresh fruit sauces, one being raspberry. The main course was breast of veal with a dressing that wasn't made of bread. I didn't understand whether it was vegetable or fruit.

TV is having special programs all day to show the Queen's activities. I laughed the other morning when a reporter spoke of Liz and Phil. I bet this is unheard of in England.

This morning on TV a reporter talked to people on the street about the Queen's visit. Some were thrilled, some could care less, and one homosexual man said there are lots of "queens" in S.F. and he could see nothing special about this one! The police are trying hard to keep those Irish demonstrators away from the Queen.

Some supervisors refused to attend the reception for the Queen. Actually it was all for the best. Two flaunt tarnished, flawed life styles. I'd say it is a good miss for the Queen.

At 11 AM there was a TV program on the Queen but just at that moment I had a phone call so I missed the first five minutes. The Queen and party went to Davies Symphony Hall. Sometime I want to take a tour of that hall. Twenty nine San Franciscans paid for a half hour of entertainment for the Queen. First the mayor gave the keys of the city to the Queen. It was a real key that would unlock the door at Mission Dolores which was the center of S.F. when it was established. Mary Martin was next and she explained how she had met and entertained the Queen previously. She sang GETTING TO KNOW YOU and a few words were changed to suit the occasions. Then Tony Bennett sang I LEFT MY HEART IN SAN FRANCISCO. Through all this the Queen never cracked a smile. Unique to San Francisco is Beach Blanket Babylon and they had the performers from there come to Davies Hall and do a program. Their quarters are quite dumpy and no place for a Queen, but Davies Hall is fit for the best. The singers and dancers were dressed in black and white gay 90's costumes. One woman wore a hat that was 6 feet across and it had many buildings of San Francisco on it. The pyramid building, TransAmerica. stood out. Another woman had a hat that had Big Ben, Parliament and I think Buckingham Palace. Doors on Big Ben opened and behind the doors were pictures of Charles, Diana and Little William. The door on the right had the Queen and on the left Prince Philip. They opened the doors several times. Thru all this Philip was animated but the Queen didn't register any emotion till she saw the London hat. I got choked up. It was so impressive. Remember my letter about Beach Blanket Babylon? I have never forgotten those hats and wonder how anyone can sing and dance with such heavy, cumbersome things on their heads. No where else in the world can you see anything like Beach Blanket Babylon. This lasted only half an hour and then they were on their way to Palo Alto.

They took the Bay Shore freeway and no cars were allowed in front of or behind the motorcade for two miles. Boy! This freeway is a busy highway that passes the airport and some people were upset not to be able to get to the airport. Passengers thought they would miss their flights but the pilots couldn't get to the airport either.

Along with the San Francisco TV commentators was a reporter from the London Daily Mirror. He thought the Queen was animated! He was asked what he thought of those two hats and he said England would expect that kind of extravaganza from the U.S. He also said he had expected this to be a routine trip but" you Americans have turned everything topsy turvy." He went on about the Queen staying in an hotel and dining in a "Chinese" restaurant. Unheard of! Trader Vic's is more Polonesian. I don't think it would like to be called Chinese.

This day my mother and I went to Pinole so we missed lots of the Queen's day. We did see a little bit that night. The Queen had lunch at Hoover House on the Stanford Campus. I didn't have a pencil in hand so I only know she was served chicken and asparagus. Twenty Students were invited to the luncheon, along with some notables. One boy was elated because the Queen asked him what he was studying and when he said the classics, the Queen said she didn't know anyone ever studied the classics now. The kitchen help were students, all dressed in long white dresses. They lined up as she was leaving and she walked over and spoke to them. Then the motorcade went to Hewlett Packard, a computer manufacturer. The Queen had requested this. The owner was her guide. When asked if he thought the Queen understood everything he told her, he said he thought he did a pretty good job of explaining. A good way to avoid making that judgment. The Reagans are giving the Queen a computer from Hewlett Packard. Coming back everyone was shunted off route 280. On the news tonight they said security has never been so tight in San Francisco. We have a Queen, a President, ambassadors, as well as cabinet members. Two blocks from any spot the Queen is has to be cleared. Secret service men surrounded her. In England, she stands alone but here they were even in front of her. I think in England nobody walks in front of the Queen.

The newspapers in England have stated that the Queen had bed and board accommodations in S.F. I wouldn't call the Presidential suite at $1700 a night bed and board. Her entourage occupied 46 rooms, too, and rooms at the St. Francis start at $100 a night and most are much more.

3/4/83

Last night we probably didn't see any more of the Queen than you did. We saw her briefly entering and leaving and we heard the toasts of the Queen and Reagan in their entirety. We saw Shultz and Wineberger. We heard Steve Bechtel who owns the company Gene works for was there. We weren't surprised. He keeps a low profile but he is one of the wealthiest men in the U.S. and has one of the three biggest engineering firms in the world. I wasn't impressed with the Queen's dress. The sleeves were a distraction with bows just below the ears which did not allow her jewelry to show off. And it should have.

Reagan is having a cabinet meeting today so I assume the whole cabinet was at the dinner.

The Queen left by plane for Sacramento this morning and her first stop was Sutter's Fort. Fifty people in period costume performed the tasks of 1849. A man dressed as John Sutter took the Queen around and explained things. Nobody was allowed muskets and tomahawks. From here the Queen went to the capitol and the governor entertained her at lunch. The Nut Tree restaurant provided the lunch which was served in the rotunda. The main course was filet or sole, stuffed with crab and shrimp and wrapped in a crepe with a white wine sauce. I've often had this but without the crepe. The crepe seemed unnecessary. The governor had one hundred guests but he did not invite the legislators, just the leaders.

Back to San Francisco in Air Force two and on to the residence of the British Consul General where seven hundred fifty children of British heritage greeted her. Inside one hundred eighty people of British heritage had tea or wine with the Queen.

Then back to the royal yacht. From a helicopter we saw the empty streets and the traffic jams on nearby streets. I thought Gene would be late getting home tonight but he was on his way before the Queen started back

MARCH 5TH

Last night the Queen entertained the Reagans on the royal yacht. It was their thirty -first wedding anniversary. 60 people were invited to the dinner and afterwards there was a reception to which more were invited. The Reagans stayed overnight on the yacht. All we saw was the Beat Retreat at the end of the evening. Everyone gathered at the side of the yacht and watched. We did not learn what was served.

This morning the Queen and the Reagans left San Francisco. The Reagans went back to Washington.

The Queen and party flew to Merced and then took cars to Yosemite. Three secret service men not in the motorcade were in an accident and all were killed. This was chilling.

She will stay at the Ahwahnee Hotel in the Park. The Ahwahnee is old but she will have the VIP suite. Saturday night we played bridge with a young couple who honeymooned at the Ahwahnee. Before they left, they made a reservation for the same room for their first anniversary. They appeared on that date but for some reason they couldn't have that room. They were given this VIP suite to make up for the disappointment. Alex said you had to have a special key to operate the elevator to the suite. He said the bathroom was as big as a regular room. Alex said the view from this top floor suite was spectacular.

So now we know somebody who slept in a room that the Queen slept in.

Gene took his camera to work and he took three pictures of the royal yacht as it sailed past his window. The window was dirty and it was raining so he may not have gotten much.

The excitement of having the Queen in San Francisco is over. As she left this morning they shot off fireworks and released thousands of balloons. It was raining so it wasn't effective.

Breakfast was served on pier 50 for the people waiting to see the Queen take off. Private organizations did this.

All of the Queen's visit to San Francisco. was paid for from donations of wealthy people in San Francisco, not tax payer's money. We only learned this when somebody complained about the cost to San Francisco of the visit.

At 11:24 AM today the Britannia sailed into the bay and Gene, at his desk, saw it sail by. I didn't know this yacht could easily be converted into a hospital ship.

Breadbaking
Earthquakes, Preparing for Africa, Yakoff Smirnof

JUNE 13, 1983

Dear Jacqui and Will,

I've been cooking! Last week I had a luncheon, we had a dinner party and I had to take dessert to a bridge. I took lemon cheesecake and it was a smashing hit. At the moment I'm making poppy seed bread.

Since we bought the Cuisinart in April. I've done nothing but bake bread and rolls. Gene is getting very spoiled and I'm afraid soon he will refuse to eat anything but home baked bread. Most recipes make two or three loaves so I give all but one away. Yesterday I made parker house rolls. When my mother saw them, she said she hoped I wasn't t going to give any of them away. They were excellent and I didn't. Maybe learning to make bread wasn't such a good idea. Previously on Sunday I only had to put the meat in the oven, cook a vegetable, make a salad and sometimes a dessert. Now I have to get up early so I can make rolls and have them ready for dinner. I haven 't time to read the paper till after dinner. I could have saved myself a lot of work if I had never started this breadmaking. Too late smart!

Last fall Gene decided to have his check deposited in the bank by Bechtel. He got fed up standing in line to cash his check. Friday Gene got an extra check at work. It seems they messed things up last fall and Gene never got credit for one check. Bechtel discovered the mistake and so paid him his back wages. Last November I complained because we were short of money. We did have some big expenses., like a new refrigerator and Christmas, but still we felt pinched. Now we know why.

At bridge Saturday night one of the young girls was telling of a super fruit salad. Over a bowl or fresh cut up fruit, you spread plain yogurt. On top of that you sprinkle grated Swiss cheese. Sounds so simple, I think I'll try it.

Today I went to the bank. An elderly man was complaining. He had a money market account certificate but no bank book. He wanted a bank book and unless he got one, he was taking his money out of that bank. Banks are certainly changing the way they do business.

Formerly when I wanted to send money overseas, I went to a special teller. Recently I wanted to pay for a reservation on an Irish boat. I went to the special teller and was told any teller now does this. The regular teller wanted to charge me $1.55 for an Irish pound. It should have been $1.23. I said no way would the pound have gone up that much over the weekend. She said Ireland was a part of England and that was the quote.

I informed her that there is a free Ireland called Eire. She should look that up. She called downtown to check and they confirmed what I said and quoted $1.20 a pound. You have to watch people. Schools have done a poor job and this girl hadn't learned that there is an independent Ireland and only the northern part belongs to England. Money going to Dublin was a dead giveaway that it was going to independent Ireland, Eire.

My mother was overcharged a dollar in the grocery store. She raised a fuss. The checker got excited, corrected the mistake, made another and gave my mother more than she was supposed to have.

JULY 18, 1983

Dear Marguerite and Ed,

Last September Mary and Bud invested in a time share condo at South Lake Tahoe. They have the use of it one week a year. They invited us to spend this past weekend with them and we were delighted to accept.

Saturday morning we left at 8:20 and arrived at 12:20. It was just two hundred miles, door to door. The condo is like an efficiency apartment, a room which doubles as living area and bedroom, bath and minuscule kitchen with doll sized sink and refrigerator, microwave oven, toaster and coffeemaker. We slept on a sofa bed.

Mary's birthday was Sunday so I took along a chocolate cake which we had for lunch. In the evening the men barbecued steaks outside on a grill. Afterwards we drove eight miles to a ranger station where, around a campfire, we saw slides about the trees of the Tahoe area. It was cold.

We had all had so much air that we slept soundly all night. Nobody snored or, if one did, none of the rest of us were awake to hear it. Ceiling to floor drapes separated the living room area from the bedroom but we had to walk thru the bedroom to get to the bathroom.

After breakfast we drove to the Tallac area of Lake Tahoe where years ago wealthy families had rustic homes. Now the governments owns them. We walked around and came upon a flower called the Snow Plant, sarcodes sanguinea. Stem and flower were fire engine red. It is about a foot tall. I don't know why it is called a snow plant because it doesn't come till after the snow is all gone. I looked in my wildflower and gardening books and I can find no mention or this, either under common name or botanical name.

Since we planned to eat early we just snacked at noon. The best places to eat at Lake Tahoe are the casinos but the wait is extremely long. We got there at 5. At the Sahara Tahoe the wait was more than an hour. Mary and I went to Caesar's and the wait was only 15 minutes so we took a number and went back for Bud and Gene. It was buffet. Cost $5.99 a person. Terribly cheap. The biggest problem is that even with a teaspoon of everything, it would be too much. We picked and chose but even then we were stuffed. Everything looked so good.

The casinos would go broke with people like us. Gene spent a total of two dollars. After a short time we returned to the condo and played bridge.

Today after breakfast, Gene and I left for home, arriving at 1:20 PM

Gene and I had a good time but a time share is not for us. Mary and Bud have this for 30 years and then it reverts to the corporation. They pay a yearly maintenance fee. They can bank their week and use it someplace else where this corporation has condos. They can't let their children use it unless they are there with them. We think a time share is a financially poor investment. Just the thought of having to spend a week each year for the rest of our lives at Lake Tahoe is boring. We want to see and do different things on each vacation. Oh, well, to each his own.

We traveled exactly the same distance going and coming and yet we got better mileage coming home. It is all downhill coming home and all climbing going, between Sacramento to Lake Tahoe. We go from sea level to 7000 feet.

AUGUST 4, 1983

Dear Catherine and Larry,

Remembrance of those wonderful kimmelwick rolls we used to buy in Buffalo and gaining confidence in my bread making, I decided to try my hand at these rolls. I looked through my five shelves of cookbooks and found not one recipe. I called the county library information service. They searched the county library system and found not one reference to them. They said they would consult the Oakland library. They did and today they called and said they went through 22 appropriate books and still no reference to them. The Oakland library wrote the Buffalo library and the Oakland library informed me it might be weeks before the Buffalo library answered. I hope they can get the recipe because both Gene and I love "beef on wick".

Back in the Buffalo-Niagara Falls area beef on wick restaurants were as popular as hamburger restaurants. Bakeries sold kimmelwick rolls and if you had thinly sliced beef, you could make your own beef on wicks. I understood when we lived there that kimmelwick rolls were made only in that area and that the recipe was jealously guarded.

When we lived in Ann Arbor either the president of GM or Henry Ford had a private plane fly to Buffalo, when his daughter made her debut, to bring back kimmelwick rolls which were served at breakfast after the dance. Just thinking about them makes me hungry for some.

There are lots of Polish people in the Buffalo-Niagara Falls area. I vaguely recall some one saying this might be a recipe immigrants brought to the U.S. I wrote a friend of Polish ancestry but she didn't know and neither did her mother.

Another thing we dearly love is croissants. Connie Huffman made croissants in her food processor and sent some over. They were wonderful rolls but not true croissants. I used her recipe and mine turned out just like hers. I guess you just can't make true croissants in a food processor. My next project is to make croissants in the traditional way. Today Connie came over and we spent six hours rolling out the dough, rolling butter into the dough, sixteen layers. After each time, it went into the freezer. We ended up with eighteen croissants. We ate some, Connie took some home and we had six for dinner. A whole days work for this. I bet if time, freezer use, oven use and ingredients were added up, we would have spent more than twice what these croissants cost in a bakery. And they weren't as good.

Connie Willey called a few minutes ago. She lives outside Boston. She and her daughter are arriving Tuesday so I will go to the airport and pick them up. They will stay with us till Friday when I'll take them into San Francisco where they will attend a craft fair on the weekend. After that, they plan to drive to Carmel for a few days. Returning from Carmel, they will stay in San Francisco a few more days. I'll spend one day with them when they return to San Francisco.

NOVEMBER 25, 1983

Dear Ruth and Bill,

It is the day after Thanksgiving. We are relaxing. Gene is looking at the Army-Navy game.

We had a quiet Thanksgiving. We invited the Huffmans who have three grown daughters, all living three thousand miles away, who couldn't be with them that day. Linda, who lives in West Virginia, is being married here on January 2nd so she will come for Christmas. Her future husband is from the San Francisco area. It is to be a small wedding in the Huffman's living room with only parents, brothers and sisters present. Yesterday after dinner we played a little bridge and about seven we nibbled left overs.

Thanksgiving and the whole month of November has been extremely rainy. BART did some repair work on one of its tracks and disturbed a drainage canal. An apartment compex was flooded as a result. People repaired the damage and two weeks later the same thing occurred.

Gene's group at work had a pot luck luncheon on Tuesday. Gene volunteered homemade rolls. Some people decided it was easier to contribute money and have things purchased. Bechtel hires people of all nationalities so all kinds of foreign food appeared at this luncheon. Gene said the Russian food appealed to him the most. My rolls are made with instant potato flakes and are light and fluffy. Gene got compliments on the rolls and even a request for the recipe. Gene said all the homemade food was eaten but the store bought food was left. Tuesday I had to see a new doctor because our doctor of eight years has a problem. He has been absent from his office for six months. He was back and treated my arthritis and now he is unavailable again. We like this doctor but we are uncomfortable with the idea that he might not be available when we really need him. My mother is eighty nine. Who knows when we'll need a doctor? So I had an appointment with a new doctor recommended by a nurse friend. I was so excited and upset about having to change doctors that my blood pressure went sky high. Tuesday, Audrey, the nurse across the road, took my blood pressure and it was normal. The new doctor advised me to stop taking the arthritis medicine. I did for two days and I was in real pain so now I'm back to taking it again. I hate to think I might have this pain the rest of my life but the doctors assure me I will. I never realized how wonderful it is to walk without pain until I got this arthritis.

This month San Francisco voted a second time on banning smoking in the work place and it was passed. Now Gene won't have to breathe smoke when working. When Gene comes home, I smell tobacco smoke on Gene's clothes,face and even his hair. Employers have to provide a place for smokers or else ban it. Even if a room is provided, air is circulated so it would just come back to the working place. Windows in these buildings do not open so no fresh air can enter thru windows. I can see this might be a problem for employers. We are glad the tobacco companies did not win this time. They spent millions to defeat the first law.

JANUARY 31, 1984

Dear Margaret,

Today is Gene's birthday. He opened his card from me this morning. No time to open his present so he will do that tonight.

The cake is in the oven. Now an hour has gone by and the cake is iced and the dishes done. Although I knew what Gene's answer would be, I asked him what kind of cake he wanted. His usual reply, "Any kind, as long as it is chocolate." The card I found had a picture of an Acoma pot on the outside. I knew I had to buy this card when I saw it because we had visited Acoma and went on a tour with a Texas woman who bought a pot. There was one for $300, one for $500 and one for $800. I think she took the $500 one. Those Acoma pots are pretty and different but not much use since they don't hold water.

At Thanksgiving I ordered white shirts for Gene. He takes a 15 1/2, ordinary size, but the sleeve length is 36 inches. 34 and 35 inches are the longest stores carry so it had to be ordered. Today the Arrow salesman called and said it would probably be March before the shirts arrived. They have to be made specially. In Ann Arbor there was a store that did carry shirts with 36 inch sleeves. Guess there are lots of men in that area who need them.

My last bread class was yesterday. We started out with twenty eight and yesterday there were only twelve. Some just come to pass the time. One woman said she had just had a $20 manicure and she wasn't going to knead bread and spoil her manicure. I like pretty nails but I never have them because I have to clean the oven, wash the floor and do all sorts of things which would spoil a manicure.

When I first started taking the bread class, the teacher showed us a book she would use, THE COMPLETE BREAD BOOK. It was attractive and we all went out to buy the book. No store in Concord or Walnut Creek had it. I even went to Berkeley and didn't find it there. I wrote the publisher at two different addresses and both letters were returned. Now I've written Crown because Crescent is a division of Crown. No answer. Chain book stores did not have this title on their computers. It isn't listed in BOOKS IN PRINT. I wrote all this in a letter to a cousin of my father's in New Jersey and on a day he was snowed in, he called a bookstore in a mall nearby and they had the book on sale! It is a 1977 book so either the store had it in stock for several years or else got it as a remainder. Chet called and asked if I had been successful in getting the book. When I said no, he had them send me the book.

I don't think we have had more than one loaf of store bread since I started the class. And very few since we bought the Cuisinert last April, Making bread is such fun and the smell of baking bread is WONDERFUL.

The picture of Gene and the goodies shows a Xmas stollen that I learned to make in bread class. I made it three times and two times it was fine and the third time it spread out instead of getting higher. Those croissants were the best I've ever made but they still aren't perfect. They could be a bit flakier. I'm not sure what to do to make them so. I followed the recipe exactly. The kolacky is between the stollen and croissants. They are Czechoslovakian in origin. I filled some with a date mixture and the others with apricot. I don' t know which I like best. The pie is an apple pie and the other things are Christmas cookies. I didn't make so many Christmas cookies this year since Gene was only home one week in December. The picture of me shows the magnifying glasses for makeup without my glasses. I can't see without my glasses and there isn't room to brush my eyelashes with the glasses on. I didn't know such glasses could be purchased. Too bad I didn't have eye make up on when Gene took the picture. I'll do this for social occasions but not for grocery shopping.

On February 15th my mother will turn 90. We are planning a dinner party of about 17. I shall have to have people sit at card tables and the food will be buffet style on the dining room table. I don't plan any entertainment because it is a Wednesday and most men will have to work the next day. Out here men have at least an hour's commute. Most leave for work about 6:30 AM. A couple men leave even earlier because they finish work at 4 PM, instead of the usual 5 PM.

APRIL 26, 1984

Dear Eunice and John.

Earthquakes have character. They are not all alike. Two days ago we had the biggest I've ever experienced. I'm beginning to sort them out. There are three I remember vividly.

One night Gene and I were sitting on the love seat in our family room when suddenly our house seemed to rise a foot in the air and then plunge back to earth with a real jolt. When it landed again on the foundation, you felt that jolt.

A month ago Gene was in Pennsylvania and I was alone with my mother. This time our house seemed to jerk sharply to the right and then to the left and there was a terrible rumble. Never before have I heard the rumble. All the rest of that evening our house creaked and groaned. Ordinarily our house doesn't make noises.

Wednesday we had a 25 second quake and I felt as though our house was a boat, bobbing around on the water and it bobbed and bobbed. This kind we have had before but not a 6.2 magnitude. It is scary. Each time I become immobilized.

The Calaveras Fault is close to our house, less than half a mile. It runs right along the freeway. Usually it is the San Andreas fault that is talked about but the Calaveras has done quite a bit of damage. We feel the earthquake when it occurs in either of these faults but we really know it when it is on the fault where we live.

The national news had the earthquake story but the local stations did the story in depth. We had lots of pictures of the destruction of those $300,000-$500,000 homes in Morgan Hill. One man was sitting on the edge of his bed, putting on his socks when suddenly a huge armoire fell on the bed, within an inch of him. Inside the houses in Morgan Hill, everything was overturned and things in cupboards were scattered all over. It was a mess. The school library shelves were bare because the books were on the floor.

The only thing in our house affected was the shower door in our bathroom. It blew open. Many people reported doors being opened by the earthquake. A neighbor tried to call me but her phone was out or order. She came over and I tried to call her and our phone was out of order. Inside of forty five minutes both were working again.

My mother was on her way through the dining room and living room and just as she got to the railing separating the two the quake struck. She thought she was going to fall and grabbed the railing and for twenty five seconds she hung on and rolled back and forth. I watched her and saw, beyond her out the front window, the hanging plants on the house across the street, swinging back and forth. Our wind chimes chimed and the measuring cups hanging in our kitchen clanged. I could see the corner of our house moving back and forth.

A friend was at a coffee hour when her chair started moving. She thought she was dizzy and going to faint but almost at the same moment a woman became hysterical and another one shouted "Earthquake."

When an earthquake occurs, I'm tongue tied. I can't say or do anything. I know I should go to a safe place but still I sat between two large windows, one quite close.

On TV people at Pier 39 were interviewed. A foreign couple who couldn't speak English got their thoughts across. The reporter said earthquake and the woman moved her head sidewise rapidly and the man used his hands to make a ripply motions and their eyes told the rest of the story. They were funny.

Two twenty year old men from Kansas, on vacation, were interviewed. They said, "We blew it! We were on a bus and we didn't see or hear a thing. We spent $285 to get here and now we have to go back to Kansas and tell all our friends we missed the best part of the vacation."

It is true, you don't feel an earthquake when riding in a bus or car. In high rise buildings you get a real thrill. I get enough of a THRILL in our one story home.

On radio one man said he was gardening when the earth began to roll and ripple. I've seen this and it is quite a sight and gives a real sensation.

JULY 11, 1984

Dear Marion and Bob,

My DAY was made ! My WEEK was made !! My YEAR was made !!! The most wonderful thing happened to me at the library today. I was borrowing two novels, two biographies and a book entitled, HAVING A BABY by seven women, one of which is Jan Yanehiro, a hostess of a TV show, Evening Magazine, which comes on each night at 7:30. The library clerk looked at the books and said, "You aren't having a baby, are you?"

"No," said I, "But I'm flattered that you think I might be."

"Lots of women in their forties are having babies today" she said.

To have anyone think I might be in my forties is the greatest compliment I've had in a dog's age. I came directly home and was thrilled to tell Gene what a young wife he has but he just said that the library clerk couldn't have been wearing her glasses. A put down if ever there was one but I'm still on cloud nine because the clerk only saw me from the breast up so it had to be my face and not my figure that made her think I could be in my forties and having a baby.

Of course, at the moment I'm probably walking like I'm in my forties. My arthritis has stabilized and I'm in no pain and I'm not limping. I even walked a very steep flight of stairs in San Francisco. The escalator in the BART station wasn't working so I had to walk up and I made it in the normal fashion but coming home we ran into another non working escalator and I had to take a step at a time and always with the same foot so I was really walking like an old lady then. The medicine and this terrible hot weather are probably responsible for my much improved condition. I just wish I could remain as I now am.

JULY 13, 1984

Dear Raedina and Milton,

Today we went into San Francisco for a retirement luncheon given by Bechtel for nine people, one of whom was Gene. It was held at the World Trade Center, an exclusive club. I think a couple of the presidents have membership there, at least that is what one of the Bechtel officials said. There were twenty three of us in all, with wives and Bechtel personnel. The room faced the bay and my place at the table gave me a beautiful view of the Oakland Bridge and the interesting boats in the bay. The table was most attractive, white linen cloth, pink napkins and the most beautiful florist table arrangements I've ever seen. There were two made up of various shades of pink roses, dianthus, baby's breath, and a kind of fern I've never seen. The leaves were only the size of a new born baby's little finger nail. This fern connected the two arrangements and came out each end. There was stephanotis entwined. At each wife's place there was a little vase with three roses, two dianthus, baby's breath, fern and an orchid. We were told to bring these home with us. After a little speech about each retiree, gifts were given. If you worked for Bechtel over twenty years. you got a clock, ten years a thermometer-barometer. We already have a barometer-thermometer we never use. Each person was given a personal letter from the president, engraved on copper and mounted on a board. What we will do with this stuff, I don't know.

The lunch was delicious. A crab appetizer, beautifully arranged on endive, with a sauce, on a flat plate. Broiled salmon, sugar pea pods, new potatoes in jackets. Dessert was was ice cream covered with apricots and a dash of whipped cream accompanied by little cookies.Next came a tiny cream puff which had been iced in various colors and swirled with chocolate. I was impressed with the quality of the food but mostly with the superb service. I'd like to go there more often but we never shall because we don't know any members who could take us. A photographer took a pictures of each retiree and his wife. It was a lovely send off for each retiree. Our only regret is that this couldn't have occurred two and a half years from now when Gene would normally be retiring.

AUGUST 9, 1984

Last Thursday we decided on our vacation and Friday morning we paid for it. Today our vouchers and tickets came. I have been laying aside clothes and washing others to take on the trip. Gene has been doing the same thing.

I have been amused by some of our friends. One said the island of Oahu is just too commercial and should be avoided entirely. I want to see Honolulu. Another said there is nothing on any of the other islands so why did we want to go to Hawaii, Maui and Kauai. Two points of view. We want to see as much as we can. I read about the island of Nihau. Aside from the people who live there, only doctors and a few government officials are allowed on this island. The island has been owned by one family for years. The people who live there work for that family and the family supplies clothes and shelter. No automobiles are allowed. Children go to elementary school on the island and then go to high school on other islands. No tourists are ever allowed. Usually the children return to the island after getting an education. Sounds sort of like slavery. I understand you can see this island from Kauai.

MARCH 2, 1985

Dear Phyllis,

Since we will be flying a LONG time, we think we should rest in Frankfurt. We have a non stop flight from S.F., then a rest of a day in a Sheraton Hotel, and then another all night flight to Nairobi. The travel agent inquired and a double bed in this hotel is $104 and twin beds are $71. Logical? No. Gene objected and I said I could only tell him what the travel agent told me. However, I called the international reservations number for Sheraton hotels and the operator confirmed these prices. Laundry is twice for single beds and it takes twice as long to make two beds and yet two beds are cheaper. We think we shall sleep in twins and save the $33 it would cost us for a double bed. King and Queens are even more. They certainly do things differently in Germany. When we ask for a double bed here, we often get a room with two double beds and we pay for just one.

Last night I made a comment about the amount of money we are spending right now. Gene replied, " Yes, we are spending money just as if we HAD it!"

I made brioches and they just came out of the oven. The top knots didn't stay top knots but became a part of the brioche. They are good but not exactly right. Too much work for the result, I think.

Do you know T. Boone Pickens? He is a millionaire oilman who buys oil companies as we would buy a loaf of bread. There was a seven page article about him in TIME. He has a corporate jet and he has a pillow on it which says, "If you must smoke, please step outside. "

We are entertaining at bridge tonight.

This morning we were eating breakfast and my mother looked out the living room window and asked if that was snow on top of Mt. Diablo. It was. First snow this winter. It is 2:30 now and the snow is gone.

MARCH 9, 1985

Dear Adelaide.

Yesterday I read a novel about Ireland, A GREEN JOURNEY by Jan Hassler, which expressed the preconceived notions that Irish people have about Americans, namely, that Americans are full of beans and Americans get mugged once a week. I won't spoil the story by telling you about George and the mugger. Do read the book. It is good.

Today I went into S.F. to apply for our new passports.Everyone else was told to sit down and wait till their number was called. I was told to write my check and that was all. I don't understand why it was so easy for me.

Then I went to buy a new part for Gene's electric razor. I wish he would buy a new one but he thinks he can fix this one. I looked for a pair of sneakers. I had ordered a pair from a N.Y. store that specializes in narrow widths but even they didn't have any that were narrow enough for me. I did find a pair in Concord, wrong color and too wide. If I use an insole, they won't be so wide. I could find neither the right color nor my size in San Francisco so I'll settle for the wrong color and a bit wide.I do want sneakers for Africa.

We have to have visas. Previously our passports have been stamped and there hasn't been a charge. Both Kenya and Tanzania require a fee and pictures for our visa. This is most unusual. Here goes another hundred dollars.

The snow on top of Mt Diablo melted during the night. It has been there for a week and this is unheard of.

MARCH 19, 1985

Before I plunge into my busy day, I'll write a few lines

Colette arrives a week from today for a three week visit. So today I must clean thoroughly. It is 9 AM and I've made a chart of each day and put down what we shall do and eat each day. I've made out a grocery list for tomorrow and will buy all but the fresh fruits and vegetables for the next three weeks. Between now and the time Colette arrives, we'll be busy with Book Review, dentist., yellow fever shots, cleaning and of course caring for my mother.

I'm planning a luncheon while Colette is here. It will have to be a tray luncheon because I can't get twelve around our dining room table.

I hope the Pan Am strike is over by the 26th. Her flight from Paris to NY has not been canceled but the one from NY to SF has been. I called Pan Am and they said they would put her on a flight of another line. WHICH ONE? San Francisco now has two different terminals. Which one will I go to? I'll call the day before she arrives and hope they can tell me what flight to meet.

I don't expect to do much letter writing while Colette is here.

Yesterday my mother and I went shopping. I couldn't find what I wanted so we went to Oakland and Berkeley and didn't find it there. I'll have to make do. I did see a joke egg and decided to buy it. It is a plain white egg, rubber, but it looks real. My foot pained last night so I lay on the sofa. I told Gene about the egg and attempted to get up and show it to him. He insisted he would get it but I over ruled him. I picked up the egg, riveted my eyes on Gene and dropped the egg. When it hit the floor, the egg bounced. You should have seen Gene's horrified expression and then his big smile. He said I was pulling an April Fool trick prematurely. Gene's expression was worth the cost of the egg. I hadn't planned to fool my mother but she also got fooled. I left the egg on the table and went to the garage. My mother came along and, expecting to see ornamentation on the other side, she picked it up. She was surprised to find it soft. The egg really looks real. I'll fool others who come into our house.

After we returned home, I made pecan tassies and cookies to be served on Colette's visit. My mother saw them and asked if I was going to give some away. She is annoyed when I give away things she likes.

APRIL 30, 1985

Dear Emma and John,

Beginning today I may have the car every day. Gene has been negotiating for the last two months with a German who works at G.E. During the winter he drove to San Jose Monday morning and home to Pinole Friday afternoon. He wants a paying rider but what he is asking is almost as much as the cost of his Mercedes. "No soap," said Gene.

Next he proposed Gene drive to Rudgear Road. He suggested Gene buy a second car just for this. No, again. At times he was actually begging Gene to ride with him but he refused to pick Gene up at home. He lives 20 miles beyond Concord so this was on his way but he said he would waste ten minutes. Finally his price came down so Gene agreed to ride to Lafayette with him. Then Gene would take Bart and a bus. The big advantage is that Gene gets home in a little more than an hour, instead of 3 hours on Bart and two buses. Gene checked out being picked up at the Walnut Creek Bart station and found it would add only 3 minutes to the German's time. The German checked this out and found it true so he agreed to lengthen his ride by three minutes and pick Gene up at the Walnut Creek Bart. So four days a week I drive Gene to Bart. The fifth day the German doesn't work so Gene will have long commutes each way every Friday. Friday is one day Gene WON'T drive. Too much traffic coming home. Gene thinks this guy is really queer and so do I. By having Gene ride with him, all the expenses of his car are taken care of. So it is a good deal for him but he was greedy and wanted to make a great profit in addition.

Tomorrow some "big wigs"" from G.E. headquarters in Schnectady will be at the San Jose plant and at noon the engineers are invited to have a sandwich and soft drink with these men at a park near the plant. Westinghouse and Bechtel never did this. Of course the lunch isn't much but the fellows get to meet the big shots.

Yesterday our passports were returned from the Kenya Consulate where they were sent for visas. I wasn't home so they went back to the post office. Today I'll pick them up and tomorrow I'll send them to the Tanzania office at the UN to get Tanzania visas. Guess Tanzania doesn't have a consulate in the U.S.

We didn't have rain this month and now California is almost all brown. Now California is truly the Golden State.

Fifteen or twenty years ago Colette had leukemia. She was very ill and not expected to live till she went to a doctor in Paris who had just studied in the U.S. He had come to learn about chemotherapy. He gave Colette chemotherapy treatments for a few years and she did get better. Of late years she has seen the doctor only once a year but just before her visit here, the doctor said that in 1985 he could consider her cured because this was the first time she did not have leukemia cells in her blood. Her medicine came from the U.S. so Colette is predisposed to like medicine as practiced in the U.S. Of course France now uses chemotherapy and I imagine produces its own medicines. Colette came down with the drippy cold the night before the luncheon I gave in her honor. I ran for the CONTACT. She took a capsule at 7 AM and after watching the TODAY show for two hours, she suddenly discovered that her head cold was gone. She was delighted. She took two more capsules and that night she asked to be taken to the drug store where she bought two packages to take back to France. I wonder if they don't have antihistamines in France.

I've known a couple of Americans who became ill while vacationing in England and they report they received excellent care. In each case it was an emergency. I do think foreigners get better and quicker care than Englishmen. In fact, I think animals in England get better care than the English people. I don't think they have a socialized medical plan for animals.

Colette was interested in our Easter customs. She saw all the candy eggs and bunnies, etc. She said in France only real eggs are given and the real eggs are hidden outside in the gardens. The Easter bunny does not enter French homes. I'd hate to put anything outdoors in California. The snails would cover the eggs in a few minutes flat. I wonder how the eggs are fairly distributed when older and younger children are searching together. Colette's grandchildren must be exceptional because Colette says Laure holds back and lets the two younger children find the most eggs. How considerate.

Each Wednesday Colette take her three year old grandson on a walk in the woods while his mother goes folk dancing. One day Colette got a little lost and missed a turn and they walked three miles. She said she was tired and she knew Joel was too but they had to walk three miles back. She said little Joel did not cry or ask to be picked up. The next week he was just as willing, as usual, to go walking with his grandmother.

When Colette was here we went to the library. I'm the library's best patron. Colette was impressed with our library, She thinks it is superior to French ones. She wanted to look up something and when she saw a French encyclopedia, she stopped right there. Colette says she could live in this area and be happy but she couldn't live in the New York area.

Roses are in bloom now. Camellias are long gone. Iris are blossoming. Our tomato plant has tomatoes on it. Our yard is pretty now.

JUNE 3, 1985

Dear Eleanor and Matt,

Yesterday Marguerite and Ed had dinner with us. Marguerite was one of the triplets who went to college with me and Ed was at Hobart at the same time. We haven't seen each other since graduation. Last fall Marguerite and Ed sold their home in Allentown, Pa and moved to Florida. They plan to spend six months each year traveling with their trailer. They left Florida in March and will return in September. They have a son in San Jose whom they visited for two and a half weeks. Ed says they will come again in two years. Marguerite and Ed say their days of parenting are over. They raised five children and now they want to be free.

Ed said they found the traffic in California terrific, especially around Los Angles. When they entered the freeway in Los Angeles, they found they were in lane 6 and they should have been in lane 1 where trucks, trailers and slow moving cars are supposed to be. They were driving a suburban and pulling a long trailer. How to get over, they didn't know. Along side them on the right came a little car and the man indicated by thumb that they should be in lane 1. Marguerite nodded her head yes and then threw up her hands to indicate they didn't know how to get over to lane 1. The driver pointed to himself and indicated that he would help them. This driver slowly decreased his speed so there was a long spot in front of his car. Ed moved from lane 6 to lane 5. Then the driver moved to lane 4 and reduced his speed so there was another long space in front of him. Ed moved to lane 4. The driver did this again and Ed was able to get in lane 3, then from 3 to 2 and finally from 2 to 1, it took 5 miles to do this. Then the driver waved at them as he moved back in the fast lane. Ed was impressed with the helpfulness of this California driver. Traffic around the San Francisco area was bad but their son took over the driving so it wasn't so scary for Marguerite and Ed. It is true that you really need to know what lane you should be in.

After three hours at our house, they headed for Donner Summit, four hours away. I just heard Donner Summit had four inches of snow yesterday. I know Marguerite and Ed were not expecting to run into snow. They certainly weren't dressed for it. Their trailer can be heated so they were probably comfortable. I hope they don't meet more snow but they may in the Rockies.

Marguerite and Ed stopped at Joshua Tree National Park on their way West. Marguerite had an experience similar to mine a few years back. She backed into a prickly pear cacti plant and you know where the thorns penetrated. I touched a teddy bear cacti, looking so soft, and I got long needles in my fingers. Gene had to use pliers to get them out. Too bad Marguerite had this happen to her but it makes me feel better to know other people do dumb things.

Tuesday Evelyn invited me and another friend to lunch at the Round Hill Country Club. This country club is surrounded by lovely houses and is in an expensive section. Afterwards we drove to Blackhawk which is a private area, fenced and guarded, and where all the houses are mansions, costing millions. Live in help and gardeners are a must there. It is out of the Davidson class but this doesn't make me unhappy.

Today I went into San Francisco for a free Ikenobo lesson, given by the visiting professor from Japan. Ikenobo teachers were contacted and told they could only send Caucasians for this lesson. It was video taped and pupils were interviewed. The room was jam packed. The professor gave a lecture in Japanese with an English interpretation. Then we all made an arrangement. The professor checked each arrangement. I had to remove some leaves and that is all. My arrangement was photographed separately and I was proud because not all were. Only two were interviewed. This program will be shown in Japan on July 2nd. I don't know the purpose of this program. Maybe it is to show the Japanese that foreigners like their ikebana.

Wednesday morning I was looking at the TODAY SHOW and Yakoff Smirnoff was interviewed. He and his parents escaped from Russia eight years ago. They now live in Los Angeles. They just bought some movie star's home. He speaks English without an accent, is handsome and has a wonderful sense of humor. He said, not too long ago, his mother got a phone call from a TV station and they asked if they might interview her about her famous son. She speaks some English and replied in the affirmative. The last words of the person telephoning were "We'll shoot you Wednesday morning!" When Yakoff returned home, his mother told him about this call and asked why they wanted to shoot her. He said he didn't know but to be on the safe side, they would take a two weeks vacation.Yakoff went on to say he was reading the newspaper and there was an ad which said BIG SALE-LAST WEEK. Yahoff asked, "Why do they want to make me feel bad by telling me they had a big sale last week and I didn't know about it?" I told Gene these tales and he also got a laugh. Gene Shalot said he heard Smirnoff at a nightclub and he was just as funny there as on TV. He seems to have no set form but just answers questions. Gene didn't repeat Yakoff's jokes. If I lived near New York, I would want to visit that night club.

Saturday we had a garage sale and sold some junk and extra things we had. We took in $70.60. Half of this was for a TV set Gene had in Pennsylvania. A realtor advertised for thirteen families and we had a lot of traffic at our sale. People asked for odd things, old whiskey, post cards, golf balls and clubs and other things we didn't have. Even a dog house.

It is hot here today. Yesterday it was 101 and today it is expected to get to 102. I was just out in the back yard for a minute and I noticed that the camellias were getting sunburned.I came back in, got a sheet, went back out and put the sheet over the camellias.

21st anniversary
Unplanned African sojourn

JUNE 27, 1985

Dear Marilyn and Dave,

Our marriage came of age today. It is 21 years old. In 1964, the year 1985 looked a long way off but it raced along these 21 years.

Gene put on a good suit this morning and his black socks which he wears for funerals, wedding and special occasions. I wonder what they thought at work when they saw him so dressed up.

I met him at Lafayette BART station at 5. Our destination was the Carnelian Room on the 52nd floor of Bank of America. We had planned to eat here last year on my birthday but instead we went to Hawaii. We were given a window seat from which we could see so clearly Twin Peaks and the San Mateo Bridge. We chose the sunset dinner which is less expensive than a la carte. The food was excellent, attractive and the service was superb. Our waiter was most friendly and attentive and the busboy was very polite. We were so impressed. On the way home Gene said we should go back there on his 65th birthday. I had the crab and seafood chowder in a tomato base, and poached petrale sole. The sole was swimming in a sauce dotted with golden caviar. Liquefied caviar had been worked into the sauce in a scroll pattern. Three pieces of asparagus radiated from the sole. There were sour dough rolls and bread and half a cracker. That half of cracker was about twelve inches in diameter, about the size of a dinner plate. We just broke off a piece. Both of us took our dessert from the dessert cart. Gene had a green salad and beef, well done, and to his mind done to perfection. We were impressed.

Seated near us was a couple. The man was about our age, very well dressed. precisely groomed, hair and mustache well clipped and the woman looked as though she had just gotten out of bed and had not yet combed her long hair. What did these two people have in common?

After dinner, we each stopped in the restrooms. The faucets were gold. One attendant turned on and off the faucets and the other handed a towel. Gene got the same attention in the men's room.

Mary and Bud gave us a box of Godiva truffles and we planned to have one tonight but we were too stuffed.

Tuesday Mary and Bud has us over for dessert which was a decorated cake. We were embarrassed to accept so much from them. Both the

Godiva and the cake are very expensive. We don't give such expensive presents and I make a cake for special occasions, but it isn't decorated.

JUNE 28, 1985

Gene and I woke up this morning still thinking about our anniversary dinner. Gene mentioned that the woman with the uncombed hair was the worst dressed woman in the restaurant. I agree. Actually everyone was well dressed. No women in pants or men in leisure suits or sport shirts. The Maitre d' and waiters were in tails and tux so I guess that sets the tone of the place.

It was 97 here when I left for San Francisco. Yesterday and it wasn't even 67 in S.F. A cool wind was blowing and I was a bit chilly.

The hostage situation is riveting. Ordinarily I don't have the TV on but I do now because I want to hear any new developments.

July 5th is the last day at G.E. for the fellow who drives Gene to San Jose. He got his termination notice Monday. After that Gene will have to go by BART or drive and he hates to drive. Gene is sure his job will terminate soon. However this three months job has lasted 10 months. Gene isn't going to look for other work. This time he will really retire.

AUGUST 3, 1985

Dear Dorothy and Lars,

Yesterday Gene left work early. I met him at BART and we visited the immunologist where we got our cholera and gamma goblin shots. We had yellow fever and Typhoid-tetanus in March. We picked up our malaria pills, which we take two weeks before departure, on the trip and six weeks after. Since we first visited the Immunologist, the U. S. Health Department in Atlanta has issued new directions about malaria medicine so our old prescriptions were torn up and new ones given us. One pill, Fabazar, has side effects and can only be taken if you actually contract malaria. We read about this in the NY Times and I called the doctor's office. They didn't know this, so they contacted the U.S Health department and changed their recommendations. We have never seen the immunologist, just his nurses. We were given four sheets of directions, told to read them and do as they said. I'll take them along with us. I think written directions are good because patients might forget.

At this visit Gene volunteered to be first. He stood up and pushed up his sleeve. The nurse said he had to sit on the table because too many people faint when given a shot. Neither of us do, but we did as she said.

Then the nurse told Gene to drop his pants and climb on the table with his stomach down. I was sitting next to the table and my eye level was just at the top of Gene's' behind ! I've never looked at Gene at this angle before ! Then came my turn. The shot in the buttocks was no problem but in two hours both of our arms were good and sore. Today they are still sore but we are not affected in any other way. Now we are ready for Africa ! I told the nurse that we were spending an awful lot of money to make ourselves uncomfortable.This trip is the most expensive we have ever taken and the hardships will be the greatest—rough roads, heat, polluted food that we can't eat, undrinkable water, insects we must not let bite us, you name it. Yet, we still want to go on a safari.

This past week was busy. Our Australian friend, Dave, and his nineteen year old granddaughter came to visit us on their way back to Australia. They arrived Monday and I drove to the San Francisco airport to collect them. Tuesday I drove into San Francisco and we went to Golden Gate Park but we spent more time on our way home at UC Berkeley. Dave and Heather explored and I sat in the Common and watched the people. There were lots of tourists but what impressed me most were the girls without bras. One big girl was a sight as she jogged along, with everything bouncing.

Wednesday we went to Sacramento and Dave and Heather went thru Sutter's Fort. I waited in the car. After lunch in the capitol, we had the capitol tour and each time I do this, I learn something new from a different guide. From there we went to Old Town which now has lots of horse drawn carriages and will soon have a boat to ply the river. On the way home we made a stop at the Nut Tree.

It is more difficult to entertain now since I have to go for Gene. My menus have to be such that I can leave food for half an hour, or more, if Bart is late. It was easier when I didn't have to go for Gene. Oh, well, the job will soon end.

Thursday I put our guests on BART at 9 AM. They were going to the airport to deposit their luggage, then come back to San Francisco for the rest of the day. Their plane left at 9 PM. I had an appointment for a permanent which I had to make the first of June for the first of August.My hairdresser has a full schedule of weekly customers and my six months appointment has to be worked in. I couldn't cancel because I have to have my hair short and easy to care for on the trip. I understand the dust is terrible and sometimes it is necessary to wash your hair twice a day. Dave has been in San Francisco before and knows it quite well so I'm sure they got along o.k. Thursday was a terribly busy day and Friday I caught up on all the things I would have done Monday, Tuesday and Wednesday. Today I'm typing up notes on 3x5 cards and we'll refer to these on the trip and add personal observations.

AUGUST 5, 1985

You wouldn't believe the strength Gene has in his hands. When he puts the top on the peanut butter jar, I cannot get it off, and I get mad each time I try. Our TV has push button changers and he pushes with all his might. This means my gentle touch won't work. I fussed about this so he took it apart and fixed it but within a year he has it right back to impossible. Usually I take a bath in the main bathroom but while Dave and Heather were here, I had to shower in our bathroom and I couldn't turn on or off the faucets. Last Thursday all my aggravations came to the surface and I made a list of things Gene had to fix. Gene said he could fix all but the faucets in the shower and for that we would need a plumber. Friday I called a plumber. Saturday Gene decided he would tackle it. Toolate. However, Gene would have needed special tools we don'thave so it was a good thing I had engaged the plumber. Cost of the plumber $45. Cost of washer $1, Labor for fifteen minutes $44.

A couple weeks ago I had six in our car and one woman used all her strength to turn off the air conditioner ventilator and knocked out two little shutters. It works so easily. I can't understand why she was so rough and strong. Gene didn't fix this, nor any of the other things I had on my list. My aggravation showed in my silence and Gene knew I was cross. He didn't like being given the cold shoulder so he got busy and fixed everything on my list.

Our front bedroom is a mess. Suitcases on the floor. Bed covered with clothes and other things to take with us on our safari. I would pack these things but Gene would only unpack and repack, so why bother.

The safari jackets I made New Year's weekend need some way to secure the pockets. We have grippers instead of buttons. The pockets and flaps are too thick for grippers. We decided to use Velcro. Velcro is wonderful but the gummy part on the back is sticky and I can't get the needle through it. Gene tackled this last night and he broke needle after needle. Today I found some Velcro without the gummy side. It will be easier to do this kind.

Friday we received a big box from the tour with our travel bags, tags, itinerary, instructions. Today we received our tickets. Now we are completely ready for take off.

AUGUST 21, 1985

Dear Helen and Herb,

On Sunday I asked Gene to Xerox a map of Nairobi from a library book I had. He agreed and put the book in his lunch bag. Monday I had to return to the library a book which was due, and I took back 3 others not due. This left me with eight books to take back before we leave on our trip. When I returned from the library. I wanted to take some more notes from EAST AFRICA. I could not find the book. I searched the living room, family room, bedroom and two bathrooms where I usually read. The book wasn't to be found. I knew it wasn't among the returned. When I picked up Gene. I told him he would have to help me search for the book.

Gene said, "Is the book you are looking for the one I have in my lunch bag?"

What a relief! I had completely forgotten this. The forgetting bothered me and that night when we were in bed and Gene's arms encircled me. I said that I really felt old because my memory was so bad that I couldn't remember one day to the next what I had done with a book.

"Don't worry, dear, I'll always take care of you," said Gene.

In January I began reading about Kenya and Tanzania. I borrowed every book the library had. Recently I wanted to see again one of the books and when looking it up, I discovered the library had acquired in July and August two new books, EAST AFRICA and KENYA. These were the best ever and I've taken copious notes which I typed on 3x5 cards. I also decided I wanted to know more about tanzanite, a gem stone discovered in Tanzania in 1960. I visited a jewelry store in Walnut Creek that makes its own jewelry and the man showed me a wonderful book on gems when I asked for prices. Tanzanite was only found in Tanzania and Tiffany's bought most of it. It is very expensive. Both of these countries have some semi precious gems mined there. This store did not have any tanzanite. I tried three other stores but none of them had a piece of tanzanite. One man said he could get a stone but the price would compare with a diamond of similar weight and size. Now I really want to see the stone and also tsavorite and malachite. Malachite is an opaque stone and not valuable, but pretty. The first jewelry store had some of this. The last jewelry store owner said the mine of tanzanite had been completely emptied and the source was now nil.

We aren't taking much money to buy things because the books say there is little to buy, outside of native things like baskets, masks, etc. Also we'll have little time for shopping. We arrive in Nairobi on August 27th at 7:10 AM after an all night flight from Frankfurt. So we shall have to rest and may have just a few hours to look around. On September 5th we have an afternoon in Nairobi. Nairobi, a city of a million people, has not one department store. Some of the lodges have gift shops but the tour information says everything is overpriced. We won't be in any other cities or towns in these countries. At one place the van will stop and the natives will flock around the van with things to sell. I won't buy. I like to look, consider and compare. Besides what they offer seems like junk to me.

I had requested information from both tourist offices but these are poor countries and have little to send, not even maps. So I've had to get my information from books.

Today I took my mother to the beauty parlor. Tomorrow we shop for food for her and Connie G who will stay with her. Friday Gene has to have the car. It is his last day working for G.E. and he has to sign out at a building several miles from where he works. All my last minute things will have to be done Thursday.

We are going out to dinner on Thursday, my birthday. I've already had two birthday cakes. Connie made me one and yesterday my mother made me one.

SEPTEMBER 16, 1985

Dear Emiko and Yuchi,

So why didn't you receive a card from Africa? It's a long story but briefly I'll fill you in on what happened.

We left home on August 24th and flew directly from San Francisco to Frankfurt. We had a night at the Sheraton connected with the airport. On the 26th we did a little sightseeing and that night we flew to Nairobi. We over nighted at the Hilton in Nairobi and left on the 28th on our safari.

Shortly after lunch on this first day of the safari, we made a stop at Lord Baden Powell's grave and there I met my Waterloo. I fell and seriously hurt my right ankle. I knew I needed medical attention but I urged the van driver to go to our overnight tree top stop. When we arrived, I had such a swollen ankle and was in such pain that I said I would need to get back to Nairobi. The driver was a little annoyed with me but I wanted the other couple not to miss anything. Had I said I needed to get medical attention, they may not have arrived for the night viewing of the animals. After much short wave radio communication, arrangements were made for me to be transported back to Nairobi by air ambulance but we had to drive a distance to the "airport." The "airport" turned out to be a strip of macadam. By 8 PM I was in the Nairobi Hospital and very soon afterwards I was in the operating room where pins were placed in my ankle. At about midnight I was brought back to my room, directly from the operating room. I was there eight days and we missed all the safari in Kenya.

With the doctor's permission, we took the Tanzania safari. I was accompanied by crutches and a wheelchair. It was pretty rugged. I do not recommend a safari in a wheel chair.

We arrived home September 12th. I'm to see my orthopedist tomorrow. Now that I'm home, I can lie on the sofa with my foot elevated and there isn't as much swelling.

Sitting up with my foot hanging down is uncomfortable so that is why this letter is short. A few minutes at the typewriter are about all I can take.

At the hotel in Nairobi, I purchased lots of stamps and I brought them all home with me. So you see, lack of stamps is not the reason why you didn't get a card.

NOVEMBER 9, 1985

Dear Annette, Claude, Laure, Clare and Joel,

Boy, have I looked forward to yesterday when the cast was to be removed. From October 14th till yesterday I was getting along pretty well, walking in my cast for three minutes each hour. I was even walking more than three minutes an hour. So I planned yesterday afternoon to take the car and go Christmas shopping. Gene said he was going to miss me. Up until now he knew where I was and what I was doing every minute but once again mobile, he never would know what I was doing.

Huh! I left the doctor's office in the wheel chair! The cast was removed and you never saw such a mess and smelled such a stink. I had tears. The doctor couldn't understand and called Gene aside to talk to him. The doctor said it looked good for such a terrible break. I'd hate to see what it looked like if it didn't look good. There was much dead, rotted skin, in fact from my big toe to my knee it was this way. The color of the whole area was a black-red. The doctor said he could put on a new cast but 10 1/2 weeks was really long enough to be in a cast. He said I should use crutches. I'm not very stable on crutches so it was decided that I will put some weight on the foot and some on the crutches. I have an appointment for the next two weeks with a physical therapist, who will give me whirlpool treatments and manipulate the ankle. I go back to the doctor on the 22nd for another assessment.

I was looking forward to my first bath in the tub but even that wasn't what I expected. The doctor's assistant suggested that when I got home, I take a shower and try to get all the crud off my foot and leg. I did this but it didn't all come off. Then Gene put cream on it and we tried to wipe it off. Rotted skin is sticky. We got some off but when I got in the tub and really rubbed with a wash cloth, most of it came off. You should have seen the bath water with all the floating debris. The stitches were removed September 17th and replaced with plastic strips and these didn't come off till I soaked in the tub.

Now my leg and foot are a purplish red. I did have, yesterday, some real dark spots where there was dried blood under the skin from internal bleeding after the operation. There are still some spots with dried skin that isn't ready to fall off. All the skin is crackled. Just to run your finger on the skin gives a sensation. My ankle is not the same size or shape as the other one. I hope it won't be permanently deformed. The doctor said it is swollen, but the swelling is deep inside because the skin is taunt over the ankle. The stitch marks are an angry red. I thought by this time they would have disappeared but they are very evident.

I weighed myself this morning and I'm ten pounds lighter than when we left in August. I think I've gained since we got home. Gene is also ten pounds lighter.

Everybody has troubles and actually mine are minuscule compared to our friend, John. He has had 12 pacemakers in 13 years and recently he had another when his pacemaker failed in the middle of the night. The new pacemaker did not respond as the others have so he had to have further examinations. It was found one artery was clogged and two valves in his heart are malfunctioning. At Stanford, they suggested that one valve be repaired and the other valve removed and a valve from a pig replace it. John went to Chicago last week to get a second opinion from a heart specialist. That doctor agreed. Now John goes back to Stanford for further talks. I wouldn't give two cents for the rest of John's life. John is concerned about these operations since he has a pacemaker. They had a difficult time inserting the lead wire to the heart this past time. John is a very upbeat person and optimistic and I hope all goes well, but I wouldn't count on it.

NOVEMBER 26, 1985

Dear Joan and Barney,

Friday the 22nd I visited the doctor again. He said I could do whatever I could tolerate, including driving the car. Saturday I drove to and from the library with Gene as a passenger, in case I experienced pain. No pain, just some prickles such as a needle might make. No more whirlpool baths required, just soaking in hot water several times a day. The skin on my leg is still rough and red and my ankle and leg are still hot to the touch. I still limp but eventually I should walk normally. The doctor said he never expected such marvelous results because my breaks were so bad. He thinks I'm a tough cookie! I'm so happy to be independent again. Gene says he is going to take a picture of me because he expects now I will be off in the car a lot.

The physical therapist and her assistant were disappointed that I would not be having more appointments. She kept outlining all the exercises she would be giving me later. I can see how she would miss the $45 for each fifteen minutes of whirlpool baths and the extra for each exercise. I can move my foot up and down and around for nothing and I will do so. We don't need to pay $15 to have her watch me do this.

A few days ago Gene raided my sewing box and took my tape measure. Since then the tape measure has been within his hand's reach at all times. When I lie down on the sofa with my foot elevated, Gene appears with the tape measure and measures each ankle. If I'm still there an hour later, he is back measuring again. As we look at TV in the family room, he does the same thing. He wants to know just how much it swells with activity and how much it shrinks when elevated. There can be from 1 1/2 to 3/4 of an inch. I'm amused and I've renamed him Mr. Tapemeasure.

Monday the 25th our neighbors came over for the evening to see our slides. Sandy is often away for two to three weeks at a time but these past two weeks he had been driving to Los Angeles one day and back to San Francisco the next day. He got home at 6 PM Monday and left at 5:30 AM Tuesday morning. I served Mamie Eisenhower's famous pumpkin chiffon pie. It is a high pie normally but with whipped cream and pecans, it is really high. Usually it draws raves. Sandy and Betty ate every bit of their piece but in the course of the conversation we learned that they don't like pumpkin pie. Betty's mother makes two pumpkin pies for the holidays and she eats one piece. Everyone else says they are too stuffed for dessert. Betty's mother wonders why the pies are left. I almost served apple pie and now I wish I had.

Tuesday the 26th we had a luncheon for my friend, Pat, her mother and her mother's nurse. The mother is 95 and can do nothing for herself. It is sad. Everything I served I had never made before and surprisingly, each was very good. About a year ago Pat gave me a recipe for Mediterranean Bread that she got from Sunset Magazine. I decided to make that for the luncheon. It is a rich bread with four eggs and has whole ripe and green olives baked in it. It was wonderful! I'm going to make this for Thanksgiving and take a loaf to Connie and John. It is so pretty when sliced.

NOVEMBER 28. 1985

It is 9 PM and we have just returned from having Thanksgiving dinner at Connie and John's. Connie had called the daughter of a long ago friend to get some addresses and discovered the daughter and her family were going to be alone on Thanksgiving so Connie invited them to come for Thanksgiving and spend the weekend. I think this was a mistake. Both Connie and John work, Connie gets up at 4:30 each morning and is in bed by 7. She is always tired. So this weekend should have been a time to relax and rest. Instead she let herself in for preparing a big dinner and entertaining this family of four for the weekend. The kids weren't bad but they were fidgety. John had laryngitis yesterday and couldn't say a word. Connie had a wonderful dinner. She is a superb cook and everything was tasty and pretty. They entertain beautifully but they do two things which drive us wild. They keep their house COLD. They have a fireplace with an ornamental log but this doesn't give heat. We dressed warmly but we were freezing before we left. Gene's hands were like ice. Also they don't believe in light. Two candles on the dining room table and the fireplace were the only light. Being a reader, I want lots of light and I like to see people's faces when I talk to them. So although we enjoyed the dinner and we like Connie and John very much, we were glad to come home.

John enters Stanford University Hospital on December 9th and will have open heart surgery on the 10th. He expects to be in the hospital two weeks. I invited them to our house for Christmas but they may not be able to come. Actually it would probably be better for John to be in our house where it is warm. They do have lots of colds and I think it is from a cold house.

NOVEMBER 29, 1985

I did not sleep last night. I was too full of that wonderful turkey dinner. Gene couldn't sleep because I couldn't. I thought I should go lie on the sofa in the living room. Gene said if I did, he would join me so I stayed put. We eat our holiday meals about two in the afternoon and by bedtime we are not so stuffed. It was close to six yesterday when we ate this dinner.

I have just stuffed our turkey and put it in the oven. Although we were out for the holiday dinner, we are having a turkey at home because we love left overs.

I took fresh rolls and a loaf of the Mediterranean bread to Connie's for dinner. Only Gene and I ate the bread and everybody else ate the rolls. So one day the bread is a terrific success and another day it is ignored. That's life!

DEC 8, 1985

Dear Colette.

After eleven years our garbage disposal no longer disposes so Thursday Gene bought a new one at twice the cost of the original. After installing it Friday, he decided we would have lunch out so that the drain could seal better without water running through. We went to Mac Donald's. As we were driving out of the parking lot, a young girl and two fellows in an old white pick up truck suddenly backed into the right front of our car. The girl, the driver, was eating a hamburger and paying no attention. She was totally disinterested in what she had done. She had on the tightest jeans possible. She had a Florida driver's license, no insurance information and the truck belonged to somebody else. Her story was that her husband had the insurance information, he was at work and couldn't be reached and the insurance agent was in NY state. She took down no information about us so apparently she didn't intend to report the accident. We had to call a tow truck to come and lift the truck off our car. I was disgusted. I think we may have a time collecting,

The day before, Wednesday, Gene and I did our weekly grocery shopping. I had a list of ingredients for Christmas cookies and as I put things in the cart, Gene took them out. He said he had coupons at home for these items and we would wait till he had the coupons with him to buy them. After two stores we did go home, unload and collect the coupons. Then we bought all the stuff. When we unloaded in the garage, we don't remember what happened. I haven't been carrying anything because I need both hands to help me up the two steps. If I had a bag, I probably put it on the bench next to the door and expected Gene to bring it in. Gene may have grabbed the bag of groceries, thought it was trash and put it in the garbage pail (the garbage was collected about an hour later) or he may never have taken a bag out of the cart when he loaded the stuff into the car trunk. At any rate, the next day we didn't find my mother's cereal. I made the cookie dough but couldn't find the M and M candies to decorate the cookies. We know the missing items cost more than $5 and we saved less than $1 dollar with the coupons. Gene had to go and buy all these items a second time. We are having a spell of bad luck!

Until a few months ago, the lending period at the library was four weeks, no matter whether books were old or new. I go thru at least five books a week so I often have ten books. Now they changed to a two week period. I've been busy with Christmas activities so I didn't get one book read. I kept it and it is now three days overdue, due to our not having a car and I owe a .15 fine. Gene says with my overdue fine, I must think money grows on trees!

DECEMBER 20, 1985

Dear Phyllis,

Monday, December 10th, our good friend, John, entered the Stanford University Hospital and the next day he had open heart surgery. John went into surgery at 6 AM and was returned to intensive care at 5 PM. During that time two of his heart valves were replaced with two pig valves. The operation was technically a success but the patient died. His heart was surrounded by adhesions and it took too long to free the heart for repair, even though he was on a heart bypass machine. Connie called us the night of the operation and said John had not regained consciousness and was bleeding internally. At that time they were planning to reopen John,in an effort to find the cause of the bleeding, but during the night they decided the bleeding was because the blood was not coagulating They gave some drugs and the condition improved. Connie wasn't alarmed because the doctors did not tell her about the adhesions and because they said being unconscious was an advantage since John would not be moving his body. Friday Karen, their daughter, called and said John had still not regained consciousness and she felt things were not going well. We didn't hear over the weekend so on Monday afternoon I called Linda's in-laws where Connie, Linda and Karen were staying. which was near the hospital. Connie said John still wasn't conscious and they had scheduled a talk with the doctors that evening. Then they learned the worse. John was brain damaged due to the unconsciousness and his heart would never function normally. He was alive because he was on a life support system. Tuesday Dec 17th, a week after the operation, John died, John was approaching sixty but he acted like a forty year old.

John lived a full, productive, active, interesting and outgoing life. Everybody liked John. He put himself out for others. He never complained or talked about his problem. We'll miss him terribly.

The day before John died his other daughter, Jo, in Indiana gave birth to a daughter so she wasn't able to be here.

We have been really sad. I made four quarts of bean soup, a jello fruit salad, cooked a ham, made a pie and Christmas stollen. The jello salad didn't set because I put fresh kiwi fruit in it and this prohibits the jello from setting. We delivered these items and a poinsettia on Wednesday afternoon. Our car was being repaired so Mary drove us over.

John donated his body to the medical school. A memorial service was scheduled for Thursday afternoon, after which Connie had an open house. Gene and I were asked to help by making and serving tea, coffee and fruit punch. Connie and her family had set the table and arranged the cookies.

I cry easily. Gene doesn't think it manly to have tears but he did have tears at the service and one other time. He couldn't help himself. We feel we have lost a good friend.

When Linda came to be with her mother, she left Bob at home in West Virginia with their eight months old baby, Kate. Bob is a devoted father and fully competent to care for Kate. He does it all the time since both Linda and Bob have full time, responsible positions. Kate is crawling and standing while holding on to something. Bob had Kate on the sofa with him. She was wiggling around and he was afraid she might fall off the sofa so he put her on the floor between his knees. She hung on to the sofa and all was well till she let loose and her little face hit Bob's knee and she got a black eye.

The next day on the flight to San Francisco the stewardess noticed Kate's black eye. Bob was getting the luggage from the carousel and

Linda was holding Kate and talking to the neighbor who brought her to the airport to meet Bob and Kate when the stewardess, co-pilot and a policeman approached. The policeman asked Linda about the black eye. She didn't know. When Bob came with the bags, the policeman questioned him and made out a report. Bob is suspected of being a child abuser! Child abusing and child molesting surely are getting a great deal of attention in the U.S. Maybe too much. We know some grandfathers who are afraid of hugging their grandchildren.

At the memorial service Kate played with a button on her mother's shoulder. She pulled it and "talked to that button." In order to quiet her, they gave her a bottle. Finishing this, she became active and made lots of happy vocal noises. Bob took her to the back of the church and she quieted down but the minute he came back to the seat she would talk again. At the at home she crawled on the floor briefly but everybody wanted to hold her so she went from one stranger to another with no tears.

Ever since we got back from Africa, we have been trying to get a refund for the Kenya part of our trip. Scantravel didn't want to give anything back, but they agreed to give 1/8th, about $500. I complained. It did no good. I wrote ASTA and Better Business Bureau. Both say they will investigate but I have little hope of a decent refund. Travel companies demand payment months in advance. They often don't get documents to the customers till the last minute. They make sure they aren't gipped. They don't care about the customer. I only know of one or two that treat customers fairly. What we need is a traveler's bill of rights.

DECEMBER 31, 1985

Dear Dot and James,

This isn't my day! I went to the library and wanted to Xerox some information about an author whose book I will review. I only had.15 and I needed.30 so I went out to the car and borrowed.15 from my mother, all the change she had. I had a $10 bill but the library could not change that. I needed to Xerox three pages and each is.10. So I put the money next to the place where you insert it and opened the top. There was an income tax form somebody had left. I put it on top of the machine and did one page. When on the second page a little old woman came along and asked if I had found an income tax. I pointed to it and put my third sheet in the machine. When I went to put in my two nickels, there was only one. That little old lady had ripped me off for .05!

When I came home, the mailman had come and left a letter from Jennie, our English friend. I mailed one to her this morning at her new apartment in Saltburn by Sea. She had moved December 17th from Easington. Her letter was like a story book. She sold her home to the postmaster in Easington in November and bought an apartment in November. She had new carpets and several other changes made in the apartment. The postmaster sold his home, which was also the post office, to a couple who wanted to be the new postmasters. Suddenly the new couple began to find fault and finally backed out. The postmaster was selling because his wife had died in September and he didn't want to be in that house for Christmas, because of the memories. When the postmaster's deal fell through, he committed suicide and so Jennie's deal fell through. I guess Jennie got out of the apartment sale but she lost all she had invested in the carpets and other things she had done. My letter went to the new apartment. I wrote a card to the postmaster in Saltburn asking that my letter be forwarded back to Jennie's old address in Easington and took it to the mailbox at the Plaza where Gene had mailed my letter that morning. The mailman was just emptying the box. I stood there and waited. When almost all the letters were out, there was my letter on the bottom. I asked if I could have it back and change the address. I showed the card I had written to the postmaster in England, but the mailman, who spoke little English, would not let me have the letter to change the address. It was a long letter and I hope Jennie eventually receives it. She left yesterday for Spain for two months.

FEBRUARY 6, 1986

Dear Lois and Fred,

I do have the nicest husband! Yesterday we learned by mail and newspaper that my favorite jewelry store is going out of business and everything is 50% off. Two young men own the store and they make a lot of their jewelry. They don't have much stock and not trays and trays of things. What they do have is tasteful and different. They don't sell watches. I go there because of my arthritis. They enlarge rings for me and they do the work on the spot. All others send it away. Gene wanted to get there when the store opened so I would have a good choice. There were about five women buying and we two lookers. I didn't see anything I couldn't live without. I don't wear all the jewelry I have. Before marriage I never left the house without earring. I seldom wear them now. There were some lapis necklaces I liked but, even at half price, they were more than I wanted to pay. I bought nothing. What an opportunity and I blew it.

I took money, pinned to my bra, to Africa with me because I thought I might get a piece of tanzanite or malachite. Had I found something I really liked in tanzanite, I might have purchased it. Gene was surprised to have me hand him a wad of money when I was getting ready to go to the operating room in Nairobi.

FEBRUARY 7, 1986

Today Mother, Gene and I had lunch with Pat, her 95 year old mother and her mother's nurse. We went to the Sizzler because my mother insisted. Pat makes jewelry and she made my mother a pair of drop earrings with real garnets for her birthday. My mother was given a piece of carrot cake with a candle by the Sizzler and they sang happy birthday to her. We came back here and I served cream puffs I had made that morning. Pat's mother can do nothing for herself. It is sad. The nurse is wonderful and the mother is beautifully groomed and dressed and given the best of care. Were Pat's mother in a home, she probably wouldn't live a week. When this nurse takes a vacation and another takes over, there is always a crisis and Pat never knows if her mother will live another day.

Mother's fracture

Retirement, Bridge party in the dark

FEBRUARY 16, 1986

Dear Raedina and Milton,

Friday night we played bridge and we were talking about hospital costs with Ginnie, who is a retired nurse. She said recently a friend had a father in the hospital and on the bill was a $15 charge for a podiatrist. This was questioned and it turned out it was for cutting the father's toenails. Ginnie said when she nursed, the nurses cut the toenails at no extra cost. Boy, they charge for everything today. Think of the cost of the accounting for all this.

Friday we took my mother to the Terrace Tea Room for lunch. This is run by volunteers and all the profits are given to the hospital. The only paid person is the cook who has been with them for years. Tips also go to the hospital. There is no choice of food. This was national health week so they featured health food. It wasn't the good meal we usually have there. The fresh fruit salad and blueberry muffin were good but the crepe filled with eggplant and zucchini was unappetizing. My mother was given cranberry yogurt ice with a candle and again they sang happy birthday to her. She liked this.

Next to the restaurant are two stores I like to visit, one sells kitchen and gourmet things and the other crystal and specialty foods. Gene put my mother in the car and came in the store with me. I found a bread and soup book and Gene found a bread book by the Culinary Arts Institute in San Francisco. This is a wonderful cooking school and anyone who graduates from it can immediately become a chef most anyplace with a salary of more than $30,000. I was about to buy both books but Gene pointed out we probably could get them at discount from a book store. I don't need any more cook books since I have a few hundred. The bread book has some unusual recipes and Gene says my soups are poor. They are watery and he likes thick soups. He is only satisfied with my bean and pea soups.

Speaking of soups, there is a store that sells health foods and we went there to get yeast from Europe which seems better than American yeast. The store has barrels of all kinds of flour and broth powder. We bought buckwheat flour and I'm going to make pancakes. I like waffles better so I seldom make pancakes. We bought candied papaya and I used it in Hot Cross buns and they weren't too bad.

Last Monday morning I went to wake my mother and she said she couldn't get out of bed. Something happened to her right side and she couldn't stand on her foot. I could see she hadn't had a stroke but I didn't know what was wrong. We got the typing chair and rolled her to the bathroom and then to the table. She was really hurting and when I suggestedthe doctor, she immediately agreed. Wow! My mother hates doctors so this was a real surprise. We got an afternoon appointment. The doctor thought it was arthritis. She has had three attacks recently. Eachtime she would wake in the morning and twice it was her hand andwrist. She would be in real pain for a week and then it would go away after she dosed herself with aspirin. Next it was in her spine and this time in her hip joint.

We had arthritis medicine for this and I started giving it to her. The doctor said he wanted X-rays, though, to be sure. So off we went to radiology. She had one set, then another. They found she had a hairline fracture of the hip. The radiologist consulted the orthopedist and he manipulated her hip and said he too believed it to be a fracture of the hip bone. Gene went to rent a wheel chair. The doctor said my mother was too old for an operation to stabilize the hip with a pin. He said the fracture had not splayed so with no weight on the hip, it would heal. Tuesday, Wednesday and Thursday my mother used the wheelchair. Thursday she had no pain and she decided she wasn't going to use the wheel chair. We had an appointment with the orthopedist and at first she refused to go. Finally we got her there and more x-rays were taken and there is a fracture. When we drove into the garage, my mother said no to the wheel chair and walked into the house. Gene and I tried to persuade her. She got really mad and threatened to move to an hotel. The situation got pretty sticky so we decided to let her have her own way. I called the doctor and told him this and he said to let her have her own way. The doctor knows my mother and when she gives him a hard time, he just winks at me. The orthopedist doesn't know my mother. My mother is

walking to meals and the bathroom and we hope this little walking does-
n't splay the fracture. How did she get this fracture? The doctor said she
could have turned over in bed or just stepped on the foot getting out of
bed. Bones ninety two years old are brittle.

I had a call from my aunt Lydia on Saturday. She is 82 and on
Monday she had a lens replacement. She had to stop driving because she
couldn't see. Her eye was frozen and she knew what was going on all the
time the doctor was operating. She was operated upon at I PM and one
hour after the operation, she went home. She lives alone. Tuesday she
went back to get the bandages removed. When she returned home, she
said it looked as though her house had all been repainted on the inside
and that a lighter color had been used. It was so bright. Five days afterwards she was seeing beautifully and really thrilled at the success of the
operation. These lens replacement operations are wonderful.In
November she had a gall bladder operation and a couple years ago she
developed diabetes. She sailed thru the gall bladder operation with no
difficulty.

Later that day

A few weeks ago Gene and I cleaned our cupboards in the kitchen.
We threw away things we never use, like frying pans and things we had
more than one of. I just now looked for a griddle and, by golly, I must
have thrown that away. I haven't used it in 21 years. Wouldn't you
know? Oh, well, the waffle iron has griddle pans and we'll use them. I
finally found a recipe for buckwheat pancakes in the Fannie Farmer cook
book. None of the other books had it. Guess they are too old fashioned.

FEBRUARY 17, 1995

Saturday, the actual day of my mother's birthday, we invited some
friends in for lunch and I served the food my mother especially likes,
seafood au gratin with shrimp, clams, crab, scallops and mushrooms.
Baked potatoes, cabbage salad, pumpkin bread and angel food cake and
ice cream. Just as we were finishing, a car drove up and a young fellow
delivered a basket of spring flowers to my mother from a friend of mine
in Syracuse. So it really was a gala affair. Sunday I baked a ham because
this is my mother's favorite meat. She received lots of cards and she has
them all displayed in her den. I think she rated her birthday a success.

MARCH 12, 1986

Dear Linda and Bob,

Our Chinese neighbors came to see our African slides and brought a cake they purchased in San Francisco. I was embarrassed. They also brought us gifts from their trip to China. So I've been taking over bread and rolls occasionally, but I can't get ahead of these people. We are always accepting more than we give. Recently Sue gave us some finger jello which was so pretty. Hing asked Sue to make it for his boss's birthday party at the office because everybody was dieting. His cohorts wanted the recipe so Hing put it on the computer and gave me a copy. I took it to an AAUW meeting yesterday and it disappeared very quickly.

Since making bread I've felt the need of a good kitchen scale to weigh the dough. I wanted it in both ounces and kilograms. I haven't found one here but I thought I might get one in Germany. I never got in a department store in Germany. Before Christmas I took my mother to a drug store and there we saw a Japanese scale with five pound capacity. Just what I wanted. I was preparing to buy it when my mother bought it as a Christmas present. Now I can have two loaves of bread the same size. Recently we made hot cross buns. Gene refused to use the scale and we had some big ones and some small ones. The second batch I insisted he use the scale and this time the buns came out in uniform size. Gene has said we are going to have to enlarge the kitchen to accommodate all my bread making equipment.

The other night Gene said he felt ashamed. I was surprised and asked why. He said sometimes I seem to be working all day and he is sitting reading or doing cross word puzzles. He said he didn't mind that I worked when he was working but now he doesn't think it is right for him to sit and me to work. Actually he really does help. He sets the table at night and makes the salad. I've been letting him vacuum while I cleaned the kitchen and bathrooms. We get thru the cleaning faster this way. Retirement is an adjustment for both husband and wife. I think it was made easier for us since those first few months I was incapacitated. Gene did everything while I was in the wheel chair and on crutches. Slowly I've worked my way back into my usual activities. The first time I made bread Gene got everything out for me. I stood on one foot and had the other resting on a stool. Then I taught Gene to knead. Gene likes to do things alone but we have worked out a system that works most of the time, not all. And now that I go grocery shopping with him, he has adjusted to my way. When he first went alone, he didn't compare prices and he was in a hurry but now I have trained to him look and he has taken a real interest in coupons. Yesterday he was pleased with himself when he got a $1.19 roll of paper towels for.19. A doubled.50 coupon took a whole dollar off the price. We never buy expensive paper towels but we could afford this with a coupon.

It is now the next day and Gene and I went to Oakland this morning. He had an interview at 10 AM. Although Gene is all set to retire March 15th,, he felt he should answer a Westinghouse ad. Tuesday he had another interview in San Francisco and he came home relieved because it wasn't in his field at all. So if all this comes to naught, he will be happy.

I wanted to visit Ratto's which is near where Gene interviewed. It is a gourmet grocery store of international items in a terrible section of Oakland. I would never go there alone. It looked like a dump on the outside and wasn't much better on the inside, but what unusual and expensive things they carry. I wanted dried mushrooms but they were five times the price of fresh. The Frugal Gourmet on TV gave a recipe for Polish pot roast and I'm making this on Sunday but I'll use fresh mushrooms.

On our way home. we stopped in Orinda and I took Gene in Phairs, a small exclusive store that carries women's clothes, fine china, silver and crystal. They did have something I want but only three and I needed eight. So we bought nothing.

I had planned to have lunch out but we got home at 11:45 AM, even with these stops. I now have a corned beef brisket cooking, along with cabbage which came free with the purchase of the brisket. St. Pat's day is four days away but we'll celebrate with an Irish meal tonight.

The terrible rains we have had flooded many people's homes but what a beautiful countryside we now see in this area as a result of the rain. The hills are so GREEN. Everything looks so fresh. It was absolutely beautiful driving to and from Oakland.

MARCH 19, 1986

Dear Isabel,

Today was a busy day. Gene and I left home before 8:30 for our weekly grocery shopping. We returned at 10 and then went to the travel agent to pay for our tour and airline tickets. We were there one and a half hours because the tour was booked solid and we had to make a change. The tour is for the end of August and this is March. I thought people were not traveling to Europe this year. It can't be true if tours are booked solid.

I had fifteen minutes to change clothes and have a bite to eat before I took off for my book review. There was a larger than usual audience which was most attentive, laughed and made comments as I talked. I think it was a success. Helen, who recently had cancer surgery and will have more next week, came and said she came because I was the reviewer. I was flattered. Betty came and told me she had to leave early but she was going to say my review was good before she heard it! When I finished, she was still there. She then said she decided the review was more interesting than her other meeting so she stayed till the end. Two other women came and said they had never read any of the books I reviewed but by the next review they would certainly have read all the books by Jeffery Archer and Ann Tyler. Peg, the volunteer librarian at the Rossmoor library, was formerly a librarian at the University of Rochester. She hasn't attended any of the reviews for the past three years because we changed the day of the week we met and she had a conflict. Afterwards she told me the Rossmoor Library didn't have all the Archer and Tyler titles but she would buy them immediately Comments like this really pleased me. However, I know it wasn't my review. The books made the review so interesting. I talked fast and covered a lot of territory. Now I'm relieved. I can read anything I please and forget about a book review till next fall when I'll volunteer again.

MARCH 22, 1986

Today we went into San Francisco with Virginia and Don to see the flower show. Other years I've entered the ikebana show but this year I didn't. This was a smaller show than usual but of exceedingly good quality. Afterwards Don drove around San Francisco and we ended up in the Richmond district of S.an Francisco for lunch. The Japanese cherry trees in Golden Gate Park were just a little beyond their prime.

Beach Blanket Babylon
Earthquake, Emergency hospitalization

MARCH 29, 1986

Dear Phyllis and Jay,

Thursday I went to the doctor for what I supposed to be my last visit for my ankle. He said to come back on the anniversary of the fractures and he would x-ray it again and make a determination as to whether he would operate and take out the pins. I was SHOCKED! I understood these pins were to be there for the rest of my life. He said for a thirty year old person, they always remove them but for somebody my age, sometimes. On safari there was a young man who had previously done the same thing and he eventually had an infection and had to be operated upon. He was skiing again and being very athletic. The doctor kept asking me if I had pain. I don't. I'd hate to have the pins taken out. There would be big holes in my bones and I would think the ankle would be weaker, but I sure don't want an infection. Gene says we'll get a second opinion in September.

This morning Gene and I were eating a late breakfast and suddenly we felt a gentle movement. I looked at Gene and said. "I feel an earth—" and at the word earth there was another much stronger but still gentle quake. The first was a like a slow rock in a rocking chair but the second was a more vigorous rock. There was a distinct rumbling noise, too. Gene got the full effect because he was looking out the window when he felt the first one.

Tomorrow our Easter activity is going to be anything but Eastery! We are going to see Beach Blanket Babylon at Club Fugazi in San Francisco. It is listed under theatre but I think it is more like a night club. They have eight new giant headpieces for this musical which is entitled BEACH BLANKET BABYLON GOES ROUND THE WORLD. Remember when Queen Elizabeth was in San Francisco? They had part of this show for her. I wanted to see that. When Gene read in the paper that they were doing a similar thing, he suggested we go. It is expensive. We are going to have a once in a lifetime experience. I tried three times in one day to get tickets and Easter Sunday afternoon was the only time available. Each time I was put on hold and one call cost $2.67 and I never got to talk to anyone. Finally when I did get a person, I complained. about the cost of these long distance calls and the guy gave me a different number to call the next day and that is how we got these tickets. We waited a month for the tickets so I hope the show is worth the cost.

Gene is out trimming the bushes. I just went out to him and the smell from our orange tree which is in bloom is heavenly. Our other orange tree has no blossoms but we only planted it last year. We have four rose bushes in bloom and the rest all have buds. The African daisies are in full bloom and make a blanket from the street to the back fence. This is the prettiest season at our house. Gene planted dahlias this week and next week he will plant tomatoes. Our camellias are gone. March in California is different from March in Geneva!

So much happened last night in a couple hours that I could not swear on a stack of Bibles that what I'm going to tell you is the truth! This is what I think happened.

At 5 PM we were having a turkey sandwich. We had dinner at noon so it would be easy to prepare for bridge that night. The lights went out. Friday night our lights were out for more than two hours but it didn't bother us because we were in bed. I wasn't worried because I assumed PG & E knew the problem and could easily fix it. Gene got out candles and we finished the meal by candlelight. I did the dishes by candlelight. The lights flickered on once. They flickered a second time and maybe were on for about five minutes. Gene blew out all the candles and put them away. They went out again. Again Gene got out the candles and I prepared my hors d'oeuvres by candlelight. I wanted to know how long the lights would be off so I called PG & E. The line was always busy. If not, a recording came on and we were told to hang on if it was an emergency. I thought it was an emergency. I needed to know whether to cancel bridge. How could we play when we couldn't see? Who wanted to play cards with no heat? How could I prepare my hot hors d'oeuvres with no oven or even make coffee and tea?

At 6:30 we called Mary and Bud and asked if we could bring the food and drinks to their house and play bridge there. They said O.K. Gene got out big boxes and put the candy dishes in them and the boxes in the car. I called the other couples and told them to go to Mary and Bud's. Then the lights came on. So I called them and told them to come here because we again had power. Hardly had I done this when the lights went out again. Gene got more boxes and put the lemon meringue pies in them. I tried to put on my make up. I called everybody again and told them to go to Mary and Bud's. I finally got PG & E and asked how long we could expect this outage to last. The man said eleven hours, just like last night. I said we didn't have eleven hours last night and he said they were able to restore some sections in two or three hours last night but it would be six or seven tonight and could even be eleven. Finally about 7:15 the lights came back on. Packing everything up was a mess so I called everybody again and told them to come here, but to bring a flash light. Then Gene and I really worked. I finished the hors d'oeuvres. I was making something new, wrapping brie cheese in a pastry crust. It was supposed to go in the oven at 6:45 and bake half an hour and then rest till 8. Well, I put it in as soon as I could but it didn't have enough time to rest and so it was runny. Good but runny. It was pretty, too, because you made flowers from the pastry and put them on top.

My mother undressed and got in bed. We dug out blankets for my mother because she is always cold, since her heart functions at a low level, and because she couldn't use her electric blanket.

Mary called and said they were all set up and so why not come there. She is a compulsive talker and I had to be rude and shut her off. I said no we were having it here and I didn't have time to talk. Gene and I were just ready at eight when the guests arrived. WOW! And the lights stayed ON all the rest of the evening. The house behind us had lights but the houses to the east of us were without electricity for blocks and blocks. No street lights, either.

EASTER SUNDAY NIGHT
MARCH 30, 1986

We left home today at 12:30 for BART and immediately got a train into San Francisco. A fifty foot walk brought us to a bus stop and along came a bus for North Beach where Club Fugazi is located. The doors open at 2 and the performance begins at 3. I thought this was a nightclub but it isn't. It is a SMALL, old theatre. Downstairs are small tables and you may buy coke, Sprite, and Calistoga water on Sundays and beer and wine the rest of the week. Nothing is served once the revue begins. We bought non smoking seats but it was requested that nobody smoke during the performance, in consideration for the singers and audience. I didn't see a single smoker. I could reach out my hand and touch the stage. We had a terrific view. The music was loud. We laughed and enjoyed every minute of the one and a half hours.If you blinked, you missed something. I've never known an audience to be so mesmerized. Cameras are not allowed. I put a piece of paper on our table and for about ten minutes I jotted down headgear. Suddenly an usher came and asked if I were taking notes and when I said yes, he said he would have to confiscate them because the revue is copyrighted. I quickly handed them over so I wouldn't miss anything more. On the back of this paper were some addresses and some shopping needs.

The story is that Dorothy has a fairy godmother who is helping her find somebody to love. The music is bits of songs we all know. Dorothy first goes to Rome and here she meets a woman with a huge hat that is a pizza in a box. Other hats are Rago spaghetti sauce and Boy R D cans. There is a song about a honeymoon and a person in a new moon shape comes out with a another in a honey jar. Somehow a person with a chow mein hat comes into this but I didn't get this because the usher was talking to me then.

Next she goes to Paris and here Dorothy meets some people who have trash cans on their heads and they sing and dance with these on their heads. Three men dressed as black French poodles sing and dance and they are wonderful. They have wiggly tails and bows on them. One woman has a street light on her head. Another woman in a toast costume sang about being the toast of Paris. Next Dorothy went to London and here she meets the Queen who had a hat in the form of imperial margarine with a crown on top of that. The beef eaters did a song and dance. Dorothy came on with a hat in the shape of a can of Royal crown cola and there was a crown on top of this. Dorothy turned into Mary Poppins and suddenly she was on a hook and flew out over the audience. Then they went to Hawaii and there were hula dancers and singers and they had palm trees on their hats. The finale came when Dorothy returned to the U.S. and finds Mr. Right who is Bruce Springsteen. Then came a woman with an enormous hat which was the world and there were various important buildings, such as Big Ben, Eiffel Tower, Leaning Tower of Pisa, etc. Lastly was the hat of S.F. and you saw Ghirardelli Square, Golden Gate Bridge, the Pyramid building, Bank of America, etc. These last two hats were electrified and suddenly they glowed. I've never had one and a half hours pass so quickly and once the show began I forgot I was sitting on the hardest seat imaginable. Gene said this was a real fun thing and he enjoyed it. I did too. Gene and I aren't night life people but we certainly enjoyed this. Bus and BART got us home a little after 5:30 and we have been talking about this ever since. I'll never forget those hats. I'd guess they were maybe six feet tall and six feet wide and they rested on a head. They must have been heavy, yet the dancers didn't show it. What an experience. I could go again.

This morning at 3:56 our bed suddenly moved rapidly forward and backward for about a minute. No up and down jolts in this earthquake but it was pretty strong, a 5.3. Yesterday it was a 4. The epicenter yesterday was by the freeway between Berkeley and Orinda., the nearest yet. Today it was near San Jose but since it was so much bigger, we felt it more. I didn't sleep the rest of the night.

APRIL 28, 1986

Dear Bonna and Wayne,

At the moment we are waiting for the mailman before we go to the hospital to visit my mother. Last week my mother had some sleepless nights. Thursday she couldn't eat breakfast and left the table to sit in the living room. When I asked why she did this, she said she couldn't breathe and she was dying. There was some fancy footwork while I called the doctor and got dressed. He said to call an ambulance but I thought we could get her to the hospital sooner. Later I realized I made a mistake because the paramedics would have used oxygen in the ambulance. Usually I think Gene drives too fast but on the way to the hospital I thought he drove too slowly. When Gene drew up to emergency, I rushed in and shouted we had a heart attack patient in the car. Immediately a nurse started out with a wheel chair. I said she needed a stretcher but they insisted on the wheel chair. Again I was wrong. She needed to be sitting up and not lying down. Her breathing was so bad that her whole body was twisting and she was gasping. I was sent to sign her in. Then we had to wait a few minutes before a nurse came for us. Now there was a doctor, four nurses, two paramedics and two security guards in her alcove of the emergency room. Everybody was functioning so efficiently that the doctor had to give almost no instructions. Why the security guards were there, I don't know. The doctor sat Gene and me down and said my mother had congestive heart failure and had already been given medicine but I was to prepare myself for her death. He said it in a nice way. He wanted to know what measures I wanted him to take. I said no heart lung machine just to keep her alive as a vegetable. He asked if I would be comfortable with this decision. I've thought about this so it wasn't a snap decision and I knew this was my mother's wish too. The doctor then asked if we were comfortable watching and Gene said no. I did not want a memory of seeing her die. So we went outside the curtain. When my mother was able to talk, the doctor asked her questions but my mother kept telling him to ask her daughter. Both the nurses and doctor kept coming out with questions. Finally the doctor came and said he had talked to our doctor on the phone and he asked some more questions. Later he came back and said my mother was a fighter and that he was going to admit her to the hospital, that she would recover and would even go home.

We were impressed with the ease and efficiency with which this life threatening situation was dealt. Later a nurse came and said my mother was being sent to definitive care, her room was 253 and she would show us the elevators. Neither of us had ever been in a room in this hospital. When we walked into my mother's room, she was sitting up and talking as though nothing had happened. She was hooked to an IV., to oxygen and a monitor. Our doctor came to see her on his lunch hour.

We came home for lunch and just as we were about to go back to the hospital our doctor called. He explained more fully what had happened and said my mother would probably only be in the hospital five days. He was so kind and answered my questions and volunteered information so that I really understood what had happened. Some doctors wouldn't take the time to do this. I appreciated it.

APRIL 28, 1986

Over the weekend our doctor was not on call so he sent a cardiologist to see my mother. He changed nothing. Today both the internist and car-diologist saw my mother. They took chest X-rays to see how the fluid was disappearing. My mother is pleased and impressed with her care. Today she started complaining about the food so Gene says she really is better.

The first hour in her room she was puzzled as to toilet facilities. There wasn't a bathroom connected to her room and this is a really mod-ern hospital. I walked up and down the hall and only found one a long distance from her room so we assumed she would have to use a bedpan. When we returned in the afternoon, my mother was all excited about the collapsible toilet. Next to her bed was a cabinet with a small steel sink on top. A U shaped door was on the front and this is pulled down and, voila, there is a toilet that flushed. Amazing. So a patient only has to stand by the bed, turn around and sit.

The first day when we rushed home for lunch, I cut two roses and stuck them in a vase, but it wasn't an ikebana arrangement. Every day thereafter, I took an ikebana arrangement. On the window side of her bed was a cabinet so we had a mini Ikebana show. The second day I walked in with an arrangement in one of my expensive, unusual containers (vases).

"Oh, you brought one of your best vases", exclaimed my mother.

She was so pleased. The arrangements have elicited much comment from nurses and people stand outside her door and look in to see them. My mother calls out and invites them to come in and see the arrangements.

Yesterday my mother really complained about the food. Gene says she is surely getting better. Complaining is a good sign. However, my mother tells us she would not be alive had she not come to the hospital. She is so right about that.

TUESDAY 4/29/86

When we entered my mother's room today, she told us she was coming home at 11 tomorrow. They had her walk around the bed today. We had another ikebana arrangement and a few minutes after we arrived three nurses came to see them. One was Japanese and she said when she lived at home, she had the opportunity to learn ikebana and wouldn't. Now it is too late and she wishes she had. The doctor admired the roses in an arrangement and said he had a rose garden. So those flowers have been a highlight and certainly have brought extra attention, non medical, to my mother.

Each day I've taken things up in a plastic bag that said SURPRISES FROM SINGAPORE. My bag of tricks. Now I'll retire the SURPRISES FROM SINGAPORE and wait till I need them again.

Today the home care coordinator who is an RN and a PHN came to visit us. She suggested a walker and my mother agreed. We have been urging a walker for a long time. This afternoon they will deliver the walker and teach her to use it. I hope it works. The coordinator suggested we have a visiting nurse come for a couple weeks. She will take blood pressure and access progress. Then after that we will have a home care person come to help her bathe. My mother is quite subdued and willing to do most anything. Some change!

MAY 8, 1986

Dear Phyllis,

We thought things were going well with my mother but on Sunday we had MORE FUN! I went to make our bed after breakfast and then to make my mother's. Gene came and told me my mother was in her bathroom and needed me. Both of us went to her. She was sitting on the john, unable to talk and very weak. We got her back in bed and she said she was dying. She thought she was having a stroke. I took her blood pressure and it was normal for her but something was very wrong. I had been given a number to call at the hospital where a nurse is on duty to answer questions and help people who have recently been in the hospital. The nurse said to call 911 which I should have done immediately. The fire department near us responded immediately and within a minute or two an ambulance was here. The firemen tried to get my mother to talk but she did not respond. They asked her what her name was, where she was and who the president is. They asked her to raise her foot, squeeze their hands, etc. She just lay there. So they decided to take her to the hospital. I went in the ambulance and Gene came in the car. He got there before we did. In the emergency room they monitored her heart, gave her an EKG and a blood test. We were there four hours. The other side of the curtain two heart attacks came in and were sent to a room. In another spot was another heart attack and a young girl who needed emergency surgery. My mother slowly roused and by the time we left, she was observing all that went on and making comments. What happened is that she strained a bit while having a bowel movement and her heart could not take the strain. The blood was not pumped to her head. As you can see, she isn't very strong. The next morning she had a little seizure at breakfast. We gave her prunes and that was too much food. She needs small meals. Medicare sends two nurses three times a week, one to monitor her heart and the other to bathe her. Both are very nice and Mother likes them. She gets around slowly on a walker.

Today we took my mother back to the doctor for a checkup. As we drove past the hospital Gene said he was hanging onto the wheel very tightly so that it would not turn in the hospital drive. Across the street from the hospital are medical buildings and this is where the doctor's office is. She had another blood test. She told the doctor there is nothing wrong with her. I think my mother is a natural Christian Scientist, even though she is a Presbyterian.

Last night there was an item on TV about Pan Am. The Pan Am counters at the airport are empty. Employees are being laid off. A 747 has 300 economy seats and right now not more than 20 are occupied on European flights. Americans in this area are just not going to Europe.

Today we went to our travel agent and booked a Westtour to Alaska.

We couldn't get the date we wanted but we did get a reservation. You can hardly get the travel agent on the phone. Karen's phone rang constantly when we were there and she had four people on hold all the time. Karen said a man came in today and wanted to book a TWA tour to southern Europe. Karen expected to have no trouble booking this since she has done nothing but cancel reservations for weeks. However, TWA has been canceling flights. There was one in July that seemed to have enough people and the man could get that. TWA must be hurting, too. The six agents in the travel bureau were busy and there was a waiting line for all six of them. All those people who canceled European holidays are now making other reservations.

Jan and Ingrid of Norway are coming July 20th to visit us for a week, after two previous weeks with other Americans. We suggested a trip to Yosemite for three days but it takes 10 days for an airmail letter between the two countries so we haven't received their reply. Gene was getting nervous about reservations so I called. Yosemite is completely booked, even the expensive accommodations. We called outside the park and finally located a motel. If Ingrid and Jan don't want to go, we can cancel. We shall have to do the same thing at Lake Tahoe. I bet anyplace in the U.S. will be crowded this summer.

Reagan told in his speech from Tokyo about terrorism at the American Embassy in Paris that was aborted the day before scheduled. He said French people daily stand in line to get visas and if the bombing had taken place many Frenchmen, as well as embassy staff, would have died. Those darn terrorists! Last night on TV I heard the tail end of a news item and I believe it said at least 50% of Americans who had booked trips to Russia this summer have canceled. I know China and Russia were popular vacation spots this summer. They were judged safe from terrorism but now with the meltdown, they no longer are. I know tours in Russia were sent back home a few days after the meltdown. Actually those in Russia did not know of the meltdown till they got phone calls from relatives back here.

I guess Australia, Hawaii, Canada and Alaska, as well as the U.S. are the favored places to vacation this summer.

MAY 21, 1986

Dear Ingrid and Jan,

When we were in the hospital packing my mother's belongings in preparation for her coming home, the nurse asked which of us was my mother's child. My mother said, "They are BOTH my kids!" She absolutely refused to name her birth child. I think a statement was made by this response, don't you?

My mother ate little those two weeks before her heart attack. We knew she wasn't feeling well and so did the doctor but I didn't know how seriously ill she was. Since my mother returned home, her appetite has been wonderful. She eats everything and leaves nothing on her plate. Sunday we were sitting at the table when my mother said, "I thought you would never learn how to cook meat, but in the last two weeks you really learned!" She ate two helpings of meat. Actually the meat was cooked the same way I always cook it.

Today Gene and I did the weekly grocery shopping. I bought a fourth of a watermelon and we each had a piece for dessert. It was sweet and good and we all thought it an excellent melon. Gene said he knew I made good choices and he rolled his eyes. I knew this was a backhanded compliment. What he really meant was that I made a good choice when I said yes to his proposal. Seems to me in this house you have to catch compliments in a disguised form.

Until Saturday night, we didn't leave my mother alone, except for once or twice when we went to a store for not more than half an hour. Saturday night we played bridge and I left the medicine beside my mother's bed and told her what time to take it. When we came home, I took her to the bathroom. Today I went to a meeting and left her 2 PM medicine out and told her to take it. She did. A few minutes later Gene came in with her medicine. She took it. It looks to me as though she is getting good care, maybe too good, if she gets double doses of medicine.

Sunday both of us were home all day and suddenly at 5 PM I realized I had forgotten to give my mother her 2 PM medicine. It is either feast or famine. Both medicines need to be spaced. However she had no problem.

MAY 27, 1986

Today I went out to buy a dress, dressy material but plain style. I found nothing.

Tonight I was looking at TV with Gene and raised my arm and Gene took a price label off that said $1.29. Somehow it got stuck there. I asked Gene it he would buy me for $1.29 and he said if I were new he would but not now when I'm old! Huh!

I want to take bread to two friends tomorrow so tonight I made tomato bread. Smells wonderful. It is made with tomato sauce that has been laced with Italian herbs. It will be tomato color. The recipe can be used with spinach and beets, too. At Christmas it might be interesting to have red and green bread.

On Friday the 23rd I had some periondontal work done, upper right and upper left. Upper left is getting better fast but upper right still pains. I think there are stitches in the right but not the left. I will see the periodontist this Friday and maybe he can make me more comfortable. The day I had this done I was given medicine to numb my mouth. 2 pills at 8 AM. 2 at 3 PM. Marilyn was in town and was to have lunch with us. I tried to help Gene set the table and my hand wouldn't hold anything. I dropped a good cup and it broke into tiny pieces. Marilyn doesn't see me often. All the while she was here my speech was slurred and before she left I went to sleep. What a hostess. Marilyn left about 3 PM and the periodontist operated at 4 PM. He also gave me another anesthesia. Gene had to put his arm around me and lead me to the office. After it was over the nurse brought me to the door and she had her arm around me. I was holding an ice pack on my face. Gene's arms replaced the nurses when she opened the waiting room door. Two men were sitting in the waiting room. They jumped up to open the door for Gene and me. They could see he had his hands full. If they were timid, they must have been scared to see me in such a wobbly, dependent state and wondering if this was their fate. Saturday Gene did the cooking and again I tried to help. I dropped the Swedish meat balls and their sour cream sauce all over the kitchen floor. Gene escorted me from the kitchen. I'm back to normal now. However, at night I still take the codeine so I can sleep. Frankly I'm getting pretty tired of doctors and dentists. Seems we had had more than our share of both since last August. There has to be a let up soon.

FRIDAY THE 30TH

It is 9:30 AM and I just returned from the dentist. I had a 9:30 appointment with the periodontist and I was back home on the nose of 9:30 I got there a bit early and didn't even get a chance to sit in the waiting room. I was whisked into a chair and in no time flat the stitches were removed. Everything was o.k. even though I've had a miserable week with throbbing and pain. Next week I go again but I assume it is just to make sure all is healed properly. I'm glad that is behind me.

MAY 31, 1986

Dear Julie-Anne,

My mother is doing remarkably well. It appears she will need to see the doctor every two weeks. Last week he discerned an incipient problem so the medicine was doubled. Problem solved for now. My mother is a fighter. I know this and the emergency doctor told me this. Our regular doctor knows she has a will of her own. Sometimes this is good and sometimes it is bad. She has decided she is no longer going to use her walker. This is bad. If she falls, she will probably be bedridden for the rest of her life. I tell the doctor I am concerned about the quality of her life and not the quantity. The same is true with me. I'd rather have less quantity but good quality.

Gene killed all our grass, rather weeds. Now he is attempting to get the dead sod up. Yesterday he rented a sod cutter. Gene isn't used to such hard physical labor. I was afraid he might have a heart attack. My mother was too and she kept coming to me and telling me I should make Gene stop. I tried but he refused. All I could do is get him to rest a bit but when the darn machine is hired by the hour, that is hard. I wanted him to pay to have the sod removed. He refused but afterwards he said had he known it would be so hard to remove the sod, he would have paid.

A baby for us!

Luggage tags

JUNE 21, 1986

Dear Chet and Bess,

I was taking a bath when the phone rang so Gene answered it. It was for me. Wrapping a towel around me, I went to the phone in our bedroom. I listened and then said, "We'll take the baby." Rushing into the hall, I called Gene and my mother and announced that I had some tremendous news. We were going to have a baby! Their eyes opened wide and they stared at me. Was I out of my mind? Then the tale unraveled.

Connie Huffman had called. Her daughter and son-in-law were coming to San Francisco this week to attend a conference. Both are medical researchers at an eastern university. A long time ago Linda asked her mother if she would care for the baby this week.

Connie said she would take a week off from work to do so. She sees her grandchildren so seldom, she thought this would be a good time to enjoy Kate. Well, the government had something brewing in relation to Connie's work at the naval air station and they had suddenly called a meeting for Tuesday and Wednesday in Washington. She was told she had to go. The other person who might have gone retired last month and as yet there was no replacement. Connie tried to get somebody from an agency to take care of Kate but all their care givers were booked. Connie asked if I knew anyone and the only person I knew was myself, so I told her to bring the baby here. I was taking care of my ninety three year old mother and a fourteen month old baby couldn't be much more work.

What a relief for Connie! They will bring a crib and high chair and the rest is up to Gene and me.

Last night we played bridge with Ginnie and Ed who have four small grandchildren. Their house is permanently equipped, with two cribs, to take care of babies. This week both cribs were occupied for two days and nights. During the first night Ginnie was awakened with a thud noise. Thinking one of the kids had fallen out of bed, she hopped out of bed and discovered it was Ed who had fallen out of bed. Instead of asking if he were hurt, she said "Don't make any noise and waken the children." Ed just turned sixty-five and this is the first time he has fallen out of bed in their 40 years of marriage.

JUNE 25, 1986

Linda and Bob brought Kate at 9:30 AM. We were ready and waiting. Kate is a sweet baby, not noisy and quite content to follow us around and to play with her toys. She usually has an hour nap from 10 to 11 but she had a 2 3/4 hour nap yesterday.

She didn't seem to want her solid food or as many bottles as I was told she would take. Linda called in the evening and I told her this, but she wasn't worried. After Gene and I put Kate down for the night. we said this baby business is a cinch. We were very happy with "our baby." Kate usually sleeps through the night and wakes at 7 AM. She woke at 2 AM and I changed her and gave her a bottle. She woke at 2:45 and I fed her again. She woke at 4:30 and I fed her. When she woke at 6, she got another bottle. Her forehead was hot and she upchucked on my shoulder. I called her parents who were in Anaheim. Bob said to give her some baby Tylenol. She sometimes does this so they weren't concerned. I said I thought she had a fever and if I got worried, I was taking her to the emergency room at the hospital. Bob said o.k. Kate certainly wasn't herself. I rocked her and Gene rocked her and about 9:30 I decided we needed help. I was so worried tears oozed from my eyes. On the way to the hospital I braced up. When I signed Kate in, the admission person said they might not be able to treat Kate because I wasn't related to her. I told them both parents were doctors. A little white lie. Both have their Ph D in medical research, but aren't practicing physicians. A young resident saw Kate, made us repeat our tale and said he would examine her but couldn't do anything because we weren't related. He sent Gene home to get Linda and Bob's telephone number at the hotel. While I was holding Kate and he was listening to her heart and lungs, she upchucked all over me again. Then he had me put her on the table. She screamed and immediately he saw the problem in her mouth. She had a possible strep throat. He took a culture. I saw her throat and it was red and raw. It took almost two hours till the results of the culture came back. It wasn't a strep throat, but either a virus or a bacteria. He didn't know which. He gave a prescription, but we couldn't give the medicine to Kate till we found out whether she was allergic to penicillin.

The doctor said to give Kate warm sponge baths every hour to reduce the fever and not to give her milk, but clear liquid.

We got home at 12:15 and I called the hotel but neither Linda nor Bob were in their room. The hotel operator said they would page the parents and leave a note in their room to call Norma. They gave me the number of the convention hall and I called that. About a half hour later we had a call and it was the operator of the convention hall who said they couldn't locate Bob but they would keep trying. Finally at 4 PM he got the message. Linda had been giving a speech and Bob was chairing a meeting and the paging was only in the halls, not the meeting rooms. Bob said she had had penicillin before and it hadn't hurt her so give it to her. Gene rushed to the drug store and in a few minutes the medicine was "down the hatch."

Gene and I ate both lunch and dinner in shifts, first Gene and then me. We held her all day long. I had heard that babies with high fevers sometimes had convulsions. I wanted to know what was happening every minute and the only way I could do this was to hold her. She seemed to be most comfortable on our shoulder. By 7 Kate had improved. She was alert and lying in Gene's arms while he was looking at a ball game. When I took her, she was less hot. I decided to take her for a walk in her stroller. She sat up and looked around. This was a real improvement. She even sat on the floor for a short time and played with her toys. However she was getting tired so we gave her the apple juice, doctor said no milk, and the Tylenol and put her to bed. Linda called and I told her the encouraging news and she and Bob decided not to return. I said we were coping. Connie will be home tomorrow and then she will take Kate. I'm tired. I think it is from the worry.

At midnight you could tell Kate's fever had lessened. She was much less hot. We woke her and changed her and attempted to give her the medicine by spoon but she kept pushing Gene's hand away. So we put it in a bottle with apple juice. She went right back to sleep and I had to waken her this morning at 8 for more medicine. Connie called before this and wanted to come for her but I said to delay till I had bathed and fed her. The doctor said we could give milk today but inside of 10 minutes it was up and all over me again. Again Gene offered the penicillin in a spoon and again she refused it. So more apple juice and penicillin in a bottle. She knew the difference between plain apple juice and the doctored apple juice so we had to offer one and then the other and fool her. I didn't have too much success but Gene took over and he got it all down her.

Connie came when I said I was ready. She walked over to take Kate from my lap but Kate burrowed herself into my bosom. She was having none of her grandmother. We all sat down. I put Kate on her feet between my knees and Connie attempted to call her but she climbed right back up in my lap. When her parents left her, Kate was perfectly content. She is used to staying with a caretaker. Finally Connie just had to take her from me. She screamed all the way out to the car and was still crying as Connie drove away. I'll never forget her eyes. They seemed to be telling me we were rejecting her and she didn't like it one bit. Two days bonding between "Grandma and Grandpa Davidson" was pretty solid, probably because she was sick.

I can see why the hospital was reluctant to treat Kate. We were strangers and didn't know her history. I knew she was fourteen months old but not her date of birth. We could have been kidnappers. Our tale sounded like a cock and bull story. When I told Connie this, she said Bob and Linda should have given us power of attorney.

My mother was thrilled to have a baby in the house. She sat and watched her and was so happy when I put Kate on her lap. I stood right near, though, because my mother is frail. My mother got herself a cup of tea before we got home from the hospital. How she got it to the table, I don't know. She can't walk without both hands on the walker. I questioned her but she gave me a vague answer. I got lunch for her then but in my worry and excitement I forgot my mother's 2 PM medicine. Too busy with Kate.

In each of the last three months, April, May and June, Gene and I have used the emergency room at John Muir Hospital, twice with a life threatening situation with my mother and this time with Kate. We think they do a good job. Gene said Wednesday seems to be a slack day because they weren't busy yesterday. Each doctor we have seen has been good.

Connie said today she was glad we had Kate, since all this happened. Her neighbor who golfs offered. She is a grandmother but not a practicing one because her children live far away. Her husband would have cared for Kate while she golfed but he likes the bottle pretty much and his bottle doesn't contain milk.

My arms ache today. Having 20 pounds in them for all those hours caused this. Gene arms are stronger and he doesn't ache.

I can see that Gene would have made a good father. Gene regrets that we didn't marry ten years before we did. He says if he knew then what he knows now, he would have proposed then. Can't blame me because I was ready.

Gene never passed Kate's door without checking on Kate and sometimes he would leave TV in the family room and go to the bedroom and check on her. When she was on the floor playing, and nobody was around, Gene was on the floor with her. She was such a good baby, it would be hard not to love her.

After Kate left this morning, I finished our weekly grocery shopping. Gene did a bit yesterday. I've just made bread dough and the bread is baking. I'm taking Connie a loaf, stopping to xerox this letter and then I'll clean house. Gene is out in the yard working on our concrete edging. He has only a little more to do and then we'll have a neat yard again.

MY DAY AUGUST 22, 1986

Dear Gertrude,

Today I'm doing nothing. It is my birthday. On TV we saw an advertisement for cheeseburgers, 2 for .99, so this noon that is what we had. Tonight we have reservations so I won't have to prepare dinner. I did make bread this morning but that is all I've done today.

My mother has always made me an angel food cake for my birthday. I bought the cake mix yesterday. Today I put all the ingredients in the bowl so my mother could beat it in the mixer and put it in the pan. Well, she just stood, spilled some of the stuff and then asked what she should do next. She just wasn't connecting. It was pathetic so I told her to leave it and I would do it. Something went wrong with the cake and it was a failure. Gene went to the store and bought a cake

The bread did not bake in the usual time. I made barbecued spare ribs on Wednesday and you were supposed to put wax paper over them. Gene thinks the wax from the paper evaporated and got on the thermostat in the oven so now the oven temperature is not correct. We are going to clean the oven and see if this helps.

Bud has a birthday on Wednesday, five days after mine so we are having a joint birthday dinner on Sunday. Ordinarily Mary invites us to her house for my birthday but I suggested we celebrate both birthdays at once at our house. Mary and I don't think alike. She thinks spending money and eating out is the way to celebrate a birthday. I think preparing something special at home and baking a cake shows your love. I can see eating out on my birthday because Gene isn't a cook but I feel I should make special dinners for Gene and my mother. Mary is going to bring fresh fruit and ice cream. I'm going to do a gourmet pot roast, a 24 hour salad, vegetable and the cake.

I took my mother to the doctor this week and he says she is doing wonderfully. Her hands and feet are always ice cold because her heart is not functioning normally but for her condition her progress is great. I wish I could say the same for her disposition. She is very strong willed. She keeps telling me she is cooking while we are on vacation. I have menus and supplies all ready and have discussed them with Connie. I try to get across that we are paying Connie for this but I doubt that it sinks in. My mother used to be a good cook but at ninety two she isn't capable. Her attempt at my birthday cake showed this.

OCTOBER 1986

Dear Eloise,

Letters about our trip have been sent and maybe some of what I have in this letter will be a repeat, but I hope not.

I had an appointment with the orthopedist on September 25th. I was supposed to have this on the anniversary of my broken ankle but we were on vacation then so we made it thirteen months later. At this time a decision was to be made as to whether the screws would be removed. They are always removed from young people but sometimes not people my age.

Upon returning from vacation, I did my Christmas shopping because I thought I might not be walking very much if the screws were removed.

The news was good, in fact excellent. The bone that wasn't in position had worked itself into position. I'm not having any trouble and there is no infection, so no operation. What a relief! Gene and I went with the idea that we would ask for a second opinion if he wanted to operate. Gene had contacted the insurance company and he knew just what was required for a second opinion. The doctor said that if trouble is going to occur, it usually occurs in the first year but he recently had a much younger person who only had one small pin and she had trouble after four years, The doctor stressed that if I have any pain at all, I am to see him immediately. We hope I never do have trouble.

Gene got new glasses last week. Instead of going to one of the cut rate optomerists, he went to a full price one. His eyes were examined by an ophthamologist and he had a prescription for tri focals. When he got the glasses, they weren't right. The bi and tri focals were too high and Gene had to hold his head in a peculiar position to read or look at TV. The ophthalmologist always checks our glasses after they are made. The strength was as prescribed. The optical company had to make new glasses for Gene. Now they are right.

Immediately after we returned from vacation, I had some head congestion and in a day's time it had gone to my lungs. It worsened daily and finally after twenty three days I saw the doctor. Neither Gene nor I could sleep at night. My cough was terrible and my chest and stomach muscles are sore from so much coughing. Nasal passages and ears are clear. People think I have whooping cough. I had x-rays and was given an antibiotic and cough medicine with codeine in it. The codeine did the trick. It knocked me out and I slept most of the time. I'm slightly better today but Gene is doing the housework. I do the cooking. Neither Gene nor my mother got it. I thought it was just a cold and what can you do for a cold? No cure yet. I have to see the doctor again on Monday and if I'm not better, the doctor says he is giving me a powerful shot. I can raise nothing in coughing and you can hear a rattle. So as per instructions I'm filling a large pan with boiling water and putting my head over it and then covering the pan and me with a big towel. The doctor says this will loosen it up. So far it hasn't. I'm not very lively. How did I get this? Who knows!

We have worked on our slides and have a slide show of Alaska ready. We showed it on Tuesday. Beforehand I told everyone about my cold so they could back out if they were afraid of catching this. Nobody did. The doctor said nobody could get this once I took the antibiotic. The germ would be killed.

Not a very interesting letter, I know. That is why you haven't received one before. Next time I'll try for a better letter.

We hope you are well and that this germ is not floating all over the U.S.

OCTOBER 31, 1986

Dear Eunice and John,

On our trip I observed on Ginger's luggage some identification tags made from plastic net. I learned how to do it and have made at least fifty. I can't think of any more people to give them to so now I'm making coasters, which have a more complicated pattern and so take longer. One morning I brought these to breakfast and Gene says I'm obsessed with them. I'm not reading so many books because this takes up my time.

I took my mother to the doctor recently. She is still doing extremely well. She must feel better because when I ask her to go out with us, she goes. For awhile she preferred to stay home. She has even asked to go in some stores. She isn't fussing about the walker and once when we forgot it, she was very upset.

This month my mother had a letter from a niece who is a year younger than I. She and her sister and both husbands are coming to San Francisco on vacation and she will call my mother. Zoe was a tomboy as a kid and not well behaved. Neither my father nor I were happy with her. I remember only too well some of the things she did. She had white rats. I do not like rats or mice. One night my parents stopped briefly at her parents' home. She came up behind me and put a rat next to my face. I was a well behaved kid. I had to be with my parents, but I screamed bloody murder. My father and hers made her stop tormenting me with that rat. I've never forgotten this. Once we were guests at dinner at her parents' house and corn on the cob was served. Zoe took a bite and the corn was too hot so she plunged it into a goblet of water and the goblet overturned, broke, and water went all over the table. Her manners left something to be desired. Her father tried very hard to make his children behave but the mother would countermand any decision he made. If the father said no, the children would ask the mother and she would say yes. Bessie, the middle child, was like her father and behaved normally. What to do! I decided to let bygones be bygones and invited the four to dinner. I hadn't seen these cousins in maybe forty years. Well, Zoe is much improved. Although I have reservations about her for her previous atrocities, we had a pleasant dinner and evening. Age has improved her. There were no lulls in the conversation because there was so much to catch up on. I knew nothing of their children or their life. It was like meeting a stranger. My mother enjoyed seeing them. She has kept in touch over the years. They came here the second day of their vacation and returned for dinner again in the 9th day of their vacation. They may never see my mother alive again. They left for home, back east, on the 10th.

Our dwarf orange tree has fifty three oranges. We had nine last year. We picked them at Christmas last year but they will be ripe before that this year. Our Japanese persimmon has forty-one persimmons and we have eaten two so that means it had forty three. These are hard like apples and sweet. We love them. Regular persimmons pucker your mouth. Our pineapple guava has too many guavas to count. Last year we had one guava and it disappeared when we were on vacation.

Our Alaskan slides are now in order and we are beginning to have shows. This past week Gene was pushing me to have people in to see them. This is a switch. Usually I am the one who wants to invite people.

Nurses week

Gold sweater, A unique Christmas present

NOVEMBER 17, 1986

Dear Emma and John,

I'm not reading books, or writing letters because I'm spending all my time making plastic net coasters. Gene is disgusted. He thinks I shouldn't be doing this and looking at TV at the same time, but I can't leave it be.

We have had five shows of our Alaskan slides and will have a sixth tomorrow night. Friday night we had two sets of neighbors, our Alameda friends and Connie. Half way thru the show, the phone rang and it was Darren, our neighbor's son, who wanted to talk to his mother. When his mother returned to the living room, she said they had to leave immediately because her father had just had a stroke and been taken to a San Francisco hospital. In minutes Sue and Hing were San Francisco bound. The next day Darren called me. His grandmother had called an ambulance and wanted her husband taken to a certain hospital but the ambulance driver said they could only take him to San Francisco General. At San Francisco General they did not want him, so they tried to get him sent to the hospital his grandmother wanted. No beds were available so he was sent to St. Mary's. Darren said his grandfather had a paralyzed arm and his face was distorted. Yesterday we spoke to the Wongs and learned his whole side is paralyzed. This hasn't been the Wongs year. Hing's father died suddenly in the summer from a brain tumor. So our slide show wasn't as lighthearted as it should have been. Things like this make you realize that there but for the grace of God go I. We are all vulnerable.

I noticed the Wongs did not return last night after an afternoon visit to the hospital. Now I wonder what else has happened.

I made a chocolate cheesecake to serve Friday and it was good but extremely rich.

Saturday Gene and I went to John Muir Hospital because it was NURSES WEEK and they were celebrating by having a tour of the Surgi Center. We were there for the first tour. Our group was all very knowledgeable adults. Questions and comments were technical and medical. Other tours had children. First we had a demonstration, on a cloth-filled dummy, of knee surgery. All the instruments were beside the table and as the nurse inserted the instruments we saw it on TV on the opposite side of the table. It is marvelous what can be done with just a little hole as big as a penny.

Then we went into a room where they do cataract operations. Again instruments were out and we could touch them. I bet there were a hundred. We felt the lens implants. There was a plastic model of an eye that came apart and each procedure in the operation was demonstrated. I wondered how they kept the eyelid open They have a little gadget that does that. We saw what a detached retina was. The nurses did everything a doctor would do in an operation and it was most interesting.

Following this, we had a demonstration of a hip replacement. Boy, that socket is heavy! Again there was a dummy to work on. Then we saw some head trauma surgery and I was impressed with the electric and manual drills that go thru the skull. A doctor has to have carpentry skills for this. We had been scheduled to go to the operating floor and see something about open heart surgery but a real operation was in progress so they brought down a machine to show us how the machine recovers and extracts red blood cells and puts them back in the body as heart surgery is being performed. I'm simplifying all this.

Finally we went into the Invitro fertilization clinic and saw a movie of a woman who actually had this done at John Muir. The doctor who does this talked to us. They use ultra sound to scatter the eggs in the ovaries so they can collect just six. It was most interesting and the Surgi Center was crowded. People brought children but this wasn't for children. We were all required to suit up, a body suit, plastic slippers over shoes, and plastic caps over our hair. There are about 10 beds in the Surgi

Center where surgery is done on an outpatient basis. Not all I've described is done on an outpatient basis.

John Muir hospital has just become a trauma center. It was a good general hospital but now it will have a 24 hour trauma unit and a helicopter port. New buildings are being added and it is a mess right now getting in and out of the parking lot and to all the doctor's offices that line the whole street across from the hospital.

Saturday afternoon Gene and I took a walk. Gene always holds my hand when we walk and it was a good thing he had a hold of me. My foot caught on a root that hung over the sidewalk and I would have gone down had he not jerked me back. I have a shoulder socket that is painful and I can barely comb my hair, but this is better than a fall.

Saturday night Gene decided to do something to my mother's glass clock on the book case in the family room. Somehow he knocked the clock and one of the Hummels to the floor and both broke. It wasn't his day.

I took my mother to the doctor on Thursday. This time he had to make some changes in her medicine. She told him we watch her like a hawk. I think this is a compliment and shows we are trying to take good care of her but she thinks we watch her too much. I think she is lucky. Recently she wanted to do some Christmas shopping. We went to Cost Plus and two other women were on walkers and one in a wheel chair. This consoled her and today she wanted to go to a drug store.Now the ice has been broken and she feels better about people seeing her using a walker.

Gene wants to go to a store and I need some items for my dinner party tomorrow night. I must stop.

NOVEMBER 19, 1986

Dear Marge and Roy,

Last night we had parked in front of our house a two weeks old white Porsche and a Maserati of a couple month's age. We were entertaining our affluent friends. I'm not saying this in a derogatory manner. Both couples are two of the very nicest we know. Both men appear unaggressive, have exquisite manners, and super intelligence. They don't flaunt their wealth or success.

Toby's hobby is cars and he has seven of them. Besides the Porsche, Toby has a Jaguar, a classic Thunderbird that they drive in antique shows and two Volkswagens. The other two I don't know. The problem of having seven cars for two people is that they don't all get driven equally and some have batteries that go flat from lack of use. The one they drive the most is the Volks van because they sit up high and can see so well.

Beside the Maserati, the other couple have a BMW the wife drives and a Volkswagen the son drives. When the two men were discussing the merits of cars, Gene and I just listened.

Gosh, think of the problems of having 7 cars. Which car to drive? Gene says Toby should be fair to each car and designate a car for each day of the week. Our life is so simple. We drive the only car we have. I wonder if I know anyone who has a Rolls Royce. If I can think of someone, I'll invite them to dinner. We might as well entertain the top of the line. No Hyundis for us

This morning Gene and I did our weekly shopping. We had a quick lunch and I went to book review. Jeffrey Archer's book was mentioned and the lady from the book store said a MATTER OF HONOR was his best book yet. Poor Jeffrey Archer! He does get himself in some messes but he always lands on his feet with a book based on his experiences.

When I came home, the mail had finally come. This was a good day. We had a Christmas card from Isabel. We had a Christmas package from Colette and a gift from Ingrid and Jan. The gift is a lovely 24 karat gold tray! WOW! This is a thank you for their July visit. We expected nothing and wanted nothing and we are bowled over with this gift. We have never sent them a gift after visiting them. Oh, yes, we did mail an ikebana container after our last visit but its value was negligible. Had we known they were going to do this, we would have discouraged them because it was a joy to have them and we didn't want or need to be repaid for hospitality.

The telephone rang just after I got home. It was Mary and they had been away over the weekend and had brought us something and wanted to deliver it. What a day! You would think it really is Christmas.

NOVEMBER 27, 1986

Dear Mary,

I'm thankful for a mother who brought up a son to be responsible, helpful and to have a guilty conscience when I work and he sits. Today Gene and I shopped for last minute things for Thanksgiving dinner and for bridge on Saturday. Then together we cleaned the house. Twenty years ago I could have done the whole thing but I've slowed down recently. Tomorrow Wilma and Russ will share our Thanksgiving dinner. I'll have only the turkey to prepare and the pie to make. Setting the table with all our good dishes is a bit of work but I want to use them.

I wasn't scheduled to have bridge till January but Therese got into a mess. Workmen installing double paned windows have torn the house apart and broken some things and her house is upset. Ginny is next on the list but she is going to a reception on Saturday and won't have time to prepare for bridge so I was asked and what could I say? I've entertained a lot this month with six slide shows, some dinners and I was looking forward to relaxing but I'll postpone this for a few more days. I'll have to stop having company so I can concentrate on cookie making.

Last week Gene picked persimmons because the birds had started to eat them. Today he picked half of our orange crop. We had our own oranges for breakfast and they were wonderful. Two weeks ago two friends brought lemons and limes. I had to give some to neighbors because I couldn't use them all.

I'll make lemon meringue pie for bridge but still I'll have lemons to spare.

FRIDAY THE 28TH OF NOVEMBER

Thanksgiving went well. I had the turkey in the oven by 9 AM and the pie made by 10 so I had some time to relax before dinner. Our guests left by 5:30 and I relaxed the rest of the evening.

My mother has been giving me a rough time ever since she was in the hospital in April. She expects when she pays her medical bills and submits them to Medicare that she will receive reimbursement immediately. Well, the system has a two months lag normally but in her case it has been 7 months.

Firstly the doctors have joined a firm called Omega who do their billings. The firm is less than a year old. It hires young people and things do not go smoothly. The doctor's hospital visits and two other services rendered in the hospital by the doctor were lost. It was a few months before I complained and this was discovered. A girl I talked to was supposed to take care of this but she quit. Another girl knew nothing about it when I complained a second time. This girl said all had been sent to Medicare. I called Medicare and they said it had never been received. I called the doctor and his office resubmitted it to Omega. Still nothing. Then I called Omega. Another excuse. Finally on Wednesday after several more calls from me and one from the doctor to Omega, a new girl, 3rd, promised to look into it and call me back. She did call back at 5 PM but at 2:30 the mailman delivered a check for all but $44. The girl was mad because she had spent time trying to figure this out. I pointed out that the mail wasn't delivered till 2:30.

I think in the U.S. we get good medical care but the financial part is a something else. There should be an easier way to submit bills and get repaid. If it weren't for me, I don't know how my mother could cope. What does an old person do who is alone and maybe not mentally as alert as when younger?

The joys of getting old ! Each month we have a session with my mother over her checkbook. I try to balance it but sometimes I have to get help from Gene. Sometimes my mother leaves off the cents on checks. Once she deposited a $205 check and she put down $209. When my mother makes a mistake and she has more money in the bank than she thought, she is pleased but when she ends up with less, then she tells me I'm messing up her checkbook. My mother tells me she never had all this trouble when she did it herself. I'm not saying my check book always balances perfectly but when it doesn't, I look for my mistake and usually it is my mistake. Only once did the bank make a mistake.

DECEMBER 10, 1986

Dear Jacqui and Will,

Things are progressing nicely toward Christmas. I'm on target and I like that.

Last week I told Gene I was going into S.F. on Monday to see the decorations in the store windows. Gene said he would accompany me. This is nice but I could see more by myself.

Sunday we had a call from friends who had two extra tickets to the Christmas luncheon of SIRS. We postponed our trip and went to the luncheon. The entertainment was good but I felt old being with so many elderly people.

Tuesday we went by BART into San Francisco. Gene had decided just what we would see but I thought otherwise. I had proposed this trip so he gave in. We went first to Gumps where the windows had puppets based upon the production of Beach Blanket Babylon. The puppets were mechanized. You could pick out notable people in the audience. The hats were like those in the performance. I thought it was wonderful but Gene said it wasn't Christmasy. True, it wasn't. Then we went to I. Magnin. Puppets again. Ladies of olden times. Dressed beautifully. The puppets even had rings on their ringers. The windows depicted a story of a woman and her lover on a canal in Venice. Again not Christmasy. Our last stop was Neiman Markus. In the rotunda they did not have that ugly gray Christmas tree they have previously had. They had eight reindeer on wires at various levels of the store. There was a modernistic sled. You had to use your imagination to make a sled of those boards.

I had told Gene I did not want to shop in S.F. I just wanted to look. We passed the Galleria and decided to walk through. One store had metallic sweaters. I've long wanted one. In previous years I've seen them for $500, then $350. I didn't buy. Guess why! This year I've seen them for over $100. I decided to wait till after Christmas when they might go on sale.

In the Galleria there was a store for petites. Petites are not for me but I did check the price and it was below $100. I tried the small size on and it fit. I had already received a Christmas present of money so I decided to use it for this. It might buy a sleeve and Gene could pay for the rest. I'm delighted. A gold sweater will go with anything.

We had a croissant sandwich and came home. I took my mother out while I did some errands.

Today is Wednesday and we shopped and mailed our packages and Connie's at UPS. Sometimes I've waited an hour but today I walked in and there wasn't a person in line. It was 12:50 PM. Lunchtime must be a good time to go to UPS.

On the way home we stopped at Payless and bought a Noble fir, the kind of Christmas tree we like.

This week our neighborhood was shaken when an older man stalked a twenty five year old girl who was walked her dog near her parents home. He had made a pass at her and she rejected this married man who lived across the street from the apartment the girl shared with another girl. On this day the man followed her car and when he found her walking alone, he shot her in the head and then he killed himself. People in their front yards saw the whole thing. The little dog stayed till the girl's body was taken away and then he ran to her car. The police traced the car and found out the girl's name. Only the roommate knew the connection between the girl and the man. Refusing an old man's advances was enough to cause him to kill her. IMAGINE! I can't believe this happened a couple streets from our house,

CHRISTMAS NIGHT

Dear Raedina and Milton,

We had a quiet Christmas, just the three of us. I took my mother to the doctor Tuesday for her regular appointment and the doctor asked our Christmas plans. When I said we were having a quiet Christmas, he said, "Good. I want YOU to relax." I prefer company even If it is work.

Before I ever knew Gene and a few years after I became a career girl I bought a gold watch which was expensive but supposed to last my lifetime. Maybe the works would have but the gold bracelet wore out. I had it repaired but it couldn't be repaired any more. A new band was as expensive as a new watch of equal value. So for a few months I went without a watch. For all these years I've been hoarding birthday and Christmas money and I had enough for a new watch of equal value, at five times the cost. For more than two months I've been looking. Just before Christmas I found the watch. It had to be small enough to go thru my wedding ring and the bracelet had to be gold. It is Swiss and has a sapphire crystal. Gene said he was giving this watch to me for Christmas. We never exchange such expensive presents. I said no but he insisted. I told him not to buy another thing but I saw him sneaking other things in the house. This morning we were gathered around the Christmas tree and Gene wanted to know whether I wanted my present first or last. I said last. So my mother and Gene opened presents and I some from friends and then came this big package that couldn't be the watch. I took off the paper but couldn't get the gift out of the box. Gene helped me and, lo and behold, it was a toilet seat. You should have heard the three of us laugh. We all laughed till the tears came. For about three years I've been suggesting a new toilet seat because the enamel has come off in spots. I agree with Napoleon, "It is but a step from the sublime to the ridiculous !" My new watch is the sublime and the toilet seat is the ridiculous. Who else got a toilet seat for Christmas? I might have been the only one in the U.S.

We have been hearing on TV that Christmas buying has not equaled last year's. The Davidsons haven't just contributed to those sales. We have boosted them.

JANUARY 10, 1987

Dear Ingrid and Jan,

Last night we had dinner at the Storms' home in Orinda. Orinda is in the hills and houses are far apart and there are no street lights. The Storms had Thanksgiving dinner with us and apparently they think we are big eaters. A hugh baked potato, fillet mignon, big enough for the two of us, was served. I felt I must eat this but I was stuffed ail evening and I didn't get to sleep till 3 AM. When a host has gone to the trouble and expense of preparing a wonderful meal, I want to show appreciation. You don't show appreciation by leaving half a meal. Somehow I'm going to have to convey to people that less is more.

Tomorrow we are invited at noon to the Cape Cod for either brunch or dinner in honor of Pat's mother's nurse who is having a birthday. I'll bake a birthday cake,

Today I received a package from Connie W in Boston She is artistically talented and had made some Christmas decorations out of plastic net. I had written of seeing some but being unable to get the directions. She sent two with directions so I shall start making them for next year.

Boy, am I showing my age. I just looked at the calendar and this morning there was an AAUW meeting which I wanted to attend. It is now 2:30 and the meeting has long since been over. A one track mind.

Last night I wore my new gold sweater with my royal blue suit. It looked nice and I was warm. Gene nearly froze. Our friends are 60 degree people and we are 70 degree people and 72 in the evening. My mother sits in bed in her nightie and we have to keep our house warm for her. When Gene got in bed, I thought I had a piece of ice next to me. His body was that cold. Gene says if we can't be warm what is the use of our money? We can be cold when we are dead but when we are alive we want to be warm, even if it does cost us money.

I would love to wear my gold sweater and blue suit tomorrow but I'll wear a blue blouse because Pat gave me a necklace she made of polished stones encased in gold wire. The stones don't show up on the gold sweater but they do on the blouse. Pat's house is warm so I can wear a light blouse and short sleeves.

JANUARY 29, 1987

Tuesday night I made a dish of sweet potatoes, chicken and mushroom soup that I got from a magazine. It was o.k. but I won't try it again. Wednesday night I sliced an egg plant into 7 pieces. I put four in one dish and three in another. Then I layered mushrooms, onion, 2 kinds of cheese, bacon, tomato slices, tomato sauce, left over zucchini and summer squash, rosemary and oregano. I baked it an hour. There was too much for us so I took the dish of three over to Betty, our neighbor. We each had a piece and there was one left over. I asked Gene if he wanted it and he did. My mother also wanted it so I cut it in half. This is the first time either Gene or my mother has ever wanted a second helping of eggplant. Betty called yesterday and she wants to come over and copy my recipe. I have no idea of amounts. A fluke. To make something really good from bits and pieces!

Tonight we are going to a slide show on Holland in the spring at a nearby church. The photographer is a professional and his pictures are perfect. He uses three big screens.

Tomorrow noon we are going to a Chinese restaurant that serves a prawn dish my mother likes and in the evening Gene and I go to bridge.

Sunday is Gene's birthday. I asked what kind of cake he wants and he said German Chocolate. What a surprise! There is coconut in the frosting and Gene doesn't like coconut. Recently Gene ate some fruit cake I had made for my mother. It is a white fruit cake and has coconut. I made coconut cookies like we had in Costa Rica and he ate them too. Gene never fails to surprise me.

I bought a doll and I'm making doll clothes for it. I'll give it to Kate when she comes this summer.

Chez Panisse
Mother's 93rd birthday

FEBRUARY 4, 1987

Dear Colette,

This is birthday time in the Davidson household. Gene became 65 on Saturday, the 31st. So now he is a SENIOR CITIZEN. Frankly I think it is more exciting to be celebrating a 21st birthday. There is more look ahead time and less aches and pains, although Gene seems to have no aches and pains. My arthritis brings home my age to me.

On occasions like this we celebrate without regard to cost. This time at Chez Panisse in Berkeley because Alice Waters' restaurant is reputed to be one of the best in the country. She is credited with being the person who started nouvelle cuisine and transforming rich French cooking to food with delicate sauces. Two weeks ahead I called for reservations but none were available till Tuesday the 3rd of February. So on the actual day we celebrated at home.

I invited the two Connies over for dinner since I was preparing a birthday dinner. Connie G is alone for a month while her parents are away and Connie H is alone all the time now since John died in December. We had Gene's favorite noodle pudding, ham meat balls with a sweet and sour sauce, fresh fruit salad, corn and kidney beans. Of course chocolate cake and ice cream.

Last night we dressed up, I with my new gold sweater and Gene his black suit, black socks and diamond tie tac. Gene usually wears white socks and when he puts on black socks you know he thinks this is a dress up occasion. Although we weren't over dressed, we were probably the most carefully dressed people in the restaurant. This restaurant is in a restored house on Shattuck. There is no parking so we rode around the block a couple times. Downstairs the restaurant holds 48 people. Tables are close together with just enough room to get between. At the back is an open kitchen where you can see the chefs working. The day before the restaurant called to check if we were really coming and told us the menu. It was roast lamb and Gene doesn't like lamb. Only once did he like it and that was at Jennie's in England. Otherwise he won't eat it. There is only one selection each night. When I said my husband didn't like lamb and maybe we should change to another night, the person calling said we should tell the waiter and a substitution would be made. This is an expensive experience. We are glad we went but we wouldn't pay this price again. The appetizer was a pork paté, with the pork coarsely ground, surrounded by pickled red grapes, pickled carrots and parsnips on spinach leaves. It was pretty. The soup was a watery soup with a white fish, shrimp and squid. Parsley and onion floated around. Breads were baguettes, and some kind of leavened, very hard crust, round, sour bread made with yeast from grapes in France. It was a coarse bread and you really needed to chew but the sour taste was excellent. I had the lamb, and between three small pieces were chopped wild mushrooms. I did not think the lamb was cooked enough. It was more red than I like. Finnish potatoes which I think were boiled and then browned. Very good. Vegetable was cubed carrot with small cubes of ham and cheese.

The cheese was slightly melted to hold it all together. The salad course followed the entree. It consisted of tiny leaves of various greens with a light oil dressing. For dessert we were to have a puff pastry prune tart but the waiter brought chocolate pave with creme anglaise. It wasn't cake, nor torte, nor brownie. It was moist like a brownie but light like a cake. The waiter said the pastry did not come up to their standards so this was a substitution. Service was good but there was much waiting between courses. We were there two whole hours. Gene was brought a steak and it was excellent. He didn't ask for it well done, but it was and this he liked. It looked like fillet mignon. We are happy we went.

I think we have eaten in three of the best restaurants in the area, Ernie's, the Blue Fox, and now Chez Panisse. Even though the surroundings are old and the food rich, Gene thinks Ernie's was best. I thought we had the best service at the Blue Fox and the food was excellent. Upstairs at Chat Panisse is a cafe. Here you chose from a menu and there are no reservations. It is a little less expensive.

At Chez Panisse there were three other couples as old as we. All the rest were younger. How do these young people afford such prices?

Across from us was a couple in their 30s. They came in after we did. The woman stated they were vegetarians and did not eat meat, fish or poultry. She asked for a vegetarian menu. Of course, they had only one menu but there was no hassle. The woman was sort of loud and brassy but not really objectionable. The man said nothing. First she ordered a bottle of wine. When she found out the price was $50, she changed her mind. They selected something else. They were brought the pork paté and again the woman went thru the vegetarian bit. Finally the waiter understood that they would have bread and wine only. They were brought an appetizer but I couldn't tell what it was. There was a substitution for the soup because it had fish. For the entree they were given spaghetti with a white sauce. As we left, I could see the spaghetti hanging from her mouth and she was sucking it in. I wonder why vegetarians come to a restaurant that has no choices. Both the man and woman were thin but the man wasn't as thin as the woman. I suspect he ate a regular diet when he wasn't with his wife.

Alice Waters was seating people last night. Although her food was good, I'm not buying her cookbook. I think Alice Waters has a gold mine. The cost of our meal, multiplied by 48, comes to over $3000 each night.

The cafe brings in extra, too. I'm appalled to think of what that couple paid for spaghetti.

Now Gene's birthday is over. Next on the program is my mother's birthday on the 15th when she will be 93. I'm gearing up for that. I'm having a brunch for 18. We'll have to get up EARLY that morning. The Friday and Saturday before I'll be busy all day.

FEBRUARY 16, 1987

Dear Jennie,

My mother's big day is over (her 93rd birthday yesterday), and so is mine (first brunch I've ever prepared). Two things I've learned. A brunch is more work than a dinner and I've slowed down. I had the brunch, not that I thought it easier, but because it wouldn't conflict with other activities of the guests. Church goers could attend early church and late Sunday dinners could still take place.

Since my mother has gone from a size 14 1/2 to a size 6, she needed some new clothes. One day we got three dresses and a jacket. Shopping was difficult because she can't walk far. She can manage to walk from a curb into a store but if what she wants is on a second floor, she can't use the escalator and usually the elevator is not close to the front door. She got a blue-lavender or a lavender-blue two piece, long sleeved suit dress. with a selt belt. She had jewelry that went perfectly with the suit. My mother wanted her picture taken so one day she dressed up and we took several pictures. Her heart failure last April made her think she wants a good picture to send to friends and relatives so they will remember her now and not as she may become as more time goes by. When she was having the pictures taken, she insisted that the walker not be in the picture. She stood next to the wall with me just out of camera range so I could grab her if she started to fall. She reminds me of a baby just learning to stand. Babies stand for a moment and then go down. Without support my mother would do the same.

I wanted this party to honor my mother but I also wanted it to be interesting and enjoyable for the guests so I decided we would celebrate everyone's birthday. I made table favors from plastic net and attached an individualized printed slip with birth date,(minus year), other well known people born on the same day, important events that occurred on the day, and songs of that year. We each read what was on our slip. The most birthdays were in August and February, 3 each. I researched songs from 1894 to 1975. Up until 1970 we all knew the songs but after that they weren't familiar. Everyone was interested to know with whom they shared a birthday. Ginnie shared one with George Shultz, even the year. She doesn't like him one bit. Now we only have to look up George Shultz to know how old Ginnie is. Nobody else revealed the year they were born.

Mary and Bud had just returned from Florida and brought us some shells. I nestled a needle point holder with pink camellias, lavender carnations and purple eupatorium against some driftwood on an aqua enameled tray for my table arrangement. It was quite effective and there were many comments.

As I said, a brunch is more work than a dinner. For a dinner I serve an entree. vegetable, salad, rolls and dessert. Five items. For this brunch we had juice from frozen concentrates of various fruits. On a 22 inch diameter plate, Gene arranged sliced oranges, watermelon, kiwi, melon, papaya and strawberries. Much was left over. There was a baked sausage egg dish, individual quiches of shrimp or crab, corned beef Hawaiian (in a pineapple sauce), cranberry salad, lima bean salad with a mustard dressing and a grape, cucumber, apple salad with a sour cream dressing. The breads were croissants, Babka (inside swirled with chocolate and nuts) and Mediterranean bread (ripe and green olives inside). I also served a Norwegian Kringler which might be considered either bread or dessert. I served it with dessert because it is sweet. Two cheeses, Brie and Havarti. I had a Scandinavian cheese slicer but nobody knew how to use it. For dessert there were pecan tassies, mock strudel and a lemon cake, four layers with lemon filling. I planned to put a meringue on the cake just before it was served but decided a butter icing would be easier because I could make it the day before. See what I mean! This was more work than 5 items.

We asked that no presents be given. My mother didn't need or want anything. I had a hard time thinking of something to give her and finally ended up with candy and cookies and fruit, munchies she can eat as she does her jig saw puzzles.

One guest brought me a magnet that said NORMA IS THE WORLD'S BEST COOK. I was flattered, even though I know it is far from true. This guest also said I must have gotten up at 5 AM to prepare the food. Actually I was days doing it.The tassies, strudel and quiches were made days before. Saturday I did the kringler, and salads.

Another guest and her husband said it was the most perfect party ever. When you have worked hard, it is nice to hear things like this, even though you take them with a grain of salt.

Gene was wonderful. He set up the tables in the living room. He helped in serving and clean up. My mother couldn't manage a buffet so he filled her plate. Gene is exceptionally kind and thoughtful to my mother.

It is now 24 hours since the end of the party and things are back to normal. All the good dishes are back in the cupboards. Table cloths and napkins have been washed and ironed. Silver dishes and trays are wrapped in plastic and back in the cupboards. The gold tray Ingrid and Jan sent us is back on display. That is one nice tray. It doesn't tarnish and

shines beautifully. A lot of effort went into this party but it was worthwhile and satisfying.

MARCH 6, 1987

Dear Ingrid and Jan,

It's that time again. We unpacked our collection of eggs today and
they are now on display. We are running out of room to display them.
This year we not only have them on the fireplace mantel but also on the
raised hearth. We have 4 baskets and one large plate, too, a total of 174
eggs from at least 16 countries, England, China, India, India, Mexico,
Turkey, Germany, Israel, Australia, Switzerland, Italy, Russia, West
Germany, Poland, Hungary. Sri Lanka, Japan and some from the U.S.
Some are hand made, some machine made, some natural. One egg is cut
out with a dental drill and is fragile.

This year we got one in Alaska with 3 bears painted on it. Some are
really old and the colors are fading. They were made in Czechoslovakia
about the time of WW I. We even have a hand worked picture egg and
the stitches are so small I had to get a magnifying glass to look at them.
I don't know how Connie W ever made such small stitches on this
Ukrainian egg. The material is framed but the egg is puffed and padded
to make it three dimensional

I started this collection 30 years ago when I bought a panorama egg
to accompany THE COUNTRY BUNNY AND THE LITTLE GOLD
SHOES. I used to read the story to the kids at school and show the egg.
After I married Gene I bought 6 old eggs from a woman who brought
them with her when she emigrated to the U.S. from Europe. She advertised in the Buffalo paper and one day I took a friend and her children
and drove miles away to buy them. As I displayed them and talked about
them, friends began giving us eggs as gifts.

Remember my telling you about clerking at the AAUW rummage
sale on February 7th? I had the treasure table on which was a Perugina
egg. Immediately I decided to buy it. For several years I've seen these in
the candy department in Macy's. They have fantastic prices. If memory
serves me, they can be $40. This egg was $10. I still thought it too much.
The clerk I relieved said she had been told prices could be reduced. When
the chairman came by, I asked what the egg could be reduced to. She said
it was a collector's item and it could not be reduced. A lady came by and
picked it up but when the clerk said it was $10, she brought it back.
Another lady did the same thing. The chairman came by and asked why I
wanted the egg and I told her of my collection. She said actually the egg
was sold to somebody working in the kitchen. She took it to the kitchen
but on the way was waylaid and left it with some real junk. I was afraid

the other clerk would sell it, but she didn't. Just as I was about to leave the chairman came by and told me the lady in the kitchen had decided she didn't want the egg so I could have it. I said I didn't want it for $10. She suggested $7. I said I would pay $5. She agreed. It is the biggest egg in our whole collection. It is 8 1/2 inches in length and 6 in diameter and 19 in circumference. I don't know the year of this egg but it was designed by S. Mantovani. Needless to say it will never be worth what a Faberge egg is. I called Macy's to see what Perugina eggs are selling for this year but they haven't been unpacked and the clerk didn't have the bill of lading. In a few weeks I'll go have a look.

Did you ever taste Perugina candy? I never did. I wonder if it is worth the price. Sunday's paper advertised Perugina chocolates at $10 for 8 3/4 oz, about $20 a pound.

Return of baby
Garage sale, Wong disappearance

MARCH 20, 1987

Dear Kathryn,

It is 8:00 PM and Gene and I have just given up our baby! Kate, who was with us last year, and who was with us again yesterday and today. This time she did not get sick. We fell in love with her all over again. She is so sweet and good. She is tiny. She will be two on April 12th but she weighs only 21 1/2 lbs and that is exactly what she weighed last June. She still doesn't talk. She understands everything but gets everything by motioning. Gene got a special kick out of having her look at him and wiggle her finger to indicate she wanted him to come someplace with her. When I would be working in the kitchen, she would put her arms around my legs and hug. She likes to be held and given a bottle before going to bed but she can drink from a glass and does.

Gene loved to hold and feed her. Gene is an old smoothie when it comes to Kate. We marvel that Kate will stay with strangers and not cry. She eats very little but, with us, she sat in her high chair and fed herself.Sometimes we offered food if we didn't think she had enough. She slept 11 1/2 hours last night. We were glad her parents took this two day vacation so we could have her. Tonight the parents came to dinner and once they were in the house things were different. She refused to sit in the high chair and went from lap to lap. She refused to eat. She was a different child from the one we had. She wasn't bad or naughty, but she wasn't the easy child we knew. Gene and I looked on in amazement.

Connie H, the grandmother, borrowed toys, bed, high chair and stroller. Gene wheeled her to the grocery store and was he proud. She had an adorable Sesame Street house and store which she could take apart and play with. She had a plastic "erector set" that you could make cars and trucks with. Gene made trucks. I went to the library and borrowed books but they brought books and they had some wonderful ones. One called, ONE GREEN FROG had Gene, my mother and me buffaloed. It was a clever counting book and the frog had an eye that was a hole and every page had another hole in the same place. It was a cardboard book.

The last stanza of the book was:

A CROWD OF SPOTTED LADY BUGS SCURRY ALL ABOUT.
CAN YOU FIND THE TWO THAT ARE ODD-MAN OUT.
LOOK CAREFULLY

I saw that one lady bug was green and all the other 33 were either red or cerise. So I asked Gene to look. There was one with a tiny hole for an eye. Gene studied it and said it must be the one with the hole in the eye. Today my mother was reading the book to Kate and she said she couldn't find the second one. So a book for a one year old buffaloed us oldsters! However, it is a wonderful book, first published in Italy, and illustrated by an Italian. Grosset and Dunlap published it in the U.S. and made the text in English.

My mother was wonderful with Kate. She wasn't jealous at all. My mother was constantly trying to make Kate talk. She even lifted her to her lap. I was horrified. Last week my mother forgot to use her walker and she took five steps, lost her balance, made a complete twirl and ended face down in a living room chair. I was lying on the sofa. I saw the whole thing but with my arthritis, I couldn't get up quickly enough to catch her. My immediate thought was a broken hip but we were lucky!!!

My mother did her jig saw puzzles only when Kate slept. Otherwise she was watching her or talking to her. When my mother went to the bathroom, Kate would run to me and get my attention by pointing her little finger at my mother and laugh. She thought that walker was so funny!

The bird of paradise is front of our living room window have grown taller than the window sill so Kate couldn't see out. My mother saw Linda and Bob drive up and she was going to lift Kate up and stand her on the sill. Fortunately I was able to do this before my mother could. Exertion is something my mother can't take. Her heart isn't up to it but her spirit is. She still thinks she can do more than she can. At times my mother attempts to carry something in one hand and use the walker with the other. A walker operated by one hand is just as dangerous as a car, maybe more so.

APRIL 13, 1987

Dear Ivy and Hubert,

We had a most interesting weekend participating in a garage sale with our neighbor, Betty, her mother, sister and a friend. It was held in Betty's garage which is immaculate, not like ours.

Although Betty's living room was like a picture out of HOUSE BEAUTIFUL, she wanted a change after thirteen years so she has been redecorating for the past six months. She sold many thing but still had two overstuffed living room chairs so she decided to have a garage sale and asked if we wanted to join her. At first we didn't think we had much, but we found things we hadn't used since we moved to California and decided we could sell these thing. Betty put an ad in the newspaper and I made signs which I put up Friday afternoon. The sale was from 9–4 but on Saturday people were pounding on the door before Betty had breakfast. Early birds are usually people who want to snatch up the best and then resell it at the flee market that day. People even called to ask if they could see things the night before. Betty had a 1982 Datsun with less then 40,000 miles, which looks like new, was for sale and was parked in the driveway.

The chairs sold as soon as we opened. A young girl and her mother came and the car appealed to the girl. She wanted it but had no money. The mother said her father would not help her. The girl said her grandmother would lend her the money. She wanted to drive the car and Betty let her take it. She was gone for several hours and I wondered. When she brought it back, she said her father refused to even look at the car. The mother said she should consult her husband and the girl responded, "What's he got to do with it? It will be my car." How long can this marriage last? The girl had only been married 2 months. However she did take it to show her husband and he took it to his father who said the girl was impulsive and he thought she should shop around. Betty had a deposit on the car and she had a waiting list of people who were interested. Today the girl was going to her credit union to see if she could borrow the money,

NEXT DAY

The girl's father came today and wanted to take the car to his mechanic and Betty let him. When he brought it back, he said something had happened to the car on his return from the mechanic and it was making a terrible noise. He drove it two houses away and turned around and Betty said the noise was terrible. The car hadn't acted like that before he took it. She thought he had done something to the car and would claim it wasn't worth what she was asking. I sent Gene over and Gene checked the front left wheel. He said the nuts were loose. We were having company for dinner and Bud went over and confirmed what Gene said but neither could get the wheel cover off. Betty called her friend and her husband came over and he couldn't get the cover off but eventually he discovered there was a special tool in the trunk that would remove the cover. They found that all the bolts were off except one which was just barely on. The wheel could have come off at any moment.

This man put on the bolts and tightened them and there was no noise. Betty called the girl's father and said she didn't think much of his mechanic and the man said the mechanic had not removed the cover. Liar! Betty said she either had the money tomorrow morning or else she was contacting another buyer. She was through with fooling around with them. I don't blame her.

We had all kinds of people at the garage sale. Lots of real fat women. I mean big enough to be the fat lady in the circus.

Two people stood out. One was a man who came on Sunday. Sharply but casually dressed. Stylish hair cut and beard, both white. He walked up the drive and said that since he had given up the booze, he was visiting garage sales. Nobody said anything. He barely glanced around. There must be a story connected to that man.

Another couple, nicely dressed and clean, came. He appeared to be a senior citizen but she was younger. She wanted a bottle of perfume I had for sale for $3.50. The man wanted her to look at a comforter. She wasn't interested but the man bought it and it cost more than $3.50. Apparently the woman was afraid to ask the man for the perfume. They weren't poor, judging by their car and clothes. I felt sorry for the woman.

Tonight I talked to Betty and she said she, her mother, sister and friend had discussed the man who had given up the booze. They said that before he got out of his car, he reached down, got a bottle and took a swig. Why did he mention this?

APRIL 20, 1987

Dear Bonna and Wayne,

Friday I went to ikebana with Virginia. Both Gene and Don are retired and our lives are different with retired husbands. The program was over early and I suggested we make a couple stops on our way home. Virginia was delighted. We felt like two kids who skipped school.

In one store I saw an egg I didn't have and in another I saw an egg that I thought was a real chocolate egg but it wasn't. It had that white sugar around the edge and a flower on top. Very different from anything I had. I didn't buy either because I thought they were overpriced. Today I took my mother for a ride and I got both eggs at half price! Some stores already had their Easter things put away. In two other stores I found four more eggs so we now have 188. Phyllis from Tennessee sent me one that had been given to her. My friend, Pat, found a large ceramic egg made in Hawaii and she filled it with candy and an amethyst egg so this season we added a total of nine eggs to our collection. Gene is going to have to make an egg stand to display these eggs.

MAY 29, 1987

Dear Ruth and Bill,

Our neighbors, Hing and Sue, live across the street from us. They have two children, neither of whom lives at home. Diane graduated from UC Berkeley and is working on the peninsula. Darren is at UC Berkeley. Two weeks ago both Sue and Hing had vacations.

During that time Diane called us and asked us to check on her parents. She had been trying to call them for two hours and the line was busy all the time. Diane said her mother never talked on the phone that long. I looked out the window. The car was gone and the newspaper was still on the front porch. I assumed they were away. Gene went over and rang the doorbell. He pounded on the door. No answer. He tried to go behind the fence but the gate was locked. Diane called back later in the morning and we reported all this. She called again in the afternoon. In the meantime I had gone to their next door neighbor and peaked over the fence. All seemed to be o.k. Diane asked if we would leave a note for her parents to call her immediately they returned.

Shortly after this Darren called and he reported that he hadn't been able to get his parents all day. We told him about Diane's calls. He also asked us to tell his parents to call him immediately they returned. That evening Diane called again. She gave us a phone number where she could be reached till 9 PM. After that she was coming over to investigate.

About 8:30 PM Sue and Hing drove up. Gene rushed out and told them the story. They said their phone stopped working the previous evening. They decided at 11 PM to go to Yosemite and they left at 2:30 AM the next morning without telling their children their plans. They came in our house and Sue phoned both children.

Next day the phone company came early in the morning. They checked outside and all was o.k. To come inside the house would cost $65 so the telephone man asked Hing to check his phones. Two gave off a busy signal but when he picked up the answering machine receiver the busy signal stopped. Something had happened to the answering machine and this caused all the phones to have a busy signal.

The next day Sue brought over a box of Chinese cookies which are wonderful, so tender they crumble as you touch then. I've never eaten such luscious cookies.

This morning our phone rang and a woman said she was Miss Wright of the.......... law office and she wanted to get in touch with Hing Wong who lives at 2160. She stated that we live at 2155 and asked that we give Hing a message. His telephone was not listed. She said it was very important. She gave me her phone number and told me her hours of work. I was astounded and asked how she got our name and phone number and she said she cross checked. I don't know how you can do this. I thought about this. What to do? I decided to call Hing at work. I didn't know his extension so I called the company and was transferred to Hing. He took down all the information and said he wanted us to have his work number and gave it to me. Hing's business is not ours but I have to admit to a bit of curiosity about all this.

We really have been involved with these neighbors.

Accident in France

Party in England, What's new in honeymoons

MAY 24, 1987

Dear Phyllis and Max,

Recently I've had two interesting letters, one from England and one from France. Ordinarily I don't repeat what somebody else wrote but each had two accounts that I think worthy of telling.

Colette reported (her own words) I HAD A LITTLE PROBLEM WITH MY CAR. A VERY BIG DUTCH LORRY HURTED ME ON THE BACK LEFT WING. THE DRIVER SPOKE DUTCH AND I FRENCH. WHAT A PROBLEM! THEN WE DISCOVERED WE CAN SPEAK ENGLISH. NOW I LEAVE MY CAR FOR TWO DAYS. I MUST ASK MY FRIENDS TO CIRCULATE DRIVING THOSE TWO DAYS.

When I was studying French, Colette was studying English. As you can see she kept up her English but I didn't my French. I wish I could express myself as well in French as she does in English.

Jennie, in England, reported that two granddaughters were celebrating their 21st birthdays a few days apart. Apparently the English make much of 21st birthdays and Suzanne's parents invited lots of people to a party, all age groups, grandparents and contemporaries, parents and contemporaries, and Suzanne's contemporaries. Because it was Easter weekend only sixty eight could accept. They had a disco in the dining room. Tarzan appeared and delivered a kiss-o-gram and slung Suzanne on his shoulder and cavorted around. Forty people stayed overnight. A good time was had by all.

However the good time did not last. Jennie got home at 2 AM and from then on she was running to the loo. Suzanne called the next day to report she, her sister and mother were feeling poorly. Her father was in bed and feeling terrible. Her grandfather was in bed and very ill. Shortly after the call he had to be hospitalized. The terrible sickness caused his heart to "pack in". I don't know what this means but it is what Jennie reported. Suzanne's father is a veterinarian and his two partners were also very ill. One lost 18 pounds in 3 days. The brother's girlfriend fainted at the railroad station, hit her head and had to go to the hospital and have stitches. Two guests were rushed to the hospital with suspected peritonitis and before food poisoning was suspected one had his appendix yanked out. Over more than forty people were affected, some with just nausea, some diarrhea and some with both. As the calls came in, Suzanne's mother decided this was a case for the Ministry of Health. They got right to work and samples of food were taken. Suzanne's mother had cooked a turkey. She had a butcher cook, ham, lamb. beef and chicken. While the inspectors were working on this case, there were calls from a wedding party where the guests became terribly ill. The next day there was a christening party and these guests became ill. All had eaten food prepared by the same butcher. The only meat found to be o.k. was the turkey Barbara prepared. They were sorry everyone was so ill but glad it wasn't the turkey. Jennie said she dragged for a week. The other birthday girl was too ill even to open her cards and presents on her birthday. Victoria's father had been ill with a heart problem for more than 6 months so they did not attend the party. They delivered Victoria to the party but declined food and were on their way in a few minutes.

Victoria's own party was to be at her college and her college friends were invited. Victoria gave invitations orally so she didn't know addresses and phone numbers and couldn't cancel the party. Victoria has an apartment.Victoria's mother took Victoria and Jennie to the college. Jennie and Victoria just looked on as Victoria's mother prepared the food and served it. There were thirty four at this party and nobody got sick. There was a family dinner scheduled on Victoria's birthday but since nobody in Suzanne's family was well enough to attend and Victoria and Jennie were ill, it was canceled.

I don't think all these people will ever forget Suzanne's 21st birthday.

JULY 7, 1987

Dear Dorothy and Lars,

Yesterday's business section of the N.Y. Times had an article entitled WHAT'S NEW IN HONEYMOONS. In case you didn't know, here's the latest.

FOR MANY COUPLES THE HONEYMOON IS NO LONGER THE FIRST TIME THEY ARE AWAY TOGETHER SO THEY WANT MORE VARIED AND INTERESTING TRIPS. THEY ARE TAKING ART TOURS OF EUROPE, ARCHEOLOGY TOURS IN MEXICO AND CENTRAL AMERICA, SCUBA TOURS IN THE CARIBBEAN, SAFARIS IN AFRICA. BICYCLE TOURS IN FRANCE AND FOR $2000 AND $3000 THEY ARE RENTING YACHTS IN THE SOUTH SEAS AND THE CARIBBEAN. Honeymoon couples are older, more sophisticated and earning higher incomes, both having jobs. Of course there are some honeymooners who want seclusion and they are renting cottages on uninhabited islands, Petit St. Vincent in the West Indies and Peter Island in the British Virgin Islands. These rent for $3,600 a week.

Niagara Falls was the honeymoon capital in the 1940s and 1950s but Niagara Falls lost out in the 1960's. Actually the largest areas devoted to newlyweds is the Poconos in Pennsylvania where a suite rents for $260 a night and are booked solid several months in advance. Here they sell romantic ambiance—heart shaped beds and tubs, mirrored walls and four foot deep in room swimming pools and whirlpool baths shaped like a champagne glass. The champagne glass is made of Plexiglas and is 7 feet tall. You climb a ladder to get in.

Almost makes you went to get married a second time, doesn't it?

JULY 18, 1987

Recently I. had my book review luncheon. Fourteen were invited but only twelve could attend. I reviewed A GREEN JOURNEY by Jan Hassler. Amazingly some of these college educated women never read a book! Well, I'm no athlete. To each his own. However, even the non readers enjoyed the review. We meet at 11 and I review till 12. We break for lunch and I finish up around two. I thought this was an excellent book. It is a novel. The story reveals a theme which I thought was portrayed well. From a remark one person made I knew she missed the point completely.

AUGUST 20, 1987

Dear Phyllis and Jay,

Gene is just besotted with a slender female with huge brown eyes and a beguiling manner. She is 28 months old. I'm not jealous but I am astounded at Gene's behavior. Yesterday we took Kate shopping with us. Gene put Kate in her car seat in the back of our car. He picks her up as though she would break into pieces. We went to four grocery stores. At one Kate pointed her tiny finger at the candy at the check out and nodded her head yes. I shook my head no. We had enough at home. Some kids would have had a tantrum but Kate didn't. At the last store Gene hopped out of the car and got Kate out and put her in the cart seat. We proceeded into the store and did our shopping and when we came out, Gene couldn't find his car keys. They were still in the ignition and the motor was running. Do you see what I mean by being besotted? Kate is cute. She doesn't speak much but she gets her way by indicating what she wants.

When Kate visits with her parents, Gene and I get no attention. She is the same with her grandmother. We wanted to take a picture of Kate and her grandmother but Kate wouldn't leave her parents. I picked up her wooden jigsaw puzzle and dumped it at her grandmother's feet. She immediately went over and picked up the pieces and put the puzzle together. I quickly took the picture.

With her parents absent, she follows us around and often she throws her arms around my legs and hugs me. We took Kate to the library. She seated herself at a little table and looked at books left on the table while I selected books to read to her.

After this Kate and I took the elevator to the mezzanine and when we looked down, she saw Gene and pointed and called to him but her voice is like a whisper so he didn't hear her. As we exited from the elevator, she saw Gene about 20 feet away. She ran from me to him, zigzagging among the library users and then she hugged one of Gene's legs. He was thrilled but too shy to pick her up in this public place and hug her so he just patted her head.

Kate's attention span is excellent and she will listen while a whole book is being read to her and if she likes it, she will turn it back to the beginning and have it read again and again and again. After the third time, I use another book.

Arriving at the library, Gene reminded me to lock the car doors on my side. When we came back to the car, the doors on Gene's side were unlocked. Again he forgot because he was so concerned and taken up with Kate. I never had this effect on Gene.

We had Kate Monday, Tuesday and Wednesday. We shall have her Friday and Saturday too. Today she will come with her parents for dinner. While I was at the kitchen sink preparing dinner, I was surprised when Gene suddenly dropped to the floor and hugged my legs. So I got a Kate hug even though Kate wasn't here. My mother missed Kate today because Kate often appears in my mother's sitting room. She knows my mother has candy and will give her a piece.

I dropped a bag of Lorna Doone's on the kitchen floor. Those cookies crumble easily and there were crumbs all over the kitchen floor. Kate took in the situation and when I said I would have to get the vacuum cleaner, she nodded her little head and seemed to be seriously thinking how to clean up the mess.

Kate's grandmother, Connie, is moving from her home to a manor in Rossmoor. While realtors are showing her house, we have all her valuables stored in our front bedroom. It is safer this way. We recently had one real estate agent who was a thief. After showing a house, he would go back alone and take what he wanted.

AUGUST 24, 1987

We can't think of anything but Kate. Today she returned to West Virginia. Yesterday Connie took us out to brunch. Kate would have little to do with us till we said good-bye and then we got a kiss and hug.

My friend Pat had to take her mother to John Muir Hospital. I guess she had a small stroke. She wasn't admitted but was sent to a convalescent hospital where she stayed a week. During that time her mother's engagement ring disappeared. It consisted of one big diamond with eight smaller ones surrounding it. Since the mother can't talk, she doesn't know who took it. The hospital said Pat should report this to her insurance company. Pat did this but she also reported it to the police. The hospital said they couldn't keep track of who cared for whom. The police investigated but nothing came from it. In telling this story to others, I learned of one woman who was in the same hospital. When she was bedridden, she would see patients in the hall wearing her clothes. When she was ready to be discharged, she went into other rooms and collected her clothes from other patients closets. This happens in some convalescent hospitals.

Our house seems so empty without Kate. Aside for a minute when her parents dropped her off, she never cried. She has a sunny disposition and smiles easily. She doesn't fuss about naps but she is cross if awakened before her sleep is finished. She is a joy to care for and we told her parents we would take her anytime.

SEPTEMBER 3, 1987

Dear Marion and Bob,

Monday night we were just getting ready to go to bed when the phone rang and somebody said, "Hello, Norma. this is Marge Miller." For a minute I couldn't think of whom this might be. Then it came to me that it was Marguerite She was one of the triplets I went to college with. After marriage, she became Marge. She was at Crater Lake and could stop to see us on her way to San Jose where her son and family live. I said I would have dinner for Ed and her.

Marguerite and Ed left Fort Myers June 1st and plan to be back on October 1st. With their air stream trailer, they headed for Alaska, making stops in the lower 48 to visit their children. Each summer they flee Florida because of the heat.

They had lunch with Ed's cousin who just moved to Rossmoor from Hawaii but who expects to move to San Diego because it is too cold here in the winter. I haven't worn a coat since we moved here, but we aren't as warm as Hawaii, I know.

After dinner we showed our Alaskan slides of last year and they relived their trip because they saw some of the same things we did. Only they had much longer to see Alaska. We also showed a few of our African slides. The contrast of the few animals in Alaska with the many seen in Africa was tremendous. I thought they would see more than we did but they saw three bears at a distance and a wolf. We saw three bears at a distance and a moose. I can see seventeen deer at Rossmoor in the early evening or two or three any time in the day. So for numbers you can see more wild animals at Rossmoor than in Alaska. Both of us were disappointed not to see more animals, but we both enjoyed Alaska and its scenery. The evening went all too fast.

On my birthday we had Kate so we did not celebrate. Today we went into San Francisco for lunch at the California Culinary Academy, a famous cooking school. We got off BART at Civic Center and walked several blocks, seeing many bums sleeping on the lawns or lounging around on steps. It spoils the area.

We had a short walk for lunch. On the mezzanine a la carte lunch is served but we chose the lunch in the dining room. The left wall is window and you see students working on food. The main kitchen is behind a glass wall at the back. Our waiter was in his second semester and this was his first week in the dining room. He apologized because he didn't remove unnecessary silverware and he forgot to remove the salt and pepper before dessert. For $13.75 you get appetizer, entree and dessert. The food is beautifully presented and it tasted good too. Gene had sole wrapped in lettuce with maybe onions and mushrooms between and covered with a sauce. For dessert I had three small cream puffs, floating in a chocolate sauce. with kiwi fruit and sliced strawberries. I couldn't pronounce the name of my dessert and the waiter said he also couldn't. On Friday noon, Thursday and Friday nights, they have buffets. They were working on the buffet items today. A round plate as big as a card table had part of a turkey with a mold inside and all kinds of decorations. In front of the turkey were sliced meats. The students worked slowly to make the food picture perfect. We noticed the students were mostly men and when I asked, I was told two thirds of the students were men. Buffet dinners cost $23.50. I want to go to one of them one day.

We walked back to BART via Turk Street. Wow ! I held tightly to Gene. ODD characters. Girly shows. Male dancer show, with men entirely nude. I've forgotten how it was billed and asked Gene but he couldn't remember either. However, he said I wasn't going back to find out!

Toby hospitalized
Roger and black dog

OCTOBER 31, 1987

Dear Marguerite and Ed,

What a week! We have friends who live in Orinda and have seven cars. I've mentioned them before in my letters. They do beautiful professional slide shows about their trips and give the shows free to organizations and churches. Toby golfs a lot. Leta has taken ikebana lessons with me. Toby is a people person and Leta is quiet and reserved. Just before we went on the cruise, they went to Germany and Bavaria. We had a card from them. This trip was off and on because Leta had broken her pelvis in June. They canceled and then at the last minute made new reservations and bought new plane tickets.

I was too busy to call them the first week we were home. The next week I called off and on and got no answer. Monday I called again. No answer. Tuesday we read in the SIRS bulletin that Toby was out of the hospital after surgery and would soon be back on the golf course. I called almost every hour that day and never received an answer. Wednesday Leta called me. Toby had been in the hospital three weeks. She wanted to talk to Gene and me and would come on Thursday. Thursday she called and said Toby was so bad that day that she would have to come on Friday. Gene bowls on Friday but Leta had lunch with my mother and me.

Suddenly on October 7th Toby became very ill and at 3:30 AM Leta took him to John Muir Hospital. They operated at 8 AM. He had an obstruction in his small intestine. They operated again when Leta called in a specialist. The specialist opened and closed and said things were a mess. Toby is being fed intravenously and may never again have food. Leta says he daily becomes weaker.

Before this happened, they had purchased a condo near us. They planned to take two years to clear out their house, sell it, and buy two side by side condos which they would make into one big condo. Meanwhile they would live in the condo near us. Leta has not gone back to the Orinda house to live. It is a lovely house with a great view but isolated. She asked Gene and me to go back with her and help her clear out the house. She also asked us to drive her to S.F. if Toby is transferred there. They have no children so we may be very busy helping them.

Connie Huffman is redoing her manor at Rossmoor, new white carpeting, matching walls. Connie asked Gene to hang pictures, and to reorganize her closet. Gene is a busy person with these women asking for his help.

I was so upset yesterday I forgot to bring in the mail. Sometime after midnight I remembered. I was restless and Gene woke and I told him that today's mail was still in the mail box. Gene went out in his pajamas and brought it in.

For a few days Toby was in intensive care. Next to him was a young girl whose boyfriend had thrown her out of the window. She had broken bones and internal injuries. Leta wasn't sure she would live. How's that for a boyfriend ?

Saturday I took part in a survey about retirement homes. People of our age and income were being surveyed to find out what we wanted in a retirement home. I answered the questions on a computer and after an hour was given $30. I never earned $30 easier. I used the money to buy Gene a Christmas present.

Leta called Friday and said Toby was being transferred to the UCSF hospital. They thought they might do more for him than John Muir Hospital. Since then she has heard things. The doctors may be great but patients see interns. Waits of six hours in the emergency room occur. A neighbor was there in a four bed room and when a patient was returned after surgery, she was put in the wrong bed. Another had something taped to her arm which said she was allergic to certain medicines.When the wrong medicine was about to be given, the neighbor raised a fuss and the medicine wasn't used. Her husband says that hospital is a zoo. The neighbor says John Muir is a country club compared with UCSF. UCSF is immense. In John Muir a nurse cares for only three patients in definitive care. The patient load at UCSF is much larger. Yesterday the surgeon said Toby was not being transferred to UCSF, but two other doctors said he was. All three doctors say Toby's illness will be long and when asked how long they said maybe a year or more. Imagine the bills for this.

NOVEMBER 11, 1987

Dear Phyllis,

About midnight on Sunday night I began to have trouble. I went to the bathroom and in less than 5 minutes, I went again. By morning I knew I had a urinary infection. I had one twenty three years ago and this was exactly like that. Gene timed my getting up and when twenty minutes came between visits, he thought things had quieted down.

At 6 AM Leta called and asked if we could be at the hospital by 8 to talk to Toby's doctors. Leta wanted to transfer Toby to UC SF. She felt he was dying. Only one doctor showed up by 9:30. Leta wanted Gene and me to ask questions and help make a decision. We decided that for the present Toby would stay at John Muir. It is doubtful he would get better care at UCSF.

I had a dental appointment at 10 AM but the new receptionist had scheduled two of us for this time. I gladly bowed out and made another appointment.

I knew I had to see a doctor on Monday. I called and got an appointment with our internist at 5:15. By noon I was in such pain, I called again and asked if there were any cancellations, would they please call me and I would be there in ten minutes. The nurse put me on hold and then said they would work me in at 2:15 while another patient was having an EKG.

The doctor said on the average women have urinary infections 2.5 times a year and if I only had two in 23 years, my average was way above par. The medicine worked quickly and by bedtime I was much more comfortable. In the evening Gene conked out on the sofa. I had wanted to sleep in another room but he insisted I stay in our bed. We both slept soundly Monday night but I did get up 5 or 8 times. At the moment I still have some infection but it is bearable and getting better hour by hour.

I talked to our doctor about Toby. He is the internist on the case. There is a gastroenterologist and a surgeon too. Leta wants a specialist from S.F. but he won't come. Toby will have to be fed intravenously for the rest of his life but the doctor said this could be done at night when he sleeps and he can live a more or less normal life. The doctors all say recovery will be long. I asked our doctor how long and all he could say was that this condition took a year to build to a climax and it was going to take a long time to unclog what took a year to clog. I thought my mother was hooked up when she had congestive heart failure, but Toby has many, many more tubes and drains.

My mother wants and needs a new hearing aid. Today was a free day so we went shopping for one. The place was on a second floor and we almost went back home because my mother cannot go up stairs and there was no elevator. However I drove around back and the second floor was even with a parking lot. The man is coming to our house on Thursday to make molds for both ears. I hope her hearing improves greatly.

NOVEMBER 21, 1987

Dear Shizuko and Kaoru,

Yesterday I rode to the ikebanaI meeting in San Francisco with Shig and Jennie. Gene took me to Shig's and Harry took us to Jennie's. It poured but nobody complained because if we don't get rain in the winter, we will have a drought next summer. Just one rain greens the hills and California begins to look pretty. Traffic was slow, it took a long time and we were late.

My mother is getting two new hearing aids. She has had only one in her glasses but now she will have the kind that fits in her ear. When she had the hearing test, I was amazed at what she doesn't hear. She has a 96% loss in one ear and 85% in the other. I've been annoyed with my mother because she mispronounces words she used to say correctly. Some sounds she doesn't hear at all or hears differently. No wonder she often confuses what I say. Usually Gene and I can talk and my mother doesn't know what we say. Now with two aids we'll have to be careful. However, even with two aids, her hearing will not be normal.

I've been making Christmas ornaments, about sixty. Some are Rudolph, whose mouth opens when squeezed and out comes a Hershey kiss. One is a three-dimensional Santa and the other two-sided. I almost have my Christmas shopping done. I have everything wrapped and our front bedroom looks like Santa's workshop.

My mother's bank statement came today and of course it doesn't balance. I worked on it without success. Gene is now working on it. We may just accept the bank's record and forget it.

Gene's sister, ten years older than Gene, teaches tap dancing to Sr. Citizens and has been doing this for several years. They have been on TV but on Dec. 13th they will dance at the Kennedy Center in Washington. Isn't that great?

Christmas catalogs have been coming in and Gene has been ordering cakes and petit fours.

We visit Toby at the hospital every other day. He has been there six weeks and has not had a bite of food or a sip of liquid all that time. He is being fed intravenously and will be for the rest of his life, we are told. Recently they removed the tube from his nose and throat and he can talk much better. They talk of sending him home but he will need constant care. I doubt Leta is up to it. Her broken pelvic bone is still very painful but she has ignored the pain and devoted herself to Toby.

Tomorrow I go to Rossmoor to sell UNICEF cards. Gene will drop me off and then go to Orinda, pack things in our car, pick me up and together we will unload them in the Evans condo. Their condo is only 1.5 miles from our house and we pass it every time we go out. Today I told Toby his hospital bill should be reduced because he had not had a meal in all these days. Toby thought it was a joke and laughed. What goes in thru tubes is probably far more expensive than food. Toby is getting weary of the hospital. I wonder if the doctor's talk of going home is just to bolster Toby's spirits.

ANOTHER DAY

Today another person and I sold $288 worth of UNICEF Xmas cards at a bank which provides space for us. This bank has a free lending library of current best sellers. It took up a whole corner of the room and the book cases were at least 5 feet high. The depositors of the bank can borrow these books free. Current newspapers of New York and Los Angeles are on a table and there are lots of comfortable chairs and free coffee. This is a social area, well used by those living in Rossmoor.

THANKSGIVING DAY 1987

I've been putting final touches on our dinner and Gene has been a big help. Gene held the turkey while I stuffed it. He enlarged the table, put on the table cloth, got out the good dishes and then set the table. He still didn't miss any of the football games.

As I was typing this in our front bedroom, I heard a dog barking ferociously so I looked out the window and saw our lawyer neighbor backed up against a car with his garbage canister in front of him. A big black dog was in Roger's driveway and would not let Roger back in his garage. The dog looked MEAN. I went to our door and suggested that Roger back up and come in our house and then maybe the dog would go away. As Roger started to do this, the dog came at him, so Roger went back to the car. At least he was protected front and back but not on the sides. Kathy, his wife, came out on the front porch. Roger with his back to the bushes along the drive inched his way to the garage with the canister always in front of him. He made it.We never before saw that dog.

Wilma, Russ and Leta will be our guests today. Toby is to be given broth for his Thanksgiving dinner, the first food he has had since Oct 7th. Leta thought her presence might dampen our spirits but I insisted she come and urged Toby to do the same. He did and she gave in.

Next week Toby may be sent home for awhile, with a battery of round the clock nurses. They now think he has Crohn's disease for which there is no cure. It is irreversible and the damage was extensive. Other problems will soon develop. Toby doesn't know this. I admire Toby because he knows there is no light at the end of the tunnel, yet he doesn't let us know this.

JANUARY 3, 1988

Dear Millie and Jim,

Christmas is a busy time for all of us but this year it seemed especially busy for me. I made eleven different kinds of cookies, plus other odd things. We packed tins and gave them away. Our Christmas tree was the freshest we have ever had and it still is up but we will take it down today or tomorrow.

Christmas day Toby and Leta were with us, Toby being discharged from the hospital Dec. 12th. He is on a very restricted diet but he is eating and originally he was told he would be fed intravenously for the rest of his life. Three doctors will assess his case in February.

Toby told me that the day he was discharged an administrative nurse he seldom saw came in his room and told him she would miss him more than most patients because each day she poked her head in his room to see his unusual flower arrangements. I took an ikebana arrangement every other day. One was just 5 aspidistra leaves and this caused much comment. No credit to me. All you have to do is follow the rules and if you follow the rules, you can't go wrong. After all these weeks of looking at these arrangements, Toby said he marveled at the simplicity of the arrangements. THAT IS THE ESSENCE OF IKEBANA.

Toby learned the most important principle of ikebana by observing. Leta is a flower arranger but she does mostly western or American style. She was too busy to make arrangements while Toby was in the hospital. The wife of one of Toby's friends told Toby she couldn't compete with the arrangements he had so she took magazines instead. I'm not really an expert ikebana arranger but comments like this make me feel good.

Christmas day I let the fresh peas boil dry and burn. I was too busy to pay attention. I was chagrined. Even a moron can do this. I didn't tell anyone. I just opened the window to let out the smell and put the peas in the disposal. Nobody knew I intended to serve peas. No use advertising my mistakes.

Tuesday after Christmas we invited Toby and Leta again for dinner because I was having turkey puff and every ingredient was something Toby could eat. I built the rest of the meal around his dietary requirements. It wasn't the prettiest or best meal I've ever served but for once Toby felt he was eating a normal meal.

Thursday I told Gene we were going out for lunch. I wanted to eat somebody else's food. I chose a Chinese gourmet restaurant. Usually my mother refuses Chinese food but we got her a shrimp dish with snow peas. There were lots of big shrimp and she loves shrimp so the meal was a success.

My friend Pat's mother died Dec 26th. She was ninety eight and had round the clock nursing care in her home for eight years. When we first knew her she was alert, drove a car, lived alone and was taking a course in Spanish. Then came Parkinson's and what a change. Near the end she kept confusing Pat and the nurse. Thursdays were the nurse's day off and Pat had complete responsibility. Other days Pat usually took her mother and the nurse out, often for lunch. Saturdays and Sundays she tried to keep for her husband. The superior care Pet gave her mother is probably why her mother lived to ninety eight.

Toby and classic thunderbird
Heard, Hurd, Herod, Baking for a dog

JANUARY 28, 1988

Dear Millie and Jim,.

Toby and Leta are clearing out their Orinda home while living in the condo near us. Toby has decided he must get rid of some of their seven cars. The first to go is the classic Thunderbird. It originally was Leta's car. They belong to the Thunderbird Club and through the club they learned of a man who wants an antique car to restore. Toby contacted this man and told him it needs a lot of work but the man wanted to see and drive it. So Toby drove it over for the man to see. The man liked it and offered $10,000. Toby came back and told Leta and they decided to ask $11,000 but take $10,000. Toby went back with the counter offer and the man accepted it readily. Toby said they would like cash. The man said cash was no problem and $11,000 it would be. A few minutes later, the man said he had decided to give Toby $12,000. Toby said, "We just agreed on $11,000 cash." In the next breath, the man said he didn't want people to hear of this deal and think he was cheating Toby so he would stick with the $12,000. On Saturday the 16th the purchase took place. Leta's parting remark to Toby when he left to deliver the car was that she hoped the check wouldn't bounce.

When Toby returned., Toby told Leta she didn't have to worry about the check bouncing. He then emptied his pockets of $12,000 in actual money. What Toby and Leta meant by cash was a check, not payment spread out over a period of years. When Toby was so surprised at the cash, the man said you said cash and cash is what I'm giving you.

Monday was a holiday so for a weekend they had $12,000 in their condo. They went to the bank first thing Tuesday and got rid of that money. I laughed as Leta told me this and I laughed with Gene when I told him this tale.

FEBRUARY 11, 1988

Dear Helen and Herb,

When Connie H put new carpeting in her manor, she asked if we wanted any of the old which looked like new. It was a soft blue green. I took a piece and asked Gene if he would install it in two of our bathrooms. It sat in our garage for a month or more. Gene did nothing. There were other things I wanted done so I made a list, gave it to Gene and said I wanted all this done in one week. Gene did everything in one day, except for the carpeting. First he laid the carpeting in our bathroom and it was a success. We decided the green of the main bathroom didn't go with the blue green carpeting so Gene painted that and he did a super job. I looked for new shower curtain and matching window curtain. I could find nothing the right size. Finally I bought two shower curtains and cut up one curtain to make the window curtain The bathroom now has a soft look to it.

Awhile back Connie H asked me if she could use our telephone number when she advertised a bed for sale. Saturday morning we got a call about the bed we had for sale. I almost said they had the wrong number and then I remembered. I took the number of the caller and said I would have the owner of the bed call back.

Connie not only works week days, but weekends and she must have worked every night this week. After three calls, I called her at work and asked when she would be home. I gave her all the numbers to call. The first man came immediately and took one look at the bed, mattress and springs and handed over the money. They were almost new and looked brand new. All Saturday, Sunday, Monday, Tuesday and Wednesday we had calls. None today so far. We could have sold 100 beds from this ad. Everytime the phone rings we are ready to say "That has already been sold."

I have been so busy I almost forgot Gene's birthday but Gene's brother's early birthday card alerted me and I got busy on that.

Our front room chairs went to the upholster on January 26th. They were returned on February 9th. They look nice and we are glad to have the living room looking normal again.

For the moment we have put off having a new tile roof. We haven't settled on the tile color we want. We think we'll wait till December.

In my spare moments I've been taking notes on Spain and Portugal.

Now I must decide what clothes to take.

Yesterday I read Masterpiece by Thomas Hoving. Thomas Hoving was director of the Metropolitan Museum of Art and also president of Tiffany's. He has written a few books and MASTERPIECE is wonderful. I stayed up one and a half hours after our bedtime last night so I could finish it. I just had to know how it ended. I recommend it highly.

SATURDAY THE 13, FEBRUARY

I just wrote the date of today and that brings back memories because it was on Thursday, February 13, 1964 that Gene proposed. I' ll never forget. Since the next day was Valentine's day, I expected at least a card but I got neither a card nor a call. Since then Gene has learned that little things like cards are important.

My mother's birthday celebration has begun. She has been getting cards all week and enjoys displaying them. Yesterday my friend, Pat, called before 9 AM and invited my mother and me to have lunch with her and her mother's former nurse. I probably mentioned that her mother died Dec 26th. The nurse was visiting her daughter at the time but she came back and is now living in Pat's mother's manor till the sale is completed.

Monday Pat and Bob and will stay a month in a condo on a golf course in Sarasota. Pat can golf while Bob does some consulting work. For several years Pat and Bob have had, in Grass Valley, a retirement home which overlooks a golf course. They have gone there weekends. They couldn't retire there while Pat's mother was alive because there were inadequate facilities for someone who needed round the clock care. It is such a tiny place. Pat put their lovely manor up for sale and sold it immediately. Pat had a landscaper make the entrance a Japanese garden and it was very distinctive.

I'm sorry Pat will be moving 2 1/2 hours away. We'll miss those luncheon sessions and phone calls. Pat has been wonderful to my mother when we have been on vacation, Always she called, visited and took my mother out to lunch

Aside from the fact that Pat grew up in a wealthy home and I didn't, we have much in common, both only children with mothers to care for. Pat is a no nonsense, get things done person. She is outgoing and has lots of friends here which she will miss in Grass Valley.

She will also miss her grandchildren. She has spent every Thursday afternoon with them since they were born. Now they are in school she picks them up after school. Pat was an excellent mother and her two children show the result of her work.

Pat liked Rossmoor for its activities. Bob prefers not to have close neighbors so their new house sits 400 feet back from the road. It is rather isolated.

I'm losing a real good friend. The one thing Pat is not is a letter writer. She doesn't sit still long enough to write letters or read many books. She is too active for this.

VALENTINE'S DAY

We got up early so we could go to Berkeley and have breakfast at the Bridge Creek Restaurant which is part owned by Marion Cunningham who revised the FANNIE FARMER'S COOKBOOK. This restaurant serves only breakfast. No reservations and even at 9 AM there was a long waiting line. The restaurant is in a converted house and sits on a hill, as do all houses in Berkeley. Difficult for my mother to get to the house because of the steps. We three had 3 different reactions to the restaurant.

To me the food was superb. I had a cheese omelet, three pancakes, strawberries (about a pint) and hot chocolate. My mother said the food was o.k. My mother had buttermilk pancakes, coffee and orange juice. Gene didn't say anything but his face expressed his feelings. I think he expected a buffet type brunch. He said he saw nothing he wanted to eat but he ordered a glass of milk and eight buttermilk pancakes. The pancakes were small so eight wasn't too much. Everything was pricey and a la carte. I think the prices just overwhelmed Gene. I'm happy we went there once. I'd rather have quality food than quantities of ordinary food. I have to agree with Gene that we have been to some wonderful brunches and, for less money, we saw more food than we could possibly eat.

The Bridge Creek restaurant is 100% non smoking. When Orange county banned smoking there were complaints that restaurants lost customers. Not so in Berkeley and Berkeley was one of the first communities to ban smoking.

Now it is February 15th, my mother's real birthday. We are taking our Chinese neighbors to a Chinese restaurant in Rheem Valley. My mother likes the shrimp here.

It is a gorgeous day. Blue, cloudless sky and so clear you can see for miles. Hills are GREEN. Warm enough to go without a jacket. Fruit trees and flowering shrubs are in bloom. Mustard covers the fields. This is the pretty season in California and not summer when it is brown.

SUNDAY, FEBRUARY 28, 1988

Dear Audrey and Glenn,

We didn't make it. Almost though! If it hadn't rained yesterday, the whole month of February would have been dry and we would have broken a one hundred twenty four year old record. The weather this winter has been wonderful, warm and sunny, but terrible because of lack of rain. We will pay for this come summer.

This is the time we should put on a new roof but we are delaying till the end of the year. Probably it will rain every day then. We haven't found tiles with a color we like. I know there will be many tile roofs in Spain and maybe there will be a pastel green house with a red roof and I will get a better idea of what our house will look like.

Toby is gradually getting back to his normal activities. This week he attended a Board of Directors meeting of a credit union he manages for a small company. Toby wanted a small job when he retired, not for the money, but just to be busy and with people. It takes only two or three hours a week. Somebody else took over when Toby was so ill but now he wants to resume this. Toby took a bottle of champagne to the meeting and announced that the champagne would go to the person who guessed the closest to the cost of his nine and a half week stay in the hospital. Only hospital costs. Not doctor's bill. Nobody was close. $117,000. and $34,000 was for intravenous feedings. That would buy a lot of groceries. For $507 a day it was just a drip and not lobster, crab or steak. Toby and Leta aren't discouraged. They are resigned to his diet and have given up any thought of traveling outside the U.S.

We have invited Toby and Leta for dinner on Saturday and I've been going thru cookbooks. Toby can have chicken or fish, pasta, no fresh fruits, cooked asparagus and cooked beets, canned pears, peaches and apricots, no spices. We are having fish, fettucine Alfredo, asparagus and beets, pear-sour cream mold and an apricot cake. This is fine for one night but for the rest of your life? it will get boring.

I admire Toby because he is cheerful and he makes you feel good to be with him. He has a wonderful disposition, is most intelligent, courtly, gentlemanly, tactful, quiet but forceful, and he has a subtle sense of humor. He attracts people like honey does bees and he enjoys meeting everybody.

I shudder to think what Toby's doctor's bills will be. The doctors get paid even if they just walk in the room and ask how he is feeling. I assume they studied his chart before each visit and that is what they are being paid for. Fortunately their insurance, like ours, has a catastrophic illness clause and that is what this was.

Tuesday night we had a phone call and I did not recognize the voice. The woman said she was Joan, daughter of Mary Hurd. I know slightly a Mrs. Hurd. After a little more conversation I understood, she was Joan, daughter of Mary Herod, a cousin of my mother who lives in Hamilton, Ontario. Joan and Barney were in S.F. and Mary insisted they see my mother and me. I invited them for dinner on Thursday. They were leaving Friday. Joan was a child when last I saw her. We have heard much about Joan and Barney over the years.

Barney retired a few years back, I suspect early. He first was a carpenter, then a contractor. Having been terribly busy all his life, Barney was at loose ends in retirement. They read an article about the Canadian equivalent of the Peace Corps. Barney applied and in four months time they were in New Guinea and Barney was teaching carpentry. They had a two year hitch. They had some interesting tales to tell.

Their car was stolen four times. but on a small island there is no place to hide a car and it always was found and returned. One week before their return, they went to a farewell party and when they came home, they found their house had been broken into. Ice cream cartons and melting ice cream were on the floor. Beer had been drunk. All their stereo equipment had been taken.

They took their malaria pills every Sunday but nevertheless Barney had an attack of malaria.

When Barney had to be away overnight, somebody had to stay with Joan because the natives raped white women who were alone. In their immediate area there were sixteen rapes and age seemed to make no difference.

Their house was near the airport and when people arrived and heard them speaking English they came to visit. They entertained lots of people they never before had seen.

Joan had taken along her box of recipes. They bought their food from a government agency so they did have familiar Canadian food.

Conversation flowed easily from 3:30 PM till 9 when they had to go back to San Francisco because they were leaving at 8 the next morning. As they were saying good-bye, they said they were glad they had contacted us. They did it as a duty because Joan's mother insisted but another time they would come because they wanted to.

When I had my mother's 90th birthday party, I wrote Mary and described the party and gave some of the recipes of things I served. One was noodle pudding and this recipe came from Gene's sister. Joan read the letter, took the recipe and in the last four years has made it a great deal. She said her daughters and friends have asked for the recipe so it has circulated. Joan asked if I would give her another good recipe. I chose untossed tossed salad and she was delighted because she has to take a salad to a couples club meeting next month and this will be it.

Friday night Leta called and I barely understood what she said. She has the bad bug that is going around and they would have to cancel tomorrow night's dinner. She is trying to stay away from Toby.

All our travel documents have arrived. After the 13th, I'll start packing.

Last Friday Gene had a wonderful bowling session. He was top in score for the whole league and top in several categories. The other 3 on his team were elated and poured out this news. This week it was the opposite. Gene was bad and so were his team mates and they lost all four games. That is the way the cookie crumbles.

MARCH 1, 1988

I was worried about Leta all weekend. I just called. She got steadily worse over the weekend and holed herself up in the bedroom with the adjoining bath. Toby had the rest of the condo to himself. Leta wasn't eating so Toby had to get his own meals.

I cooked some turkey drumsticks and added to the broth some ten vegetables I had pureed. I called Toby and said I was bringing it over to Leta. He met me outdoors and said he was going to eat it too. I reminded him onions and celery and maybe some other vegetables he couldn't have were in the soup. He said he was taking a chance because it was so finely chopped. I hope he doesn't have any trouble because of this. I also took a jar of soup over to my neighbor who just came home from the hospital.

For a long time our garage has been a MESS. Today I told Gene I was going to scream if he didn't clean it up. The garage is his job. He dared me to scream and I did so now he is cleaning it up. It looks 80% better already and he hasn't finished. When Gene worked and had little time, he got things done. Now with all the time in the world, he gets little done till I complain.

This will have to do for now. I have work to do.

MARCH 19, 1988

Dear Emme and Ken,

These two weeks before we leave for Spain and Portugal have and will be busy. We had company for dinner. I gave a book review, went into San Francisco to help set up the flower show and today Virginia, Don. Gene and I went to the flower show.

We got half way to S.F. and I remembered the tickets were home. We didn't go back for them. I went to the ticket office and the treasurer was there and remembered that she had received my check so she let us in. HURRAH! We walked in the door and lo and behold. there on the table opposite the door was my arrangement, the best spot in the whole auditorium, I thought. How did it rate that? Not because my arrangement was best, although Gene graciously said he liked it better than any of the others. It was of two birds of paradise and one leaf, the top of a piece of umbrella palm and a piece of faciated willow.

The arrangement I loved was very different. I consisted of crystal cylinders filled with blue or lavender colored water, iridescent paper similar to saran wrap and white orchids. These cylinders were on a extra large mirror of irregular shape. The cylinders were filled with water right up to the top. The arranger put a pebble in the paper and folded it over so the orchids stayed in place and didn't float to the top. Those iridescent colors sparkled thru the colored water. Not all cylinders had water. All had a small amount of paper, though. The paper was slightly crushed and this enhanced the effect. The paper is quite new and can be had only at the flower market. It was the most different arrangement I've ever seen and it deserved a prize but in ikebana no prizes are given because flower arranging is an expression of the soul and who can judge a soul.

Our club has a yearly membership at the Flower Mart so we can buy flowers for our programs. In this way you get them really fresh and you get different flowers than you would from ordinary florists.

After the show we went to Lychee Gardens and had a Chinese lunch. This is the same place we went with our Chinese neighbors. It again was excellent.

My book review was a success. Nobody went to sleep and nobody walked out. We had a good turnout and those women sat for one and a half hours and listened attentively to me and made comments afterwards. They were most complimentary. However, it wasn't my reviewing. The book was good. Several people went to the library and wanted to borrow the book. The book was AT THE DROP OF A VEIL by Marianne Alireza. It was published in 1971 and was the story of married life to a Saudi, twelve years when she lived in a harem. I was going to contrast it with NOT WITHOUT MY DAUGHTER by Betty Majmoody which is new. AT THE is a happy book, for the most part., but NOT WITHOUT is a bitter book. I don't think things have changed much in the Middle East, although women can now be educated. If they attend college, and if the professor is a man, they sit in one room and the man in another and lessons are televised. The women have phones so they can ask questions. Mrs. Alireza had an article on women in Saudi Arabia in the October 1987 NATIONAL GEOGRAPHIC.

Two hours after we went to bed last night Gene and I were still awake. I complained of the smell in our room. Gene used a deodorizing spray but he said the smell was coming from outside. We closed the bedroom window and opened the bathroom and it wasn't so bad. Two hours later I was still awake. Today we think the smell came from a flowering shrub against our back fence. A week ago we had another sleepless night and that time we blamed it on the refineries on the bay. They used to do this at night till they got caught. We live miles away but the wind must have been in the right direction for us to get it.

Duty calls. Dirty dishes. Preparations for company dinner tomorrow night. Bread making. I'm going to be busy this afternoon.

MAY 13, 1988

Dear Pat and Bob,

I have a word of advice. Avoid, if possible, germs from Spain. They are devastating, or at least the kind I picked up was. We hadn't been in Spain long when I got this respiratory infection. Unfortunately there was no nasal discharge and no sputum came with the racking cough. Had there been, I would have been well much sooner, I think. Today is day forty three of this illness and I think today I'm starting on my way back to health.

The doctor thinks it probably was walking pneumonia. We know from x-rays it wasn't lobar pneumonia. We have spent a fortune on medicine that did no good. One medicine caused a drug reaction and the inside of my mouth was covered with sores. Food and tooth paste hurt terribly. The respiratory infection caused an embarrassing, uncontrollable and uncomfortable urologic reaction and a most painful gynecological condition. I just wanted to scream from this gynecological condition. The doctor gave me three different medicines. The first worked not at all. The second, he said. would clear up the condition in three days, and he gave me a three day supply. It worked for 18 hours of the first two days and not at all on the third day. Yesterday I got a new medicine and all yesterday and all last night I was comfortable. So now, maybe, I'm almost well. I'm still spraying my throat and we hope this will cause the sputum to raise from the pleura.

May 1st my mother had a small stroke. She was in the bathroom and came out immediately to Gene and me. She hadn't had breakfast and wasn't dressed. We sat her down in the living room. I could tell something was wrong but didn't know what. All at once her mouth twisted and her left arm and leg went numb and I realized she was having a stroke. I went for the blood pressure kit and her blood pressure was in the low stroke range. Gene got her some breakfast and I hurriedly dressed because I expected to rush her to the hospital. Within ten minutes her face was o.k. and she regained feeling in her arm and leg. She was scared and so was I. Yesterday she had an appointment with the doctor. I had seen him on Monday and alerted him to this. He said a slight stroke like this is a TIA. The doctor asked my mother how she was and she told him she was fine. He questioned her a great deal but she would not admit to any problems. Finally I told my mother to tell the doctor what happened. She got mad at me for telling him. He increased her blood pressure medicine and we are giving her aspirin to thin her blood. These last twelve days she appears normal. However, I understand that even with an TIA some brain damage is done.

So much for all that.

Last Year the doctor said the pants I wear are too heavy for our weather and I should buy pants of a lighter material. So I've been shopping.

Saturday night we are entertaining Connie H and Frank. Frank and his wife Bess were good friends of Connie and John. John died at Christmas one year and the next Bess died. Both like to play bridge so I've invited them to dinner. I'm not matchmaking, They are just friends and we four enjoy each other's company. Connie is on a diet and Frank has had two angina attacks and two angiplasty procedures so he is on a heart diet. My menu was hard to decide.

A week ago I bought Bernard Crayton's NEW COMPLETE BOOK OF BREADS. I have his first book and use it a lot. I made a cheese bread from the new book that is out of this world. I was looking for a roll recipe for tomorrow night and I found a chapter entitled BAKING FOR DOGS! Clayton reports that he has received many, many thank you letters from dogs that have been given his dog biscuits, some from the dog next door, the dog down the street and from dogs who just like them. The recipe can be tailored to a dog's taste, sweet with sugar, honey or molasses or it can have added vitamins. Clayton used Timothy, a Cairn terrier, as a test animal and he reported Timothy loved them and begged for more, but even though they were bone hard, there were none left because Bernard Clayton himself ate them!

Last week there was an article in the N.Y. Times about prices in Japan. It was reported that you can buy one cherry for $16. Yes, that is sixteen dollars for one cherry.

Since I've been sick, I've been confined to the house pretty much. One day I felt good enough to make another outfit for Kate's doll. It really took me two days. Gene says he is getting jealous of the doll because I spend so much time on it. I told this to Connie H, the grandmother of Kate, and she said she didn't feel sorry for Gene because she thinks he gets more than enough attention.

JUNE 22, 1988

Dear Lucy and Lucien,

Summer has finally arrived and the weather is hot and so is Norma. I'm not hot from the weather, though. I'm riled because I can't get through to the Medicare system. Here is the story. April 30th I had an x-ray at a Walnut Creek lab to see if I had pneumonia. I sent Medicare a $49 bill for this. May 11th I received a check for $60 for a mammogram from a Santa Rosa lab and I've never been to this lab. I called and was told to cash the check and then send them a personal check for $60. This I did. I also had to resubmit the bill. June 20th I received a thank you for my personal check but no payment for the lab bill. I called and was told everything had been processed and they had no bill and to resubmit a third time. Then I was told claims go to Chico and problems to San Francisco so now I should consult San Francisco. I almost wish I had been dishonest and kept the $60. Gene says this would have messed up his Bechtel insurance because he has to attach a bill and we have no bill for the mammogram which I never had. I wonder if we'll ever get the $49. The above was really simplified but that is the gist of the problem.

Since the news came out about cracklin oat bran, people are really buying it. The clerk at the store says the boxes just jump off the shelf and their supply is gone in a few hours. He expects a new shipment tonight so I guess we'll have to go to the store tonight if we want it and we do.

We think we have found the tile for our house. It isn't red and it isn't orange. Two houses in this area have this tile and we looked at them and liked what we saw. Now for estimates.

We had a letter from Jennie in England and she has been house sitting for her veterinarian son and his wife. They have recently been burglarized. She had the care of a dog, cat and lamb that had been hit in the road. Mike stopped to see the lamb and discovered its hind parts were paralyzed. No bones broken. He thought it might be a temporary paralysis so he put it in the orchard under a tree and each day Jennie fed it and moved it to a clean spot but on the fifth day it died. The dog was with Jennie the whole time but she never saw the cat. Just before Mike left, a farmer called and needed some medicine for a cow so Mike went to his drug shed and got the medicine. He didn't notice the cat came in with him and was still there when he locked the shed. The cat was in the shed the whole nine days. Jennie said the cat came out with its tail in the air and very perky but a few pounds less.

Remember my telling you a couple years ago about Jennie's granddaughter's 21st birthday party and how more than 40 people got sick? The butcher was sued. He has insurance but nothing has been settled because some people are still having trouble from the salmonella. I didn't know the effects lasted so long.

We will be married twenty four years on Monday and we are going to Remark's Harbor House in Vallejo for dinner. It doesn't seem like twenty four years.

At the moment caraway rye bread is baking in the oven and our house smells heavenly. Does anything smell better than baking bread?

JULY 11, 1988

Dear Catherine and Larry,

After Gene returned from his SIRS luncheon meeting today, we visited Karen, our travel agent. Our final payment for the Canadian Rocky tour was due.

We were to have been four but now we are three. Adelaide wrote me one day and said that she was in the hospital and would not be able to go on the trip with us. She had had a freak accident.

One morning she went to church and as she was sitting there the kneeling rail fell on her leg and it made a big cut on the skin covering the shin bone. The skin is thin there and the cut opened up wide and bled profusely. She had to see a doctor and I think stitches were necessary. The darn thing became infected and she had to see him again. This time things were so bad it was necessary to hospitalize her. She is on crutches. She doesn't think she will be healed before we leave.

While she was in the hospital, I called her and things are even worse than she described in her letter. Adelaide was happy to join us but I can see that doing that is impossible.

Gosh, you would think just sitting in church would pose no hazard. One never knows when an innocent action will result in a dire circumstance.

So we shall be just the three musketeers.

AUGUST 5, 1988

Dear Eleanor and Matt,

We have had a busy week. Kate, 3 years, 3 months, arrived on Friday morning, the 29th. Her parents left for a weekend in the wine country. The previous day they had brought Kate for a couple hours so she could get used to us because she hasn't seen us in a year. Kate is a dear little thing, small for her age, with a soft, quiet voice, and brown eyes that are almost black. She is a little angel and she eats like an angel, almost nothing. She still has a bottle. I'm concerned about her not eating.

Kate loved to call me in our bedroom, order me to open our walk-in closet door and turn on the light. As soon as we both were in the closet, she would run out and close the door, leaving me inside. Then she ran down the hall and into the living room. She would stand just inside the door and occasionally peek out and laugh when I came out of the closet. The same thing happened when she went to the bathroom. I would go to help her but she was only getting me in the bathroom so she could close me in. I learned later that she goes to the bathroom by herself. She was having fun.

She went to bed without fuss. She made no fuss when her parents left. Connie came Saturday night and took her home with her. She expected to have Kate alone for a day but the parents returned on Saturday night. When the parents are around, Kate has time only for them so Connie didn't get close to her granddaughter.

Sunday they all came for dinner. Again Kate would have nothing to do with us because her parents were present. Monday we didn't see Kate but Tuesday Connie took us all out to dinner. Kate didn't have a nap that day and she just sat on her mother's lap. Wednesday we didn't see Kate but Thursday we had her for the day while Connie and Linda shopped. Gene wanted so to hold Kate but she wouldn't go either to him or my mother. Once he got her to sit on his lap but as soon as I sat down, she came over and got on mine. She doesn't sit much but she does like to be held and loved.

Kate told her grandmother that our middle bedroom was hers and when her father came, she took him in the bedroom and said it was hers. She thought one side of our table was hers and she didn't want her parents to sit there too.

Last New Year's weekend I made clothes for a doll. I gave Kate the doll the first day. I wrapped the clothes and hide them, so Kate had lots of presents for two days. The doll had three pairs of pants and tops, a christening dress and slip, a sun dress, two party dresses, bonnet, sweater, bootees, bunting, nightie, blanket, diapers, comb, brush and bottle. When I gave her the doll, she only wanted to change the diaper. She didn't play with the doll much. Her parents brought puzzles and books and I had lots of books. I read all the books three or four times. We took lots of walks and she did lots of somersaults on the front lawn. It was a real joy for us to have Kate.

Our dining room table extends and will accommodate one board. It is too small so I asked Gene if he could make a new table slide and boards for it. We both got under the table to see what could be done and discovered the name of the maker of the slide extension. With the name, I called the maker and ordered a new slide extension. Gene is now studying how to remove the old one and install the new one. Then he'll have to make new boards and we'll have to have new pads. Our table used to accommodate six but now we can seat ten.

I've had some interesting books from the library. One was A TASTE OF MY OWN MEDICINE by a doctor who had cancer of the throat which wasn't diagnosed correctly. His field was not cancer of the throat and he was hesitant when an intern discovered this. Even though he was a doctor he was afraid to let others work on him and he misunderstood things they said. This doctor says that now he understands and appreciates far better his patients worries

I also read EMERGENCY DOCTOR by Goldfrank who is head of the emergency room at Bellvue in N.Y. If ever a president comes to N.Y. City, Bellvue will be where he is taken if he gets ill or wounded. So each visit is preceded by visits from the Secret Service who go over the Emergency Room and its procedures very carefully.

OCTOBER 10, 1988

Dear Phyllis,

A little after 7 this morning the phone rang. I hadn't used my voice for eight hours so it was husky and the caller thought I was Mr. Davidson. The call was in response to my letter inquiring about reservations on the skyline Drive in June. I was advised to call January 2nd if we want a room in June. Any letter before Jan 1st is ignored and probably after January 2nd no accommodations will be left. National parks are very popular.

After breakfast I made bread. Gene got ready to go to SIRS. After he left, Leta called. Toby had a visitor and so Leta was able to go in the bedroom and talk freely with me. She said Toby had been told he had an advanced case of cancer of the liver and he wouldn't live much beyond Christmas. My bread rose and fell. I tried to bake it but I finally threw it out and started over. I felt it was better to listen and talk to Leta than tell her I would call back. A good loaf of bread wasn't nearly as important as listening and sympathizing. A miracle occurred last year when Toby resumed a somewhat normal life after being diagnosed with Crohn's disease, so he has had about six months grace. I assured her we would help and support them.

My Christmas card list is a mess. Many change of addresses so I did the whole thing over. Now the envelopes are addressed and the Christmas letter included. Only stamps are needed before mailing.

This isn't Christmas card weather. It was 91 yesterday and in the high 80s today. However our front bedroom looks like Christmas with wrapped packages.

I'll have to get that bedroom back to order because Leta will come stay with us when Toby is finally hospitalized. She isn't resigned to Toby's death. They are in the process of getting their Orinda house ready for sale. Toby can do nothing but rest while Leta works. Toby is discouraged but his mind is keen and he can give Leta good advice.

I've prepared scalloped potatoes and ham, made a salad and cooked a vegetable. I'm just about ready to serve dinner.

Dinner is now over and the dishes done. I've worked eleven hours without a break. We didn't get mail today because they declared this Columbus Day so I didn't even rest while reading the mail. The news is on TV so I'm going to sit down and relax. Who says a housewife doesn't work?

NOVEMBER 20, 1988

Dear Lois and Fred,

All this month I've been writing letters but none have come your way. They have been business letters with regard to the items we are selling for our friends, Leta and Toby. If I haven't been writing letters, I've been visiting antique stores. I know nothing about antiques so I must bone up and become smart enough to make good deals. Fortunately Toby and Leta just want the stuff sold and are not holding me to top price. However, I don't want to be cheated. We know if we didn't sell to dealers, we would get more but it would be difficult to find buyers. A garage sale wouldn't do.

Stored in the rafters of the Evans garage were some barrels that came from Leta's mother's home. We found some chipped soup and dinner plates of Haviland china and some silver. The silver was in good shape. There were three sterling serving pieces, two spoons and a fork. The rest of the stuff was plated but good, a covered vegetable dish. trivet. sandwich plate, candy dish, platter and a couple other pieces. We also found seven oriental plates with lots of gold on them.

So I started out to sell these items. The first offer of $86 I refused. I finally found a silver dealer who would give me $125 for the 3 spoons. He wasn't interested in the plated ware. I almost took this but our friend Connie H met me and she said she would buy it for her daughter at that price. Toby and Leta said o.k. so this deal wasn't too hard. I got refusal after refusal about the china because it was chipped. Then Leta found a matching platter that was in perfect condition. This made a difference and finally a dealer made an offer for everything and I grabbed it.

I took the seven oriental plates to oriental stores. I learned they were from the Meiji period in Japan and were made in Yokohama. The artist name was on the plates. Unfortunately they were made for export and no oriental dealer wanted them. The oriental dealers want only items the Japanese use. I only got $90 for the plates.

Toby's family had a bronze urn. It was huge and corroded. I thought it ugly. I got no offers till one day I found a man who offered $50. I quickly called Toby and he said to take the offer. An hour later the man had changed his mind because he said it was Mexican and not oriental and Mexican things are not so valuable. After some more conversation he agreed to his original offer and I handed it over immediately.

This antique business is not an exact science. Boy, am I learning.

Remaining was a Louis E. Rea painting and a diploma from Washington College with the signature of Robert E. Lee as president and these two items have taken all the letter writing. I wrote four persons who buy autographs. I got an immediate offer from one, two were interested but quoted no price. All wanted to see the diploma. We decided to

have it photocopied. They actually photograph the item and we get a
negative. I wasn't about to send the original diploma. That diploma has a
story that goes with it and here it is.

Toby's grandfather was Oliver Perry Evans and he was a descendent
of Oliver Hazard Ferry, famous in the War of 1812. His grandfather went
to Virginia Military Institute and, while there, his unit was called to be a
back up at the Battle of New Market. They got caught in the middle and
these eighteen year old boys, led by Toby's grandfather as color bearer,
fought hand to hand and captured the hill. There was a painting made of
him which hangs in the Museum at VMI. In 1961 LIFE did a six issue
spread on the Civil War. On page 62 of the January 6th issue of 1961 there
is a reproduction of another picture of Toby's grandfather with the flag.
The Beverly Hills man first offered $800 for the diploma but with the Life
magazine and the fame of the grandfather, he raised it to $1000. I wrote
the other two dealers and said any offer must be more than $1000.

After Toby's grandfather graduated from VMI, he went to
Washington College where Robert E. Lee was president. The diploma is
from Washington College which is now Washington and Lee University.
The diploma is dated June 20, 1867. His grandfather completed a course
of study in the School of Law and Equity. He later became a Supreme
Court judge in San Francisco. Actually the painting resembles Toby. The
grandfather was 6'2'. Toby is 7 feet and may be an inch or two more. We
think Toby could have looked like that at 18. I'm still dickering about this
diploma with the R.E. Lee signature.

I'm also working on the Louis E. Rea painting. It was purchased from
world famous Gumps but Gumps does not want to buy it back. I have a
tentative offer for $800–$1500. Somebody heard about it and is coming to
see it in a few minutes. Toby and I decided not to take an offer till we
have the painting appraised. Rea was written up in an art book and it
said he was one of the finest landscape painters in California. The painting is of a scene in Marin County and shows the golden hills and valleys
in the summer with a few low, scrubby, green trees in the left hand corner. It is typical of what California looks like in the summer, the Golden
State. So my next project is to take it into San Francisco and have the de
Young Museum appraise it.

All this has been time consuming but most interesting for me and an
added interest for Toby because I have kept him informed about every
letter and contact. Toby is now racked with pain and morphine no longer
dulls the pain from the cancer. The radiation treatments have been
stopped because the side effects were worse than the cancer.
Chemotherapy has been stretched out because it was so debilitating.
Although Toby's body is in bad condition, his mind is as keen as ever.

I was just interrupted by the dealer who looked at the painting. He
offered $350 and it wasn't even considered.

Toby has others helping him sell his motor home and the Jaguar.

November 6th I started to come down with the same illness I got in

Spain last March. I used my left over medicine but when that didn't help, I went to the doctor. He gave me other medicine which I took for a week. I got no worse, but I also got no better so I had another appointment. The doctor said he was going to use the "big guns", powerful medicine, a shot, ten additional new pills per day and a nasal spray. Last April I had a crown put on a tooth and ever since I've had a throbbing in my right cheek. When I mentioned this to the doctor, he sent me for a facial x-ray and, by golly, I have a sinus infection. The doctor thinks I've had it for 6 months and it just spilled over and caused all this trouble. So I was given Actified with codeine which caused me to sleep day and night for two days. Gene woke me to eat. I'm some better but the doctor thinks it will be a week before I'm completely recovered. Our new roof should be completed in a day or two.

It is Sunday afternoon. Dinner is over. I've read the newspapers. I'm going to make out my cookie baking list and think about Christmas.

DECEMBER 25, 1988

Dear Emiko and Yuichi,

Monday, Dec 5th Gene and I went into San Francisco to see the store windows and we were disappointed because they were not Christmasy.

We had been looking at a word processor, Magnavox 450, in Macy's in Concord for some time. Last week we decided to buy and went to the store, only to find out they were sold out and were not going to be able to get more. Why, we didn't know. So we decided to look at Macy's in San Francisco. That store had three which the clerk said would be sold that day so if we wanted one, we should buy it then. We presented Gene's new Macy's credit card but this had a $400 limit. They wouldn't accept our Visa card. The sale had to be check or cash. We never carry that amount of cash and we had just paid our bills and hadn't that amount in our checking account. Finally I said I had a Macy's credit card which I had had for years and it was good for the amount of the sale, but if we used this we would lose the $100 and the 10% discount the Concord store would give us. The clerk verified all we said with the salesman in the Concord store and said she would give us the same deal as the Concord store. She rang up the sale and we started to give our address for delivery and she said this had to be a take sale. We didn't see how we could carry such a heavy bulky package but she said it weighed only 25 pounds and it was boxed and they would put a rope around it for carrying. So it was a done deal. We left it in the store till after we window looked and had lunch and then carried the word processor to BART and brought it home.

Everyone was surprised at this deal. You don't bargain with big department store like Macy's. We never intended to bargain. We didn't understand about the payment business but a few days later we did. Magnavox is no longer making word processors and Macy's planned to get rid of all they had that day. Maybe this wasn't such a smart purchase. We may not be able to get ribbons and discs for a machine no longer being made.

It is now Christmas night and almost bedtime. We had a lovely day. Gene forgot to set the alarm so we didn't get up as early as I wanted, but I did have the turkey ready and the pies made in time for dinner. We also looked at the items in our Christmas stockings and unwrapped the mountain of presents under the tree before Leta and Toby came at 2 PM. Everything in their stockings was either eatable or consumable.

We spent a long time at the table. Toby could not eat everything but he had a full plate. We had two hours of interesting conversation after dinner and then they went home.

Last week when I stopped to leave some fresh bread, Toby was home alone. He said he felt he was sitting on a time bomb because the doctors said he wouldn't live past the New Year. I think he has a bit more time because the last cat scan showed the cancer is the same size as previously. Toby told me that at the November meeting of SIRS he was given an award and at the end of the meeting a man came up to Toby and said if money would cure his problem, he would provided the money. Toby was touched.

DECEMBER 26, 1988.

There was snow on Mount Diablo Christmas Day and today people are taking their children up to play in it. They get excited about snow out here. They closed the road so people are walking up. Gene is glad he no longer has to shovel snow.

FEB 12, 1989

Dear Dot and James,

To date, my mother has had two birthday celebrations and her birthday isn't till the 15th. A week ago today we went to Campbell for dinner with Maryann and Dick. Maryann surprised my mother with a birthday cake and present. Maryann and Dick were upset when we arrived because, shortly before, the electricity went off and when it came back on, the furnace did not, so the house kept getting colder and colder. They had a fire in the fireplace and an electric heater near where my mother sat. We didn't feel the cold. I did worry about them that night because the TV said pipes would freeze if houses were insufficiently heated. They went to bed and kept warm and next morning called P G & E who asked if they had pressed the reset button. They didn't know they had a reset button but now they do and won't be fooled again when the electricity goes off. My mother was delighted with this first surprise birthday celebration.

Yesterday we had our official 95th birthday celebration. I've been working on it for weeks. It wasn't the right day but Saturday is a good day for a brunch because working people can come. The first person who was invited was Leon who is on Gene's bowling team but he refused because he said two events in one day were too much. Leon has a dance band and they were going to be performing that night for six hours. Gene's teammates are 79, 80 and 81 years old but all are active and last year Gene's team came out in first place for the year so they aren't such slouches. I understood. Three couples were away for the weekend and one had a class. I ended up with 16 acceptances.

I prepared a folded menu and on the inside cover had a list of those present and a statement concerning my mother's 95th birthday. I did this on my new word processor. When people came, I gave these out. As did Princes Andrew and Edward at the wedding reception for Charles and Diana, I announced each person. The Princes used a rattle but I used a bell. They said, "Coming up, one King of Norway, King Olav." I said, " "Coming up, one bowler or one bridge player, flower arranger, or what- ever." Almost nobody listened but it did create a bit of amusement and some comment. We didn't have name tags but everybody used the menus to connect people with names. The day before the party Leon decided to change his mind and come so I added his name to the menu and rearranged the seating. We had three card tables and a combined card and little kitchen table for five. Table one went directly to the dining room table that was covered with food. Table two went to the coffee and tea on the chest of drawers in the dining room, tables three and four went to the desk which is now in the hall under the clock and they had a choice of guava juice or orange-pineapple juice. Then everybody went to the place least crowded. It worked well.

On the dining room table were the following: curried fruit—pears, apricots, pineapple, cherries, baked in a honey curry sauce, a layered seafood salad with smoked oysters and whitefish, a clam casserole, a crab casserole, Northwest hazelnut turkey bake., shrimply delicious, oven fried scallops, ham pasties, chocolate swirled babka, cheese bread and peanut butter bacon rounds. This concoction was on English muffins and was baked. At the end we had an Hawaiian mardi gras cake which is a white cake made with four eggs and lots of candied cherries, pineapple, papaya and macadamia nuts. I used our dinner plates and everybody had a full plate and nobody wanted seconds.

Our friend Toby may be slowly dying but he made the party. After dessert, he gave out seven balloons and the men blew them up. Then they started batting them around and everyone got into the act.

Everybody was talking but watchful of the balloons and it was a sight to see all those waving arms and balloons going every which way. My mother was amazed. It was like a kid's party in this way, but the conversation was adult and most interesting.

I had no program but I did ask people to tell where they were born, how long they lived in California, how many other states they had lived in and how many foreign countries they had lived in. Each response brought comments. I also asked people to tell what came to mind first when a state was mentioned. Iowa— Everybody thought corn. Missouri—Show me. People left about 2 PM and just as they left, Connie G came and she ate left overs. She was the one with the class. She stayed a couple hours and then Gene and I tackled the dishes and cleaning up. I had a twelve hour day and I could just barely walk after this. Being on my feet this long played havoc with my arthritis, but today I'm almost back to normal. I had a twelve hour day on Friday too, getting ready for the party.

Today we had several phone calls and the most complimentary things have been said. I think the reason why people enjoyed the party was that we were crowded and you just have to be friendly when everybody is so close. Gene was the most silent person of the group, as usual, but he did glean one bit of interesting information. Ken was a drama teacher and Leta majored in dramatics in college. Leta told Ken she had been in one movie before her marriage. It was with the Ritz brothers. I wish I could see that movie.

Near the end of the meal, I discovered that I had fooled a lot of people, one of whom was Gene. I had smoked oysters in the salad and everybody thought the oysters were mushrooms. Gene refuses to eat oysters. The oysters tasted like oysters when eaten individually, but with all the other ingredients they just blended in.

My mother is to have three more birthday celebrations. We are taking her out for either lunch or dinner on the actual day of her birthday. I suggested two nice places but she rejected both. She likes shrimp at the Sizzler so we may just go there to please her but either of the other two are far superior.

On the 22nd Mary and Bud are taking us out to lunch for her birthday and then we'll come back here and I'll have cake for Connie who also has a February birthday.

On the 22nd Connie H and Frank are taking us out for a birthday lunch. We are going to Marie Callender's. Not many people get five birthday celebrations, do they?

On the 15th, I'll tie all the balloons to the mall box.

Our baby returns

Persian rug, Garage doors up and down on own

MARCH 1, 1989

Dear Halys and Gordon,

Today we received a letter from the Pasadena Rug Market in response to one of mine and thereby hangs a tale.

Gene is always entering contests and sometimes he needs to buy a magazine. A couple years ago he subscribed to ARCHITECTURAL DIGEST. I loved looking a this magazine in the doctor or dentist office but I would never buy it because it is too expensive. Gene didn't see anything else to buy so along comes this magazine each month. At the back of each issue is the California Collection, unpaged pages of advertisements from California businesses. The March 1989 issue showed a picture of a Persian rug whose pattern is exactly like that on our drapes. I showed it to Gene and we decided to write and ask the size and price. A small one could be a nice accent to our living room, we thought. The letter said the rug was a Persian work of art and had previously belonged to the founder of the Serafian Loom and is one of the finest examples of Persian rugs. It has over 2 million knots. They found it difficult to quote a price for such a masterpiece; but for this 3x5 foot rug, they are asking $24,000. Correct! Twenty four thousand. We had a good laugh. My mother was passing by so I asked her if she would like to buy us a present. My mother said if it was something we really wanted, she would buy it. What was it? I showed her the picture and she asked the price and then she just walked away. Another good laugh. Gene's final comment was that I had good taste. Those drapes also have a story. When I bought my house in Niagara Falls in 1961, I wanted a gold drape with an orange -peach pattern that I had previously seen in a downtown drapery store in Buffalo. I returned to the store but it had gone out of business. I tried all the drapery stores and described this shiny material with this Persian pattern. On my way back to Niagara Falls I stopped at a little drapery store in Kenmore and that man knew just what I wanted and showed me a sample. I ordered enough material for drapes for the living and dining rooms. I had the man make the living room drapes but I made the dining room ones. When Gene proposed, he said he wanted nothing but the drapes and refrigerator from my house. I had different ideas and we almost canceled our wedding because of this. When Gene realized that, if he wanted me, he had to take my furniture, he gave in. We sold most of his furniture, except for two bedroom suites and a couple chairs. My dining room drapes fit perfectly in Gene's house. My living room drapes were one panel short in width of each drape. I went back to the man who sold me the material and asked if he could order two more panels. He thought he had some left over from my drapes. He searched his warehouse and he had just two lengths. I bought them and added a panel to each side. Good thing because this material was no longer being made. My drapes went perfectly with the rugs and walls of Gene's house. So we both were happy.

Then we moved to Ann Arbor and guess what? The drapes fit both the living room and dining room and again went with the walls and rugs.Two and a half years later when we moved, the drapes were rotting from the sun. Our first prospective buyer wanted the drapes but we didn't want to leave them. They would fit in our new house in California and would serve the purpose till we could find something else. After a year I started looking for new material. I finally narrowed it down to two samples and I took Gene one Saturday to make the final selection. I didn't like either of these as much as our old drapes. Gene also liked neither as well as the old drapery material. We decided to think about it over the weekend. On the way home we stopped at a small furniture store I had never been in. We looked at samples. The owner of the store was friendly and Gene told him we had drapes we really liked and described the material. The man said he would look in the decorator stores in S.F. and see if he could find something close. A couple weeks later he called and said he had some samples and one was just what we described but the orange color was just a bit different. It seems the copyright had expired and a new company had purchased it and was now making the material. We ordered enough for our living room and dining room and I made the drapes.

I think we'll pass on the rug!

MARCH 15, 1989

Dear Connie and Herb,

Today I gave my book review at Rossmoor to AAUW. I reviewed I AM OF IRELAND by Elizabeth Shannon. After talking one hour, I started talking fast so I could finish but Selma indicated I was going too fast. I said I was doing it purposely so I could cover all I wanted to say. She said nobody was in a hurry, to take my time and finish because everybody was interested. I talked for one and a half hours. Nobody went to sleep and nobody left. When I finished, the audience began to talk. It was most interesting because they remembered what book I did last year and the year before. I was flattered. They really knew the contents of those reviews. It wasn't that the reviews were so good but rather that the audience was so intelligent. I really felt that the work involved in preparing the review was worthwhile since so many enjoyed and were stimulated by the review.

A mistake was made in the AAUW bulletin and my review was scheduled for the 22nd of March. Selma requested a correction and the new article was enlarged and most flattering.

Yesterday I went to an AAUW luncheon at Rossmoor. There were only 47 present and the membership is about 250. Meetings of AAUW are poorly attended but interest groups do quite well in attendance. I think the national organization is out of tune with local chapters.

Last Friday people in Contra Costa county began having trouble with garage door openers. Some just wouldn't work. Some people came home to find their garage doors open. One woman said her garage door went up and down 20 times. Everybody called the garage door opener companies. They didn't know the cause of the problem but a couple days later they said there had been a solar flare and this may have damaged the openers. Good way to sell more openers.

Yesterday somebody got smart and figured it out. This person had a friend who worked on Mt Diablo on a Navy project. The friend confirmed that the Navy had a station on top of the mountain and was doing an experiment and using a certain frequency. Any garage door with this frequency had trouble. They will be doing this till the middle of May. Garage doors work on a low frequency and can't jam anything but anything else can jam a garage door opener. Mary and Bud's garage door is operated on this frequency and they have been having trouble. The Navy will not confirm this. The man who figured this out had his friend turn off the experiment and had people use their garage door openers and they worked perfectly. Then he called the man on the mountain and he started transmitting and again the garage door openers wouldn't work.

On my mother's birthday and the day before, l was on my feet 12 hours each day and after that the arthritis in my knee was very painful and I could not stand from a sitting position and this was bad when I used the toilet. Last week the doctor told me to take more medicine. I'm now on two pills a day and I'm much better. I'll do this for a couple weeks and then go back to one pill a day because the side effects are bad.

I've just finished reading VIEWS FROM THORNHILL, a collection of newspaper and magazine articles which appeared in the BALTIMORE SUN and HOUSE BEAUTIFUL. Dee Hardie writes about her life bringing up four children in Maryland. It is a really good book.

MARCH 17TH, 1989

Yesterday the Navy admitted that it was to blame for the garage door openers not working. They have changed their frequency and all the openers are working properly again.

This morning I was doing the dishes and listening to the TODAY show when I heard that there was to be a segment on women in Ireland and I guessed it might be Elizabeth Shannon. It was. I was thrilled. She was dressed tastefully in a red dress and was most attractive. She was asked if any of her interviews affected her and she said two stood out, one about Annie and the other about the Sisters of Terror. Both of these drew comments in my review. How I wish my audience had been able to see Elizabeth this morning.

Wilma called this morning and she had two purposes, one to invite us to have dinner with them in a restaurant in Orinda and the other was to tell us about the wills she and Russ are having prepared. She thought I might have some knowledge about something they are interested in. At the end of the conversation she invited us to their funerals. No time was specified!

MARCH 29, 1989

Dear Raedina and Milton,

Last night I made an amazing discovery. Absolutely delicious. Entirely original. Norma flavor. On our first good night kiss I detected a sweet fruity taste on Gene's lips. In our almost 25 years of marriage I've never experienced this before. Subsequent kisses got even better. I asked Gene if he had cleaned his teeth and he had and he had also washed his face. When Gene washes his face, he really washes and face cloths last like paper ones would. I asked if he had eaten before coming to bed and he had eaten a stale hot cross bun. I made them Saturday. Those kisses were irresistible. So here is a love potion I will share with you. I'll either send the recipe or make the hot cross buns and send then and they will work even if stale. Only candied cherries, pineapple and papaya were in the buns. Wine or other foods are not necessary or even desirable. Just eat the buns. Of course, you are on your own until you get that first kiss.

APRIL 3, 1989

Saturday we had dinner with Wilma and Russ. They served a milk punch at their house. We had the main course at the Vintage House and then returned for dessert to their house, followed by a game. They don't play bridge.

I was on my exercycle this morning and two male Mallard ducks and one female ambled across the sidewalk outside the family room. Gene checked their progress and they stayed quite awhile in our driveway and then went onto the road. We had things to do so had to give up watching them. They apparently live nearby because it isn't unusual to see them in our yard. I think they come to have a swim in our neighbor's pool.

Last night we had Mary, Bud and Connie for dinner because they have a thirty seventh wedding anniversary on Wednesday.

Leta called this morning and reported that Toby has been having terrible headaches and loss of memory. The doctor thinks his cancer has reached the brain but Toby doesn't know this. Toby is to have a brain scan on Wednesday.

Leta asked if Gene would watch out for Toby when he goes to SIRS next Monday. Usually Toby goes with a friend but the friend can't go because of the illness of his wife. Gene goes with Leon but this time Gene will call Toby and say he is going alone and invite Toby to go with him.

I read in the newspaper about a book called FABULOUS FIBER COOKERY which helps reduce cholesterol. I tried several book stores yesterday but none had the book. Last night I located the book and we purchased it this morning. I've gone thru it and made out two different menus for two different dinner parties this month. This is one of those Nitty Gritty cookbooks which used to be published in Concord but now are published in San Leandro but sold all over the US. Each Nitty Gritty cookbook deals with one thing, i.e. seafood, bread etc.

Another hot day. Records are being broken for this time of year. Air conditioning was on yesterday and will be today and the sprinkler system must be on for the plants.

MAY 1, 1989

Dear Andrea,

This morning I threw a book at Gene. Was I mad? Not really. I was working at the kitchen sink when the phone rang. Gene was doing his cross word puzzle with the TV on. He didn't hear the phone. I couldn't hear what was being said on the phone. I wanted Gene to turn down the volume on the TV. I waved my arms, pounded with a glass on the counter but to no avail so I flung the cookbook at Gene and this got his attention. He turned down the TV.

Leta was calling to ask us to come stay with Toby for a couple hours while she did some business. I'd say the last roundup is near for Toby. Lack of food the last two days has caused Toby to become so weak he can't walk. Leta is calling two doctors this morning because they do not know how bad things really are. I hope they put him in the hospital.

3:30 PM

The oncologist was in conference when Leta called. The nurse took the message and the oncologist told Leta to bring Toby to the hospital for a three day stay. Leta, having urgent errands, asked if we would take Toby and she would come as soon as she could.

We were sitting in the waiting room when Leta was paged. I answered the phone and explained my husband and I had brought Toby instead of his wife. The oncologist had never heard of us and was definitely annoyed.

After seeing Toby settled, we returned to their home where we had to wait for Meals on Wheels. This was the first day they were to have Meals on Wheels. Gene came home and got lunch for my mother. Then Gene came back and I went home for lunch. When I returned, the food had been delivered but we had to wait till the internist called. Leta wanted him to know what was going on and she also wanted him to know he was to be on this case with the oncologist. We then returned to the hospital to visit Toby. Already some tests had been done and an IV had been started for his dehydration. Toby is ready to give up. He doesn't want any more pain.

I really felt queer being in their condo without them. Gene sat in Toby's chair and, when and if Toby gets home, he can say like the papa bear—somebody has been sitting in my chair. Gene also looked at their TV. I took along a book and read.

MAY 3, 1989

Yesterday Toby had an MIG along with a lot of other tests. The MIG showed three cancers in the brain. Leta was told he would be in the hospital two weeks and after that will have to go to a convalescent hospital. I don't think anyone should be kept alive just to suffer. Leta was told there would be personality changes. Living with such pain, terrible headaches, nausea, so weak he can hardly eat, talk, or walk is not my idea of life.

MAY 5, 1989

Yesterday we went to the hospital to feed Toby and we were amazed to find he was almost back to normal. He didn't have the strength to cut his meat but otherwise he fed himself. He was cheerful and alert, and, as always, we had a really nice visit.

Gene bowls today so I shall go alone to feed Toby. Yesterday we took an arrangement and while we were waiting for Toby's bath to be finished, we had four compliments on the arrangement. I went out early this morning and picked some more flowers for another arrangement,

So what else is new in our life. Not much. Fortunately my mother is o.k. and doesn't resent all the time we spend on Toby.

My ikebana teacher's husband had an ulcer operation a couple weeks ago and he came home yesterday. He only eats Japanese food so I can't take anything I might prepare. I've decided to take a cantaloupe. We have been buying tiny cantaloupes lately. They seem to be sweeter than the larger ones.

When we have our health, we have everything, don't we? Money cannot be compared to health.

MAY 12, 1989

Dear Isabel,

Today was Gene's last bowling session for the year and we invited Leon to have dinner with us. Leon picks Gene up each Friday and brings him home so this means I can have the car. We are happy to invite Leon for dinner.

I went alone to visit Toby today. I met Leta coming out and she said Toby had just gone for radiation. I returned home and worked on my dinner and went back a couple hours later. Toby was alert and immediately asked about Gene's plumbing experience. Last week Leta reported one toilet ran all the time. She wanted to know what plumber to call. I said no plumber. Gene would fix it. We stopped on the way home and Gene tightened something and that fixed it. Toby wanted to pay Gene and when I said no, he said at least they could pay for parts. We had a bit more conversation and then Toby asked me to close the door because he was cold. I suggested we put his pajama tops over the hospital nightie to keep his arms warm. I told Toby I was going to put my arms around him but I didn't think Leta would mind and he smiled. He doesn't have enough strength to raise up, even from a sitting position. So I rested him against me and then put his arms in the pajama top. This formerly big man is now a featherweight. We talked a little and then I left. This was one of his better days as far as I'm concerned but this may not have lasted more then minutes. Leta didn't find him lucid this morning.

We just had dinner home today but tomorrow we plan to go to the NUT Tree. Toby's condition may change our plans, though. For a period this morning he was not conscious. This afternoon his eyes fluttered and then he slept. The end is near.

Yesterday Leta moved in with us and she will stay till after Toby departs this earth. Last night the doctors told her that if she wanted to say anything to Toby, that was the time.

This morning she went over early to give him his breakfast and then she called us. The doctor was there and told her this probably was the day. So we went over to be with her. I doubt Toby knew we spent the morning there. The physical therapist came and made Toby do some arm and leg exercises. Then they took him down for radiation. WHY! We came home for lunch and as soon as I finish this, I'll go back till 3. Gene will go and stay till 5 and then Leta will take over. Leta will come home and take a nap while Gene is there. She doesn't sleep nights.

MAY 18, 1989

Our days are so mixed up now. Everything is running together in my mind. The routine now is that Leta goes to the hospital at about 8 and stays till 1 PM when I relieve her and Gene comes at 3 and relieves me. At 5 Leta returns and stays till Toby is bedded down for the night. Toby appears to sleep most of the time. Leta talks to him but I just tell him I'm there when I come and say good-bye when I leave. I don't know if this registers.

I cry because I remember this handsome, well adjusted, super intelligent, friendly person who was always so interesting. What I see is a human body wasting away and unable to communicate. To me this is a living hell. It is so undignified.

We canceled everything this week. Few friends come now that Toby isn't conscious. In fact, only one comes.

Tuesday Leta was leaving the hospital parking lot which is immense but still not big enough for all the cars. A man wanted her place and he didn't wait for her to go forward and attempted to get in her spot and hit her bumper. He backed up and took part of her bumper. She was so upset she didn't get his insurance information. The man said you take care of your car and I'll take care of mine. His was more damaged than Leta's. Toby gave Leta this VW for Christmas. When I told Gene about this, he said he would look at it in the morning and maybe he could fix it. The black part of the bumper clamps on to the main bumper and Gene was able to put it together but there are two little holes in it.

One night this week my mother met Leta in the hall as she was going to bed and they stopped. My mother said, "I could say a lot to you, but it would be just words." Leta came and told us this and later I heard her telling others. She felt more was said in those words then all the talk others had said to her. I was proud of my ninety six year old mother.

Most nurses are good but last night Leta asked one to do something for Toby and the nurse said Toby had a fever and she couldn't do it. The doctor stopped in a couple minutes later and Leta told him that the nurse said she couldn't do this because Toby had a fever. The doctor said Toby never had a fever and he checked and Toby didn't. After the doctor left, the nurse came back and Leta told the nurse that the doctor said Toby did not have a fever. The nurse popped the thermometer in Toby's mouth and when she took it out, she said, "Well, how about that!" Was the nurse lazy or just perverse?

Actually I think John Muir Hospital is an excellent hospital and I was pleased when my mother was there. Oncology is a whole different world. Many there are terminal. Most don't stay as long as Toby. Toby is lucky they are keeping him. They will keep him as long as they are treating him and I think that is why they give radiation every day, even when they know it is useless.

I can't sleep nights and so Gene and I overslept this morning. My mother came and pounded on our bedroom door. We both were startled and jumped out of bed. I lost my balance and grabbed the bureau. Gene was so groggy he came crashing down, knocked the lamp off the bureau and landed at my feet. I was in a panic. I asked Gene if he was hurt and rushed to open the door and see what was the matter with my mother. She thought we were sleeping too long and wanted her breakfast. I could have shaken her! Both Gene and I could have broken bones. Thank Goodness, we didn't.

JUNE 1, 1989

Dear Mary and Dave,

When Toby's blood pressure fell on Monday, I knew the end was near. Toby was comatose when I stopped after my permanent. Leta sent me home and asked for Gene to come. When Gene came home, I called and said I would come in the evening but Leta thought she should come home for a brief rest and advised me to do the same.

After a bath, she was called to the phone and it was while she was talking to a friend that the conversation was interrupted by the operator who said she had an urgent call for this number. The friend hung up and Leta was told Toby died at 8:45 PM.

The convalescent hospital had called the undertaker but we felt we should go and collect Toby's things and see that things were done properly. We were there by 9:30 but the undertaker did not come till 11:30. I made repeated calls. My guess is that the driver would have waited till morning since Toby was to be cremated.

Our short driveway has a curve and in his excitement Gene backed into the door of Leta's car which was parked there. It was a gentle bump but it made a dent in the door.

None of us slept Tuesday night. Wednesday we had to go to the mortuary where papers had to be signed, obituary written and decisions made. Today we went to Oakland to the mausoleum. Leta had to decided whether to use the family niche or buy a new one just for the two of them. She finally decided to buy one just for them.

Tonight the internist called Leta. He is a very caring man and it was a comfort for Leta to talk to him. None of the other five doctors called. Other calls have come. Some are welcome and say the right things but some say things which hurt even though they aren't mea

Today would have been their 50th wedding anniver
brated it by going to the mausoleum! Toby died two da

Toby had said he didn't want a service but people
to have one. Suggestions were made to Leta and we
nothing appealed. Both Leta and Toby liked the Northbrae Co..
Church in Berkeley so we visited it and Leta decided this was the place.
At first the service was to be in the fellowship parlor but then the minister
took us into the chapel. I have never seen such a beautiful church. Leta
still favored the simplicity of the parlor till we were ready to drive out of
the parking lot and then she changed her mind. I went back in and told
the minister the service would be in the chapel. The ladies of the church
will serve coffee, tea and nut bread after the fifteen minute service.

Leta says we are a buffer between her and reality. True.

So the memorial service will be Friday, the 9th, Leta's birthday. What
a way to celebrate a birthday!

Saturday we had invited Maryann and Dick for dinner. Leta ate with
us and entered into the conversation and it was a restful break from the
sadness of the week.

Sunday Leta had to decide what dress to wear to the memorial. A
couple months ago she had purchased a new dress to wear when they
went to out to dinner on their 50th anniversary. It was a lovely print chiffon over lavender but it had a party look and this was no party. She chose
a yellow shirtwaist chiffon which was dressy but not too dressy.

Boy, has our life ever changed since May 1st and especially the last
week. I wonder if it will ever return to normal.

JULY 16, 1989

Dear Emma and John,

A couple weeks ago there was an article in our newspaper about
parking in San Francisco. I know parking is a problem in many places
but in San Francisco it is unique because San Francisco is on a peninsula
and there is no place to expand. The only way is UP. S.F. has the highest
density of cars in the world, 10,000 per square mile. Each day there are
280,000 more cars in San Francisco than there are parking places and each
day two hundred fifty illegally parked cars are towed away. Each week
the tow company auctions off fifty unclaimed cars.

Even parking in front of your own home is a problem so now residents pay $13 a year to park in front of their own homes but it doesn't
guarantee a spot will be available. One resident in San Francisco tells his
friends, "If you want to visit me, you will have to parachute in." However,
San Francisco does benefit from the problem in this way—San Francisco

.es in $40 million from parking citations yearly and $40,000 per day .om parking meters. Do you wonder we always take BART into S.F.?

Yesterday Leta left us for Kensington Place, an active retirement community. It is new and only half full. Each resident has a little apartment, bedroom, bath, living room and small kitchen. You must take one meal a day in the dining room but you may have all three it you desire. Leta choose to have lunch and dinner in the dining room. Cleaning and washing is included in the monthly fee. It is like an apartment hotel and is most attractive. I hope Leta will be happy there but she really wants a life care place. If you become permanently ill, you cannot stay there.

Our friend Russ had a stroke June 20th, right after breakfast. Wilma called 911 and Russ was taken to Kaiser. Wilma was told Russ would go home in two hours and was sent to buy medicine but before the two hours were up, Russ was paralyzed and comatose and he remained this way till July 14th when he died. Although Wilma has a driver's license, she seldom drives and she refused to drive to the hospital. For 10 days neighbors took her. Then she didn't get to the hospital at all for 4 days. I took her once and then the minister started taking her. I was unimpressed with Kaiser's care of Russ. It may be cheaper but I think it doesn't compare favorably with care at John Muir.

Yesterday for his 80th birthday Leon, Gene's bowling pal, was given a party by his son. Guests were family with children, and a few friends. The invitation was for 2 PM and no presents. Did this mean birthday cake and drinks Lunch? dinner?. We assumed just birthday cake.

The son's home was circled with streamers saying HAPPY BIRTH-DAY BASH. So many cars caused us to have to park on another street and walk quite a way.

When we arrived, we found a complete bar and lots of cold soft drinks which were consumed more than the liquor because it was a very hot day.

At one point Leon was talking to some men when suddenly he lost consciousness. 911 was called. He was put in a reclining chair and ice was put on his head. Oxygen and an EKG were administered. Leon refused to go to the hospital. Leon had previously told us this happened to him recently three other times and none of these times had he even had a drink. I felt the party should be over and we should go home but others felt Leon would be hurt. So we stayed. My guess is that Leon had had only breakfast. The temperature was over 90. These two things could cause him to faint.

More than 100 people attended but by five o'clock half of them had gone home. The grandson told us dinner would be served so we rushed home and prepared a meal for my mother and then went back to the party. Dinner was wonderful with a great variety of food. Leon's dance band played music the first part of the party and then some young professionals in tux came and played the rest of the time. After dinner there was a magician and he was excellent. At 8:30 PM just before the two birthday cakes were cut, Gene insisted we had to leave because something, probably a spice or the barbecue sauce, had not agreed with him. We didn't get a piece of cake.

The son's home is so large that it required two big air conditioners. The backyard was concrete on one side and a pool on the other side. The back of the yard was a big bank that went to the street above. On top of the bank was a gazebo and this is where the musicians played. Many tables were set up and each had a plastic awning over it. There was an enormous barbecue built of bricks. A couple times a year the son and his wife entertain big groups in this back yard. The son is in the insurance business. I suspect some of the entertaining may be associated with business. They must have had lots of practice because they entertain beautifully.

Hal is another of Gene's bowling pals. He is widowed and lives alone in Lafayette. Next Friday he will be 79. He remarked during the party that on his birthday, he would wake up and say to himself, "Happy Birthday, Hal" and that would be his celebration. This made me feel sad so when we got home, I asked Gene if we could invite him Thursday night when I'm having a birthday dinner for Mary and Gene said yes. I'll bake two cakes and we will celebrate both Mary's and Hal's birthday.

Today's paper had an article on the front page about the selling price of homes in this area. Realtors laugh when anyone asks for a $100,000 home. You need to start at $200,000 here. Prices have gone sky high this year.

Flour catastrophe

the BIG ONE? Kate again

AUGUST 10, 1989

Dear Marge and Roy.

This isn't my day

This morning as I cleaned the sink, I noticed that the water from the faucet was dirty. I didn't understand why but I didn't say anything to Gene. Then I went to take a bath and I had a tub full of dirty gray water so I called Gene. Earlier he had noticed the toilet water like this. I called the water department and they came out. It is now 2:30 and the water is clean again. I don't know what they did but, whatever, it solved the problem.

After lunch I decided to make a ham roll for dinner. New recipe but it looked good. Ground ham, cheese, onion and mushrooms are rolled in pie crust and baked. The cupboards in this house are just a little too high for me and I have to stand on tip toe to get things down. Well, I didn't get a good grip on the flour and five pounds of flour fell out on me, the stove and the floor and I said, "Damn." Gene just filled the canister yesterday. What a mess. We got out the vacuum cleaner and sucked it all up. I think I'd better not try to do anything more today.

On our June vacation, we took one big suitcase for both and we hoped to do the same on this trip. My clothes are all packed, except for a raincoat. I read that it rains a lot in Austria so I mentioned to Gene that we both better take a raincoat. That was too much so we had to unpack the suitcase and repack two smaller suitcases. Gene isn't happy. He thinks I'm taking too much. Maybe so but I have to be prepared for both summer weather and cool weather in the mountains.

I know Europeans do not wear pants as much as we do so I have four dresses but all are light weight. Gene just tried to talk me into removing some clothes I packed. No soap. Maybe I'll have room for purchases with two suitcases.

Connie and Andrea from Boston are in San Francisco and will come for a visit on Saturday morning. We'll have Sunday together and they will leave on Monday morning. I'll wash the towels and linens and clean the two bedrooms after they leave. On Tuesday I'll clean the house and Wednesday I'll finish shopping for Mother and Connie. I have 23 days of meat and fish in the freezer so I'll only have to buy fruits and vegetables. They will have to buy fresh things a couple times while we are gone. I have all the menus prepared and all the recipes typed. It isn't simple to take a vacation and also prepare for Mother and Connie.

Well, enough of this. I'll try not to do anything more today. Maybe tomorrow will be better for me. I just hope I don't spill anymore flour.

OCTOBER 18, 1989

Dear Eunice and John,

Last night just as we three sat down to eat our dinner, our chairs began to move and I said, "EARTHQUAKE". Gene had placed some teriyaki chicken wings on my plate before he went to the garage to check our gas hot water heater. It is attached to the wall and was o.k. Then Gene went through the house. He found the bedroom and bathroom doors had closed. Mother and I just sat and said nothing. We were too frightened. This was the worst quake we ever experienced and we later learned it was the worst since 1906. It seemed to last so long and we just rolled from side to side. I saw the hanging plants outside the dining room window swing wildly and the chain on the cuckoo clock was really swinging. After Gene came back to the table, we served dinner and ate.

The first quake was at 5:04 and all electricity went off. Gene got his battery operated radio and put it on the table. We felt two more quakes and the radio announcer felt them too. One came at 5:25 and the other at 5:30, the first being a 4.8 and the second a 4.5. I finished dinner and started washing the dishes. While I was standing at the sink, the floor began to roll and the roses outside the window were waving back and forth. This was a 5.4 quake. These 4 and 5 quakes we have experienced before and we are used to them but the 7.0 lasted so long. It really was frightening. For dessert we had a choice of fruit, cookies, ice cream, but I decided we would have none of these. Colette gave us a can of pudding, Mont Blanc les pastels. She had served it and it was wonderful. I had been saving it for a special occasion. The radio said this probably wasn't the BIG ONE. Well, I decided that if the big one was still to come, we would at least have this dessert. Who knows if we will survive the big one. So we ate it. This pudding has fruits exotiques. I don't have a French-English dictionary so I cannot tell you what they are.

At one point during dinner I went outside and looked at our new front roof. Gene went out back and checked the roof and chimney there. They seemed to be o.k. but you should have heard the tiles on our roof moving against each other. What a noise.

At 6:41 PM we again had electricity so we turned on the TV. The TV stations were operating on emergency power and now almost a whole day later still are. Electricity has not been restored in San Francisco. Stop lights are not working and neither are the telephones.

At one point we saw neighbors outdoors and I went out to talk to them. The Smiths were walking home from Bart and Sid said he walked as though he were drunk. Linda said she thought she had suddenly become very dizzy. Hing was at work a few blocks away and he said his building shook. When he arrived home, he found everything on the kitchen table was on the floor. Sue works in San Francisco and at the time Hing didn't know about her. Before we went to bed we called Hing and our phones were working. Sue had called and she had to walk down 42 floors in the Bank of America building. She was going to stay overnight with her mother-in-law in San Francisco. We tried to call Maryann in Campbell but we couldn't get through. Today Sue called me at noon. She reported that it took six hours to walk down those forty two flights of stairs and find surface transportation to the Golden Gate area of San Francisco. Her legs hurt terribly. She talked to her boss today and he was stuck in an elevator in the Bank of America building for three hours. The boss said nobody was to report to work till the building had been checked. Today BART was running so Sue came home.

Kathy, next door, was having a conference with five teachers from her school. We saw the teachers run from her house to their cars and head home. After checking their homes, they returned and worked till 10:30 PM. Roger teaches on Tuesday nights so he left his law office a bit early and was in Oakland when the quake came. He and ten other men crowded into a stranger's van and came home. Their swimming pool really was creating waves and overflowing.

All evening we were glued to TV. We were so lucky here and we are grateful. After we went to bed there were some strong aftershocks but we didn't feel them. Just before we went to bed we heard on TV that the Red and White fleet was going to ferry people from Market Street in San Francisco to Jack London Square in Oakland. They were trying to get buses to take people to the BART station. Eventually some people did get home very late last night. People in hotels in San Francisco had no lights. The fires were terrible. Worse was the collapse of 880 in Oakland. Our TV has been on every waking moment.

This morning at 5 AM Connie H called from Cincinnati where she had gone Monday. She saw the earthquake news on TV but nothing about Rossmoor. I reported all was well at our house and I had not heard of any damage at Rossmoor.

Wilma called and her electricity hadn't come back as soon as ours. She lit candles and her smoke alarm went off so she called 911. They told her to open her windows and they came to investigate. They said the candles were the cause of the smoke alarm going off and to douse the candles.

Right after dinner Gene got out candles and flashlights but we didn't need either.

Gene and I went grocery shopping this morning. The first store, Fry's, closed last night and didn't open till 7 this morning. All aisles were three feet deep with stuff from the shelves. Worst was the liquor section. No carts were available because all were being used to put stuff back on the shelves. It took them fourteen hours to clean up. Another store was closed seven hours and three were closed four hours each. All reported the liquor sections were the most badly damaged. The stores had a different smell. Liquor. This afternoon I went to a drug store and the smell there was a sweet smell, mouthwash, shaving lotions, perfume.

Today the TV reported that Bechtel was asking all their structural and civil engineers to report immediately. Good old Bechtel to the rescue.

Friends and relatives have been calling all day and, boy, do we appreciate the interest they have taken in us.

On TV people were asked not to light matches or candles last night and today because gas mains have been broken and gas is escaping. They never said don't smoke. Just don't light a match or lighter. I wonder if the smokers got the message.

My ikebana teacher called this morning. She lives on top of a mountain and has a wonderful view. She checked her house and the chimney had separated from the house. She had a flower arrangement on top of her TV. It fell over and broke. She had some special vases on display and two of these fell and broke.

I called the women who were to go to S.F. with me Friday and said no way would I drive north or south and try to get into San Francisco.

Nobody expected it.

Leta was on her way to dinner when the lights went out. She returned to her apartment and went to bed. She never looks at TV or reads a paper. At a sorority meeting next day, she heard people talking about a canceled world series but she paid little attention because she wasn't interested in sports. She knew nothing of the Bay bridge collapse, the 880 collapse or the fire in S.F. I couldn't believe this.

My mother just came out and she wanted her medicine so she could go to bed. She said she is depressed. Too much bad news all last evening and all day and it gets worse. At ninety five she knows what is going on and frequently call us to tell us to look the station she is looking at. Thank God, she still has an alert mind and can feel the enormity and sadness of this catastrophe.

When the quake occurred some drivers of cars on the bridge thought they had flat tires or mechanical difficulties. When they realized it was an earthquake and that part of the bridge was gone, many abandoned their cars and ran backward to land. That is a long bridge. So tow trucks were called and cars were hauled back to Oakland if they were on that side of the break. If on the other side, they were hauled to San Francisco. Then crews and emergency personnel could get to the site. Tonight the TV is telling people who abandoned cars to come and get them and that there will be no charge for towing. People are really scared when they abandon a car because cars today cost a bundle but what is money compared to your life

It is now 9:45 PM the day after the earthquake and I was just able to get Maryann in Campbell. Maryann had chosen Waterford Crystal when she married and had a cabinet full of it. The cabinet doors opened and the crystal fell on the floor and broke. One of Dick's speakers was broken. His turntable was tossed to the floor. The refrigerator door came open and stuff fell out on the floor. Kitchen cabinet doors opened and stuff fell out and broke. Juices. etc. Maryann said she washed her kitchen floor four times today. Everything in the bedroom was tossed around and in some cases thrown from one side of the room and hit the opposite wall. Marks were left on the wall. Every room had some damage. Dick's books and records all ended up on the floor. As of this moment they don't have electricity or water. Maryann plans to go to work at Apple tomorrow and will take a shower there. Their sidewalk has buckled. They don't have earthquake insurance. Almost nobody does because it is so expensive and the deductible is so great. I feel so sorry for them.

Yesterday morning we shopped for groceries and after that we were glued to TV right up till the time we pulled up the blankets, turned off the light and went to sleep. This morning I baked bread because we had only one slice left. Between 8 and 10 we have had at least four phone calls, one from Kaoru in Japan, one from Ingrid and Jan in Norway and another from Italy, collect, from somebody we never heard of.

We heard on TV this morning that a few cars have been unearthed from the collapse of the upper highway onto the lower highway, maybe 5 out of the 200-250. The cars were flattened so that they were ten inches high. On one program a doctor said the people in the cars were so crushed that bodies were the width of a dime.

We heard on TV today that there have been 1400 aftershocks but we did not feel them.

We live in the East Bay and going from our house into San Francisco is twenty-five miles. If we had to drive into San Francisco we could go north and over the Richmond and then the Golden Gate Bridge or we could go south and over the San Mateo bridges, but this would be a long way. We won't even go in by BART. The ferries have helped business people.

People are really shaken up. Strangers talk to you about the earthquake when you are in public. Today we aren't turning on TV except for the news. Seeing this tragedy gets just too depressing. We don't see that there is anything Gene and I could do to help.

I thought you might be interested in the nitty gritty.

NOVEMBER 3, 1989

Dear Mary,

Our life certainly has been different these past few days. At 9 AM on Halloween Connie, Linda and Bob dropped off Kate. Then Connie drove Bob and Linda to the airport and they took off for a medical convention in Phoenix. For a minute Kate cried but immediately I took her to see her surprise and all tears stopped. We brought the doll house out in the living room and put it on a card table, along with all the furniture. Actually we had more furniture then the house would hold. Gene's week of making furniture brought much joy to Kate and she really played with the doll house.

This morning we went grocery shopping. Usually we do six stores on Wednesday morning but Tuesday, before Kate came, we did two so we only had four left to do. Kate yawned all morning. I thought she was tired. We had lunch and I had prepared a noodle dish with shrimp and peas. When Kate saw the one dish on the table, she asked us why we didn't have lots of things on the table. I said we would for dinner but this was lunch. Kate is never a good eater so I wasn't surprised when she ate almost nothing. I baked special cookies for her. She took a bite and said she didn't like them. I think she ate some banana and maybe a few grapes. That was all. After lunch I put her down for a nap and she slept three hours.

Connie came for dinner and we had a turkey meat loaf, asparagus, cauliflower, and cabbage salad. Again Kate ate almost nothing. Connie sad this was par for the course. Halloween we dressed Kate in her ballerina costume that Linda brought. She had never been trick or treating because they live in a remote area on a lake and theirs is the only year around house. Gene and Connie were to take Kate trick or treating and I was staying home to give out candy but Kate wouldn't go unless I went with them. I went to the houses on the court and then I returned home and Gene and Kate and her grandmother went to a few more. Kate was timid about this. We didn't have many children. Kate always went to the door with Gene when the kids came. Some little kids were adorable. One little boy was a bumblebee. After Kate's grandmother left, I gave Kate a bath and put her to bed. It was 10 PM. I checked her a couple of times and she wasn't asleep. The third time I checked, she was crying softly. She said she wanted her mummy and daddy. I called Gene and he carried her out to the family room and I rocked her. Then Gene took over the rocking while I undressed. We put her back in bed and all was o.k. I can understand this. It has been a year since she saw us and being with strangers at this age is trying.

Wednesday we shopped again. In the first store Kate said she wanted a doughnut with chocolate on top. I said we would not buy it in that store but in another store where the doughnuts were better. Kate accepted this. When we finally bought the doughnut, we sampled a pumpkin doughnut and decided to buy three for us. Kate piped up and said she also wanted a pumpkin doughnut. She is a smart little thing and she knew that 4 doughnuts were needed. That afternoon I had a hard time getting her to nap and she really had only twenty minutes before her grandmother arrived. With a lack of rest, she was out of sorts.

After dinner, I rocked her. Connie said she would do this but Kate would have nothing to do with Connie. This really hurt Connie.

Kate wanted me to play with her and her doll house so I did. I had the mummy and daddy going to a party. Next night when Connie played with Kate, she had the daddy going to work and the mommy working at home. I was lying on the sofa end I laughed because this certainly showed our personalities. Connie is a workalcoholic, working nights, Saturdays and Sundays often. She talks a lot about her work. I always felt you left work at the workplace and seldom brought work home. Gene never talked about work at home.

We had learned from the night before so this night I held and rocked Kate before putting her to bed. Gene also held her and rocked her. Kate is apparently used to lots of cuddling and we both were willing. In bed, she was quiet but she wasn't asleep at 10:30 when we went to bed. I understand this is normal but not desirable.

Tonight Kate went into my mother's room while she was watching TV and she jumped and jumped on my mother's bed. My mother didn't say anything. For somebody ninety six she certainly put up with a lot from Kate. I think all the commotion made for interest in my mother's bland life,

Thursday morning we let Kate sleep as long as she liked and she woke smiling. I had a doctor's appointment at 11:30 and Gene and Kate accompanied me and sat in the waiting room. Kate had some sewing cards and she did these while waiting. Afterwards we stopped at a grocery store to get something on sale which hadn't come in yesterday. At the check out Kate pointed out something and I thought she meant a man at the far end of the store was Gene. I said no but she still kept pointing. Finally I realized she wanted something hanging in a plastic bag. It looked like cotton cloth, maybe cotton panties. I said no. Then she said it was cotton candy. I looked and that is what the label said. What awful looking cotton candy! I said no and Kate threw a tantrum. Wow! We had never seen this before. When Gene attempted to lift her from the cart, she flexed her knees and held on with her hands and he couldn't get her out. Finally she let me take her out. I put her on the ground and I thought she was going to run away. Gene picked her up and put her in the car seat and was she mad at Gene! She could do it herself, she said. Lots of screaming on the way home. When Gene tried to help her out of the car she went to the other door and would only let me help her.

Once in the house she returned to normal and after lunch we went out doors so she could blow bubbles with the bubble pipe we had for her. She didn't want to come in. Finally I did get her in bed by 3 PM. Shortly after that her grandmother arrived and she woke Kate. Kate wasn't rested and had lots more tears and ate no dinner at all. Connie decided to take tomorrow off and take Kate home with her that night. I didn't think she should but she is the grandmother. Connie said they were having a cake and ice cream at work in the afternoon so she would take Kate with her to this. Connie had to pick Linda and Bob up at the airport at 5 PM so this meant Kate would have no nap. Connie said Kate could sleep on the way to the airport.

Next day Connie changed her mind and went to work as usual in the morning and took Kate with her. How she got past security with a child I don 't know. Connie 's boss said nothing but the boss of her boss said the child should not be there. Connie, however, did not leave. In the late afternoon Kate fell asleep. Somebody carried Kate to Connie's car. At the airport Connie tried to wake Kate. Kate raised a terrible fuss. Connie didn't want to leave her locked in the car so she dragged her, screaming, into the airport. When they arrived here for dinner, Kate was still carrying on. Even the parents couldn't quiet her down. She ran into HER bedroom and screamed and we tried to eat dinner. Finally Bob went in and after a considerable time, she quieted down and came out to the table for her grandmother's birthday cake. She was her sweet self the rest of the evening.

From all this, I deducted. Kate needs to go to bed early each night and she needs a nap each day.

On this visit, Gene really enjoyed Kate and she was loving with him till we refused the cotton candy. Gene said we won the battle but lost the war. I felt like a failure but when Kate acted like she did last night and her parents were here, I no longer felt like a failure. After dinner when she returned to normal, Gene and I were back in her favor. Thank goodness.

NOVEMBER 27, 1989

Dear Colette,

Thanksgiving weekend is over and things are back to normal.

On Wednesday before Thanksgiving I drove to Orinda to pick up Wilma. She only learned to drive this year and she says she is too nervous to drive here, even by the back roads. I told Wilma to bring something to do because I would be busy with my Thanksgiving dinner and unable to entertain her. I also told her we would not have breakfast till after the turkey was in the oven and the pie made.

Hal, Gene's bowling pal, came at 1:30 and we ate at 2. The stuffing this year was part whole wheat and it was tasty. After dinner we asked our guests if they wanted to see our vacation pictures and both did so we showed Disneyworld and Virginia. Then we had the pie which we were too stuffed to eat at the end of the meal. Our guests were game for more slides so we showed France. It was almost 8 when Hal went home. It was a lovely day for us because we had company and it reduced the loneliness for Wilma and Hal.

Hal's wife has been dead for some years and he lives alone. His daughter lives in Arkansas. Hal is most appreciative of home cooked meals and he makes me feel good about my cooking with his compliments which are sincere and not overdone.

Wilma worked all her life till retirement. Wilma said she and Russ never had an overnight guest or stayed overnight with anyone in all their fifty years of marriage. Hotel overnights were all she knew. We met Wilma and Russ on our trip to Alaska and later invited them to dinner. They returned the invitation and I think this was their first entertaining. When both worked, they ate their evening meal in San Francisco so that they could avoid the commute rush. I took Wilma home Friday morning and Saturday Wilma called and said she had had three days of no crying and she had her first whole night of sleep. Since Russ died, she has cried every day and spent part of each night looking at TV in bed.

Today Wilma called and said a niece of Russ' had visited her yesterday. The niece had never seen Wilma or Russ and she is about 50 years old. The niece wanted to see where Russ is buried. He isn't buried. He was cremated and his ashes are behind the altar in the church waiting till the church builds a mausoleum. There are three or four other boxes of ashes there. Wilma opened the door and stepped inside and fell into the organ. She was hurt but didn't immediately go to the hospital. After a couple hours, she went and she has a broken rib. Wilma said 1989 was the worst year of her whole life. Wilma wasn't crying so maybe being with us did help.

Wilma called yesterday and asked if Gene end I would attend a cock-tail party on Dec. 20th at the Orinda Country Club. She had an invitation from a realtor who was giving the party and Wilma wanted us to go as her guests. I thought the realtor was inviting people who would be apt to sell or buy a house in Orinda and we would do neither. Since we did not have an invitation from the realtor, I felt we would be crashing the party so I refused. Wilma and Russ went last year and Wilma said the hors d'ouevres were out of this world and the Country Club was beautifully decorated. I would like to have gone but I felt we would be like a fish out of water since we do not have MONEY and only people with MONEY can afford to live in Orinda.

Wilma's house is located on the golf course pond and its water is used for the lawns of the golf course. Wilma and Russ built their house right after WWII and it is the smallest house in Orinda, I bet. Our house is three or four times as large, newer and more modern, yet Wilma's house, because of location, would sell for twice what ours would.

I called a neighbor who used to be a realtor and told her of this invi-tation. She said we should have accepted because realtors give affairs like this to make contacts and they are tax write-offs. She said the more who come, the better for the realtor. Still I would have felt we were party crashing.

DECEMBER 14, 1989

Dear Jennie,

Not having the use of my word processor has really crimped my style. I just don't write letters because I now hate to use my manual type-writer. Supposedly the print head has been shipped and I should have it by Christmas and then I'll be back in the letter writing business.

Friday the 8th I drove over the Bay Bridge and it didn't fall in! Traffic was light because people haven't returned to driving to work in San Francisco The off ramps I used were not damaged and everything was normal in Golden Gate Park.

Sunday the 10th Connie invited us to have dinner with her at the Officers Club at Alameda Air Station where she works as a chemist. Civilian employees of high rank are entitled to use the club and they may bring guests. It was buffet with forty eight different dishes. We sampled only a few and were too stuffed for dessert. My mother was thrilled because the dining room was decorated for Christmas and there was an orchestra for dancing. We returned to Frank's and played some bridge and then came home early. Again my mother was thrilled because she saw all the Christmas lights. It was a treat for her to be out at night.

Monday we were invited to Mary and Bud's for lunch but what she really served was dinner. I had left a roast in the oven for dinner but we couldn't eat it. Tuesday I needed to deliver a package in Danville and my mother needed more jig saw puzzles so we drove there. Gene went along and we made a stop at the bank for him. Lunch time came along and we were near the Courtyard in Alamo so we had lunch. Gene had never eaten here but this is a favorite place for my mother and me. The Courtyard is a tiny restaurant run by two good cooks. The prices are low and quantities more than sufficient. Places like this are rare in this area.

I consider my pelvis healed and walk normally but Friday at the ikebana meeting I sat for two hours on a metal folding chair. I mentioned my discomfort to the person next to me. She was in just as much discomfort. She has a small behind and no fat to protect her bones. My pain was not due to lack of fat! At this meeting we were supposed to bring something for sale, profits to go to the treasury. I took two loaves of Mediterranean bread, each of which contained a jar of ripe and green olives. I priced the bread at $3.50 and wondered if anyone would buy it. I apologized for the cost but explained that the olives increased the price. Immediately one of the sellers bought a loaf and the woman standing next to me bought the other one. So my bread never got on display for sale.

I may have mentioned that a few weeks ago I thought my mother was losing her memory. She couldn't find things she bought. Once she couldn't find the car and it was right beside the store. Well, the problem isn't memory loss. It is eyesight. I took her to the ophthalmologist to have an eye test and her cataracts are now so bad that only a lens replacement would help. She decided not to have the operation. She can see up close but anything further than three feet she doesn't see.

I'm back in business. The print head arrived this noon and as soon as Gene gets home from bowling and installs it, 1'll be able to use my word processor again.

One night last week Tom Brokaw on the national news told about Black Hawk Market in Danville. A pianist at a grand piano plays constantly in this deluxe grocery store that caters to the wealthy who live in Black Hawk. Shelves are automated and when you remove something from a shelf, another item appears. Black Hawk is a very exclusive community with security gates, fancy golf club and houses several million dollars in cost. Today I took my mother to see the store. The piano was surrounded by poinsettias. Fruits and vegetables are artistically displayed, not piled on the counters. Tom mentioned that the piano playing originated in the Nordstrom stores on the west coast. These stores are as big as department stores but only sell clothes. In the center of each store is a grand piano with the pianist in formal attire. There are comfortable chairs for husbands not shopping in the men's department. Nordstroms requires clerks to buy their clothing in their store at a discount and to sign a statement that they will not chew gum while working. I never buy designer dresses but I look at them. They have terrific half yearly sales and that is when I buy. My mother and I lunch there often because they have a soup and half sandwich, with salad thrown in, for a low price and it is good.

Tomorrow we are putting up our Christmas tree. It is the best tree we ever had. So full and shapely.

Santa and chimney

My True Love Drove Me Nuts in 12 Days

CHRISTMAS 1989

Dear Ingrid and Jan,

The frost last year froze the orange blossoms so we have few oranges but what we do have are large. Today we ate an orange the size of a grapefruit.

Wilma reported the cocktail party at the Orinda Country Club was great. Women were dressed to the hilt in velvet and green satin dresses. The hors d' ouevres, both hot and cold, were delicious. This was probably the only chance I'll ever have to see the inside of that country club whose yearly fee for member ship is $40,000. The hostess asked Wilma why she hadn't brought guests so I guess we wouldn't have been party crashers if we had accepted.

Twice before Christmas we went out to see Christmas decorations. On a nearby court all the houses were decorated and the lawns were filled with Christmas objects. There was music. Traffic near the court was great. Parking was available only far away. In the opposite direction there was a street where one house was outstanding. There were three huts in the front yard and one had a see saw with teddy bears and another a carousel with teddy bears and another a Ferris wheel. Santa and his reindeer were on the roof. The yard was filled with lighted Christmas trees and there were four moving characters above the garage door. This place was shown on TV. I was so impressed we took Hal to see it Christmas night and he said he had never seen anything so grand.

Both Brittany Lane and Court were decorated this year. Our neighbor had a Santa on the roof. Another neighbor had twenty five luminaries on Christmas eve. Each luminary had a cut Christmas tree on two sides. These are bags filled with sand and have a votive candle. They light the way to the door. I had never seen them before.

We had a lovely Christmas. Hal came at 1:30 and he stayed till 9. Hal is close to his daughter in Arkansas and he speaks so lovingly of his dead wife. He is a thoroughly nice man and we enjoy his company, sense of humor and real intelligence.

I'm enclosing Gary Bogue's column which made me really laugh. I hope you enjoy it too.

Yesterday we read about a twenty year old man in L.A. who locked himself out of his house. He decided to get into the house by the chimney and then open the front door for his brother. He got down to the damper and then could go no farther. His father heard him calling and tried to call the fire department. Since both men spoke only Spanish, the fire department understood there was a problem but not exactly what. The fire department took the chimney apart to get the man out. The man was having difficulty breathing because soot got in his nose, throat and lungs.

It is a good thing little children can't read because they would never believe Santa comes down the chimney after this. When we got to bed Christmas Eve, Gene said he meant to climb up and take the screen off the top of our chimney. I told him Santa was smart enough to take the screen off before he came down. At any event Santa got in our house and our stockings were filled.

Last night at 9:30 Sue called from her mother's home in San Francisco where she was staying the night because of her parents' illnesses. Sue and Hing went into San Francisco on Tuesday to shop. Afterwards Sue got on BART and went to her parents and Hing came home. In the evening Sue called Hing and for four hours she got no answer. She wanted us to look and see if the car was in the drive. We looked and it wasn't. When we went to bed at 10:30, Hing still wasn't home. I was worried too. This morning the car was in the drive so I called Hing. He said he had decided to visit the Tower record store and he spent a couple hours there. Then he went to Whole Earth and spent another couple hours there. Next he had something to eat. Sue had left a message on the answering machine so when he got home, he called her. She chewed him out and he deserved it. Sue was so worried she reported him missing to the police.

After Christmas I went in a lovely card shop. They sell quality cards but I saw one that really turned me off. It was Santa's back in front of a urinal. I didn't look inside to see the message, I thought this was EXTREMELY TASTELESS.

Christmas is over and now we can return to our normal routine.

MY TRUE LOVE DROVE ME NUTS IN 12 DAYS
BY
GARY BOGUE

Dearest John:

I went to the door today and the postman delivered a partridge in a pear tree. What a thoroughly delightful and appropriate seasonal gift.

Jane

Dear John:

Today, the postman delivered your very sweet gift. Imagine — two turtle doves! I'm delighted with your thoughtful gift. How adorable.

Jane

Dear John:

Aren't you the extravagant swain! I really must protest — because I don't deserve such generosity. Three French hens. How darling.

Jane.

Dear John:

Today, the postman delivered four calling birds. Now really, don't you think enough is enough? You're being too, too romantic.

Jane

Dear John :

What a surprise! Today the postman delivered five golden rings — one for every finger. You're just impossible, but I love it, Those birds squawking are getting on my nerves.

Jane

Dear John:

Today there were actually six geese a-laying on my front porch. Back to the birds again, huh? Those geese are huge. The neighbors are complaining and I can't get any sleep at night because of the racket. Please stop.

Jane

Dear John:

What's with you and those %$#@! birds? Seven swans a-swimming? What kind of stupid joke is this? They mess all over my house and never stop making a racket. This isn't funny!

Jane

OK Bird-brain:

I think I prefer birds: What in blazes am I going to do with eight maids a-milking? it's not enough with all those birds a-laying, but the eight maids a-milking all had to bring their lousy cows. Just lay off me, you jerk!

Jane

Hey, Fathead :

What are you? Some kind of wealthy Yuppie sadist? Now there are nine pipers playing and boy, do they play. They haven't stopped chasing those maids since they got here yesterday morning. The neighbors have started a petition to have the city planning commission evict me from my own home. You'll get yours.

Jane

John, you lousy... :

Now there's 10 ladies dancing. I don't know why I call those harlots ladies. They've been necking with the pipers all night long. The building inspector has subpoenaed me to show cause why my house shouldn't be condemned. I am getting the police after you.

Jane

Pay attention, Fathead!:

What's with the 11 lords a-leaping after those maids and ladies? The pipers ran off with the maids and all 23 of those addled birds were trampled to death by the cows in the riot., you rotten, filthy swine.

Jane

Dear Sir:

This is to acknowledge the latest gift of 12 (12) fiddlers fiddling which you have seen fit to deliberately infliction upon our client, Miss Jane B.

All further correspondence regarding our ward should be addressed to our attention as court-appointed representatives of her affairs. If you should further attempt to contact Miss B. at the psychiatric sanitarium in which she is receiving therapy, attendants there have instructions to shoot you on sight.

With this letter, please find enclosed a copy of a warrant for your arrest. Your attorney may contact this office for further information....

Badger and Cajole
Attorneys at Law

From THE CONTRA COSTA TIMES
Saturday, December 23, 1989
PAGE 3 A

The 1990's

Dear Kathryn,

If my reading is as good the rest at the year as it has been these first seven days, it will be a wonderful reading year.

At the library on Friday I got A TWIST IN THE TAIL by Jeffrey Archer, which is a collection of short stories. Absolutely wonderful. It took only a couple hours to read it and each story did have a most unusual twist. Do try to get this book.

Years ago Gene bought a phonograph player because Westinghouse was selling them cheap. My mother has used it ever since she came to live with us. Something went wrong with the turntable and it revolves slowly so the music whines. It drove me batty. Gene tried to fix it. We tried to buy another like it but they don't make this kind any more. This one played several records consecutively and had a built in speaker. Now you need separate speakers and only one record at a time is put on the turntable. For more than a year it hasn't worked properly. We recently shopped and we ended up with a record player, tape player and radio all in one. We brought it home and my mother refused to use it. Our house was silent and my mother was out of sorts. I got tapes from the library and Gene played them. Two tapes would last an hour. She liked these oldies but refused to learn to use the machine. Then Gene turned on the radio and maybe this is the solution. Two music stations were o.k. but the third had all the songs she likes. I also like this easy listening music. With no music my mother's life was so barren but now with this her disposition has improved.

Now it is dinner time and I've been working all afternoon. I'm back to my old library ways. I ordered Princeton files which are used in libraries to hold magazines and pamphlets. We buy those pamphlet cooks books at the check out in grocery stores, Pillsbury, Betty Crocker, Favorite Recipes. I love them because they have pictures and give much nutritional information. I counted my cookbooks and I have 110 hard cover ones and 449 spirals and paperbacks, a total of 559 cookbooks. When my mother was keeping house, she had one cookbook. When I'm making out a menu for company, I sometimes go through 20 of these paperbacks.

Much has been made of the bridge damage from the earthquake but little was said about the public library in S.F. All the books fell off the shelves and shelves attached to the walls broke away and fell. Today the San Francisco library reopened. It took only a month for the massive job on the Bay Bridge but it has taken 3 months to repair the library. I know the Bay Bridge is terribly important for business but having the library closed would have been more of an inconvenience for me because I'm a reader.

Flu is prevalent here. Our neighbor, Hing, is home. I called and wanted to take him some soup but he said he was too ill to even come to the door to accept it. Sue has the flu too but she went to work. She said almost everyone in her department at Bank of Americn has the flu.

Wednesday we bought some hunks of cooked turkey for .99 a pound and it usually is $4.29. We had it for sandwiches for two lunches. I went back to get some more but this was a special sale for just a few hours and every piece was grabbed up. We were dumb not to have purchased several hunks. The butcher bought ten hunks.

Today I went to the library to get two specific books but no library in Contra Costa county had them. The library will contact other counties and even the state library and if they aren't successful, they will go national for the books. We have a good library system.

The circulation computer was down today so the library clerk had to write down library card numbers and accession numbers of each book I borrowed. When the bank computer goes down, the bank is out of business. At least the library can function when the computer goes down.

The administrator of our county library system is sixty-six and he is going to retire. He was interviewed and his interview was published in the newspaper. He said only two books on the present best seller list are any good. He also said Danielle Steele's books are trash and he wouldn't give her books time of day. Danielle Steele is a San Franciscan and is making plenty because her books are popular even though they are nothing but sex and high living. The library has many copies because they are so popular. I read a couple of Steele's books and I agree with the county librarian.

JANUARY 17, 1990

Dear Ivy and Hubert,

In my last letter I reported that the S.F. library had reopened after three months. Later I read in the newspaper that only a part of the second floor was open and it would be a long time before the north wing opened. So to date 170,000 volumes are available out of the 900,000. Apparently walls have to be repaired before the sheared stacks can be reattached. Books fell off the shelves here too but the shelves were not damaged and they quickly put the books back on the shelves.

We went shopping one day and Gene bought a birthday card for his brother which said:

HAPPY BIRTHDAY BROTHER

IT'S YOUR BIRTHDAY.
JUST THOUGHT I'D LET YOU KNOW,
CAUSE THEY SAY WHEN YOU GET OLDER,
YOUR MEMORY STARTS TO GO.
It struck a funny bone and I laughed till I cried.

Monday night we showed the slides of our trip. I made bread that day and gave each couple a loaf. Virginia's husband has the flu so Virginia came alone. Virginia presented Don with the loaf of bread when she got home. They went to bed and during the night Don got up and ate a piece of bread. He said the smell of the freshly baked bread was driving him wild and, flu or no flu, he had to have a piece. How's that for a loaf of bread?

I'm on a laughing jag. I am reading Jack Hanna's MONKEYS ON THE INTERSTATE AND OTHER ANIMAL TALES. There is a laugh on every page and sometimes two on a page.

The zoo had a five ton elephant which was especially ornery and liked to throw things. It was decided the elephant could be outdoors only when the zoo was closed. One day the zoo opened before they got him inside. A family were innocently walking around when the elephant reached up, pried loose a rock from the wall, hurled it and it struck the father smack in the middle of the forehead. He went down immediately, bleeding and knocked out. Nobody saw the stone strike so none of the family knew what laid Dad out but Jack saw the stone nearby and guessed what happened. The zoo paid the medical bills because the man had to have stitches and the zoo gave the family passes, posters and what not. The family were understanding and did not sue.

Another man on the same day tried to steal a coke from a machine. He had his hand halfway up the machine when it fell over on him and broke his arm. He threatened to sue but Jack had him thrown out of the zoo and wouldn't even listen to his threats to sue.

Another day a mother was walking thru the children's zoo with her children when her shoelace came untied. She bent down to tie it and a donkey mounted and humped her. The children laughed like crazy but she was frightened and embarrassed. When she got home, she was mad and called her lawyer and wanted to sue. Upon learn how public all this would be, she decided to drop the suit and avoid further embarrassment.

We just returned from our weekly grocery shopping and we bought two more cookbooks so now I have 601.

Monday I noticed our neighbor's third car was in their driveway and this indicates something is wrong because that is the car they drive to work. I was really busy so didn't call. In the afternoon Sue called from work in San Francisco. She thought I might have noticed the car, called and with no answer, I might be worried. She explained that we had a heavy frost last night and Hing didn't want to scrape the frost from the windows, so he took one of the cars in the garage. I laughed and said, boy, do we have these neighbors trained. They feel the need to report to us.

We are entertaining tonight so I made bread and will give each guest a loaf to take home. I also made chocolate cinnamon rolls from my 601st cookbook which is Betty Crocker's IN LOVE WITH CHOCOLATE. I had most of the ingredients in the mixer when I realized there was no cocoa or chocolate in the recipe. I reread the recipe. None. I got Gene out of the bathroom and made him read the recipe and he found no mention of chocolate or cocoa. What should I do? I threw in some cocoa. I immediately wrote a letter to Betty Crocker and asked for a corrected recipe. This is a February 1990 cookbook. I can't believe the testing kitchens of Betty Crocker could make such a mistake.

During the evening I told Frank I needed help from somebody smarter than I and, since he had a Ph D, maybe he could help me. I showed him the recipe for the rolls and asked him to tell me how much chocolate or cocoa the recipe specified. He read it twice and said he couldn't find any of either mentioned. Frank knew I was joking.

1/28/90

Apparently the chocolate-cinnamon rolls were a success. Gene, my mother and I had one each. There were 12. When our guests went home, there was half a roll left so two people ate 9 cinnamon rolls. They really loved them.

I went for some blood work Thursday and the nurse said a pipe under her kitchen sink sprang a leak and she had to have buckets there for three days because she couldn't get a plumber. All she called said that due to the earthquake pipes were breaking now, three months after the earthquake, and the plumbers couldn't keep up with the demand. Last week I took my mother to the doctor and during the night the U shaped faucet in a small lab broke and water spurted out all night and one room and the hall of his office were flooded. San Francisco has been having lots of breaks in the water lines and streets have been flooded, all due to the earthquake.

1/30/90

Tomorrow is Gene's birthday and I baked a cake from a mix but I wish I had made it from scratch because I have two wonderful chocolate cake recipes. Gene always wants chocolate cake on his birthday.

Sunday we had duck for dinner and I'll never do a duck again.

Because you want the skin crisp and all the fat out of the duck, you don't cover it. You know the state of the oven after this. Cleaning the oven is one job I hate. If ever we get a new oven, we'll get a self cleaning one. From now on I'm eating duck only in a restaurant,

We saw walnut oil in a store today and I bought a bottle. I've been looking for it ever since we returned from France. Colette served a salad of lettuce and tomatoes with a dressing of red wine and walnut oil and it was delicious, but best of all walnut oil has no cholesterol.

Speaking of cholesterol, Frank had two procedures to rid his arteries of cholesterol plaque. Before the operations, his arteries were 90% blocked and now after the procedures and eating only fish and chicken, no fat, his arteries are 90% open. He no longer has angina pain and is most active. Isn't that wonderful?

JANUARY 31, 1990

Today is Gene's big day. We drove to Oakland and had lunch at Jack London Square, which is right on the bay. Because it was foggy, the view wasn't much. The food was good, but not gourmet. Portions were so large that neither Gene, my mother nor I could eat everything on our plates. At home, we would consider this dinner, not lunch. My planned dinner was omitted and we just had birthday cake and ice cream tonight. It was plenty after our noon meal.

FEBRUARY 5, 1990

Dear Bonna and Wayne,

In the Sunday Business Section of the N.Y. Times some corporate shenigans were exposed and I thought they were most interesting. Ross Johnson, former chairman of Nabisco, traveled with G. Shepard but they always traveled in separate private planes. When Nabisco was taken over, the new owners discovered that G. Shepard was Johnson's dog and he had to travel in a separate plane because he bit people.

When the J. Walter Thompson Company was taken over in 1987, they discovered that uniformed butlers delivered water in cut glass crystal on silver trays each day to the executives and they also came and took lunch orders. This cost the company $4 million a year. Expensive water! In the same company an executive had a peeled orange delivered each day and this cost $80,000 a year or $300 per orange. There was more to the article but you get the drift.

I've just finished reading ISLAND SOJOURN, the true account of

Elizabeth Arthur and her husband who bought a three acre island in B.C. They built a house and intended to live there, away from world material-ism, but after a year and a half, they knew such togetherness and alone-ness was not living. A well, written, thoughtful book and interesting in spite of no plot.

2/11/90

I just want you to know that I didn't "fall off the turnip cart yester-day." I just finished reading AMONG SCHOOL CHILDREN by Tracy Kidder, and I find this book is tenth on the nonfiction best sellers list of the NY Times today. I think it is a good book and agree that this book is worthy of being a best seller, although I think teachers are going to find it more interesting than non teachers. Apparently Puerto Rican children use this phrase to mean I wasn't born yesterday. A few minutes ago there was an innuendo on a TV program and Gene thought I didn't get it, but I told him I "didn't fall off the turnip cart yesterday."

I read in the N.Y. Times of a book published this week; MD by B.H. Kean who was physician to many famous people. He was on the faculty of Cornell Univ. Medical School for 40 years. The review was so good I went to the library and put in a reserve, even though they don't have it in the collection yet. In 1950 the doctor made frequent home calls to financier, H. Esterhase. Three months after the death of the patient, a pri-vate detective came to his office and accused the doctor of stealing a one of a kind Lalique vase which had been willed to the Metropolitan Museum. Witnesses said the doctor was the last person in the house before the vase disappeared. The doctor was so mad at the innuendo that he escorted the detective to the door and as they were passing by the sec-retary's desk, the detective shouted "There it is." It was holding pencils. Seems the day before the man died, the butler delivered a paper bag with this vase inside which held a urine specimen. The secretary thought it was so pretty that she asked the lab technician to wash out the vase and give it to her for her desk. There is a lot of the Shah of Iran in this book, too. I am anxious to read it.

Today Connie and Frank invited us to brunch at his Lordship's in Berkeley. This was in honor of my mother's birthday on Thursday. It was the best brunch we have ever had. So much seafood. A dessert table that must have been 20 feet long. I didn't sample 1/4 or even 1/8 of what was offered. We were stuffed. We came home and played bridge. I served a ham sandwich and blueberry pie before they went home, but we didn't need this at all. My mother was thrilled at this attention.

Yesterday Gene went to SIRS for his luncheon meeting and a former warden of Alcatraz prison spoke. He was most interesting and the men enjoyed him. The warden said Alcatraz was a great place to bring up kids because there was no place for them to get in trouble. The last boat from San Francisco returned at 11 PM so the kids always got home at a decent hour. He said they didn't coddle prisoners and if somebody destroyed his toilet, they left it broken till the prisoner worked enough to pay for it and in the meantime the prisoner had to use a pail. This took some months but it sure stopped other prisoners from causing destruction. My mother and I went out for lunch and I did some errands so we were away till Gene came home.

This morning Gene and I went to the third lecture of the series we joined in the fail. This one was by Antoinette Matlins who has written two books on gems. Her title was ALL THAT GLITTERS. She spoke for 1 1/2 hours and if she had talked longer, we would have listened longer. She had slides interspersed with her talk. She told of a woman who recently bought an antique necklace from Sotheby's. When she had it appraised for insurance, she found her $16,000 necklace was worth $300. Backing the stones was colored foil and this made the stones look like emeralds and sapphires when they were just plain white. The value of the necklace was only in the gold. She said diamonds have various ratings, like VVVVS I, VVVS 2, etc. This meant very, very slight inclusions. VS I means very slight inclusion. There are seven ratings of this and only a gemologist could identify these inclusions so it is wise to buy the one with the most inclusions, or flaws She told of some stones that have two parts with a substance that holds the two parts together and when put in some solution the substance shows up. Customers don't know this and can be fooled into thinking they are buying a precious stone when it isn't worth anything. She said the way to tell real pearls, cultured pearls are real pearls, is to run the pearls over the bottom of your front teeth. It won't work with false teeth. Fake pearls are slick and smooth, like a slick and smooth clerk who might have passed them off as real. Real pearls have a slightly gritty, uneven feel. I decided to try this out. Gene bought me a pin when we went to Japan the first time. It had Mikimoto pearls in it. True, it does feel different from the imitation ones I have. I have some strings of pearls and two are supposed to be real so in a few minutes I'm going to try this out. We felt this was the best lecture so far this year.

Did you read the food article on page 86 of the February 19th TIME? I did and I agree. Walter Shapiro says there's a whole generation of people who won't know what traditional food used to taste like and further more they won't care. They know only microwavable food. He says American home cooking is fast becoming a truly endangered species. He says the microwave industry is now willing to concede that the ovens have built in limitations. However there are a few things, like vegetables, that they do well. Gene has two widower bowling pals and they eat frozen food which is microwavable. If I were single, I might do this because it is hard to cook for one. I can see a couple doing this if both work but it would be too expensive for a family. Today a store had a sale on Healthy Choices and we went out to buy some dinners that Connie could serve to my mother while we are away in April. She has two evening classes and I thought it would be easier if she could use this food on those nights. It was all sold out at 1 PM. If we want it, we shall have to go at 9 AM tomorrow because at this price it doesn't last long. As long as I'm able, I'll prepare meals from scratch because I enjoy cooking.

Valentines
A sewerage plant named Trojan 2000

FEBRUARY 14, 1990

Dear Helen and Herb,

Today we each had a valentine at our place at breakfast and Gene's to me just hit the spot. There was a series of eleven pictures and all depicted exactly what I do. When I saw it, I said it matched my activities to a T. I was especially amused at the figures writing letters, lying on the sofa and reading. Gene knew this was the card for me.

Tomorrow is my mother's birthday and we are going to a Chinese restaurant in Rheem Valley where my mother can have prawns with lobster sauce. I'll make a cake and we'll have that with ice cream at the evening meal. No big celebration on her 96th birthday. We'll do that again on her 100th. We discussed going out to dinner but my mother vetoed this because she will miss too many of her favorite programs.

It has been cold here and will go down to 27 tonight.

FEBRUARY 16, 1990

A week ago when I was in a lovely store in Orinda, I saw a blue agate necklace on sale for $78. I wanted it but I needed it like I need a hole in the head. I told Gene about it. All week I thought of that necklace. Today Virginia and I stopped on our way home from San Francisco and it had been sold. Gene said I should have the store order another. What! And pay full price when I thought it was too expensive on sale? No way, Jose.

I told Virginia about my Valentine and she had a valentine story to tell. Several years ago she bought Don some jockey shorts with hearts all over them. Don refused to wear them. They have been in the dresser drawer for years. Her valentine from Don said on the outside, "I'M NOT

WEARING THOSE SILLY SHORTS WITH THE HEARTS ON THEM."
Inside it said "Look and see." She did and he was wearing them. Don
said he knew that was the card for Virginia.

We didn't get home till 4:45 and this is late for us. Gene was pacing
the floor and my mother was all upset. Virginia and I were relishing our
freedom. We both have wonderful husbands but occasionally we like to
be alone.

FEBRUARY 24, 1990

Dear Pat and Bob,

In the last few months I've learned a lot about widowhood from
observing Leta and Wilma. Toby died May 30th and Russ July 14th so
they both became widows close together. Leta couldn't bear to go back to
the home she shared with Toby. Wilma couldn't bear to leave the home
she shared with Russ. One couldn't stop crying and the other refused to
cry and choked back her tears. One surrounded herself with people and
the other holed up and met no one. Both have trouble sleeping.
Widowhood is a painful adjustment.

This past week I read a book by Hollis Hedges and the title was
NORMAN ROCKWELL'S GREATEST PAINTING. It is a novel and very
easy reading. It dealt with the subject of widows and widowers and a
widow was reading a book about widowhood and quotes from it are
interspersed throughout the book. Some advice was excellent. At times I
found it funny. One bit of advice that was given to widows was this. If
you are invited to something and the hostess says you will know everyone present, refuse. If you are invited to an affair where you will know
nobody, go. Think about this advice.

Thursday our phone bill came. I was astonished to see the January
bill had not been paid. The checkbook showed I wrote a check January
22nd. I always mail the day I write the check. I called the telephone company and they confirmed the check had not been received. I called the
bank and they said the check had not cleared. The telephone company
said recently lots of checks have been lost in the mail. I called the post
office and reported this and the postal person was indignant and said I
was the only one complaining. So where did our check go?

FEBRUARY 27, 1990

Last night and this noon the local TV news reported a real problem in
the Bay area. On Sundays and Mondays the sewerage treatment plants
become clogged. With what? Condoms! Seems Saturday and Sunday are

popular times for sex and, since safe sex is being practiced, there is a super abundance of these things being flushed down the toilets. They are wily things and don't get caught with the sludge. In the last two processes where water is being purified, these can be seen. They try to skim them out but even that isn't too successful so a lot of times they go into the bay. Now the sewerage superintendents have become social scientists. One sewerage plant is named Trojan 2000.

Last week the President was in San Francisco giving a speech to the Commonwealth Club at the St. Francis Hotel. If it weren't so pricey for membership and luncheons, I'd join. This year Malcolm Forbes was to give a speech and I'd love to hear him. This weekend ended all speeches by Forbes because he died. This week the President is again in San Francisco. This time he is giving a speech at a fund raiser for Pete Wilson at the St. Francis. The store keepers were told that once again the area would be sealed off and this time the period would be 24 hours. The store keepers were up in arms. One articulate, well dressed store owner was interviewed and he said Saks, I Magnin and Macy's were allowed to stay open and he didn't see why stores in his area had to close. He ended his interview by saying that he would just as soon the President give all his speeches in CLEVELAND

Yesterday I borrowed THE FABRICATOR by Hollis Hodges from the library. I thought Hodges was a female but no, he is male. I finished the book before I went to bed. I couldn't put it down. Quirky but so enjoyable. His books are like chocolate candy to me. I love both chocolate and his books but I wouldn't want a steady diet of either. What an imagination that author has.

Promises, promises. We were promised a big storm beginning tomorrow but last night they said the jet stream blew it away. Now we shall have only a slight bit of rain. We don't want the storm battering Europe but we pray for a bit of rain so water won't be rationed.

I must get back to my dish washing. I sat down to write this letter so I could rest.

4 water bills for same period
Wedding and baseball game

MARCH 15, 1990

Dear Phyllis and Max,

I'm exhausted and it is only 2 PM. I made bread this morning and cleaned. We had lunch and have just arranged our 207 eggs. It is quite a job unpacking them and distributing the eggs so they will show to advantage.

Tuesday we went to a lecture. Peter Lance, formerly of ABC, was the speaker and he was excellent. We learned so much about behind the scenes activities and the law suits that his investigative reporting generated. We could see that this kind of reporting was extremely stressful. He resigned from ABC and is now living in Woodland Hills and working on documentary films which expose problems. He didn't marry till he was 35. He said this kind of life is better but it is also scary. Recently there was an earthquake in the Los Angeles area and he was home at the time. He said they had just wallpapered some rooms of their house. At the time of the quake, he was in one of those newly papered rooms and, to his amazement, he saw wall paper tear and fall right off the wall in great strips. The shaking and falling wall paper were physically scary where as the law suits were mentally scary. So he concluded that life is not peaceful.

Yesterday traffic from San Francisco to the East Bay was tied up for hours. A pot hole in the Embarcadero had been repaired in the morning and by afternoon it was a big deep hole. They decided a sewer pipe had broken and were ready to replace this hundred year old pipe, but they found there was no pipe. Officials are puzzled and don't know why this big hole is forming. They think the earthquake had something to do with it, but what?

Remember my writing about the chocolate cinnamon rolls, the recipe had no chocolate. To-day I received a letter from Betty Crocker in response to mine. It said there were six recipes which had mistakes and they sent me a list of the recipes and the corrections. Gosh, you could really have some failures using these recipes.

When I took a loaf of bread over to our neighbors yesterday, Betty said the last loaf went fast. Sandy was home because his company is on strike. When Betty asked Sandy what he wanted for dessert, he said, "A piece of Norma's bread." Sandy travels a lot so he appreciates home made food.

Last night I had veal, cooked in wine with vegetables and surrounded by duchess potatoes. The dish was pretty, good and low calorie. We ate every bit and Gene said he would give me an A + for that dish. Gosh, after 25 years of marriage I FINALLY get an A +.

Yesterday we received our water bill but I didn't open it till this morning. A water bill is nothing to get excited about. When I did open it, I found not only our bill but bills of four of our neighbors. So I proceeded to their houses to deliver their bills. One just expressed amazement. The second suggested that since we received them all, we pay them all. The third man said he would only accept the bill that was the smallest. The final man just said, "Pay it" when I handed him his. I was flabbergasted when I found four bills in our envelope.

Today was the biennial flower show of Ikebana International in San Francisco. I did not enter an arrangement. Virginia and Don invited us to go with them. It was beautifully staged but too many of the arrangement had a western influence and were not pure ikebana. Afterwards Don drove a long way home and we had lunch at a Chinese restaurant. The bill was three fourths of what it should have been. Don told the waiter to check the bill. The waiter didn't so Don proceeded to point out the error. If they operate like this with other diners, they won't stay in business very long.

3/20/90

We won't pay $60 for a seat for PHANTOM OF THE OPERA, even though it is supposed to be very good. Our neighbors are going to England in April and hope to see it there for less. A person not able to get tickets in San Francisco flew to Los Angeles for the evening, saw the show and flew back. Another person went to New York to see it. Sunday night and last night it was on TV and we looked at it. It was excellent. I understand the TV show had more to it than the stage show. Best of all it was free.

I was away from home all morning and afternoon. We decided to have dinner at the Red Lobster which a friend raves about and for which we had a $6 coupon. The food wasn't bad, just very ordinary. My friend is no cook so to her this food was good. We wouldn't go there again.

MARCH 25, 1990

Dear Dorothy and Lars,

Remember my writing about leaks, developing under sinks, which plumbers now think are attributable to the earthquake in October? Well, it happened to us last night. After a dinner-bridge party last night, I decided to wash some pots and pans. I reached under the sink for soap and found it was all wet. I hesitated to get Gene because he would try to fix it and it was already midnight. When I did, I said it could wait till morning but he investigated and found that the U pipe was absolutely disconnected on one side. The shaking of the earthquake unscrews the pipes and after enough water has passed thru, the pipe gradually drops till there is no connection. Gene put it back together and it is o.k. now. I said Gene would have to check the bathrooms because maybe the same thing has happened there.

Frank's birthday is tomorrow so I made pecan raspberry torte which looked like a four layer cake. It was good and pretty but high in calories.

I had a boneless turkey in the oven for dinner when Sue called and said she was bringing over our dinner. I finished baking the turkey and put it in the refrigerator and we ate part of what Sue brought. Sue thinks because we are big, we eat a lot but we don't. Sue buys lots of her clothes in the children's department because she is small, with a tiny bone frame. She wears a size-1, Hing says, and weighs 83 pounds. She doesn't look thin, just small.

While on errands this morning Gene and I stopped at Sun Valley Mall so I could see what the Perugina Easter egg looks like this year. Chocolate Heaven had been replaced by a music box store. We weren't surprised they went out of business. You had to be a Rockefeller to afford their candy. I checked Macy's and they said they might have one or two Perugina eggs for sale this year. Gene said he was prepared to buy me one of these eggs this year. If I ever do see one, I'll let him know.

All our 207 Easter eggs are on display. We'll put them away on Easter because we leave on the 18th for our Mississippi cruise.

Our friend, Leta, put a deposit on a unit in Rossmoor in the Waterford. The Waterford is a new idea to Rossmoor because with these units you can go to the dining room for meals and your apartment gets cleaned. The other part of Rossmoor does not provide meals and cleaning. The most expensive units sold first. They are luxurious. I wish we could afford to live there when we get old.

Maryann, daughter of my friend, Phyllis, and her husband, Dick, took a foster child this month. The social worker thinks this child will be available for adoption late in the year. They are thrilled with Molly and if the adoption doesn't materialize there will be two sad and disappointed people. The only requirement Maryann and Dick stipulated was that the child be college material when grown. Maryann knows we enjoy taking care of Kate and said maybe she would ask us to take Molly for a day or two when they take a vacation. My guess is that they won't want to leave Molly. We'd be delighted to have her. On Saturday before Easter we'll see Molly for the first time. Maryann says Molly doesn't like brussel sprouts and cauliflower but she really likes chocolate cake and fruit. I think I'll have an orange glazed chicken. We all love chocolate so dessert will be something chocolate.

Linda, Kate's mother, sent a letter with an enclosure from Kate. Both Gene and I got letters saying Kate loved us. Mine read, "Dear Norma, I love you." Gene wore a fake mustache on Halloween so there was a picture of Gene with a mustache. We have these on our refrigerator door.

My mother is having a new permanent today at a different beauty school. The one she has previously gone to is out of business. She has fussed for a week and she didn't sleep all last night because she was afraid they wouldn't do her hair the way she wants it. I go to a regular hairdresser who works fast. These learners have to have everything checked and it takes such a long time to have your hair done at a beauty school.

Last night we heard that England had an earthquake. Goodness, how unusual. There was also one in Washington, near Seattle. I wonder if there is a fault that goes across the world.

People in California are upset that Harris who murdered two boys 12 years ago was given a reprieve from execution. The justice system in the U.S. doesn't work as it should and even the governor was angry that this happened. He stated his opinion on TV in no uncertain terms. Harris murdered the two boys so he could use their car in a robbery and after he killed them, he ate their lunch. The boys were going fishing. One boy was the son of a policeman and this same policeman captured Harris but he didn't know at the time that Harris had murdered his son. What is wrong in the U.S.? Why are we having so many heinous crimes committed?

APRIL 7, 1990

Dear Phyllis and Jay,

Yesterday, after helping Leta clear out her condo, I dropped in the travel bureau which is in the southern part of Walnut Creek. The personnel greeted me by asking if I had just driven there and what the earthquake felt like in a car. I hadn't felt anything (you don't in a car) and I hadn't felt the earlier one because I was sitting on the floor.

When Gene returned from bowling, my mother, excitedly, asked Gene if he had felt the earthquakes. Gene was riding in Leon's new Cadillac and he felt nothing. My mother really felt these earthquakes because they were on the Concord fault which is right in our backyard. The epi center was only six miles away from our house and three miles from the travel agency. Even though the jolts may be only in the 3-4 range on the Ricter scale, they are good sized shakes if the epi center is near. The newspaper recorded six quakes in the 3 range and one at 4.5 after dinner.

I was working at this word processor when there was a big shake. Gene ran to the garage and bedroom and then tried to stop the hanging lamp from swinging. The late news reported that we had a swarm of earthquakes and an additional seventy seven tremors. My mother decided to go to bed with her clothes on but we finally persuaded her to take them off.

There was the usual damage in drug and grocery stores where things fell off shelves. We thought everything was o.k. at our house.

Gene always checks the garage before we go to bed and last night he found the motor of the garage door opener was working but nothing was happening. He couldn't immediately see what was wrong so he disconnected it. When I was preparing for bed, I discovered that the heavy card table we have next to the wall in our walk in closet was on the floor and the hamper was overturned. No damage, though. This morning I found one of our eggs on the floor and a little duck that goes inside an egg was also on the floor.

Gene called a repair man for the garage door and he came on Saturday. He found a part broken just above the door. He replace it and once again we could raise and lower the door with the wall button. The next day when we returned home and tried to use the remote control, the door wouldn't open. Gene called the man again. His answering service said he had a huge list of people who wanted him so his return call would be delayed. Finally he came and immediately noticed that the wire leading to the motor had been snapped in two. He said the earth quake caused this. He said he was too busy to write a bill so he would send one later. This morning the newspaper reported a total of two hundred thirty six tremors, of which we felt only four. In this case our loss was the repair man's gain.

Last night my mother entertained Connie and Frank at the restaurant of Diablo Valley College where the students who are studying hotel and restaurant management do the cooking, waitressing, planning. The food was very different but excellent, for example oyster spinach soup, duck with brandied cherry sauce, salmon in puff pastry with a sauce, squash blossoms stuffed with cheese and lightly deep fried and chocolate souffle.

Maryann and Dick brought Molly for lunch yesterday. They have had her three weeks but this is the first time we have seen her. She has a large vocabulary, learns quickly but doesn't yet use complete sentences. She is book oriented. At one point her parents were showing her pictures in the National Geographic and she recognized a shadow. She looked at all our fragile eggs but didn't touch. Like most children under two years, she runs rather than walks.

When Dick put her in her car seat, he said hands up but she already had them up over her head. When the door was shut, her hands came down. Good idea. This way those little hands will not be injured in the door.

Molly is a good little eater and she especially liked my oatmeal maple syrup muffins.

We played bridge last night. Today we put our egg collection away and pack for our trip.

JUNE 2, 1990

Dear Marion and Bob,

Today I got a jolt. Connie called and said she could not stay with my mother in September when we go away. She said her parents would be away then and she had to take care of the dog. Previously they have put the dog in a kennel when her parents were away and Connie stayed with my mother.

The dog is 17 years old, crippled with arthritis and incontinent. He may even have had a stroke. A few months ago they had it operated upon for kidney stones, cost $850. Almost anyone else would have had it put to sleep.

We have been fortunate to have Connie because she neither drinks nor smokes and is absolutely honest. She doesn't have boyfriends so we don't have that problem.

Finding someone else may be a real problem. This causes a strain and probably my blood pressure will rise.

I called an older person who sits with elderly people but she is looking for a permanent live in job and she will probably find one because live ins are scarce. My mother doesn't need nursing care because she washes and dresses herself and makes her own bed. She needs somebody to prepare her meals, sleep over night and respond to any emergency that might arise. She can be alone for a few hours and often is, even when we are here.

Every time I mention finding somebody, my mother says, "I may be dead by that time". This really upsets me and today I snapped at her and said, "I can't count on that." OH. DEAR! It wasn't a nice thing to say but I've heard this just once too often.

In 1992 my class at William Smith will have a 50th reunion. I said we would go to that. Now I don't know. I wonder if it will be as bad as Gene's 50th high school reunion.

Yesterday we saw the Wellesley commencement and I thought Barbara Bush was excellent. Her delivery was straight forward, her speech brief and she hit on the most important things in life very diplomatically, family, friends and caring. I really was disgusted with the students who felt she hadn't accomplished anything in her own right. In my estimation bringing up children is a real accomplishment, if a good job is done. I was unimpressed with Raisa Gorbachev. Her speech was meaningless, even if she does have a Ph D.

I better stop now before I think of lots more to say.

JUNE 10, 1990

Dear Marguerite and Ed,

Wednesday I awakened with another urinary infection. I called the doctor but his schedule was filled and he couldn't work me in till 3:45. I had left over medicine but the doctor didn't want me to take it because I had a new symptom which might be a kidney stone. By noon I was in agony and called the doctor again. He said to report to the lab immediately and then come directly to his office. He didn't think it was a kidney stone and I started on the medicine. By 9 PM I was comfortable but not cured. I'm to have my physical on Thursday and I hope we will know what germ is bothering me.

Thursday we cleaned the house and I made a birthday cake for Leta who was coming for a birthday dinner. This was a better birthday than last year because Toby's memorial was on her birthday.

Friday was a free day for me. At 5 the doctor's nurse called and asked if I was going to be all right over the weekend. I was better and appreciated that the doctor checked on me. Most doctors wouldn't bother. Having such a good doctor is a plus in my life.

Sunday we were up early so we could take off for Campbell to visit Maryann, Dick and Molly. Molly turned two last week. She is so lovable. Maryann and Dick adore her and are doing a good job bringing her up and she is happy with them. Before Christmas they expect to know if they can adopt her. Molly showed us her toys, talked, played and was a joy to be around. She finished eating before we did and they gave her books to look at. She knew what was on each page. I mentally compared Molly with a friend's grandson who is almost the same age. We saw him recently and he just ran around wildly. They call him a disaster. I don't wonder.

Tuesday I had my regular dental appointment and the dentist said the back tooth we have been watching for ten years is now at the stage when something must be done. It has a crown and there is decay under the crown. We decided to have it removed and July 16th is the date.

Thursday I have my yearly physical. Gosh, what a week. I'll be glad to have all this behind me.

JULY 14, 1990

My physical made me very happy. My blood pressure was normal and my cholesterol was 199. Everything else seemed to be o.k.

JUNE 18, 1990

For more than a year I've wanted the two guest rooms painted but Gene never got to it. A couple of weeks ago I told Gene that either he do it or else I would hire someone and he had till today to decide. I wasn't going to nag or pressure. Gene realized his days of procrastinating were over so today we are ready to paint. I have the drapes soaking and will wash them. The label said dry clean only. They are old and I won't be sorry if they are spoiled. I'll just buy new ones.

I just checked on Gene. He has the ceiling at one end of the bedroom done and so can move on and I can do the walls. This means I sign off and get busy painting.

JULY 4, 1990

Dear Shizuko and Kaoru,

So many things have been happening.

Just a few minutes ago I finished the new drapes for the middle bedroom. After we painted the room, I noticed that the old drapes were rotting. I wanted something to match the gold chiffon bedspread. I found material for $25 a yard and some for $125 a yard, but we settled for some costing $9 a yard. I found I needed half a yard more for the valence. An extra trip back to the drapery store.They are done now and we like them.

Last year we decided to vacation in Newfoundland this year and we chose a Four Winds tour which the travel agent said was upscale, translate expensive. Not many tours go there and the ones that do are at least $1700 less. However they don't go to the Viking settlement and St. Pierre and Miquelon and these we want to see. We tried to book the first of the year and were told it was too early. We tried at Easter and were told to wait. We tried in June and nobody had booked. They had tours booked for each week of the summer but only one tour had enough signed up. We decided to go on our own.

Then we got a CANADAPASS brochure. They didn't go to the Viking settlement but the rest was o.k. Back to the travel agent we went. They had three tours this summer and the first two were all booked. The third they weren't sure about. Next day they called back and said there was room for us. We thought we were all set. We put down a deposit and the next day the travel agent called and said if we paid fully now we could get a 3% discount.

So we went over to do that and change our plane reservations from September to August. More complications. Only one flight a day so we needed a stop over going to St. Anthony. Finally, after three hours, everything was set. Karen's final question was did we want her to reserve a car for us at St. Anthony. Gene said yes. Next day Karen called and said there was no car rental at St. Anthony. If we wanted to cancel our plane reservations, it had to be done immediately because she was turning in our reservations and they were non-refundable. I asked her to wait a few minutes and called the Newfoundland Tourist Bureau. They called St. Anthony and found a motel had a car rental. I called the motel and requested a reservation. They weren't sure they could guarantee one. I said I must know then because of the plane reservations. Finally the girl said they would guarantee a car. I hope it is all settled now. What a hassle this has been.

Now the big problem is getting somebody to stay with my mother.

I'm asking friends if they know anybody. Some suggestions but nothing promising.

I'm beginning to wonder if this vacation is worth all the trouble.

We had car trouble last Friday. The belt for the generator broke. I thought this was a simple problem but it cost $17S to have a new belt installed. The car was out of commission for one and one half days.

As I sit typing, I can observe Gene at the kitchen sink. When we use the dishwasher, we have a leak in the cupboard under the sink. So Gene ran the dishwasher and found that water was bubbling out of the overflow and the kitchen faucet had a leak around the seal so the water was coming through the seal. He is putting stuff there and I hope the problem is solved.

I'm worn out just thinking of all these problems. I'm going to relax and read a book.

JULY 15, 1990

Dear Millie and Jim,

The last couple weeks have been busy ones. And interesting.

On the 7th we attended the wedding of our neighbor's son in San Francisco. Since we didn't know how to get to the church, we left at 9:30 for an 11 AM wedding. Traffic wasn't bad and we were at the church in less than an hour. We circled the church because there was no parking and finally Gene parked in a handicapped place and used my mother's sticker. The church was old but attractive. Four hundred were invited but the church was packed so I think others came. Everyone was seated at II but no bridal procession. Still no bridal procession at 11:30. At 11:40 the priest came out and said the bride and her father were stuck in traffic on the bridge because there was a game that afternoon at Candlestick Park. All the women went to the bathroom and men went outside. After awhile the priest returned and said the bride had arrived and the service would begin. Everybody trooped back in the church. It was a high mass so it was 1 PM when the service was over.

The reception was at the Knell Mansion in Burlingame. We drove slowly but most of the guests had arrived before us. We sat at a table outside in the sun and waited for the bridal party to arrive. The bridal party were delayed for picture taking. Shortly after the bridal party arrived, people began to leave. At 4:15 before the wedding cake was cut, we had to leave because I only left lunch for my mother. Traffic was bad and we didn't get home till after 5:30. We were gone eight hours. My mother had found some soup and was eating it. Not being used to sustained bright sun for a couple hours, both Gene and I had sunburned faces and as of the moment my nose is all bloody. It peeled and when I washed my face, the new skin was too fragile and broke. Our scalps were sunburned too and it hurt when we combed our hair.

We played bridge Monday night and the hostess uses a ceiling fan instead of their air conditioning. The ceiling fan evaporates the moisture from your skin but doesn't lower the temperature. The house was hot. My face got redder and redder and people asked what was the matter. I said I was too hot. The host offered to change chairs with me but it did no good. As we were leaving, Ed asked what their thermostat was set at and the host said 78 or 80 and they have a 15 degree range before it comes on so at 80 it has to be 95 before the airconditioner kicks on. No wonder I was so hot I couldn't think. It was cooler outdoors than in that house.

The rest of the week was spent searching for somebody to stay with my mother. I contacted people who advertised in the Rossmoor News. Most were in long term employment and if available would not accept a two weeks employment. Then I contacted agencies. What an education. Some agencies charged a fee to access our house. They charged the salary of the caregiver and another half of this daily fee for the agency. Agency business is profitable. I visited some rest homes and I was in tears when I left one. Old people sitting around, vacant expressions if awake, mouth open if asleep. Pure and simple vegetables. I wouldn't put my mother there.

I interviewed two. A young girl with a small child and a child care problem. An older woman wanted the job but she was so coarse and vulgar. I said I would let her know Monday.

Late Thursday I talked with Frank, our bridge playing friend. I told him my problem and asked if anyone in his Mormon church would be available. Mormons are very caring people. He didn't know but asked his daughter-in-law who is in charge of welfare in the church. At 11 PM Mary called me and offered herself and her husband. They have a family and each would take a day. I couldn't let them disrupt their life like this. The next morning Mary called and suggested a college girl who would be home August 10th. She needed to earn money. The father came to visit us and approved of the situation and called his daughter. The father is a dentist. He was a low key, gentle, dignified man with a subtle sense of humor. All three of us liked him and we were enchanted by a picture of his beautiful daughter. Apparently his children aren't coddled and spoiled. What a burden was lifted from my shoulders. What a relief!

Maryann, Dick and Molly came last night for dinner. Molly talks in a low voice all the time. It is amazing what this child says. She was enthusiastic about strawberries and she told us her Daddy was handsome. The birth mother gets to see her once a week and before the visit is over, Molly is crying and saying she wants her Mommy Maryann. The birth mother isn't physically or financially able to take care of Molly and everything about her life, including her marriage, is unstable and in a state of flux. Almost from birth Molly has either been with relatives or friends but the majority of time she has been in foster care. Her birth mother is a stranger to her. The bond between Molly, Maryann and Dave is already strong. The courts are giving the mother much time and if she proves a competent parent, Molly will be returned to her mother. If not, she will be adopted. Time will tell.

Tomorrow I am to have a back tooth pulled. I'll be glad when tomorrow is over.

I don't know about conditions in your section of the country but some unusual things are happening in our area. Last night on TV we heard about a man who had a house for sale in Alameda for over $400,000. Six months have gone by and no offers. The man reduced the house to $387,000 and still no offers. This weekend he is throwing in a brand new Mitsubishi. There will be open house and he has balloons all over the place. I hope they report whether he sells the house. This man is a car dealer.

TV also reported that houses have gone up 250% in the San Francisco Bay area since 1970. Buyers are waiting for prices to come down. The only houses selling are those for a few million and buyers in this range have ready cash.

Leon's sitting duck accident
Hal's safe deposit story

NOVEMBER 4, 1990

Dear Audrey and Glenn,

One day last week I went to Walnut Creek to buy a book for a Christmas present and I wanted to buy it at Crown where a discount is given. Since the earthquake of last October the Broadway Mall has been done over and the old parking structure demolished because the supports were damaged. Crown no longer has a back entrance but next to it was a store that was called PEA IN A POD and it had a back entrance. I entered and a clerk approached me and asked if I were pregnant. It was a maternity store and apparently people use the store and the store doesn't like it. I did it accidentally but I did not return to the car that way. Returning I went around a corner and walked thru an expensive jewelry store. They should have a thoroughfare from the mall to the parking lot. I didn't find the book.

Thursday we took our Christmas packages to UPS which is near automobile row in Concord. Car dealerships line the street. As we drove past, I suggested to Gene that we stop and just look at a Taurus. Our car is ten years old and the air conditioning no longer works so we are in the market for a new car. They had three choices but either the color wasn't right, or there were too many extras or not enough extras. After lunch at home we decided to go to Walnut Creek and look at the Ford agency. They had a Taurus in a pretty blue and it was just what we wanted but the battery was dead and their price was more than the other agency. We told the salesman we were just looking. We didn't have much choice in the make of a car to buy since we wanted a six passenger and most today are five passenger because they have a gear shift between the two front seats. Taurus is six passenger and so is Olds. We decided to stop at Oldmobile where our present car was purchased. We were just looking. They didn't have a blue one but they did have a white one and the price was lower than either the other two agencies and it had some options we didn't want but which would be nice. Both of us felt this was a really good deal. By eye contact, Gene and I decided to buy that car. They would take our car in trade and instead of fixing it, they would ship it to Mexico where cars like this sell. We could have brought the new car home with us but instead we opted to have it checked, and washed before we picked it up Friday at 3 PM. We had to pay for it on Thursday so I wrote a check that was no good and Friday Gene went to the bank and transferred funds to our checking account so the check wouldn't bounce.

Thursday night Leon called and told of an accident he had just had which would prohibit him from driving to bowling. He asked Gene to drive the four men. I told Gene if somebody else volunteered to drive, he should agree immediately because our fan belt could break at any moment. One man did offer and Gene quickly accepted.

Leon was driving north on Treat in the far right lane of a four lane highway. He stopped for a traffic light. The woman just ahead of him decided she wanted to make a left turn. She was in the right lane and needed to get to the far left lane so without looking, she backed up right into the front of Leon's Cadillac. She must have backed up with force because the Cadillac was pretty badly damaged. I never heard of anybody doing this.

Saturday morning we were invited to sub at bridge that night. That night we were so concentrating on the different gadgets and computers that we lost our way and were ten minutes late.

Saturday I took my mother for a drive in our new car and we ended up at Orchard Nursery. This was the opening day of their Christmas show of decorated Christmas trees and it is an extravaganza. The nursery is set back from the road and when I turned in the drive, I was stopped by a boy with a walkie talkie. There was no parking available near the nursery but, noticing my mother's handicapped sign, he told me to wait till a parking spot was available. The parking spot I got was next to a live elephant, with attendant, surrounded by bales of hay. The elephant wasn't more than ten feet away from the car. My mother couldn't see it. She can see to do her jig saw puzzles but she couldn't see an elephant ten feet away. Apparently she has no far vision.An elephant ten feet away is pretty hard to miss.

It is now Monday. Before I throw away the N.Y. Times, I'm tearing out the front page of the entertainment section. It was covered with pictures of Babar the elephant. It seems some woman in N.Y. city was giving a benefit dinner and her theme was Babar and this was a picture of cookies made in the shape of Babar, colored and decorated, which were favors at her party. The cookies cost $1,600 but she made a profit of $4,200 which was donated to the N.Y. public library. Now that's party giving.

NOVEMBER 19, 1990

Dear Mothers of our "Grandchildren",

Biologically they aren't our grandchildren, but they are the closest to the real thing Gene and I will ever have.

I want to tell you the reason for sending this book.

When I entered college years ago, I met Isabel Wilner who was from the Philippines where her father had been an Episcopal missionary ever since she was a child. Originally the family came from Pennsylvania. When the war broke out, her parents were interned in Santa Tomas and she heard no more of them till the war ended. Having no home to go to during vacations, she came to my parents' home. We were very close, more so than some sisters. We made a pact that we would be maid of honor at each other's wedding if we married and Isabel was my maid of honor.

We have remained close ever since, even though many miles have always separated us. Vacations have been our times to be together, otherwise the telephone and letters have kept us in contact.

So Isabel has heard much about Kate and Molly, the two little girls who have stolen the hearts of Gene and Norma.

About three years ago Isabel's Christmas alphabet poem was accepted by the publisher, Dutton, and it was published this fall. I decided I wanted both little girls to have a copy of the book and I asked Isabel to autograph a copy for each child. And here it is.

I hope this autographed book will be special and a first for each child. I'm enclosing some of the publicity relating to B IS FOR BETHLE-HEM. Knowing the background of the book should make it more interesting in later years when the child can appreciate an autographed book.

In the Book Review section of the N.Y. Times on November 11, 1990, Dutton had an ad for its new children's books and figures from the illustrations of B IS FOR BETHLEHEM are attached to each book advertised.

Isabel did not know the illustrator. Dutton contacted Elisa Kleven and asked her to submit illustrations. Both Isabel and Dutton were extremely pleased with the illustrations. They were accepted. Even the end papers were attractive. The result is a beautifully illustrated book.

I hope the girls will enjoy this book.

AFTER THANKSGIVING 1990

Dear Emme and Ken,

For Thanksgiving we had a seventeen pound turkey, one guest, and the three of us. Four servings of turkey hardly made a dent in the turkey so I suggested to Gene that we serve dinner, and not just dessert when we entertain at bridge Saturday. He thought it was a good idea if wasn't too much work for me. I told everybody they were having left overs. Two couples do not have Thanksgiving dinner at home so they had no left overs. I made a dessert but I would have made that anyway.

Hal, one of Gene's bowling pals, was our only guest. He is 80. He had a lens replacement in August and will have another in a couple days. His wife died in 1982 and his daughter and family live in Arkansas so he is alone.

Last time he was here he had this story to tell. He went to the bank to get something from his safety deposit box. He couldn't get the key to open the box. Neither could the manager of the bank. The solution was to get a locksmith to drill the lock and install a replacement lock, at Hal's expense. Hal had added his daughter's name to his box when his wife died so the box could not be drilled unless the daughter gave her consent. A release form had to be mailed and returned before a date for the drilling could be set. The day came and the locksmith entered the vault with Hal and the manager of the bank. The locksmith tapped the box with a small hammer, inserted the key and it opened! It seems the October earthquake jarred and jammed the tumblers in the lock. When the hammer made the tumblers fall back in place, voila, the key worked. Hal didn't have to pay for drilling and a new lock but he did have to pay for a service call. The earthquake did a lot of things that didn't show up immediately.

This time Hal had another story. In 1980 Hal had a radical operation. While he was in the operating and recovery rooms, his wife waited in his room. She stayed till 5 PM and then left for home, about fifteen minutes by car from the hospital. At 6:30 Hal's friend called Hal because he got no answer when he called Helen at home. Hal knew Helen should have been home long ago. He called and also got no answer. He kept calling. A nurse became curious as to why Hal was making so many calls. Hal said he was worried about his wife. The nurse said they would take over and call the police and other hospitals and that he should relax and rest. The police went to Hal's house and entered through a back door Helen had forgotten to lock. Everything in the house was o.k. but no Helen. Hal was really disturbed. The doctor was called and he put Hal in intensive care. The police turned up nothing in this area. All that night and the next day the hospital tried to find Helen. Late that day the doctor came to Hal's room and told him they had found Helen. She was in a police station in Elk Grove which is over a hundred miles from here. She had run out of gas about midnight and the police took her to a station and kept her because she seemed disoriented. Hal got on the phone and called a friend and asked him to go for Helen and take a friend to drive back his car. When Hal was again home, he realized Helen probably had Alzheimer's. He had noticed she wasn't the meticulous housekeeper she used to be and that she forgot things, but these were minor things. Hal blamed some of this on her emphysema. For the next two years Hal had to think for Helen. Eventually she had to be hospitalized.

Gene and I thought this was a terrible thing to happen to Hal when he was so sick.

Oh, yes, another thing. Before Helen ran out of gas, she got off the freeway on an entrance. She was going the wrong way and the police picked her up. When Hal was opening the mail after he returned home from the hospital, he found Helen had a subpoena. Why didn't the police realize Helen wasn't normal?

Today I sold UNICEF cards for AAUW from 9:30 till 12:30 at a bank near Rossmoor. My partner and I sold $300 worth of cards. The first day of the sale a Japanese couple bought $600 worth of cards. This was a record for all sales in all the years AAUW has been selling them. My partner and I were relieved by a woman who has no voice and another who can't see. The one who can't talk will write up the slips and the one who can't see will talk to the customers. The cards this year were the prettiest UNICEF ever had, I think.

Yesterday there was an article in the N.Y. Times Magazine section about Jeffrey Archer and it said that every five seconds some place in the world a book of Jeffrey Archer's is being sold. He never meant to be an author but he is good and I like all his books.

I hope this will be an enjoyable holiday season for you.

P.S.

I meant to have this in my letter, but I forgot. I hope I'm not getting Alzheimers.

Maryann said they bought a small child's sleeping bag to use when they go to their condo at Mammoth or visiting friends who do not have cribs. Molly loved sleeping in the sleeping bag and on returning home, she still wanted to sleep in it. Maryann agreed to this for a few days.

Maryann and Dick are doing a good job with Molly. I don't have to put my "treasures" away because she doesn't touch them. We have yet to hear her cry. Maryann and Dick will be devastated if Molly is given back to her parents.

Tonight Maryann called. I sent B IS FOR BETHLEHEM on Monday and they received it on Tuesday but they didn't read it to Molly till Wednesday night. Maryann said Molly liked the book because of the many pictures of animals and fish. FISH? What do fish have to do with the nativity? I checked the book and, by golly, there are fish. I was intrigued with the figures of many nationalities and races but the fish were the most important to Molly. Maryann is telling Molly the story of the nativity, in addition to reading the book. This is a big concept for a 29 month old child. She gets the idea of Jesus birthday easily. Molly doesn't want to turn pages. She has to see and identify everything on the page. So it takes a long time to go thru it. Her attention span is long for a child her age.

DECEMBER 6, 1990

Dear Isabel,

A week has gone by since Molly received B IS FOR BETHLEHEM. She is past looking at the animals in the book and now the content interests her. She calls the book her Augustus book. Maryann kept telling her it is B IS FOR BETHLEHEM but because the first sentence is A is for Augustus it remains her Augustus book.

Molly has become conscious of night and darkness. Previously she has only wakened in the morning to daylight and gone to bed when it was still daylight. Now she gets up when it is dark to go to day care and she gets picked up in the late afternoon when it is dark. Maryann has talked to her about evening and to illustrate her point, she showed the E is for evening page to Molly and they talked about it. Maryann tried to explain about the sun and why it gets dark and Molly seemed to understand. When Maryann talked about the sun moving around the world there was a discussion about the world. World is mentioned in this book too. Maryann and Dick will buy a small globe for this two year old child. Maryann and Dick are impressed with Molly's questions and I am too. Dick says he is going to enroll her in Harvard.

I'm busy with my Christmas activities, baking cookies, sweet breads. fruit cakes. Ikebana is having a food bazaar on Friday and I'm going to take Hawaiian honey bread.

This is a short letter but I did want to share with you Molly's reaction to her Augustus book.

DEC 25, 1990

Dear Lucy and Lucien,

It is 9:40 PM and this is my first minute to write to you. I arose at 7 AM and was very busy preparing dinner. I didn't even have my hair combed when Leta arrived for the present opening. While we were doing this, Frank, son, daughter-in-law and three grandchildren arrived. The kids got skates for Christmas and they stayed outside and skated. Mary, Tom and Frank came in. Immediately Mary spotted B IS FOR BETHLE-HEM because I had it displayed on the bookcase. Mary had been to a book review where it was on the coffee table. She was so impressed she planned to buy a copy. She wondered why I had a copy so I told her of my long friendship with Isabel. She said when next Isabel visited me she wanted to know because she would come with her book to have it auto-graphed. Tom is a vice principal of a high school and he was most inter-ested in it. He really examined the book. Mary said the book was sold in a small book store in Orinda. The big book stores here didn't carry it.

Leta went home to change and bring back Ann who has no family. She was only gone thirty minutes. Then Hal arrived. We had sixteen dif-ferent items for dinner. Afterwards we opened our stockings. At five Leta and Ann left, Hal, my mother, Gene and I went for a ride to see the lights. A light lunch followed and it was after 9 PM when the dishes were done and I collapsed on the sofa. It is now time to go to bed. I may not sleep because I'm just too tired but we had a wonderful day. I felt our house was Grand Central station today.

BOXER DAY, DEC. 26, 1990

It is now 4 PM. Gene and I were out all morning buying Christmas cards for next year. After lunch I dismantled the turkey and made turkey soup. I made olive bread because it is wonderful when made into a turkey sandwich.

By this time, after 3 days of real work, I am ready to drop. I made a list of our presents so I can write thank you letters. I haven't had time before. I am not the old Norma that could work and work. Those two days of preparation meant that I never sat down once in eight hours or more. Christmas was as bad. I know I'm getting old.

THURSDAY THE 27TH

Today we put away the presents and cleaned the front bedroom because Phyllis is coming on New Year's Day and will stay 5 days. She is staying with her daughter, Maryann, in Campbell. When I talked to Phyllis Christmas night, she said her plane from Rochester to Chicago was twenty five minutes late and she had only half an hour to change planes. She was worried she wouldn't make it so the airline alerted her ongoing plane to wait and they called for a wheel chair and rushed her from one plane to another. Phyllis doesn't need a wheel chair but they felt this was the only way she could make the connection.

You probably have heard about the terrible weather we have been having. Our cala lilies and bird of paradise are dead. Shrubbery looks sick. I don't know how much we will lose. We picked a lot of our oranges. Those we left probably won't be good but Gene covers them each night with plastic.

I made olive bread yesterday and today we had a turkey sandwich with olive bread. At Thanksgiving we made olive bread but it wasn't good. Gene is a strong willed person and he decided it needed more olives so he took more from the jar and didn't let them drain enough. They added more moisture than the bread should have. Because of the weight of the olives, the bread rises more slowly. Gene didn't let it rise enough and when it was baked it was soggy and dense. I told him his mistake and this time he didn't add the extra olives and he waited till it rose double and it turned our perfectly. Sometimes you have to let Gene make a mistake because he will have his way. I was recently introduced to some people at a church tea and Ginnie ended the introduction by saying Norma had a jewel of a husband. Most of the time I agree.

DECEMBER 27, 1990

Dear Catherine and Larry,

Over the weekend we had a terrible cold spell. The day before Christmas Gene and I went to buy perishable items we hadn't previously purchased for our Christmas dinner. Among other things, I wanted asparagus, tiny yellow pear tomatoes and strawberries. All had been frozen so my menu had to be altered.

When we played bridge Saturday night, we heard that two couples that have solar hot water heating had no hot water because the pipes had frozen. The third couple wasn't aware of the problem. This happened to many and in some cases the homes were flooded and damage was done. We don't have solar hot water heating. The cost of installing is so great that the system will wear out before you save enough on your heating bill to make it worth while. Some people can't figure this out.

Sunday morning Gene walked around our house inspecting everything to see what damage we might have experienced. The control of our sprinkler system had frozen and broken so he shut off the water. That afternoon we were expecting company and we kept looking for them from our front room window. At one point Gene saw water covering the sidewalk near our neighbor's house. He thought a pipe of ours was broken so he went out to inspect and fix it. It wasn't our pipe but our neighbor's. I called the neighbor but got an answering machine. Gene then went over and he found that they had a broken control to their sprinkler system. Apparently it had broken after Gene made his morning inspection. He shut off their water system. I called and left a message that Gene had done this. We didn't know it but the neighbors were away and would not return for several days. Boy, what a water bill they would have had.

The bird of paradise in front of our living room window is frozen. I don't know about the roots. It looks sad. Shrubs have curled leaves. Cala lilies are flat on the ground. All the greenery around our house and other houses is frozen. We hear such a freeze hasn't been know for one hundred ten years and even then it was not as bad as this.

Our orange tree was covered with oranges. We had picked the top ones which were large size and very good. Before the freeze we picked two dozen more and put them in the garage. Gene covered the tree with plastic each night. We don't know about the oranges still on the tree. Our crop of oranges was the best yet this year. Now I don't know.

Elsewhere the pond in Golden Gate park was frozen. Water from frozen pipes ran into streets and froze. People in California don't know how to drive on ice and there were several pile ups. I had to watch my step every time I went outdoors so I wouldn't fall on the ice. We needed more blankets on our bed. Sunny, warm California is a misnomer right now.

JANUARY 7, 1991

Dear Bonna and Wayne,

As of this morning things are back to normal at 2155.

January 1st we drove to Campbell to pick up Phyllis who came on the 24th to visit, Maryann, Dick and see Molly for the first time. Molly gets sweeter each time we see her. If she weren't so young, I'd keep my distance from her because she does make a PLAY for my husband. She sits on Gene's lap and to me this says, WATCH OUT, NORMA. She is only thirty months but mentally she is much older. She got a globe for

Christmas and when she took it out of the box she said it was the world and she pointed out California and the U.S. Phyllis says that Molly's reaction to anything new is "It's amazing." What a vocabulary she has and she knows so much. We are happy to have this child to enrich our lives.

Upon returning home, we did nothing but relax. Next day Mother, Phyllis and I went to Loehmann's, a discount store that sells designer clothes. On the way back we stopped at Blackhawk which is a security planned community for the nouveau riche. I wanted Phyllis to see the beautiful homes which even a million would not buy. Old money isn't interested in this community but it is lovely. The developer came from a poor family back in Wisconsin but today Ken Behring is reportedly worth three hundred to five hundred million. His house in Blackhawk has 33,000 sq feet. Ours is 2,400 sq feet.

His ball room is 10,000 sq. feet and in it he keeps his classic car collection, valued at one hundred million. He has a DC jet, two pilots, and a flight attendant and he flies all over the world and to other homes for recreation. Going back to the house, he imported six hundred tons of Utah rock and twenty seven miles of teak for construction. His house is modeled after Frank Lloyd Wright's Falling Waters. I drove up to the gate and asked if we could have a ten minute drive through because I had a guest who would like to see how the other half lives. The security guard waved us on when I said my guest came from N.Y. state. We drove around but didn't call at any of the homes!

Near the entrance of this community is a shopping plaza. Not the usual kind. This is pink architecture and the main store is the F.J. Black Market, featured on TV several times. Always someone is playing a grand piano in this grocery store. Last year it was surrounded by poinsettias. During 1990 Safeway and Longs opened in a nearby plaza. Competition forced prices down but they still have unusual foods and a wonderful bakery and meat department.

Each night Phyllis was here we looked at slides of our trips.

Thursday Phyllis, Gene and I went to Pier 39 so Phyllis could see the sea lions. This is their second year there and there were three hundred seventy. Wildlife people says they are all males, some young, some old. We had lunch upstairs at Neptune's Cafe which overlooks the seals. The food was good but the view of the sea lions was wonderful. Afterwards we walked to Fishermen'sWharf and then to Ghirardelli Square. Too much walking for me and I was in real pain next day from my arthritis. We had hoped to go to the Galapagos this year but Gene thinks it would be too much for me. Darn!

I heard about the handicapped shop and wanted to visit it. I found a kangaroo with a joey in its pocket and thought I might buy it for Molly. It was six inches high and made of felt and cost $89. Molly did not get it.

When Gene was bowling Friday, Phyllis, my mother and I explored. I wanted to go over Grizzly Peak to Berkeley but it was too foggy. Instead we went Wildcat Canyon which is not as high and not as scenic. We visited a Norwegian store on Solano. but no other stores. Coming back we stopped in Emeryville and had lunch at the Hong Kong East Ocean Restaurant which is on the bay and from which we should have seen the Oakland, Golden Gate and San Rafael bridges. Guess what! FOG! We had lousy weather all the time Phyllis was here.

On Saturday Maryann, Dick and Molly came to lunch and to take Phyllls back to Campbell. I made an Italian cheesecake. My mother and Gene refused to eat it. The recipe said it was the pride of an Italian baker. Bah humbug!

With company gone, away went our Christmas decorations and the house is back to normal.

Our cold spell is still with us. It has been almost two weeks that we have had freezing weather at night. Almost everybody reports some damage but farmers are the ones to feel sorry for. They lost crops and income.

We are looking forward to 1991 which we hope will be a good year. Most of all we hope the war in the Middle East will be averted. Our next hope is that the recession will be short and not too harmful.

JANUARY 17, 1991

Dear Eleanor and Matt,

Twice we decided on a Galapagos vacation and twice we have rejected it but this year I thought it was decided. When I was recently asked where we were vacationing this year, I replied Galapagos and Gene immediately said NO. Later I asked him where we were going on vacation and he didn't know. We made out of list of places we want to visit and I took it to our travel agent and asked for brochures. Friday I picked them up and on Saturday we knew where we wanted to go. China. With the world situation as it is, Europe is out. China isn't too stable but it is felt that it will be a few years before there is another revolt. China wants tourists badly and authorities are trying to make travel there attractive.

We decided on a Pearl cruise with a side trip to Xian. The package included 4 days in Beijing and four days in Hong Kong. Monday we stopped at the travel agents with some questions and she was able to offer a 34 % discount so we book right then.

Saturday I went to the library for books on China. One book told about the wife of a San Francisco scientist who said the number of dogs she saw was less than the number of fingers she had. Another book said there are almost no cats in China. Homes are too small and food too expensive. Another book said a man who lived in a dirt house was given an apartment on the fourth floor. He had previously kept chickens in his yard. He didn't want to give up his chickens so he shared his living room- bedroom with his chickens.

Wednesday evening we saw an Australian play, DOWN AN ALLEY FILLED WITH CATS. which had two characters, both male. It was a queer play and many people walked out.

I just read, CHINA, A TRAVELER'S COMPANION by a Chinese American who returned to China after she married and had children. This is a wonderful book and certainly gives a lot of information about life in China. She said a Chinese scientist and his wife came to the U.S. and he and his wife decided to buy a live turkey at Thanksgiving. Chinese people do not buy dead fish and chickens. The scientist did not want to wring the turkey's neck or cut off its head so he gave it some chloroform. That evening he and his wife spent the whole evening plucking the turkey's feathers. Then they put it in the refrigerator over night. Next morning when they opened the refrigerator out staggered a naked turkey. From then on the scientist and his family have eaten a butterball turkey.

The author says that hotels lock the doors of all rooms in the daytime and doors cannot be unlocked from the inside. Her brother-in-law went to China and one day he didn't feel well enough to sightsee with the group so he stayed in his room. A couple hours later he felt better and decided to explore on his own, but he was locked in the room. Since there was no phone, he had to stay there till the hotel unlocked the rooms just before dinner.

FRIDAY THE 18TH 8:30 PM

Maryann called a few minutes ago and said they had been told late this afternoon that Molly can now be legally adopted.The birth mother had sued for the return of her child but the judge denied this. The father had signed off his rights. Adoption papers cannot be signed for eight months and the mother can appeal during that time. Maryann, Dick and Molly celebrated by going out to dinner and Molly was allowed to have food that usually is restricted. Molly is too small to realize the significance of this. Often the law is not justice but in this case I think justice prevailed. From birth on Molly had not been with her parents. The marriage often presented a crisis situation and Molly was neglected and endangered. Social workers placed Molly in good foster care, thank goodness. In court the mother showed no remorse for her neglect.

So with a very poor beginning to her life, Molly now looks to have a bright future.

JANUARY 30, 1991

Dear Emma and John,

I guess we have all had times in our lives when anything that could go wrong does. We remember this. These past few days everything has jelled for me. I much prefer it this way.

Saturday I made bean soup for my mother and ended up with 3 quarts which I put in the refrigerator. Sunday I made cheese bread from a hot roll mix, the recipe for which I found in a cookbook we bought last week. Anybody can make good bread from this mix but the added ingredients for the cheese bread had my mother telling me it was the best bread I ever made.

That same cookbook had a recipe for turkey cooked in wine and I decided to make this Tuesday night.

Monday morning I made a crown jewel dessert to serve when we showed our slides that night. I had just finished dressing when there was a phone call from Bev and Will, whom we knew from our Ann Arbor days. They were having breakfast in Denny's in Walnut Creek. I invited then to visit us and they said they would be here in half an hour. I suggested to Gene that we invite them to stay overnight and see our slides and he thought this a good idea. I immediately issued the invitation when they arrived and they accepted.

For lunch we had the bean soup and the bread and the bread was an immediate success with them. For dinner I made the turkey in wine and it was tasty. I also made a salad that Maryann, Dick and Phyllis liked when they visited during the holiday season. It is made with white and red cabbage, broccoli, lettuce, mushrooms and radishes and has a dressing that is out of this world.

1/4 cup sugar, 1/4 teas celery seed, 3 tablespoons each wine vinegar and walnut oil.

Every bit of this salad was eaten the first time I served it and every bit was eaten this time. I noticed Bev used her spoon to get every bit of dressing. Both Will and Bev were complimentary about the food and both had seconds of everything. This makes a cook feel good.

I think the Lord must have been looking out for me and guiding my activities. I was so prepared for company and yet I didn't know we were having company for 3 meals. I only knew about the dessert after the slide show.

Will and Bev had spent the weekend with their son who works in the judicial department of San Francisco. Recently, because of the L.A. riots, S.F. had had protesters and in order to protect the bridges and federal buildings. the son had had an 80 hour week. This wasn't part of his job but the police had commandeered everybody they could. Another friend has a son who is in the CHP and he has had 12 hours shifts on the bridges, even though he isn't employed in that county. Will and Bev's son said the protesters were quiet till the newsmen with cameras appeared and then they demonstrated. The protesters are paid $50 a day. Who pays them?

Next morning Will and Bev left right after breakfast. They didn't have a travel plan. Their next stop was Lodi where they planned to buy wine.

Today we did our weekly grocery shopping. Tomorrow is Gene's birthday and we are having company. I'm making the foods Gene likes.

The Motor Vehicle Bureau sent a letter which said Gene had to have his picture retaken before they would give him a license. Maybe he broke the camera, but a handsome guy like Gene shouldn't have done that.

FEBRUARY 2, 1991

Dear Phyllis,

Gene liked his birthday dinner, much to his surprise. We had chicken baked in a cranberry sauce. Usually Gene won't eat cranberries but this sauce just pepped up the chicken.

We had just dealt the first hand of bridge when we four heard a thump. I rushed from the room and found that my mother had fallen on her way to the bathroom. She broke her glasses. I asked if she were hurt and she said no. I helped her back in bed and I kept checking on her. She had the light on and was just lying in her bed. She couldn't see the TV because she had no glasses. When we went to bed. she wanted the light left on all night and this was unusual. The next morning as soon as I woke, I went in my mother's room. She said she was hurting and couldn't walk. I said we would rent a wheelchair and take her to the doctor and she agreed. I didn't dare suggest the hospital but Gene came in and said authoritatively that she was going to the emergency room of the hospital. She nodded her head yes. Then I knew something was really wrong. We practically carried her to the car. They found that she had a broken pelvis and admitted her to the hospital for a few days, after which she will either go to a convalescent hospital or come home with nursing care.

My mother's bathroom has needed a thorough cleaning for a long, long time but she objects whenever we want to disturb the status quo. Now is the time for us to paint. We removed everything and worked on cleaning the walls and shower stall. Saturday and Sunday Gene will paint. I have the curtains soaking and will wash them. Her bedroom also needs to be torn apart and cleaned but we won't be able to do this unless she goes to a convalescent home for awhile.

Guess what? It is raining. A miracle. Just this steady little rain won't help the drought but it will make the grass green.

FEBRUARY 4, 1991

Things change fast. Yesterday the doctor said my mother would be discharged Tuesday. I could bring her hone or put her in a convalescent hospital for a short time, but he advised the hospital because she needs physical therapy till she can stand on one foot. The hospital booked her in a Walnut Creek institution. Gene and I inspected it. It didn't smell but it was dark and hemmed in by other buildings and my mother would have been in a crowded three bed room which was really big enough for only two. Most of the patients were vegetables or almost vegetables. On the way home, we stopped at the Ygnacio Convalescent Hospital. and this was smaller, light and airy. We both liked this place. There is to be a vacancy today but I couldn't book till tomorrow. The earliest I could call was 7 AM and I did. My mother didn't get the vacancy but there is a room with a very sick woman which my mother would have to share for a day or two. The nurse said I sounded stressed and, believe me, I was. This convalescent hospital is right behind our doctor's office, next to the orthopedist office and right across the road from John Muir Hospital. Best of all it is just two miles away from our house, so it really is convenient. They insisted my mother go by ambulance from one institution to the other, just across the road,

Today I had to go to the doctor. Two weeks ago I had something wrong with my heel. Fifteen years ago the same thing occurred and the doctor gave me a shot of cortizone. This doctor gave me inserts which made my shoes tight and one toe on my left foot was so cramped that the toenail cut into the skin and I got an infection. What next!

FEBRUARY 12, 1991

Dear Phyllis,

I feel I'm on a roller coaster, some bad downs and a few ups.

While in the hospital my mother was perky and observed all that was going on. She was given a pain killer but it was spaced out. Her spirits were upbeat. At the convalescent hospital things changed. Her speech was garbled and she slept most of the time. Once she wanted Gene and me to go to the bank and withdraw some money she had in her name and put it in my name and Gene's. She wanted us to go THAT minute. She talked about everything having a beginning and an end. I felt she had given up. She was depressed when wheeled out to the day room where patients who aren't with it sit. She made them return her to her room. Often she was too tired to eat. Both Gene and I said this isn't my spunky mother. I thought she would be better when she got home.

She was o.k. coming home but once in bed she just lay there. At 7 I thought she was breathing her last. A neighbor couple came to inquire about my mother and I let Eve look at my mother and she was amazed. I had a terrible night.

This morning we got her up but she didn't stay up long and went back to bed and slept. The physical therapist- evaluator came at 10 AM. We talked and then she went to see my mother. She did some exercises with her legs and then asked her to try to walk. She got about 15 feet and gave out. So we put her in the wheel chair and took her back to bed. The P.T. said she would come Thursday. Wednesday and Friday a nurse's aide would come to bathe her. She laid out a schedule for the next two weeks.

At noon I told Gene lunch was ready as soon as I got my mother up. Gene said he would do that. Well, this was a whole other kettle of fish. My mother came to the table, ate a little, not much, and then decided to sit in the living room for a few minutes. Gene and I sat with her and we read. All at once she said she was going into her den where she does her jig saw puzzles. I wheeled her in and right up to the table. She looked at things and turned on her radio and was content till almost 4 PM. WOW! Gene and I were amazed. At four she fell asleep in the wheel chair so I put her back in bed for an hour. We brought her out for dinner. Again she didn't eat much but still more than before. Now she is back in bed but she is sitting up and she has her TV on. This is normal. She does have some pain but the P.T. showed me how to ease this with a pillow.

It is now 7:30 PM and I just checked my mother. She was uncomfortable sitting up so now she is lying down and the TV is off but this day she made more progress than any other.

I haven't given her any pain pills. I think they gave her too many in the convalescent hospital. The physical therapist agreed. It takes a long time for the cumulative effect to wear off. Her vital signs are not normal, they fluctuate. I don't know what to make of this and neither does the physical therapist.

If my mother is laid up for six weeks, that means I will be confined. We can't leave her alone because she cannot get in and out of bed alone. The physical therapist ordered a toilet seat attachment so she can get up and down more easily and it came within two hours. Delivered and installed.

Gene will grocery shop tomorrow and I'll help the nurse.

We had bridge changed to our house on Saturday night. My mother will be in bed but I'll be here if she needs me. Saturday Maryann, Dick and Molly are coming for lunch. This will be an added interest.

My spirits tonight are better than last night. My mother has a more positive attitude. I thought just getting home would be beneficial to my mother but it wasn't. I attribute the change to the physical therapist. She showed my mother what she could do and predicted progress.

Yesterday we got new lens for my mother's glasses. When I called, the nurse in the office said my mother's glasses were over a year old and she would have to come to the office for a new test. I explained the situation and said when my mother was well enough to come, we would but right now we needed the old lens. The nurse talked to the doctor and today Gene can pick up the glasses.

The nurse has just gone. She was very nice. The pressure spots on my mother's body have disappeared now that I know about the pillows.

My mother was depressed last night but it is now Friday and a few minutes ago my mother started to sing. Things are looking up!

What happened to lost and found
Diane's art museum wedding

FEBRUARY 22, 1991

Dear Lois and Fred,

Remember the short features we used to see before a movie? Well, I've been describing the main event, my mother's fall, and now I'm going to give you a short feature.

When my mother was transferred by ambulance from the hospital to the convalescent hospital, a distance of .02 miles, the cost was $250. From bed to bed, it probably wasn't five minutes. I said this is the most expensive taxi ride she ever had.

Early February 1st we took my mother to the emergency room and it was 1:30 before a bed was available and all the x-rays had been taken. She was on a gurney. They removed her bedroom slippers and placed them on the gurney but my mother kept moving one foot and they fell to the floor repeatedly. Each time I picked them up and put then on the gurney next to her. The day she was transferred I packed up her things and checked to see nothing was left. That night I didn't recall packing the slippers. I called the sixth floor and asked them to look around the bed and closet she occupied. We were in bed and asleep when the nurse called back and said a thorough search had been made and no slippers had turned up. These slippers were a favorite of my mother because they were lined with lambs wool. I said the last I saw them was in the emergency room. The nurse said this was a different story and I should call lost and found. The next morning, early, we stopped at the hospital before going to my mother at the convalescent hospital. I inquired at the desk for lost and found. Two volunteers manned the desk and one directed me to the fourth floor and one the basement. So one called and reported it was on the fourth floor, only now it was called ENVIRON-MENTAL SERVICES, instead of lost and found. I went to the fourth floor and walked the full length and there was no environmental services.

I stopped at the nursing station and was told it was in the basement. I said Information had just called and was told it was on the fourth floor. The nurse called and she also was told it was on the fourth floor. The nurse said she was in charge of the fourth floor and it WASN'T there. Then they told her it was in the fourth floor of the NEW building. I had to go down to the third floor and walk into the new building, go to the end and then go up to the fourth floor of the new building. The outside of the new building is completed but the inside is not and the fourth floor had two little offices and the rest was occupied by carpenters and plumbers working in a large area. No rooms there except for those two little offices. Nobody was in the first office but a man was in the second. The man said I should see the girl in the other office who would be back soon. She did-n't come so eventually he came in and took the description of the slippers and said he would tell her. Just as I was about to leave, the elevator opened and out came the girl. I described the slippers again. She said she would have to go to the basement in search for then. I offered to go with her but she said no. When she got to the elevator, the door opened and out stepped somebody with the slippers neatly marked with name and date left in the emergency room. I give the hospital credit for keeping track of the slippers but I wonder about the person who designated lost and found to now be environmental services.

In library school librarians are taught to catalogue under exact name. A dog is a dog, Puppies have a cross reference,see Dogs. At least a dog and a puppy are the same thing, but how can lost and found be environ-mental services? Never in all the world would could I imagine lost and found to be the same as environmental services. What about you? Does environmental services immediately come to mind when you want lost and found?

There is a lot of gobbledy gook in our language today.

Example : When I think of an engineer, I think of a mechanical, elec-trical, civil, architectural, aeronautical engineer. A garbage man used to be a garbage man but now he is a sanitary engineer. This makes as much sense as environmental services for lost and found. Do you agree?

MARCH 7, 1991

Dear Halys and Gordon.

Last Thursday, the 27th of February was the last day for the physical therapist. Today was the last day for the nurses's aide and tomorrow is the last day for the RN. We know my mother is better because her disposition is returning to normal. Today she was definitely out of sorts because the nurse's aide did not come right after breakfast for her bath and she wanted to get dressed. I explained that the aide had several persons to bathe and she had to take her turn but when my mother wants something, she wants it then. 11:45 was just too late to take a bath in my mother's estimation. Doctors have to order home nursing care from P.Ts. RNs, and LVNs and I'm sure grateful ours did. It took a lot of strain off me and maybe helped me as much as my mother. I'll watch over my mother and help her but now she is on her own. Friday I'm taking her out to lunch. Bush said the war is over and Norma says Myrtle is well. Things return to normal, says Norma.

Actually the fracture is healed but my mother has two other problems. Her blood pressure is still not what it was. The other problem might be fatal if an operation is performed. So we just try to control it and not cure it. She is in no pain.

Last Monday I declared a NORMA DAY. I just had to have a breather so Gene took over for a few hours. I went shopping and bought a dressy pants outfit to wear on the boat when we go on vacation.

Ever since we decided on the China trip, I've been reading books on China. I'm reading Fox Butterfield's CHINA. He lived there for several years while a N.Y. Times correspondent. He says in the U.S women want equality of work with men. In China women have equality that is forced upon them and they wish for liberation from work. He made it a point to get to know many Chinese and cites examples where a wife is forced to work in one village or city and the husband in another and often they see one another and the children only once a year. People are not free to move and they are not free to find their own places to live. I don't think we will see the things he described because we will see only what China wants foreigners to see. I've read several books by persons who traveled independently in China and they had much difficulty going where they wanted to go. Fox tells about riding overnight on a train in the soft berths reserved for foreigners. At 5 AM the woman conductor opened his door and told him to use the bathroom. He was going to be on the train for three more hours so he turned off the light and went back to sleep. Again the woman opened the door and she handed him his clothes and told him to use the bathroom. He objected and she said that in a few minutes the toilet would be locked and this was his last chance before arriving at this destination. I would not like to be Chinese.

Our friend, Frank, is being married for a second time. For Mormons, the first marriage is for eternity and the second for time. So in heaven he will be reunited with Beth and his second wife will be reunited with her first husband. So what happens to a divorced couple in heaven? What happens to a second wife who hadn't previously been married? What about the never marrieds?

APRIL 1, 1991

Dear Connie and Herb,

The neighbors we know the best are Sue and Hing who live across the court from us in the brown house. Sue called one night and asked if we had received a surprise that day. We hadn't but the next day we received a lavender-pink envelope with a San Mateo return address and I guessed it was an invitation to their daughter Diane's wedding. This was not a surprise but a delight. The Wongs have two lovely children who are a real credit to their parents. We know Darren better than Diane because he came home weekends when he was at Berkeley. Diane also graduated from Berkeley. Now she works for an airline and Darren is working on his Ph. D.

We were intrigued with the invitation which was on a white card that had the faintest red threads woven into the paper. The background of the wording was a Chinese character which Sue later told me meant love. There were two tiny red hearts pasted on the invitation. We returned the reply card and said we would be delighted to attend the wedding of Diane and Jay on March 30th in the Green Room of the Museum of Modern Art in San Francisco. There was another card enclosed which invited us to a dinner on the 31st at the China Station in Berkeley. Another little card had a map of Berkeley showing us where China Station is located. The invitation to the dinner had the same character three times on the left. The top character was black, the middle one gray and the bottom a very light gray. Later Sue told us Darren designed these invitations for his sister. It seems one printer made the character black and the words were also black so nothing showed up. Diane took it to another printer who did it correctly. The word correctly characterized the wedding and attention to detail dominated all plans. We have never been to such a perfectly planned wedding.

On the 30th Gene and I left home at 4:30 and drove to the BART station where we got a train into San Francisco. We exited at Civic Center and walked to the Museum. It was still light. We knew that at one time Civic Center was populated by the homeless and not a desirable place to walk. However the police had forced them to move weeks before so it wasn't bad. We wondered how it might be when dark. We entered the Museum and walked around and did not find the Green Room. When we looked at the elevator, we saw that it was on the second floor. Before we entered the elevator, we met two women also looking for the Green Room. One asked us if we were friends of Diane. I replied, "No, her parents." Very surprised the woman exclaimed, " You are Diane's parents!" That would have been a surprise for Gene and me to produce a Chinese child. We had to say no but we certainly wouldn't mind being the parents of a girl like Diane.

As we left the elevator, Sue, Hing and Hing's mother were coming down the hall and they joined us and we entered the Green Room at the same time. I had planned to change from my walking shoes to dress shoes before entering. A picture was taken of the five of us and I was chagrined that my old walking shoes would be in the picture. Sue asked somebody to give me a chair so I could change my shoes. I was relieved after I did.

Chairs had been set up in the Green room for the wedding. The buffet reception was being held in the same room. We could see tables all set up on the balcony. Sue said after the ceremony the chairs would be replaced by tables. Diane and Jay marched down the aisle and out on the balcony. We all followed and went thru the reception line. Meanwhile Jay's softball team replaced the chairs with tables and chairs. The caterer had said it would take an hour and a half for this but in twenty minutes flat it was all done by these efficient guys. Not a glass was broken in transferring the tables.

Diane was a beautiful bride and had an exquisite wedding gown with a satin skirt, a long train appliqued with pearls, lace and sparkling bits. The bodice was of a softer material and it was off the shoulder with puffy short sleeves. The train could be removed and then the skirt was a straight skirt. Around the dress hem was a band, maybe eight inches high, of beaded work. I don't think I've ever seen such a lovely gown. Diane is tiny and she looked especially small when the train was removed. I was afraid Diane would catch cold on the balcony when the reception line formed but she didn't catch cold because she already had a cold. Darn! That may have lessened her enjoyment of the wedding.Nobody wants a cold at that time. I do know brides who had a cast on a leg, used crutches or a walker and this would be worse. There were three bridesmaids in long, close fitting, red gowns with a peplum. They were small, like Diane. They carried red and white bouquets and if I remember correctly there were lilies in the bouquets. It was such a pretty wedding party.

After the reception line, the bridal party returned to the Green Room and the bridal party passed along the buffet table. Guests signed a book as they entered and were given a slip of paper with their names and the letter of the table where they were to sit. Since we were with Sue and Hing and I had to change my shoes, we didn't sign in so we didn't have a table assignment. Sue went over and got it for us. We were at table E with another Caucasian couple and two Chinese couples. Both Chinese men were friends of Hing from his school days. Jackie had worked with Hing so that is how they were invited. Aside from we eight people all the guests Hing and Sue invited were family. We felt honored to be invited.

The bride and groom, Sue and Hing circulated among the tables. Conversation at our table just flowed. Care had been taken to get people together who would be compatible. Darren had made cards for each table which listed the guests. This is nice because sometimes you forget a name when introduced. Again attention paid to detail showed. After the bridal party passed by the buffet., a designated person approached each table and we went in order to the buffet table. So everyone at a table ate at the same time. The centerpiece at the tables consisted of a circular mirror with 4 porcelain swans, four candles and one perfect white camellia. Simple but beautiful. The swans were favors for each woman and had her name on it and a ribbon with the date and the bride and groom's name.

Some pictures were taken during the wedding and during the buffet but the main studio pictures were taken prior to the wedding on the grounds of the Palace of the Legion of Honor. In this way you can choose a lovely setting and take time to get the pictures just right.

While the 168 people were eating, Diane disappeared for a few minutes and came back in her Chinese (cheongsam) dress. It was the traditional red, form fitting, slit up the side, high neckline Chinese dress with gold embroidery on the front. The gold embroidery has a meaning, something like yin-yang. Nobody could tell me exactly. Since Gene and I are large, people think we eat a lot. The caterer gave me two pieces of beef and I took one of turkey. We thought the beef was wonderful. It was well cooked and could be cut with a fork. Sue and Hing thought it was overdone.

I learned early in marriage not to serve beef because all my guests wanted it a different way. I don't know the difference between rare and medium rare. Nobody was pleased. We only have beef when we are alone and we have it well done.

The wedding cake was three tiers and around the bottom tier were some of those porcelain swans which Diane had purchased in New Orleans and brought back on a plane. The roses on the cake were the color of the bridesmaid's dresses. The cake was chocolate with a pink filling, the flavor of which I could not identify. It was very different and so good.

Before the cake was cut, Diane disappeared again and came back in her white wedding gown. Diane was just as pretty in her Chinese gown as she was in her wedding gown.

Speaking of gowns, Sue's gown consisted of a chiffon skirt attached to a lace top that reached to the hips. It flowed. We are used to seeing Sue and Hing in clothes they wear to work, to garden, and at home but we weren't prepared to see them in formal wear. Hing looked like a tycoon and appeared most comfortable in his finery.

After the wedding dinner, there was dancing. We stayed for awhile but when one couple said they must leave because they had an hour's drive down the peninsula, our table broke up. Jackie and her husband live just beyond Concord and offered us a ride home. We readily accepted and they dropped us off at BART where we picked up our car. So we didn't find out if the homeless are still sleeping outdoors in Civic Center.

Usually the bride's mother is worn out with preparing a daughter's wedding but Diane planned and executed this wedding. Both Diane and Sue have full time jobs, yet this was the best organized wedding we have ever attended. We observed that Darren seemed to act as master of ceremonies. In a very quiet manner he kept everything moving. He also was a groomsman so he was a busy person. The girl who gets Darren will be so lucky.

So the wedding is over. NO, SIR. The next afternoon Gene and I drove to Berkeley to China Station where Sue and Hing hosted a Chinese dinner for 76. Dinner is not an appropriate word to describe it. Feast or banquet would be better. Gene and I thought we should invite Jackie and her husband to ride with us but we weren't sure they had also been invited to the dinner so I said nothing. When we were again assigned to the same table, I confided to Jackie I had wished to invite them to ride with us but since the Wongs said this dinner was just for family, I said nothing. Jackie had the same thought in reverse.

At this banquet Sue's sister, Marilyn, daughter Linda and son-in-law Ben, Teddi and Jane and Jackie and husband sat at the same table with us. Conversation was easy with Marilyn acting as hostess. Twelve courses were served. First came a platter of cold meats, 1000 year old eggs that are the color of coal and shrimp. I didn't recognize the cold meats. We ate hardly half on this platter. Next each got a quail and I was surprised at the amount of meat on this little bird. The third was shark's fin soup which is a real delicacy and served only at banquets. In Japan we were served soup as the last course. I was replete and thought this was the end of the meal. But, no, we had hardly begun. The fourth course was crisp duck skins with steam buns. I had never had either before. The fifth was the duck meat. The sixth was chicken with rice. Seventh lobster. Eighth beef with broccoli. Ninth Peking sparerib. Tenth fish with macadamia nuts. Eleventh almond jello and the twelfth fortune cookies. Besides tea there was 7 up, sparkling cider and cognac.

Beginning with the fourth course Marilyn asked the waiter to pack up the left overs and she gave us two packages when we left, the beef with broccoli and the duck. We had two meals at home from these left overs. Gene said Marilyn didn't understand English because when he said no to another serving, she paid no attention. Marilyn speaks and understands English perfectly. We never had such a delicious Chinese meal. We'll go to a Chinese wedding anytime.

I say Chinese wedding. Actually it was a wedding between two

Americans, one of Chinese descent and the other of Caucasian background.

I expect this weekend will be a highlight of 1991 for Gene and me. It will remain in our memory as one of the three best weddings we ever attended.

After this, next weekend will be dull.

MAY 18, 1991

Dear Isabel,

It is 2 PM and I've been working since we got up at 7:15 AM. Ruth and Bill, our square dance friends from Buffalo days, arrive at 8 AM on Monday so I've been cooking up a storm. I want meals so well planned that we can spend our days sightseeing. They embarked on a Panama Canal Cruise on the east coast and they will disembark in San Francisco. We are letting them come to us by BART because we would have to drive in the commute traffic if we picked them up at 8 AM. I'm tired and glad to sit down and write this letter.

Yesterday was my ikebana meeting in San Francisco and Gene's bowling banquet in the evening. I told Gene to give my mother for lunch some soup I had prepared. I said it was fortunate we had some barbecued turkey, fresh peas, and cabbage salad and I would give this to my mother for dinner so I wouldn't have to cook just for her. Well, Gene heated up the soup and was about to put the peas in the soup when he remembered they were for her dinner. However, he put the turkey on his plate and sat down to eat it when suddenly he remembered I was saving it for her dinner so he put it back in the refrigerator. Phew! My mother's dinner almost was eaten for lunch.

Yesterday I decided to wear my Austrian crystal beads which I love and wear very frequently because the stones are in pastel colors and go with everything. Stores sell these Austrian crystal beads but usually the stones are one or two colors and of a deep hue. I couldn't find them. Usually they are on our bureau. I looked in my jewel box. I took everything out of the drawer where I keep my good jewelry and looked in every box. No crystals. I looked in drawers where I have clothes, just in case they accidentally got there. I went thru my purse. I looked in the drawers in the bathroom. I put my hand in the love seat where I usually sit. Gene did the same. Not there. I finally wore something else. When I came back, I looked all over again. Then I decided I might as well resign myself to losing them. I was afraid I had tried something on in a store and left them in a dressing room but I hadn't recently been shopping. Where had they gone? Just a few minutes ago I asked Gene to help me vacuum under the cushions of the love seat, sofa and overstuffed chairs. I took the cushions off the love seat and there on the opposite end of where I always sit were my crystals. I must have been on my exercycle and taken them off and put them on the arm of the love seat and they slid down.

All the while I was busy this morning, Gene was looking for the bill for his physical which he wanted to send to the insurance company. It had been on the bureau for a couple weeks. Not there now. I looked thru all the bills connected with my mother's illness and thru my medical bills. Gene was fit to be tied. He had to have that bill. Finally he went thru all his bills again and found he had attached this bill to another bill. So the lost was found in both cases. Now the question is ARE WE GET-TING OLD AND FORGETFUL? I leave it up to you.

Those crystals have brought comments from store clerks and friends. Kate is drawn to them and once before she could talk, she took her father in our bedroom and reached her little hand up and got the crystals and brought them to me. I think she wanted me to put them on. This last time she visited, she said. "Do you know why I like those beads?" I said no and she said. "Because they sparkle." Molly is also intrigued with them and the very first time she visited us, she had to touch them. Little girls like things that sparkle and I KNOW BIG GIRLS LIKE SPARKLING STONES. Do you agree?

Last week I read someplace where baggage handlers at an airport discovered a dead dog in a dog cage. Not wanting to be blamed for the dog's death, they rushed to a pound and found a similar dog and traded the live one for the dead one. When the woman owner collected her dog cage, she screamed because she had shipped her dead dog home for burial and now suddenly he was alive.

I told this to my four passengers when we went to San Francisco. Jacqui said a visiting son brought his dog, his most prized possession. While her husband and sons were away, she opened the door and the dog slipped out. She had no voice because she had a virus, so she couldn't call the dog. She got in the car and rode around, hoping to see the dog. She intended to clap her hands and hoped the dog would come to her. Not finding the dog, she called her son and in a whisper she told him about the dog. The son said. "Don't worry, Mother. It is o.k. " She couldn't believe her ears because her son loves this dog almost more than anything else. When the son returned, he searched for the dog. No luck. A couple days later a vet called and asked if they had lost a dog. It seems the dog was sighted on Main Street by a couple that had lost a similar dog. They stopped and the woman angerly commanded the dog to get in the car. The dog slunk in. When they were home, the man decided to remove all the mud from the dog before he took it in the house and while doing this he noticed the dog tags were not those of his dog so he took the dog back to the vet and left it there.

MAY 23, 1991

Bill and Ruth were to arrive at 8 AM in S.F. and I thought they would be here a little after 9 so we were ready to pick them up at the Pleasant Hill BART station. They called after 11 and they were at the Concord station. Off we went. They had two enormous bags and two big straw bags and some other bags. They were loaded down. They neglected to tell us what ship and line they took on this cruise of the Panama Canal. It turned out to the Regent Star. We had gone on the Regent Sea to Panama. This line leaves something to be desired. Air conditioning broke down on our cruise and the ship leaked and pails were set up all over to catch the water. The air conditioning broke down on their ship, too, and before they got to San Diego the stabilizer broke so they were delayed six hours in San Diego. It couldn't be fixed so they used water for ballast. That didn't work and the ship listed twenty degrees all the way from San Diego to San Francisco. Ruth said it broke in the night and she was awakened when things fell off the dressing table. This ship will cruise to Alaska all summer. I wonder when they will get the stabilizer fixed. Can you imagine being a couple days on a ship that wasn't level?

It has been nineteen years since we were together but it was as yesterday. Letters have kept us informed. Memories have kept the friendship alive. Square dancing, a New Year's Eve party at their house, a get together at our house for both their mothers and my mother, their nice children are some of the memories we have. Ruth recalled a Christmas dinner party at our house and could even tell me what I served. Ruth and Bill are fun to be with.

Monday we went to the top of Mt. Diablo and to Rossmoor. Tuesday and Wednesday we went into San Francisco and spent the whole day. Evenings we saw slides and played bridge.

Ruth and Bill left by airport shuttle for the San Francisco airport where they will fly to Tacoma to visit Ruth's cousin for a couple days. Then back to San Francisco for an overnight and an early morning flight to Buffalo.

MAY 24, 1991

Gene had an appointment to receive his new hearing aids this morning. Gene has been deaf ever since his service in the Air Force. During our courtship in 1955 Gene wore a hearing aid that had a box he hid under his shirt and a wire went to his ear. One day Gene hugged me tightly and the hearing aid box made a black and blue mark on my breast. That weekend I had a physical and the doctor asked how I got so bruised and I had to tell him it was from my boy friend's hearing aid.

I shopped this morning and when I returned home, I began to tell

Gene about my bargains. He told me not to talk so loudly. Apparently these hearing aids are going to help.

Molly's 3rd birthday party
$1000 yard material

JUNE 2, 1991

Dear Andrea,

We left at 9:45 this morning for Molly's birthday party. We arrived at 11. The party was slated for 11:30 but we were bringing folding chairs, a salad, parker house rolls and little baskets of candy I had made for the children. The house had purple and lavender streamers on the front and there was a sign directing us back where tables were set on the patio for the parents of the invited children, relatives and friends.

Molly was in her navy blue dress. When she greeted us in the drive, I gave her birthday present to her and suggested she take it in the house. Already there was a pile of presents in the family room. Molly took me to her bedroom to show me her new bed and then she went back for Gene and took his hand and brought him to her bedroom where she showed him the bed and the railing they put up at night so she won't fall out of bed. Molly may be only three but she has an eye for a good man!

For the children Maryann had a large dish of fruit and a sherbet which the kids loved. For the adults she had salads and dips.

We were still at the tables when the man with the pony arrived and that was the end of eating for us. Dick said the pony rides would be out front on the sidewalk because otherwise all the pony would do is eat the grass in the back yard. Molly was first and she wasn't a bit scared. Each child had a turn and then a second turn. One little boy cried as soon as he was on the pony and even with his mother beside him, he was afraid. A fourteen month old baby didn't cry. The pony was rented for an hour but long before that the kids were finished with pony riding. Maryann had invited the social worker and her husband and the foster parents Molly had before she came to them. Fifteen months had intervened and Molly had no recollection of this couple, even though she had lived with them for six months. Kids forget fast in the early years of their life.

After the pony rides, it was present opening time. A little boy and girl sat down and started tearing the paper off the packages before giving the present to Molly. Just like in Japan. Molly didn't seem to mind. Maryann was busy writing down the name of the giftgiver and the gift.

My mother gave Molly, Isabel's new book, A GARDEN ALPHABET

and we gave a bond. An old lady I met collects Danbury Mint dolls and she had just received one named Molly. I asked if she was throwing the box away and she was so I took the box and put the bond, wrapped in tissue paper, inside the box. I just put a ribbon on the box because it was such an attractive box. The little boy shook the box and tissue paper and didn't find a present. Maryann spied the envelope in the tissue paper. It was the least exciting gift but it will last the longest.

After the presents, we went back outdoors for games. I'm so out of touch with small children's parties, I didn't know that pin the tail on the donkey is now place some gummed thing on Minnie Mouse. Things change.

The kids were very good and they shared Molly's toys. No one was hurt even though a baseball bat and ball were used.

The party was to end at two o'clock but it ran over. Dick's mother left on a five o'clock plane but another couple stayed over till tomorrow. Maryann will be tired tonight.

My mother looked forward to the party and said she just wanted to live long enough to attend this party. She enjoyed the kids and one little boy recited the alphabet for her.

A party for a three year old is a rare treat for us. Gosh, it is a different world from our world. I bet we enjoyed it more than any of the parents.

JUNE 21, 1991

Dear Raedina and Milton,

Today we received a thank you from Diane and Jay for their wedding present. I wrote about this March 30th wedding. Diane's mother warned us the thank you would be late in coming and I can see the reason. The 5x7 paper was the same as the wedding invitation with tiny red threads woven in the paper and love in Chinese characters at top left and the words Diane and Jay next to it. Not only did she thank us for our two gifts but told us how she used them and then she thanked us for sharing their special day. The parents had been so interested that I sent about twenty five letters telling about the wedding that I made copies for them, Diane and Darren, her brother. She wrote that she was flattered at my detailed account and that they would always enjoy it because it would jog their memories in future years. In addition was a picture of them in their wedding finery on a "baseball card." It said Diane & Jay's big day and gave the date and had that love character on the front. On the back it had "WEDDING COMMEMORATIVE CARD, SPECIAL EDITION, EAST MEETS WEST," then their names with the word, newlyweds, under that.

Next it said, "Diane and Jay first met working at United Airlines.

Now they plan a lifetime of flying the friendly skies. He wants to visit all the ballparks. She wants to see faraway, exotic places. Is Wrigley Field a faraway exotic place? Does Bali have a baseball park? Watch for future editions/'additions'!"

We had a picture thank you from our Norwegian friends and this is the second one. I think this is such a nice way of saying thank you. It took a long time to get the printing done but the thank you was so special and different.

On our 27th wedding anniversary on June 27th, we three went to Chez Dyon for dinner which Gene and I thought excellent. My mother said she never wanted to go there again. This is par for the course. Vegetables were al dente. She is so fussy about her food and hard to please in her old age. I know what she likes and how she likes it cooked so I cater to her.

JULY 23, 1991

Dear Chet and Bess,

I have been remiss in not thanking everyone who sent an anniversary card. We did appreciate them. I say Thank you. Sorry about that. The reason for the delay is that I was busy preparing for and having company.

As you know, we are in our fifth season of drought. Two Monterey Pines on the church property behind our house died two months ago. Early in the year I called the church and asked the minister if he knew they had the two dead trees. He said yes. I said there was danger of them toppling over and he said the session was considering having them taken down. Nothing happened till last night when the nearest one crashed down during the night and broke the fence of our back neighbor and their clothes drying rack. I had noticed yesterday that the tree was slanting about 45 degrees into the parking lot. The next tree is slanting slightly our way and will probably land in our back yard. I called the back neighbor tonight and asked the back neighbor if she had informed the church. She said the secretary said the minister was on vacation and nothing could be done till he returned. This made me mad. I called the police and a policeman came and looked and said he could do nothing but that the church would be responsible for any damage. WELL! If Gene or I get clunked on the head and killed, responsibility won't give us back our life. I called a member of the church and asked the names of session members. This person wanted to know what the problem was. She gave me the name of the session member in charge of grounds and building. I called this man and I got results. In a few minutes two men were here and looking at the situation and one man had already contacted a tree removal company and had two bids. This man promised that the trees would be gone by Thursday or Friday. Both said the secretary should not have said this problem would have to wait for the minister's return. If nothing happens this week, I'll be on the phone next week till something is done.

It is now 8:10 AM the next day and already the standing dead tree is down and buzz saws are going. The man didn't wait for more estimates. It paid to raise a stink.

Now it is three hours later and all is quiet in the church yard and chunks of trees are lying around but this doesn't bother me. The whole thing took about an hour but the clean up will take much longer. It is a good thing the tree fell in the middle of the night because the man behind us barbecued right where the tree fell and his kids were running around. Somebody could have been killed. The session member said he had an estimate for $700 for cutting down the tree and removing the other. I said we paid $350 when we had a eucalyptus tree removed. Monterey Pines grow six feet a year and these trees were at least seventeen years old so they had attained full growth of a hundred feet. Gene raked up dead needles and branches for a month this spring. Only the trunk and large limbs are left.

After the earthquake the Wongs water bill was inflated. Both work and weekends they go into San Francisco to visit family and friends and oversee their properties. They use very little water. They knew something was wrong and began to investigate. This past weekend Sue was ill with a cold so Hing decided this was the time to have the leak fixed. He called a plumber and got an estimate and contract and the agreement that the work would be done on Saturday. The plumber said it would take about one and a half hours.

Gene and I saw the plumber arrive at 8 AM. Every hour we noticed he was still there. At 2 PM Gene said we should go over and offer to take a second mortgage on the Wongs house. We expected the bill would be horrendous because we did not know that the signed contract called for $200 labor and $45 service charge. The plumber arrived in a white outfit and each hour he got dirtier. By five when he left, he was covered with mud.

Here in California, foundations, about one foot high, are made for houses. The house is built on this foundation and under the house is dirt. Pipes go under the house. There is only about one foot crawl space and it is dark. Gene went under our house once shortly after we moved here and he won't ever go again. Other men have said the same. You need to be a small man to crawl under these houses and one who isn't claustrophobic.

Have I mentioned we are recovering our dining room chairs? I wanted an animal pattern or the exact random pattern that is on the chairs. Two interior decorators tried to find something suitable or anything remotely possible. Finally one brought a French tapestry whose colors were perfect, a geometric design. Everybody who saw the sample loved it but I still held out for something I saw in ARCHITECTURAL DIGEST. One decorator said he found the exact thing I saw in this magazine but he did not bring a sample because it was $1000 a yard and the material was only twenty five inches wide. At this price you would think it real animal skin but it was only velour. We settled on the French tapestry for $150 a yard. Last week Gene recovered the seats of the chairs and he did a beautiful job. We are extremely pleased with the result. Actually this material is better for our decor than the animal pattern so I'm completely satisfied.

I had a stroke of luck last week. My comment to the doctor that I was having a heck of a time finding someone to stay with my mother caused him to whip out a card and write down a name and phone number. I called Sara when I got home. Everything seemed o.k. so I said I would contact her after our company left. I called Friday and Gene, Mother and I went over to see Sara and her house. She lives in a lovely section of Walnut Creek. The house is on a court and is most attractive.

Upon entering there is a beautiful living room on the right and a formal dining room on the left, most tastefully furnished. Thick carpeting. Then we came to a peach bedroom which had a big bed with a peach and lace spread and about five oversized pillows. Glamorous! This is to be my mother's room. The house was immaculate. My mother was impressed and said the house was too good for her. I think my mother will feel she is returning to the slums when she comes back with us. Sara has two rest homes and she works hard administering them. Usually she doesn't have anyone in her own home but she did have a ninety five year old woman who was too alert and well to be in a convalescent hospital. Sara has a cleaning woman and a person who takes care of this elderly woman. I feel I can go away and not worry about my mother. Sara works with our doctor and between the two my mother will probably get better care than I give her. It is expensive but far, far superior to some rest homes I've investigated.

FRIDAY THE 26TH

People from the church are fixing our back neighbor's fence today. We certainly can't complain about the church not doing their duty.

Recently Gene and I have unintentionally been playing tricks on each other. Gene goes out to work in the yard and uses the side door in the garage. I go out to hang something on the line, come back, close and lock the door. So Gene is locked out. Yesterday I was going away and went out and told Gene. Automatically I closed and locked the side door when I came back in. Then I backed out and closed the garage door with the remote. control. Fortunately Gene had his keys in his pocket so he could come in the front door.

Gene keeps telling me I'm lost. Once I was reading the paper in the family room. Gene passed thru the kitchen and didn't see me there. Returning from the garage and going to our bedroom, he has to pass thru or by every room. He didn't see me at all. When he finally returned to the family room, he found me. I say I'm not lost. I know where I am even if he doesn't. Another day I was lying on the sofa in the living room. He looked all over for me. I saw him searching and wondered but I didn't know he was looking for me. Are we getting old? Or what?

Our grass is getting green again. We are supposed to conserve water but we are no longer rationed. We lost some shrubs and we won't have many oranges but the tree is alive and a few days of watering has made it look much better.

August is going to be a busy month. Jacqueline and Will are coming to San Francisco to a wedding and we have made plans to get together. Linda, Bob and Kate will be visiting Connie and we are planning a picnic. Our Japanese friends arrive on the 18th.

As of now we have two weeks without company before we go to China. Since I won't have to prepare the house and food for my mother and a companion, I think I will have plenty of time to pack and rest up for the trip.

A Chinese funeral

Little lost girls, Flying saucer hits Gene

AUGUST 3, 1991

Dear Mary and Dave,

Thursday my mother told me the mailman was at the Wong's door. I knew this meant something must be signed for so I went over, signed and took the envelope. When Hing came home, I took over his certified letter and he thanked me and said this saved him a trip to the post office.

Friday afternoon Sue called me from work. In a very low voice she thanked me for taking the letter. I was puzzled. Sue has never called from work before. The next thing she said was that her brother had just called her at work to tell her that her father had just died. Gosh! I was flattered. You only call real friends when something like this happens.

I immediately got in the car and went off to buy yeast so I could make rolls, beef for a wonderful French stew, beans for the California bean salad and a brownie mix. The rest of the afternoon and evening I was busy cooking. Gene looked enviously at the brownies

This morning I made the rolls and they turned out great. I called Hing and asked him to take them to Sue's mother when he went to San Francisco. He was surprised that I knew and asked if Sue had called me and when. He was more surprised when I told him the time. Sue's father had a stroke six years ago and he has steadily deteriorated. He died of pneumonia.

Sue and Hing have planned a trip with friends the last two weeks of August. I'm glad this happened now so they can go on vacation and not worry.

AUGUST 10, 1991

Sue's father's funeral was at noon today. Last weekend Sue and her sisters and brother were busy making arrangements. Sue worked Monday through Thursday, even though she was quite sick. Friday she had an EKG in the morning and then went for visiting hours in the afternoon and evening. I figured if we were asked to share the joy of a wedding, we should also share the sorrow of a funeral.

So Gene and I went to San Francisco this morning. The funeral home was in the North Beach section of San Francisco. The outer room of their unit had seats like a church and along the sides and across the front at each side of a large arch were the floral arrangements. I counted thirty nine. Aside from two, they were large wreaths three feet in diameter and the wreath frame had three rows of flowers, usually carnations. At the top of each were large clusters of different flowers. There were two white streamers on each with Chinese letters. There were two sprays which must have been sent by Caucasians because they didn't go with the other arrangements. One was white and purple orchids and the other anthurium. In the room thru the arch was the casket and seating for wife, daughters, son and spouses. The son wore a black strap on his arm and around his waist. The rest all wore just black straps on the arm. Everybody was in black with no ornamentation. There were more arrangements there and the children of the deceased placed a floral wheel chair there because the father had been wheel chair bound these past six years. In the corner was a table and on it was a roast chicken and a roast leg of lamb and a bottle of sauce. What this signified, I don't know.

There must have been twelve grandsons and spouses of granddaughters, who came in two by two. All were dressed in black suits, with white starched standup collars and bow ties. Diane's new husband was one and he fit right in. The granddaughters all had non descript black suits, exactly alike. All had shoulder length black hair. I stood out like a sore thumb because I wore a beige suit. There was one other Caucasian couple and they also were dressed in black.

A Chinese man dressed in a robe like a Protestant minister spoke in Chinese. Darren, our neighbor's son, gave a brief history of his grandfather's life. Born in 1909,. he came to the U.S. with nothing and worked eighteen hours a day till he had enough money to go back to China and marry. He sired two children and then returned to the U.S. He worked hard again and went back and sired two more children. He came back and worked hard again and then sent for his family. He bought a home and started his own business. He joined the army in 1942 and served thoughout the war.

Three decorated, young soldiers served at the funeral along with a trumpeter. They will give a twenty one gun salute at the cemetery. After the speech making was over, the soldiers went to the casket and saluted. Then the audience, one by one, went up and bowed. Hing's mother who doesn't speak English waited for us and sat beside us. We followed her and bowed three times. Then you passed before the wife and children. Sue and Hing stepped out of line to embrace us. One sister and the brother especially thanked us for coming.

As we left the room two old men were stationed at the door and one gave everybody a small white envelope which contained a quarter and a piece of candy in a red wrapper with a Chinese character. A white bag signifies death. To sweeten death you eat the candy and buy more candy with the quarter. The red bag has a quarter and it signifies good health and good luck. Some people also got another red bag with a dollar. We got the dollar bag because we did something that was especially appreciated by the family. So we ended up with a total of three dollars for candy. We were impressed with this funeral.

Some people will go to the cemetery and at 4 PM today there will be a longevity meal at a Chinese restaurant. Orally all were invited to attend. We also received a written invitation as we left.Gene and I decided this was for family and friends and did not go.

Until we moved to California, I had no contact with any Chinese person. There were none in Geneva. I never had one in any school where I worked. I know nothing about their customs so a Chinese wedding and funeral are most interesting.

AUGUST 5, 1991

Dear Ivy and Hubert,

Kate and her parents are visiting Connie and yesterday I ran out to Connie's and picked up the doll I gave Kate a few years ago. She lost a bootee and needed another. I brought the doll home and made new bootees. They are difficult because they are so small. I also made a new dress, bonnet and panties, a crib robe, mattress and pillow and I was working on the sheet when suddenly my sewing machine wouldn't sew. Gene fiddled with it but he couldn't make it work. So early this morning I took it to a repair man. He said he would have it done by Wednesday afternoon. I said Kate was leaving on Thursday and no way could I get the doll clothes made in one evening. He said to call him back at five today. I did and he had it fixed. He showed us a plastic gear that had three teeth broken off. The new gear cost $8.50 but the labor was $89. I don't use my sewing machine a lot but I do use it. I asked if I could pay with a check and he said yes. I asked if he wanted identification and he said, "Yes, A smile will do." I smiled and he waved his hand. I wonder how far this smile thing could go!

Connie suggested a picnic while Kate and her parents are visiting and I asked what I could bring. Immediately she said potato salad, another salad and dessert. Connie will buy the chicken and the charcoal and Bob will barbecue the chicken. No work for Connie. She used her head. As my father would say, she used her coupe and saved her sedan. I didn't mind the work because Connie is very good and generous. When my mother has been sick, she has visited and brought flowers and gifts.

We are having this picnic in a grove at Rossmoor. The tables are a bit far from the parking lot and I didn't know how we were going to get my mother there. She can't walk 100 feet. I remembered seeing our neighbor take her grandchild for a ride in a wagon. Yesterday I saw Linda out in her drive and went over and asked if we could borrow her wagon for a few hours and she readily agreed. Gene washed the wagon because it was dirty. Linda's children are all grown up now. As we talked Linda said David got the wagon for Christmas and Debby who was almost four saw the Sears sign on it and remarked that she didn't know Santa got his toys from Sears. Linda said the only two words Debby could read at this point were Ford and Sears.

Linda had just returned from buying a new car. Sid died in April and they planned she would have new a car this year. Sid had an almost new sports car which Linda sold. I can see why. I had tears everytime I saw it sitting in the garage. The association with Sid probably would have upset Linda when she drove it. A sports car is not Linda's type anyway. It was Sid's.

AUGUST 9, 1991

I didn't tell my mother about the wagon because I was afraid she would refuse to go to the picnic. While we were driving there the wagon rolled around in the trunk and my mother said her walker never before made so much noise. Gene took the wagon from the car and I got a pillow and then we got my mother out of the car. She was surprised but she sat right down and let Gene pull her up the hill. Had we known that Rossmoor had something like a wheel barrow with three wheels, we wouldn't have needed the wagon. This is provided for people to take their picnic supplies to the picnic area. My mother could have ridden in this. Bob did a beautiful job on the chicken. Well done and not burned. The lemon poppy seed cake was a real hit. So were the salads, judging by how little was left.

I gave Kate each tissue paper wrapped article separately. I think there were nine packages.

Another Rossmoor couple were having a barbecue with their grown children and grandchildren. Eventually the kids started playing together. The bigger boys put the little kids in the barrow and took them down the hill and up the paths. The kids had a wonderful time. Manors at Rossmoor are small so these picnic area are great for Rossmoor residents to entertain.

Sunday Maryann, Dick and Molly are coming for dinner. We love being with Molly. Tuesday we will spend with Jacqueline and her husband who are in San Francisco for a wedding. The 18th Emiko and two children arrive from Japan and will be with us thru the 21st. After that I'm going to start preparing for our China trip.

AUGUST 20, 1991

We received our first Christmas catalog today. Miles Kimball. They have petrified Holstein cow's eggs and I told Gene we should have this for our collection but he said "Nix". Darn! What a conversation piece, as well as a laugh.

MY BIRTHDAY, 8/22

We went north to the Delta and had lunch at Humphrey's a new restaurant named for Humphrey the whale who made world news a few years ago by swimming up the Sacramento River. The setting is at the marina and thru the glass walls at the restaurant we viewed the boats sailing past. Soup and desserts were wonderful but the entrees were just ordinary. We are stuffed so tonight we are just having cake and ice cream. I don't make my own birthday cake so we stopped at Raleys and bought one. They had salmon on sale for .99 a pound so we bought enough fillets for three meals. What a bargain.

I just started to read THE MAN WHO CHANGED THE WORLD, GORBACHEV by Gall Sheehy. Perfect reading for the coup days reported on TV now. Did you know Gorbachev is a diabetic? I couldn't have chosen a better time to read this book. I recommend it.

SEPTEMBER 5, 1991

Dear Emma and John,

Last night on the evening news we heard about a little girl in Berkeley who had either attended her first or second day of kindergarten. At noon she followed some other children to a bus and was taken to a Jewish day care center. Her parents reported her missing immediately and the radio and the TV reported this as a possible kidnapping. Someone at the Jewish Center heard the news and told the day care workers. They knew they had children from that kindergarten but nobody by that name. Later they heard that the child had her hair parted in the middle and braided and a pig tail on each side of her face. They had a child like that. Next they heard that the child was wearing navy pants and a navy top with diagonal stripes from shoulder to waist. They had a child like that. Eventually they called the police and a squad car was sent. The picture they had was the spitting image of the child but the name was different. A policeman took the child's hand and led her out the door. On TV we saw an amazed little girl holding a hand and a policeman's legs. Reporters were taking pictures. Somebody told her to wave and she did. Next we saw the child sitting up very straight on a policeman's lap and looking at the policeman who was driving. Her face registered surprise. She did not comprehend what was happening. She had spent the afternoon at the day care center, doing a lot of coloring. This morning we saw the little girl, holding her father's hand. leaving the police station. For five hours this little girl got a lot of attention and her parents a lot of agony.

My first year in Niagara Falls, I had libraries in two new schools, one on 93rd Street and one on 79th Street. The schools had identical plans, but rooms painted different colors. On a rainy morning early in September a father took his kindergarten daughter to 79th Street School. She went to her room but the teacher was different and all the kids were different. She peaked in the kindergarten across the hall and recognized nobody. School started so she sat outside the door in the hall. Coming down the hall, the principal spotted her and asked why she was there. The principal took her into the room and the teacher said the child didn't belong there. Then the principal called 93rd Street School and asked if a child by this name was registered there. She was. And they had a teacher by the name the child said was her teacher. So the principal drove the child to the other school and called the father to tell him where his child was. It seems the dividing line was down the middle of the street where the child lived and this child was on the 93rd Street side. The father worked nights and slept days and the mother worked days and slept nights. Always before the mother sent the child off to school so the father didn't realize which school his child was supposed to go to. Had he let her walk in the rain. she would have gone to the right school. Imagine how puzzled this child was, yet she didn't cry.

SEPTEMBER 6, 1991

Today was Gene's first bowling day for the season. I decided to please my mother by taking her out for lunch and a nice ride. I had read in the PG & E folder that there was a good little restaurant in Rio Vista. I didn't remember the name or address but Rio Vista is small so I thought I could easily locate it. I knew there was a florist shop facing the street and behind the florist shop was the restaurant. I couldn't find it. I asked several people about this restaurant. Finally I went in a travel agent's office and described the restaurant. The agent knew of the restaurant but said it was in the next little town, Iselton, five miles up the river. So much for my memory.

On we went to Iselton which was established by the Chinese shortly after the gold rush days. Lots of empty buildings in bad repair. Outstanding was Le Croissanterie with a blue awning. Lovely flower shop and beside it a small nine table restaurant. You pass thru the floral shop, and in front of a glass case with pastries and beyond is the restaurant. We had a cup of clam chowder and half a croissant sandwich. A whole croissant was the size of a dinner plate. We should have had a fourth of a croissant. I wish you could have seen a whole sandwich on bread. A man and woman run this restaurant and do all the baking, which is excellent. The waitress said, since the article, business has been booming and people come from all over. I believe it. It is thirty eight miles from Concord but we plan to go again for lunch. Dinners sounded great, too. My mother was very pleased. This village is so old and out of date they don't even have parking meters!

Our bags are packed and except for toothbrushes, makeup and shaving supplies, they could be closed and locked. A week from today is China take off. I hope all goes well, no falls, no revolutions, no typhoons, none of the usual tourist sicknesses. Time will tell.

I had a letter from Colette in France and she reported that her son-in-law's uncle, who is a mountaineer, was vacationing with his wife in Italy. They had a packed lunch and stopped to eat it under a tree in a field with sheep and goats. After they were again in the car and on their way, they discovered they had left their map on the grass so they went back for it. The uncle was bending over to pick up the map when a ram butted him hard and he hit his head on a stone and was dead in a couple minutes.

Imagine!

Our doctor says he is coming to Sara's to have lunch with my mother while we are gone. My mother is thrilled and plans to take a certain dress for the occasion!

NOVEMBER 25, 1991

Dear Marge and Roy.

Yesterday Maryann, Dick and three year old Molly came to dinner. Molly is bright and very active and we love her. She is especially attached to Gene. If she picks other men in her life of Gene's caliber, she will do fine. Knowing we were going to show our China slides, which were of no interest to Molly, they brought along her sleeping bag and thought she could nap at that time but plans don't always become reality and she didn't nap.

Dave asked if we would be willing to have Molly overnight in February while they take a two day vacation on their wedding anniversary. We didn't hesitate a moment in saying yes. This would be her first overnight away from them. If this goes well, we may have her again in March. Again we would be delighted. Having no grandchildren, we are happy when someone shares a small child with us. When we had Kate our life was different and really spiced up. Even my mother enjoys seeing a little child running around the house.

Thanksgiving we will have two guests, Leta and Hal, Gene's bowling teammate who is 80. He has been with us for previous Christmases and Thanksgivings and he fits right in. He carries food to and from the table and even gets things from the refrigerator so I have two helpers, Gene and Hal. Hal is widowed but from what I see, he must have been a good, helpful husband.

We have permission to bring Leta to our house from the convalescent hospital. Gene will pick her up. She was hospitalized October 15th and one month later went to a convalescent hospital which is a dreary place. Most of the patients are not with it. Some moan all the time. Some yell. Some are vegetables. Leta is getting better so it is especially hard to be with these unfortunate people. She is looking forward to being in a normal situation.

FRIDAY, NOVEMBER 29TH, 1991

We had a nice Thanksgiving. Gene picked Leta up at 11 and returned her at 5. She was really tired, even though she rested on the sofa for awhile. Leta was never fat, but she now weighs only 100 pounds and, for her height, this is a small amount.

I was looking at the latest National Geographic in bed on Wednesday night and I read the article on Australia's pearls. I always thought the Japanese pearls were the best in the world but this article says the Australian ones are much bigger and have more luster due to the warm water where they grow. There was a picture of a $4000 strand of Japanese and a $190,000 strand of Australian so I told Gene I now know what I want for Christmas. Some Australian pearls! He said O.K. We both laughed. Yesterday Leta asked me what I wanted for Christmas and I showed her the article and picture and told her the price and she said she would buy them for me. I said this was just a joke. Most of the time Leta's mind is o.k. but she certainly is vulnerable. In former times she would have recognized this as a joke. When Hal came, we discussed this again and Hal persuaded me that I would not want two strands of pearls. I already have one. So I guess I'll have to think of something else but for the life of me I cannot think of anything I want or need. When you are young, there are lots of things you want, but at this age. your wants and needs are much less.

The newspaper today was filled with ads and many stores had three hour sales, 7AM to 10 AM. We saw some bargains and went shopping but it was almost impossible to get a parking place at the mall and to get thru the aisles of the stores. People are looking for bargains this year.

Just before we sat down to Thanksgiving dinner, we had a phone call from friends we knew in Ann Arbor. They had come to visit their son but he had made other plans. They were at loose ends. They were going to Las Vegas and would be back next weekend. I suggested they call then and we would arrange for a time for them to visit us and see our China slides. I know I should have invited them to come for Thanksgiving dinner but it would have meant enlarging the table and the table was all set. We had more than enough food for two more. Such a disruption at the last minute would have disturbed me.

As I was taking a hot dish from the oven on Thanksgiving, I burned my left thumb and I have a big blister. Everything I do hits the blister and it is annoying.

Tonight Leon is coming for dinner, left overs. He likes left overs and has none of his own.

We read in the newspaper this morning that traffic was terrible yesterday. People left the San Francisco bay area and headed east. Route 80 to Sacramento was bumper to bumper traffic and it took 2 1/2 hours to get to Fairfield which is about fifteen miles from Concord. People turned around and came back. So, many people did not eat the Thanksgiving dinner they planned. Hal just came five miles from Lafayette and he also got in a traffic jam. He got off the freeway and came a back way. The newspaper reported that telephone booths had waiting lines of people who were calling to say they couldn't get thru. It is always bad on holidays but this was the worst yet.

We hope you had a most pleasant holiday season.

DECEMBER 15, 1991

Dear Jacqui and Will,

Friday December 13, Gene and I were preparing breakfast together as we ordinarily do. I was peeling and sectioning grapefruit and Gene was going to put cereal in each bowl. Each of us eats a different cereal or combination of cereals. He was taking a bowl from the cupboard when it slipped out of his hand and landed on the marble pastry slab. It broke into large pieces and bounced all over. One piece landed on Gene's instep just above where his slipper ended. He felt it and looked down and saw blood gushing from a cut. He went to the bathroom and tried to stop the bleeding with pressure and then he put on ten band aids, going all which way. I wondered it he should see a doctor but I was going to San Francisco for an ikebana meeting and he was bowling. Gene found it too uncomfortable to bowl so he only bowled one game out of four. That night I thought we should look at the cut. It was only an inch long but it bled as he removed the band aids. Should we go to the emergency room at 10:30 PM or wait till morning? I thought he needed a couple stitches. We decided on morning and got up early and went off to ER. The doctor and nurses said it was too late for stitches. They have to be put in before six hours have passed. They used pressure tapes. He will have a scar but it won't show. However, they could see that the tendon to his fourth toe had been partially severed. The ER doctor called an orthopedist and he said he would see Gene in a week, if necessary. The toe may flop down and if so, the tendon will have to be repaired. Last night it still hadn't flopped down. What a silly accident. It doesn't hurt today but he can't get it wet for a week so bathing will be restricted. The doctor said we must keep it clean so it won't get infected but even if we do keep it clean, he said it still may get infected.

DECEMBER 22, 1991

A week has passed and Gene could have gone bowling but he decided not to. His cut is healing nicely but is still raw. Gene said my mother and I could still go out as we usually do when he bowls. We invited Leta to ride along and have lunch with us. She is almost crawling up the walls of the convalescent hospital. She can use a walker and that is easier for me to take than a wheelchair.

I delivered some cookies to Wilma in Orinda and then we had lunch. Small mountains separate Orinda from Berkeley and Oakland. I suggested we drive thru the Caldecott tunnel and see the devastation from the fire. For some time after this terrible fire people were not allowed to drive on the streets but now you can. WOW! Hiller Heights which used to be beautiful homes on the side of the mountain is NOTHING BUT STREETS AND SIDEWALKS. Burned stuff lies where the thousand houses used to be. We rode around several streets and not one house did we see. The views of Golden Gate Bridge, Oakland Bridge and San Francisco are magnificent, probably better now than when trees and houses were there. You could almost imagine that this was a war zone where bombs wiped out everything. It was a very clear day so we enjoyed the beautiful scenery but were depressed with the destruction we observed. The fire roared over the Caldecott tunnel and leveled Rockridge too. We could have ridden around there and seen the same devastation, but we had had enough. We saw the actual burning on TV and were horrified but seeing the result of the fire is unforgettable. Those unfortunate people who lost everything!

Hal called tonight and he sounded terrible. He said he had caught the "bug," translate Beijing flu. He will go to the doctor tomorrow but he probably won't be well enough to come for Christmas dinner. His symptoms matched those reported in the newspaper. Actually we don't want him to bring the flu to us and he doesn't want to either.

CHRISTMAS NIGHT

The doctor confirmed our fear that Hal has the Beijing flu and said he should not come for Christmas. We are disappointed.

Gene picked Leta up at noon. We opened our presents and then had dinner. Leta's eyes kept closing, so I suggested she take a nap. They wake her every morning at 5 to weigh her. In this way they can tell whether her edema is from food or retention of water. At five she was ready for her bed at the convalescent hospital so we took her back.

Then we went on to Hal's in Lafayette with food from our Christmas dinner. Sick as he is, Hal went to mass this morning. After mass he usually has breakfast with a couple he has known for years. Today he told them he wouldn't eat with them but they said he didn't sound bad and insisted. Hal felt pretty good this morning but tonight he was worse. He should have stayed in bed all day.

Our friends, Ken and Emme, both have the flu. Ken had it for a week and it appeared to be going into pneumonia. He went to the doctor. That very day Emme came down with it. They had been careful and Emme had moved into another bedroom but she took Ken's meals to his room.

They live in Alameda so it is too far to take food to them. I'll call in a day or two to see how they are coming along.

We had a quiet but most pleasant Christmas. My mother always has some little presents for Gene and me but this year she wasn't up to going into even one store. Her main gift is money, always the same amount for both of us. Today I got a box with twice what she usually gives me. Gene opened a present and he had the usual. Both of us thought this queer. Later I got a package with the amount Gene got and he got a package with the amount I got first, so we got the same. My mother thought two boxes would be better than one.

DECEMBER 28, 1991

In bed last night Gene said he thought my mother was trying to tell him something when he got the lesser amount first. I knew this wasn't true because recently my mother told me she didn't think a better person than Gene could be found.

This morning my mother rode with me while I shopped for Xmas cards. We left at 9:30 but this was too late and few cards were available. One man said stores bought fewer cards this year because they took a licking on cards last year. I went to three stores before I got some cards and I wasn't really satisfied with any of them.

JANUARY 2, 1992

Dear Colette,

The day after Christmas Gene called my orthopedist and got an appointment for Monday. The tendon to his toe has disappeared. No pain but he wanted it looked at.

The orthopedist said the tendon on Gene's foot had probably severed completely but he didn't want to do anything about it because, if they did open it and attach the two parts of the tendon, scar tissue would form and there would be a bump. Then the shoe would rub against this and he would have trouble. Athletes who do their thing in bare feet might need to have this done. Although I've been this orthopedist's patient for years and Gene has gone with me to lots of appointments, Gene had to pay a new patient fee.

New Year's day we had dinner at noon and nothing was left so I didn't know what to have in the evening. I was racking my brain when the phone rang and our Chinese neighbor said she was bringing over barbecued spare ribs and a Chinese chicken salad. Both were excellent. Each had a subtle flavor and no garlic in what she gave us. Sue expected to have her mother, Hing's mother and her sister. The sister called in the morning and said she had some friends she would like to bring. So instead of five the party eventually numbered fourteen.

Sue is such a busy person and especially right now when she will work from 8 AM till 9 PM each day for the next two weeks. End of the year reports have to be prepared. What a way to start the New Year.

JANUARY 8, 1992

Dear Jennie,

We went to bed at the usual time Sunday, the 5th I couldn't sleep and by midnight I had pain in the back of my left shoulder. I was perspiring so much that my hand was wet when run across my forehead and my nightgown was so wet it stuck to my body. It was 40 outside and our bedroom windows were open so our bedroom was cold. I knew I didn't have all the classic symptoms of a heart attack but I also knew something was wrong so at 3:05 AM I called the emergency room at the hospital and talked to a nurse. After listening, she told me to call 911 and have an ambulance bring me to the hospital. I said I wasn't that bad but she thought I might need oxygen and I shouldn't fool around. Gene threw on some pants and I a dry nightie and a robe and Gene drove me to the hospital. I told Gene to drive carefully because I wasn't dying but he ran a red light and this really upset me.

Nobody was in ER. They started an IV of sugar and water, hooked me up to oxygen and did an EKG. My systolic pressure was in the high stroke range but the diastolic was normal. The ER doctor decided to admit me to definitive care.

The cardiologist arrived and sat down to talk to me. He said the EKG showed nothing but that isn't always correct. He had talked to my internist who told him something of my recent problems. He said he thought I was under too much stress and stress could cause pain like this. The sweating in the cold room was puzzling and might indicate angina. Therefore he was ordering a thalium stress test the next day. Off and on I had pain and I was given nitrogylcerin tablets. My blood pressure and blood tests were taken often. My internist arrived and talked to me. Tuesday was better and I was pain free. That night the cardiologist said they could find nothing and so he assumed it was stress. He said I must put myself first. He said he was releasing me Wednesday morning. We would wait and see what happened.

Gene picked me up, we came home, I had a bath and then we went grocery shopping.

A hospital stay is an eye opener. The old woman in the room next to mine was dying. Her daughters and granddaughters stood outside my door and planned her funeral. I wonder if the old lady heard. A comatose old lady in another room was constantly being urged to breathe by the nurses. A very big man in the room on the other side had an operation Tuesday. Monday the whole family was there and they made lots of noise. Tuesday morning they were there again before the operation but after the operation nobody was there. I heard the nurse tell him that he had a large tumor that had invaded three parts of his body. The nurses would ask this man questions and his answer to anything was "EEEuuuggg, oh. boy." I heard this many times and eventually I started to giggle every time he answered this way. Finally they gave him pain medicine and for awhile he slept. I wonder why nobody came after the operation.

There was lots of coughing and in answer to my question one nurse said there were lots of flu patients. Another said the coughing wasn't from the patients on my floor but rather from the nurses. She had just recovered from the flu.

The sides on my bed were kept up. I told the nurse I wouldn't fall out of bed so they could be lowered but she said they couldn't do this unless I signed a release.

What is going to happen next? We are seeing too much of John Muir Hospital. One whole month with Leta, a visit with Gene and now this. Three times is enough, I think.

My mother knew nothing of my going to the hospital till breakfast and Gene made light of it. By dinnertime, she decided something really was wrong because I hadn't come home. She refused to eat her dinner. That night Gene couldn't sleep. Gene used to be a good cook but by Tuesday he couldn't even eat what he cooked.

My mother was waiting at the door when I came home. I guess all three of us were disturbed. We hope things return to normal.

Tonight I'm cooking pork chops in a special way with sherry and dijon mustard which we all like. I'll have a good fresh fruit salad and maybe this will make us think everything is o.k. again.

JANUARY 12, 1992

Dear Ingrid and Jan,

Our big weekend has just ended. We had Molly while Maryann and Dick spent it in San Francisco. They arrived about noon on Saturday and spent just a few minutes briefing us about Molly's habits. Then we were on our own.

First we had lunch which wasn't a great success. I had soup and an English muffin with melted cheese. Molly said she liked soup but she ate only a spoonful or two. However she did eat the English muffin and cheese is nourishing so I wasn't uptight.

After lunch she wanted to put on her pink tutu. Maryann said she had to wear a pink top and pink tights because it is too cold to have all that bare skin. Molly grabbed Gene's hand and wanted him to be a ballet dancer. He tried but he didn't toss her around the way her Daddy does. Before Christmas Maryann took Molly to a performance of the Nutcracker Suite and she saw real ballet dancing so she is very enthusiastic about ballet dancing right now.

When dinner time came, she didn't want to take off the tutu but with some cajoling I got it off and we had dinner. This also wasn't a great success. I had crab quiche and broccoli and a dish of cut up fruit. She ate all her fruit and part of Gene's and mine. The fault wasn't Molly's. I should have had food kids like, spaghetti, macaroni and cheese, hamburgers.

Molly didn't especially want to go to bed but we got her in the tub for her bath and in bed at 8 as Maryann said. She was allowed to play her tape recorder and she wanted to hear Thumbelina. It was on radio and she said she didn't want to hear the weather report. I had to get Gene to change it and finally she heard Thumbelina. I kept checking and she was still awake at 9. I turned off the tape and at 9:20 she was asleep, uncovered. The house was warm but would go down to 55 during the night. We decided to leave the heat on during the night and not open our window. Molly slept the whole night.

At 7 our alarm went off because Gene forgot to turn it off the night before. I went to the bathroom and when I opened the door Molly was standing there and she asked if she could get in bed with us. She does with her parents so I said it would be ok. She snuggled up between the two of us. Before long, I decided to get up and after washing up, I entered the bedroom to find Molly on her knees, Gene on his back and Molly kissing Gene again and again. You don't need more than one guess to know who was pleased. Soon she came out in the kitchen with me. She said she liked grapefruit and oranges but she didn't eat what I gave her. Maryann said she loves oatmeal but she didn't eat that either. She said she wasn't hungry. We didn't press the point.

This noon we had roast chicken and dressing, green beans and fresh fruit salad. Melissa had four helpings of green beans and some chicken and she ate all the fruit. Cookies and macadamia nut cake completed the meal. Then we she was allowed a couple M and Ms.

Vignettes I'll treasure

1. Gene trying to ballet dance with Molly

2. Molly on Gene's lap, rubbing her nose against his and kissing him. Boy, when somebody can divert Gene from a football game, that person has power.

3. The kissing scene in bed.

A couple times Molly called me Mom and then she would say, "I called you mom but you are Norma."

While we were getting breakfast, she was right at our heels and she would hug Gene's legs.

We read a lot of books, those I had and those they brought.

When Maryann and Dick arrived, Molly came from my mother's room and said she didn't want to go yet. Maryann thought she might miss them since this was her first time away from them overnight. She got along well. We didn't have a tear. I have yet to hear this child cry.

I bought a doll and I made two dresses, a pair of panties, 2 pajamas, a bonnet and sweater. We had a carrying basket and we put foam rubber in it and I made a mattress and sheet for it. I had a flannel blanket and I made a coverlet and pillow. The coverlet was different on each side. I gave each item separately to Molly. Later she said her surprises weren't wrapped in paper and she liked them wrapped in paper. At one point Molly was putting Jennifer, the doll, to bed and suddenly she said, "I have to hug her first." She picked up the doll and hugged it and then put it back in the basket. I can see what Maryann does with Molly. I'll remember this too.

You can imagine that our life was much changed for 24 hours.

We loved it. At least occasionally we get to play grandparents. My mother loved it too.

The cardiologist was right. He gave a definite yes to our having Molly this weekend. He said it would be relaxing but that I might get really tired The important thing was that the stress element is missing from an adult-child relationship. I much prefer this relationship to old person to old person. Actually Molly was so good we aren't worn out.

JANUARY 23, 1992

Dear Kathryn,

I had an appointment with the internist this morning. This was the first time I've seen him since my two day sojourn in the hospital. He agreed with the cardiologist that my problem was stress caused and I did not have a heart attack. Thank goodness! I'm trying to eliminate the stress and to take better care of myself. However the doctor is seeing me again in six weeks.

The doctor says he sees lots of "stress heart attacks." He told me of a man who had to drive thru the Caldecott Tunnel every day on his way to work. This is where that terrible fire was a few years ago and people were burned to death. The man would be fine till he got to the tunnel and then he had all the symptoms of angina. He was hospitalized and they found nothing physically wrong. With psychological help, he recovered.

I have a cold. I get them often and Gene and my mother never do. Neither of them has had tonsils and adenoids removed and mine were when I was a child. I asked if this might be the reason and the doctor said yes. The kind of cold I have drags on and on so he gave me an antibiotic.

On the way to get the prescription filled, I told Gene I was costing him money this year. He agreed and said he thought it might be time for him to turn me in and get a new model!

FEBRUARY 6, 1992

Today I decided to send for some file cases to accommodate my ever increasing cookbooks. I looked through the Gaylord catalogue and laid it out on the kitchen table to the page on which the files were advertised. Gene was vacuuming so I waited till he was finished and I could hear well when ordering on the phone. I returned to the kitchen and there was no catalogue. Then I went on a search. Where had I moved it? I asked Gene if he had touched it. No, but he remembered it was there. We both searched the house, every room, including bathrooms. I wondered if I had put it with the newspapers in the garage but I hadn't. I began to worry about my sanity. Ten minutes after doing something and I cannot remember!! THIS IS BAD. I gave up.

I was walking thru the kitchen and observed my mother sitting on a chair at the table, writing a note. I happened to glance at the chair and I noticed she was sitting higher than usual. Why? I really looked and saw she had taken the catalogue and was sitting on it! No wonder I couldn't find it. However, lately, I put something down and frequently I can't remember where it is. Don't say it. I'm not even going to admit to getting old.

This is the 25th day of a bad cold for me. The doctor gave me a decongestant and an antibiotic and I've taken all the pills. Still I have this deep chest cough and I'm so tired. Yesterday I lay down for the afternoon and it did help. Also Gene went to the drug store and got some more cough medicine. I'll do anything to get rid of this lousy cold.

FEBRUARY 15, 1992

Dear Ivy and Hubert,

Today was my mother's 98th birthday and we went out for lunch. It is very difficult for my mother to go out any more. She likes ham and pork chops but she can only eat soft food. I suggested Pacific Fresh and said scallops, shrimp and fish are soft. Finally she agreed to go. She ate her clam chowder and shrimp and scallops and that was the extent of her meal. I told the young waitress that today was my mother's 98th birthday and when she brought the bill, she said she had never before seen a person that old. Youth! Later in the afternoon Leta came and we had ice cream and birthday cake.

We were eating breakfast Thursday when I heard on TV the words Ocean Pearl and three hundred eighty people were picked up by another ship. I called Ocean Pearl and was told there was a fire in one of the engine rooms. Boy, are we glad this didn't happen when we were on that ship.

FEBRUARY 16, 1992

We were supposed to leave at 9:45 this morning but my mother wasn't ready so we didn't leave till after 10. My mother is not as sharp and much slower than she used to be so things don't always work out as planned. Maryann had a birthday meal for my mother with a birthday cake decorated in her honor. My mother was delighted with the attention.

Phyllis, in Syracuse, sent flowers yesterday and Connie in Boston sent candy. Most of my friends sent cards and she has a stack of then. She really had quite a 98th birthday. I'll have a big party for her 100th.

When we arrived at Maryann's Molly was at the dining room window waving at me. She had on her new pink dress and pink tights and black patent shoes. The dress has three tiers of lace around the hem. It is a dainty dress and she looked lovely in it. Molly had told me all about this new dress last time she stayed with us.

Dick said Molly had spent a lot of time and thought on the dress the doll, Jennifer, was to wear today. She finally decided on the royal blue dress I had made for the doll. I took along today some other clothes for Jennifer. I got the sleeves too tight so I had to bring them back. When I bought the doll, I didn't check the arms. They are soft but the hands are hard with fingers outstretched. Without the doll, I couldn't judge. It would have been better to have bought a doll with hard arms and then I could have had short sleeves which are easier to make.

When we were saying good-bye, Molly tried to hold the door shut so we couldn't go. How flattering. We think Molly is precious.

We are glad Maryann lives only 50 some miles away but we wish it were closer because we would love to baby sit more often.

Medical diagnosis 785.5

Molly's kisses, PSA and tears,

California marriages dangerous to your health

FEBRUARY 22, 1992

Dear Bonna and Wayne.

Yesterday we received the bill from the hospital and I nearly went into a tailspin. I was in the hospital for 54 hours and the total bill was $7,768.86, excluding doctor's bills. That is a little less than $4000 a day. For that kind of money we could have stayed in a pretty nice hotel and enjoyed ourselves. Do you want to know what was wrong with me? 786.52. Just as we classify books by subject, illnesses are now classified by numbers. A medical Dewey Decimal system. I know 785.5 is chest pain. I don't knew what .52 is but assume the 2 stands for stress.

Sue came over this morning and she brought our lunch. They are having company so she bought enough dim sum for us. We ate half and will eat the other half tomorrow. It was excellent.

Maryann called today and reported the pink dress I made for Jennifer to match Molly's is such a hit that Molly wants Jennifer to wear it all the time. Molly learned to print her name this weekend so I'm getting a thank you from Molly.

Maryann asked if we wanted to have Molly the last weekend of May and I said yes immediately. Maryann said she had no doubt the answer would be that. We also were happy to hear Molly wants to come. So we get to be grandparents again.

MARCH 8, 1992

Dear Pat and Bob,

Last night we had two couples in for dinner. Both women are really good cooks and serve beautifully. I'll have to get on the ball and try to approach their expertise.

I'm serving a sweet potato salad because sweet potatoes are the most nutrition packed vegetable and have fiber and no cholesterol and are low in calories. The main course is oven barbecued chicken breasts and a fruited wild rice. Dessert is a lemon angel torte with a blueberry sauce, light and few calories.

At the end of the meal, the comments were that everything was so different. Before we ate the comments were about the smell. Our house did smell food wonderful. Before I married Gene, he thought a house should NEVER have a food smell and the first year of marriage he was constantly turning on the fan to get rid of the smell. Now I agree some food smells we can do without but the smell sometimes just enhances the food. We have been told so many times about the good food smell of our house that Gene no longer objects. Thank goodness.

The third Thursday has passed and we still have no vacuum cleaner. We had it repaired at Christmas and it took two weeks. It came back with more wrong with it than when we took it in. We took it to another shop and when we got it back, it worked five minutes. Our vacuum cleaner is only two years old and it shouldn't be worn out.

We got out our egg collection today and now have all the eggs on display.

I bought a doll house kit today which is made of plastic canvas. I'll do all the needle work and Gene will assemble the house and furniture. We'll give it to Molly.

MARCH 16, 1992

Dear Dorothy and Lars,

To put it mildly, this hasn't been the best week of my life.

March 9th Gene went happily off for his yearly physical. His lab work had been done the week before. When Gene returned, he reported everything was normal, EXCEPT for the PSA test which was a 6 and anything over a 4 indicates possible cancer of the prostate. I was devastated. On the 11th Gene had an appointment with a urologist and I said I would go with him. He said NO. We had a slight disagreement and I was so upset I cried, so Gene said I could go with him and remain in the waiting room. This I did. When the nurse called Gene, the doctor saw me and asked if I was the girlfriend or wife. When I said wife, he told me to come too. I could have hugged that doctor.

The urologist bonded with Gene immediately because both were natives of Iowa and had gone to Iowa universities. I had gone to the library and read up on this kind of cancer. I had a page of questions but I didn't need to ask them because the doctor covered them in his talk. The urologist said a 6 on the PSA wasn't a sure indicator. He did a digital exam and found nothing. He said a biopsy should be done to make sure. The next day he did the biopsy. Afterwards, Gene and I stood outside and I was asking Gene questions when the doctor came out and asked if there was a question. I said I wanted to know what the ultra sound showed and he said there was a spot but even this didn't prove anything.

We would have to wait till the 18th for the result of the biopsy. This waiting is hell.

As if this weren't enough, my mother refused to eat on either day when we went out for lunch or at home. She has had a terrible bowel problem for over a year but she won't admit it to the doctor. I had told him what I knew and he questioned her but she always denied that anything was wrong. I took her blood pressure and instead of being high, it was low. I suggested seeing the doctor and she agreed immediately, She hates going to the doctor so I knew something was really wrong. I got an appointment that day and she went for blood work, stool and urine analysis. Wednesday I'm to call him for the results. If nothing shows, she will enter the hospital.

My mother is giving me advice in case "she doesn't come back" and she is telling Gene things he should do "in case she doesn't come back" I'm worried enough about Gene so this is just adding fuel to the fire. Gene and I are both tense.

Saturday afternoon Hing and Sue came over to see our egg display and in the course of the conversation, Hing said people at work are always telling him you can't take it with you. He responds that if he can't take it with him, he isn't going. My one laugh of the week.

WEDNESDAY, MARCH 18, 1992 3:40 PM

I've been weeping since 3 PM when we were told Gene has adenocarcinoma which is prostate cancer. He will have a bone scan next Wednesday. If the cancer is contained in the prostate, we will wait till after our June vacation because this is a slow growing cancer. I wanted to cancel the vacation but Gene suggested this and the doctor thought it a good idea. Gene will have an operation to remove the prostate cancer and he may have to have a second for incontinence. I was so afraid of this.

5:45 PM SAME DAY

The doctor's nurse just called to tell me the blood work was o.k. for my mother. We'll know about the stool report on Friday.

MARCH 25, 1992

Dear Phyllis and Jay.

We are exhausted. What a treadmill we have been on today. We left home at 7:30 and headed to the office of a radiologist who specializes in nuclear medicine. At 8 Gene had an injection of a radio isotope, technetium pertechnetate. We did some grocery shopping and then returned to the office. At 10 Gene had a scan by a synthesizing camera, up and down, back and forth for an hour. We dashed home for lunch and then to the urologist at 2 PM. His first words were that no cancer was found in Gene's bones. Thank God. I had thirteen questions to ask. I got to number six and started to cry.

I didn't want to wait till June for the operation. I was afraid the cancer would spread in the three months. The doctor said he would give Gene hormones to shrink the cancer. Actually this is better because it would be easier to get the cancer out. He sent us to the hospital where Gene had a chest x-ray, EKG and some blood work. We got home after 4. We had to stop at the drug store to get some expensive medicine which Gene thinks is to get the radio active isotope out of his body.

Tuesday the 31st Gene enters the hospital at 9:30 AM. He is booked for surgery at 12:30. The urologist will go thru his navel and down to lymph nodes and do some biopsies. If no cancer is in any of these places, Gene has a good chance of a cure. It cancer is found, there will be no prostate operation. Gene will stay overnight and come home on Wednesday.

Then he goes on a hormone.

We are to go on the trip in June. I objected but the doctor said we should. Gene will give blood before we go and immediately upon return and surgery to remove the prostate will probably be June 30th. Gene will be in the hospital seven days.

So this is the way it stands. One more hurdle next week and then we will have to put this out of our minds till late June.

We aren't telling friends here and we won't tell friends we meet on vacation. Gene's sister and two or three friends know this thru my letters, otherwise mum is the word.

Some years are good years and some years are bad years and 1992 has started to be a bad year for us. We'll hope things improve after July. We've been lucky most of our married life and we have to be thankful for this.

APRIL 15, 1992

Dear Shizuko and Kaoru,

Today may be the big day for many because IRS returns have to be in. Today is a big day for me because I gave my book review to the AAUW Book Group at Rossmoor. I mentioned CHINA BOY by Gus Lee because it is such a good book. It is a novel that reads like an autobiography and the setting is San Francisco. So easy to read and such descriptive sentences. So I spent ten minutes on it and then turned to LEARNING TO BOW by Bruce Feiler. There were thirty plus in attendance and they listened attentively. Afterwards lots of questions and comments. Many people had heard of CHINA BOY because there was a review in the San Francisco paper but nobody had read it. Nobody had heard of LEARNING TO BOW and several people wanted to buy it and give it as a gift or else just read it. I hope it is in our bookstores.

Today Gene got his advance inpatient registration form from John Muir Hospital. We try not to think of the operation but this makes it definite. As a result of the lymph node biopsies, one incision still has a scab but the other three are healed. There is still a blister in one spot.

Tonight I told Gene that after the operation and the recuperation, we are going to paint the inside of our house and get new carpeting. I said I wanted him to have something to look forward to but that I wouldn't rush it. He is to get better first and then we'll tackle this. So after the operation we'll consider paint colors and carpet samples and this will be an added interest in his life. We must look beyond July 1st.

APRIL 18, 1992

Dear Marguerite and Ed,

On March 31st when Gene was in the hospital, my mother asked to see the doctor. I was back and forth from hospital to home all day and just didn't have time to take my mother that day. However, I did call for an appointment. The doctor said he wanted an upper GI before he saw her. We arranged for that. She agreed to that but when the day came, she raised a fuss. I decided the technicians might have an easier time if I left so I went out to the waiting room. The technicians were good and calmed her down and joked with her. She wasn't too unhappy when it all was over. Next our doctor said my mother should see a gastroenterologist and we were scheduled for a 5 PM appointment today.

Between the day I made the appointment and today, my mother felt better so she was really upset to be going to this new doctor. Our appointment was for 5 PM. An elderly farmer and his wife who smelled of the farm were waiting. Their appointment was for 5:45 but they arrived at 4 PM. The old woman kept asking how much longer they had to wait. Finally the old man said he was too sick to sit there so they took him in an examining room. The longer my mother waited, the madder she got at me. She said I was always dragging her to the doctor when nothing was the matter. Finally she was put in an examining room. There she really laid into me. I was upset so I left and stood outside the door. The nurse said I ought to check on my mother. I went back in and soon the doctor came. The doctor spoke pleasantly to my mother but she was beyond being pleasant or polite. He apologized for the delay. My mother told him there was nothing wrong with her. The doctor turned to me I explained but everything I said my mother refuted. He had the results of the G.I. series and mostly it was normal. My mother's stomach was turned and had a kink. The doctor said this often happens and when it does food will not go thru. All the time the doctor was talking to me, my mother was berating me and, from embarrassment and hurt, I started to cry. The doctor put his arm around me and the nurse gave me Kleenex. Finally we were back in our car with my mother still telling me off. I have never seen her so mad. What did this doctor think? I took this all the way home in the car, but when we were in the house, I yelled at my mother and she stopped. My yelling startled her because I don't do this. By the time bedtime came, she said goodnight in a nice way. No child's tantrum would be as bad as this tantrum of an old person. Maybe she realized her tantrum was just enough to make me lose my cool.

It is now bedtime and I feel limp. Episodes like this take the starch out of me. I'm glad they are few and far between.

APRIL 20, 1992

Dear Millie and Jim,

It is dangerous to be married in California!

Today we read in the newspaper and heard on TV about the woman who poured alcohol on her cancerous, bed ridden husband and then set fire to him. She left for eight hours and upon returning she expected him to be dead. Instead he was badly burned. She got help and then the story unraveled. She had recently bought herself a chocolate bunny, but before she got around to eating it, her husband did. Since he had eaten her candy before, she decided to do away with him. Morale of the story—Don't eat your spouses candy.

Also today a fifty year old, divorced policeman, now married to a forty year old secretary, parked his car about a mile away from his house and, wearing a wig and mustache, he walked home. He was mad at his wife because she sometimes spent part of her wages on clothes. Saturday he provoked an argument with his wife as she was carrying a basket of clothes. He used a piece of clothing to strangle her. Then he put her body in her car and drove to the lonely spot where he had left his car. He spray painted WAR on her car, got in his car and drove to the police station where he stayed for more than an hour. He returned to their home, waited a few hours and then reported his wife missing. He concocted a story about how his wife was going out to dinner with a girl friend. The police found this untrue. By the next day they had figured it out. They found his clothes with the same paint on his shoes and confronted him with her murder. His lawyer says this wasn't premeditated murder because it occurred during an argument. Why did he buy the disguise? Why did he park in the lonely spot? Why did he provoke an argument? Why couldn't this working woman spend some of her money on clothes?

See what I mean! Marriage is dangerous. I better watch out because Saturday I bought a new dress. During the past couple weeks I bought two new pairs of pants and seven tops. I'm getting ready for vacation and it may not be as warm as California so I need warmer clothes. I got everything on sale so I saved my husband money. Nevertheless, my actions may have been dangerous.

I've finished the walls of the doll house and now Gene can assemble this plastic net house. I'm starting on the furniture. Molly will be with us May 30th and 31st and we will give this to her for her birthday.

During the time Gene was in the hospital, my arthritis acted up and I was in pain. Usually the medicine leaves me comfortable. I took extra medicine and I'm better. I'm beginning to think stress causes arthritis to get worse.

The Easter bunny brought each of us a chocolate egg. I PROMISE YOU I WON'T EAT GENE'S EGG.

MAY 2, 1992

Dear Helen and Herb,

I've noticed recently that my pants that used to fit seem too big and the legs seem to have lengthened. I wondered what had happen till today when Gene came out from getting dressed. He had weighed himself and he has lost ten pounds. I went in and weighed myself and I've lost eight. Both of us can afford to lose weight but we don't like the reason why we are losing. I think it is worry and anxiety over Gene's problem.

Gene got his $346 shot on Friday and the next one will be on Wednesday the 27th. The shot is good for 26 days so this will bring him within a few days of the operation.

For a few years Gene had a little growth on his face just under the bottom edge of his glasses. He also had some smaller ones on his face. He thought he should have them removed. The other day Gene showed me the place where the growth had been and I saw nothing. The flutamlde and the hormone shots have shrunk these skin cancers to nothing. I hope it is working just as efficiently on the cancer we can't see. Gene can now only feel a little indentation on the skin where the skin cancer used to be.

Thursday Sarah Yancey from William Smith College visited us. She left a little before 3 PM and was getting off BART at Berkeley to visit some other William Smithers. At 5 we saw on TV the riots, due to the Rodney King episode, in Berkeley and Union Square in San Francisco. She could have been in the midst of this. I wanted to call her but didn't know which hotel she was staying in.

Darren, our neighbor's son, was to be in a production of the Flower Drum Song in San Francisco Thursday night. At rehearsal somebody interrupted and said the rioters were smashing cars so Darren ran out and just as he drove away, they smashed the car that had been parked behind him. He parked elsewhere and returned to the rehearsal. Later that night he called his mother to say he had gotten home safely. Tonight Sue and Hing were planning to go into San Francisco to see Darren in the Flower Drum Song but both were too ill. I took over a loaf of poppy seed bread at dinner time and both had spent the day in bed. You can be sure they were sick if they did this.

On TV this morning we heard that all the malls on the peninsula and the East Bay are going to be closed today. Bank of America sent its employees home early.

Do riots solve problems? I don't think so.

MAY 6, 1992

A few minutes ago we saw Raisa Gorbachev on TV. She said that when the coup occurred her blood pressure shot up so high one arm was paralyzed and she couldn't talk. We could see this when she got off the plane that day. She probably had a TIA or small stroke. She said that when they were back in their home, she spent the first three days reading the love letters from Mikhail. Wow! it wouldn't take me three days to read the love letters I have from Gene. Not even one minute. It is not because I'm such a fast reader, I just don't have any to read. Gene wasn't a letter writer then and he isn't a letter writer now. What a relief to know Gene isn't causing me all this work.

MAY 29, 1992

Dear Audrey and Glenn,

What a week! We took my mother to the hospital Tuesday afternoon. She had a colonoscopy at12:30 on Wednesday. We brought her home about 4 PM. My mother did not know what was involved in a colonoscopy. The preparation is almost worse than the exam. She was so angry at what they had to do to her. The first exam was unsuccessful because she wasn't thoroughly cleaned out so they had to do this twice. So she was twice as mad. And whom did she take her anger out on? You guessed it. Norma. I just couldn't take it so I waited in the hall while Gene tried to soothe her. She saw me when she was wheeled to the operating room and she saw me again when she returned. She was glad I hadn't gone home. She was so weak from lack of food and the examination that she couldn't walk alone. We gave her food and she rested all night. The next day she could walk again without help.

Wednesday the doctor told me he found a small growth. I'm to call Monday for more information. Thursday I went to our internist and he had talked to the gastroenterologist and he told the internist that my mother had colon cancer. He said she could live 2 years and maybe even 5 but she might die of something else before the cancer took her. Because of her age and physical condition my mother is not a candidate for surgery. We decided just to try to keep her comfortable. My mother hasn't asked the result of the examination. I think she knows but doesn't want to hear it. So neither thedoctor nor I am to tell her unless she asks.

The internist said Gene and I should take our trip. He said he and Sara, who cares for other patients of his, will take care of anything that comes up.

Boy, this is a double whammy. I've suspected my mother had colon cancer but Gene's was a shock.

We had an appointment with the urologist while my mother was having her colonoscopy. The hospital had told us wrong. Gene enters the hospital at 5 AM on the 30th and the operation is at 7:30 AM the same day.

Linus Pauling, the 91 year old famous doctor, has the same as Gene and he is being given hormones and flutamide. He is not being operated upon. I told the urologist I had read this and he said Gene had the same option. Age makes the difference. Pauling will take this stuff the rest of his life. Once Gene's prostate is out, he will not have any more treatment. Hopefully, since it is confined within the gland, it will not appear any other place. The drugs could have side effects.

MAY 31, 1992

Dear Catherine and Larry,

What a weekend! Maryann and Dick came on Friday night and at 9:30 the power suddenly went off. Molly was in bed and when all went dark, she started to cry. Dick went in to quiet her. I didn't rush to get candles because I thought the outage might only last a few minutes. We did get flashlights and as time went on we got candles. With nothing to do, Maryann, Gene and I went to bed but Dick stayed with Molly. At first he sat on the bed with Molly, then he lay on the floor and finally he got in bed with her. At 3:30 AM the lights came back on. Six hours!. At 4 AM I woke and the light in the hall was on so I went out to turn off other lights in the house but Dick had already done that and was back in bed with Maryann.

Saturday morning Molly was in our room before we got up and she got between Gene and me. This didn't last long but she does like to cuddle for a few minutes. Molly could hardly wait for her parents to leave because I said we had twenty six presents for her, which I would give her after her parents left. She was so anxious for the presents that I think Maryann and Dick left a few minutes earlier than they had planned. I had hidden the presents all over the house and she had a ball finding them. We didn't wrap the doll house which was the twenty seventh present. Actually I think she enjoyed finding the presents more than the actual presents. When all was unwrapped, I played dolls with her.

Molly is a loving child and we enjoyed the hugs and kisses we got. At 7 PM I was reading to Molly when she yawned. I gave her a bath and read another story and she was in bed before 8 and asleep immediately. She slept till 7:50 on Sunday, a full twelve hours.

Sunday morning we took off for a drug store which had an item on sale that we wanted. Molly saw a pony she wanted. She had one like it but each pony comes with some thing different. This one had a lipstick. She let us know in no uncertain terms that she wanted this. We bought it even though we didn't think it a good idea. Another pony had a wedding veil and Molly is interested in weddings. As we paid for our things, the clerk called Gene Grandpa. What a thrill.

After dinner I got out some netting and sequins and flowers and I started to make a veil. Dick called and said they would be here earlier than expected because they got an earlier flight. We straightened up the living room and put things away. Molly wasn't ready to go home just yet so she was out of sorts when her parents arrived. We had cake and ice cream before they left and she was even disgruntled then.

As they were leaving, Maryann reminded Molly to give us a kiss. What a change! Kisses came freely when the parents weren't around. This used to happen with Kate. With no parents around, Gene and I were special and we got loving treatment but with parents around, we were nothing. I guess this is the way it should be.

Even if Molly isn't too keen about the doll house, it more than served its purpose. For a month and a half it kept Gene occupied. Construction was quite a job and kept Gene's mind off his problem.

Thursday the urologist asked Gene if he had any depression. Gene hadn't but the literature on the medicine said this was one of the side effects. The doctor has only had one patient who suffered depression and his was quite severe. My guess is that he may have had a problem before he got prostate cancer. The doctor told us today that 84 to 85'% of cases like Gene's are successful. That is encouraging.

Tomorrow Gene gives blood which will be stored and used if needed during the operation. Things are progressing.

JULY 4. 1992

Dear Phyllis,

Gene came home today. The doctor removed the drain from the incision last night. Now maybe it will heal. He still needs packing bandages because he is still bleeding. It will be at least two weeks that he has a catheter. So he will be housebound for awhile.

The pathology report was that the cancer was entirely contained in the gland. This is good news.

Gene lucked out at the hospital. The new wing was opened three weeks ago and Gene got the VIP suite on the surgery floor. It was a large room with five windows next to each other on one wall and the view was of Mt. Diablo. Gorgeous. The room had a sofa bed which I could have slept on.It had a built in desk, refrigerator, hair dryer, two sinks, six cabinets and a private bath. Room galore for flowers.

The nursing staff was excellent. We have not one complaint.

Gene put on his clothes to come home but they were too uncomfortable so he is back in pajamas, sitting on a doughnut pillow.

I'm glad he is home. It is so much easier for me. I'm exhausted, going to the hospital, taking care of my mother and cooking and cleaning.

Nitty gritty of Gene's surgery
Kate and tooth fairy, Interior decoration

JULY 5, 1992

Dear Lois and Fred,

Here is the nitty gritty of Gene's recovery.

Friday night the doctor removed the drainage tube from the incision. Saturday morning the doctor said Gene could come home. Gene called me about 9:30 AM and said in one and a half hours I could pick him up and bring him home. I rushed off and did some shopping,

Since the doctor said Gene would need a doughnut inflatable pillow, I went to buy one. I found they come in different sizes and shapes. We asked the doctor about size and shape, and he said he would order one thru the hospital. Saturday morning it came but was defective and wouldn't hold air. It was the only one the hospital had. When we got home, I started calling around. Most drug stores were closed and all medical supply places. Finally I located one in the mall.

We had a long wait for Gene to be discharged. It was the 4th of July and no volunteers were on duty. The nurse said Gene would have to wait till someone could take him to the car. Patients are not allowed to go alone.

Arriving home, I asked Gene if he wanted me to go buy the pillow first or lunch first. He opted for lunch. I didn't wait to do the dishes, but took off. When I got back, Gene had done the dishes. He couldn't sit down but he could stand so that is why he did the dishes. Now he carries a pillow whenever he changes seats. He also carries a piece of plastic in case of accidents. No accidents, so far.

Gene came home in his clothes but he soon took them off because they pressed and hurt. Loose pajamas are best. He wears net briefs to hold the pads and super sponges. In the hospital he bled a lot and three pads would be soaked.

We have plastic under the bottom sheet, plastic on the floor of the bathroom. Towels get blood on them. I'll be washing every day.

It takes more than an hour for Gene to clean up in the morning. This catheter business is a foreign procedure for Gene and takes some getting use to.

Tomorrow I call for an appointment in ten days and hopefully the catheter will be removed and Gene will only need pads. By that time maybe the incision will be healed and won't need sponges.

Gene's color hadn't returned to normal. He is usually pinker.

Gene has some discomfort from the anesthesia tube, which causes a sore throat and the voice to change. It can also cause polyps in the throat. We hope this doesn't happen to Gene.

Hing had a triple by pass on Friday and Gene had his operation the Tuesday following. Hing came home on Thursday and Gene on Saturday. I think we'll walk across the road and see Hing for ten minutes today. He is in much more discomfort than Gene.

Sue and I have our hands full. Sue is taking three weeks off from work to care for Hing. I'm tired. I didn't sleep well while Gene was in the hospital and I'm not sleeping too well now. Saturday afternoon I lay down to read and in seconds I was sound asleep, the first restful sleep I've had.

JULY 15, 1992

Dear Halys and Gordon,

Today was grocery shopping day so we spent the morning doing that.

After lunch we were relaxing when the phone rang and I answered it. A nice voice said he was the urologist and asked how Gene was doing. I replied very well and said he was sitting right there and could answer for himself. The doctor asked some questions and then suggested Gene come to his office this afternoon, instead of Friday, and to bring diapers with him. We stopped at the drug store and Gene came out carrying this big bag of diapers and he wasn't embarrassed. He walked in the office with them and still he wasn't fazed. The doctor opened the bag and took out one and put it on backwards. He took it off, put it on correctly and asked me to do one side while he did the other.

The doctor looked at the incision. It still isn't completely healed. It was a deep incision and has to heal from the inside out. It is like a cylinder that you could put your finger in. It is maybe half an inch now but it was at least 3 inches deep. There were no stitches. Stitches would have caused the outside to heal and the inside wouldn't have. Everything is progressing according to schedule. Gene is more comfortable without the catheter, but he is totally incontinent. He soaks six diapers a day. A month's supply will cost about $100. In some cases things return to normal in a few months and sometimes it takes a year. The doctor said there is nothing you can do to speed this up. You have to have patience.

The doctor told Gene he could drive again. I expected Gene to drive home because he doesn't like being a passenger but he suggested I drive home.

Our lawn needs mowing. The doctor said Gene could start the mower if it had a handle starter and not the pull kind. Ours does have a handle starter. Also he said the mower must be self propelled. Ours is, so Gene mowed the grass.

Hing is also recuperating. His leg where they took the vein for his triple by pass looks terrible. Hing had to go to urgent care because he got an infection in the incision in his leg. Now they gave him an antibiotic. Gene was given an antibiotic when he left the hospital to prevent infection. This is the difference between HMO care and private care. The HMO cuts costs by not giving antibiotics and hopes no infection occurs. Private medicine's primary concern isn't saving costs. It is preventing infection. I absolutely do not agree with HMOs and their cost cutting at the risk of a patient's recovery and well being

It takes Gene more than an hour to prepare for bed. He is very good about following the doctor's instructions so complications don't develop.

We had bridge here last night. Gene doesn't mind company because he can disappear when he needs a change but he isn't going to someone else's house where he might need a change and would have to take diapers.

AUGUST 8, 1992

Dear Connie and Herb,

Last night we had a dinner party and if the guest noticed that Gene disappeared twice and returned wearing different pants, they said nothing. Even the super absorbent diapers don't accommodate a volume that comes all at once. The doctor says this will go away as soon as the internal healing is complete.

I decided to serve a fish soup and used the recipe Midge sent me. I bought the spine of a large salmon for the base. I was surprised at the amount of fish attached to the bones. The recipe called for a tablespoon of Pernod just before serving. I didn't have any. I tried the liquor stores and one had a small bottle for $20. I wasn't going to pay that for a tablespoon full. Finally I found a liquor store in Lafayette that had miniatures for $3 so I went over and bought that. Before we went to bed last night, Gene told me the soup was really good. Some was left over and we had it for lunch today.

I was busy most of the day preparing the food for the dinner. I almost knew the fish soup recipe by heart. It called for three cups of stock and one cup of white wine. Before I knew what I had done, I put in three cups of white wine and one cup of stock. What to do? I just continued on with the rest of the ingredients and said nothing. The soup was a real success but with salmon, shrimp and scallops, why wouldn't it be? One man had a second serving of the soup,

Gene only learned to eat fish after he married me. The day before when Gene learned what my menu was, he said he wasn't going to have any fish soup. I asked Gene how it would look if he didn't eat the soup. Our guests would think the soup wasn't fit to eat. So he reluctantly agreed to have just a little.

Connie of Boston is very interested in Houghton House, 629 South Main Street in Geneva. She wanted information so I wrote to the Geneva Historical Society requesting this. I received eight pages in response. Now don't worry, I won't write all that was on those eight pages. However, I did learn some things that interest me. Gene and I had our wedding reception at Houghton House. On September 9, 1887 the Kings, who owned the house, entertained President Arthur and Governor Grover Cleveland who were on their way to the funeral, in Geneva, of Secretary of the Treasury, Thomas Folger, who was a Genevan. Imagine Gene and I having our wedding reception where two former presidents were entertained. I wish I had known this. I would have distributed this information to our guests.

In another book I found these words. STATELY CITY OF GENEVA. SOUTH MAIN STREET HAS BEEN ACCLAIMED AS THE "MOST BEAUTIFUL STREET IN AMERICA" IT IS LINED WITH 19TH CENTURY HOUSES AND CENTURY OLD TREES. THE SCENIC CAMPUS OF HOBART AND WILLIAM SMITH IS HERE TOO.

My home town. Why wasn't I more interested in Geneva when I lived there? I just took it for granted.

AUGUST 9, 1992

Yesterday was six weeks after Hing's triple bypass and he was once again allowed to drive so they went into San Francisco to visit Hing's mother. Upon their return, they stopped by to bring us a pastry. I asked Hing about the driving. He said the driving was o.k. but what really hurt was the bumps. Every bump hurts. It takes years for the breast bone to knit.

Today we had brunch with Linda, Bob, Kate and Connie at the Fisherman in San Ramon. Gene didn't want to go because he was afraid of an accident. His fears weren't realized and all went well.

I invited them for dinner on Thursday night. Kate will come and spend the day with us. Now I must stop. I need to go thru recipe books and try to find something good to serve.

AUGUST 15, 1992

Dear Isabel,

Thursday afternoon we had a treat. Kate came to have lunch with us and stay for the afternoon. That evening her parents and grandmother came for dinner. We only see Kate once a year. Last year we saw her only at a picnic. It is better when she comes to visit alone because then we can talk and really get to know each other. With no other children in our house, it is a one to one deal and can be most interesting.

I had borrowed from the library three I CAN READ books. They were on the floor with books I'm reading. When Kate discovered them, she gave a happy little cry. We sat down and she started reading me the rhyming book. There were only a couple words she didn't know. She liked that rhyming book so much she read it aloud a second time and later she read it two more times. She read the other two right after the rhyming book.

After this I read Kate ONE MORNING IN MAINE which is about Sal who discovers she has a loose tooth. Sal's mother tells her not to worry because a new one will come in right where this one falls out. Sal wonders if their puppy will lose his teeth and her mother says yes. When Sal loses her tooth, she is worried that the tooth fairy will not visit her because she has no tooth to put under her pillow.

At this point Kate interrupted me and told me Sal didn't need to worry because this same thing happened to her. She lost her tooth and the tooth fairy left her something in spite of this. "What did the tooth fairy leave?" I asked. Kate replied, " A dollar and some bubble gum".

To get back to the story, Sal joins her father who is digging clams on the shore. She asks him if clams, fish, hawks, loons and seals have teeth. Dad says only seals have teeth.

Sister Jane comes into the story and here again there was an interruption. Kate solemnly told me she was an only child. I told her I was too. She looked at me skeptically. Only, I might be, but a child?

During dinner Kate asked her father if dogs lose their teeth and he said no. Kate has a dog and doesn't remember him losing his puppy teeth. Here is a profound question. Do puppies have baby teeth?

My dinner was prepared ahead of time but there are always some last minute things to do and in this case the strawberries had to be sliced in thirds and added to the cold strawberry soup at the last moment. Kate was my shadow all the time and wanted to be helpful. She hulled strawberries and when I got out my sharp knife to slice the strawberries, she wanted to do that. I told her we wanted only sliced strawberries in the soup and not slices of Kate's fingers. She agreed. So with my hand guiding hers, we sliced the strawberries. She felt she had done it alone and was proud of herself.

NEXT DAY

I couldn't stand the suspense so I called information at the library and asked if dogs have baby teeth. The librarian took my phone number and later called back and said the 1992 WORLD BOOK said puppies have thirty two temporary teeth which they lose around 5 months of age and as adults, dogs have 42 teeth. There!. You have learned something. Maybe you already knew.

AUGUST 18, 1992

Bob and Linda left yesterday for the wine country so Connie has Kate for three days. We invited Connie and Kate to have lunch with us but Connie wanted to take Kate to the Lawrence Hall of Science so she invited us to go with them.

We left at 10:30 and expected to be home at 4 P.M. I suggested Gene take along a diaper. He said NO. I quietly tucked one in my purse. At 2 PM Gene became concerned that he was leaking. I opened my purse and presented him with a paper bag containing a diaper. HE TOOK IT. Gene has steadfastly refused to go out because he was afraid this might happen. Now we have done it and it wasn't so bad. So maybe we can go out again.

This afternoon we were looking at ARE YOU BEING SERVED and we laughed a lot. At the end Gene said he felt wet and he was. All the back of his pants. He had to change everything, diaper, underwear and pants. The problem was that he put the diaper on with the shiny non absorbent part next to his skin and the absorbent part on the outside. So it quickly rolled down the shiny part onto his clothes. It took eight weeks before he made this mistake.

SEPTEMBER 6, 1992

Dear Raedina and Milton,

Friday night we showed our Gaspe and reunion slides.

The scenery on that trip was not spectacular and didn't impress our guests. What they liked best was the then and now part. We showed the colleges as they used to be, our wedding at St. John's chapel and reception at Houghton House and then these places as they look today. We also showed our Clarence home, my Niagara Falls home. then and now. Maybe it was the personal part that made them enjoy this. I had four couples and all need to watch their cholesterol intake so I served a dessert with no cholesterol. It looked o.k. but it wasn't too tasty.

On Friday I washed our flag. In my school days we were taught to respect the flag and I hesitated to wash it. I wondered about hanging it outside on the line to dry. I consulted Gene and he said to wash it. Before I got around to hanging it up, Gene had it in the dryer, Now nobody knows I washed the flag but it certainly does look better, all nice and clean.

Molly has the chicken pox. I called Maryann to see how Molly was doing. She has a hundred pox on the front and about the same number on the back but none in her mouth, ears or eyes. She does have them on her feet. Molly is getting along o.k. but Maryann and Dave are being driven wild trying to keep her quiet and amused. Gene kissed Molly last Sunday. Since he never had the chicken pox, he could get them sometime between September 13–30th.

SEPTEMBER 8, 1992

We went out for dinner on Labor Day. My mother ordered a dinner and ate half a cup of soup, a teaspoon of the entree and a cup of tea. How does she live on the little she eats?

SEPTEMBER 15TH, 1992

Now I'm reading a novel and I just read when turtles lay their eggs in the sand, they cry. I told Gene this and wondered if it were true. He said he had seen on TV excretions from turtles eyes. Goodness, we've been married 28 years and I never knew Gene knew this. I thought I knew Gene pretty well. Wonders will never cease! After we got in bed, I was still thinking about the crying turtles and I asked Gene why they cried. He said probably because they would never see their offspring. They go into the water after laying their eggs. I said maybe because it hurt to lay the eggs. Now what do you think, either of these or something entirely new? The book, is A GLOVE SHOP IN VIENNA by Eva Ibbotson. Some stories are laid in England. A 1992 book in the U.S. but 1984 in England.

SEPTEMBER 20, 1992

This is the last day for coming down with the chicken pox. I guess Gene is home free because there is no sign of chicken pox

SEPTEMBER 29, 1992

Dear Andrea,

This morning Gene had an appointment with the urologist at 9:30. Of course, I went along. Tomorrow it will be three months since the operation. The doctor said Gene is slow in his recovery. That is Gene's nature. He is slow and deliberate and apparently this even carries over to health. There are reasons why recovery is slow. One could be an infection. The doctor did a urine test. No Infection. Another cause could be that the internal sutures haven't been absorbed. A digital exam showed nothing abnormal. The doctor said Gene could paint the inside of the house and do some digging in the garden. Not to worry! It may be a bit slow but progress is being made.

The Sunday Edition of the N.Y. Times had an article about prostate cancer on the front page and more on another. Yesterday TIME had two pages. I read both articles and wondered if we had done the right thing. I told the doctor about each and he wanted to see the articles. The doctor said Gene was in such good shape otherwise that he felt surgery was the correct solution.

Today we heard from a company that sells motor controls for drapes. I was delighted till I heard the cost. I expected it to be something like a garage door opener in cost but it is much, much more. I said," Forget it." Gene said, "Why?" Gene said he expected this cost. He thinks we should buy them. Time will tell.

We have on the airconditioner. It is 8 PM and the temperature is still in the 90s.

OCTOBER 6, 1992

Dear Mary and Dave,

In June when we visited Helen and Herb, I noticed Helen had a couple shelves of books by Miss Read. I have picked them up and put them down. However, if Helen had so many, there must be something good about them. When we got home, I borrowed one. I found it most relaxing. No sex. Just life in an English village. No psychological characterizations but you did get the gist of characters. No social problems. I read another and was soothed again. I found only a few on the library shelves and she has written over 30. I checked the card catalog and most of her books are under the name of Saint. No cross references in this computer catalog. Every once in a while I borrow a Miss Read title. To me they are like a piece of candy. Too sweet for a constant diet but really good for a dessert. Some of the same people are in each book. I can't keep the story of one book separated from another book. Easy and quick reading. Eventually I'll try to read them all, but spaced far apart.

I just finished THE LAMPS IN THE HOUSE, another English book. I realize I've been reading a lot of English books lately. Maybe I'm making the wrong assumption, but it seems to me the English novels of today aren't as sex ridden as American.

Friday night we showed our slides to four people and what to serve was a conundrum. One can't eat fresh fruit. One can't have sugar. One eats nothing with seeds and no chocolate. One has difficulty swallowing. I went round and round in my mind trying to think of something all could eat. I came up with zilch. I'll have to research my five hundred cookbooks and see if I can find something suitable.

My mother almost lives on fresh fruit. She will take some canned chicken noodle soup at noon. I cut up vegetables very fine and put them in. She won't eat homemade soup. It is a real worry. The doctor says to let her eat what she wants. Tonight we had Coquilles St. Jacques and my mother used to love this. She just looked at it. I took her fork and put one scallop on it and put it on her plate. She ate it. I did this with another scallop and finally with all the scallops. This is the way you treat a child.

Gene was a finicky eater when we were first married. I tried so hard to make good, tasty, pretty meals.One day I was so upset when he refused cauliflower with cheese sauce that I cried at the table. Gene took a taste and he liked it. I heard Gene tell somebody that he eats things because I'll cry if he doesn't. Boy. I'm glad I cried that day. Tears can sometimes do a lot more than talking. I'm not in favor of crying over every little things but once in awhile it pays off, as it did in this case.

For the next couple weeks, I'm concentrating on house cleaning so don't expect a letter.

OCTOBER 7, 1992

Dear Colette,

A celebration is in order. Maryann and Dick heard today that Molly is eligible for adoption. The law works very slowly but thoroughly and after three court hearings, the birth mother was denied the child she gave birth to but never cared for. All that remains is the paper work and then Maryann and Dick will be Molly's legal parents.

THEY AND WE ARE OVERJOYED.

Although we haven't seen it, there has been something on TV, maybe an ad for a doll, that tells how a baby comes out of a mother's tummy. Molly has seen it several times. She asked Maryann to show her where she came out. Maryann said Molly did not come out of her tummy because she was adopted. Molly knows she was adopted but it probably is just a word to her. Molly thought about this for a moment and decided she didn't want to be adopted, She was going to come out of Maryann's tummy. Isn't it sad that kids have to be exposed to all this at such an early age, before they can understand.

In years past little girls were given baby dolls to play with and they copied their parents in caring for the doll. Now Barbie dolls are sometimes the first doll a little girl gets. Activities with this doll involve boyfriend, Ken, and all sorts of grown up concepts. First things first. Wouldn't it be better for little girls to get a baby doll when they are preschoolers and wait for Barbie. I think so.

OCT. 22, 1992

Dear Chet and Bess,

Yesterday Gene had a tiny skin cancer removed from under his eye where it kept hitting his glasses. It was about the size of those colored heads of sewing pins. I left Gene at the doctor's and did an errand nearby and returned just after he went into surgery. When he came out, I gasped in amazement. The right side of his face was covered with bandage, from his hairline to his jawbone. He looked like a pirate. I wondered how much skin the doctor took. Today we went back and the bandage was removed. The incision was less than an inch long. The area under his eye is black and blue. Today the doctor put tiny pieces of adhesive tapes across the incision. Gene has to put anti bacterial material on the incision four times a day and we return next Tuesday. For those three months that Gene was given injections to shrink the cancer, this skin cancer disappeared. After the prostate operation he no longer received the injections and the cancer grew back and changed color. Even without the pathology report, the doctor is almost certain it is a basal cancer.

The pathology report was positive but basal skin cancers are only eyesores. Usually.

What a year we have been having. I'm truly tired of doctors, even if they are nice. However, we still have more appointments.

Today I had my regular visit and Gene had his teeth cleaned. This afternoon Gene had a basal cell cancer on his back removed.

Guess what! Tomorrow neither of us has a medical appointment. Whoopee!

NOVEMBER 4, 1992

Dear Marge and Roy,

It is a good thing I don't have to buy a hat today because I'm sure no hat would be big enough to fit my head at this moment. Here is the story.

When I bought my house in Niagara Falls, I bought drapery material, predominantly gold in color, with an oriental design in large blocks. When I married Gene the drapes went to his house. When we moved to Ann Arbor the drapes fit the windows in that house. When we moved to California the drapes were beginning to show wear but we brought them with us and used them until they started to shred. Then I searched and searched for new material and didn't find anything I really liked. I took Gene to see two possibilities and he wasn't keen on either. On the way home, we stopped at a small furniture store to look at their samples. We found nothing. Gene described to Bill, the interior decorator and co owner of the store, what we had and said how much we liked them. Bill said he often goes to the decorator showrooms on Jackson Square in San Francisco and he would look for something similar to what Gene described. A couple weeks later, he called and said he had some samples. One was exactly what we have. We ordered it and I made the drapes and Gene covered the valance board.

Recently we got new carpeting which is a muted orange in color but which matches furniture and walls beautifully. Our next purchase we hope will be a motorized device for the drapes. We contacted several sources but didn't find what we want. I contacted Bill again. He came out today to see what we needed. Bill said motorized drapes are used in theatres and mansions that have very large, tall windows. As he was talking with us, he remembered the drapery material and asked if he had made the drapes. I said he got us the material but I made the drapes. Then he asked about the covering for our dining room chairs. He stood in the middle of the living room and looked around and remarked about how pretty the carpeting was, how it matches so well the wood in our furniture and overstuffed chairs. He talked about the pictures on the wall and the color of the wall. He was very impressed. He would have liked to take credit for the decoration of our house. Such compliments!

Bill's price for the motorized drapery device which he could get thru an electrician was hundreds more than a hardware store for the same item from the same company. So we bought from the hardware store and Gene installed the device.

At the moment our bird of paradise is in full bloom and I recently counted fifty three blossoms. In the grocery store single blossoms are selling for $4.98 a stem. At this rate we have $263.94 outside our livingroom window. Maybe we should sell our blossoms! No, they harmonize with the living room.

NOVEMBER 8, 1992

What's new? Well, for one thing, a male student at UC Berkeley decided this week that he was attending classes without clothes, only sandals. He rode his bike to class and sat in class in the all together. Oh, yes, he did have a chain around his neck with a couple keys on it. Otherwise nothing. Next day quite a few other fellows appeared in the buff and by this time reporters and photographers were there. Pictures were taken, all back view or front view to the waist. Accidentally a front view of the fellow momentarily flashed on the screen and I missed it. Gene remarked that he was a good looking guy, all of him. He was suspended for thirteen days. I don't think this will catch on at every college. Too cold for some, but this week it has been summertime during the day. Evenings would be a bit cold. Had I known about this, I'd have driven to Berkeley. It would have added a bit of spice to my life.

NOVEMBER 23, 1992

This morning at the hospital Gene had a complete colonoscopy, his third in the last few years. Gene gets polyps in the colon. The first two colonoscopies Gene had two and three polyps but this time he had none because we have religiously followed the doctors directions, two big salads a day of raw cabbage, broccoli and other fibrous vegetables. The doctor said Gene will have to eat like this the rest of his life. Polyps aren't serious till they become cancerous. These raw vegetables inhibit polyps so take heed and eat lots of rabbit food. For once in 1992 we had good news.

1992 brought eight days of hospitalization for Gene, three for me and four for my mother. Gene had twenty nine doctor visits, Norma fourteen, and my mother six. We have no scheduled visits till 1993.

We hope you have a healthy 1993.

DECEMBER 7, 1992

Dear Ingrid and Jan.

We met Madeline and Lee on our China trip and found they live close by. We invited them to dinner and they invited us to attend a performance of the San Francisco Symphony Chorus at Davies Hall. Lee's daughter is a member of this chorus. Symphony Hall was remodeled last year and it is beautiful. We had loges seat with much room for legs and arms.

We had never been in this symphony hall and I was impressed and even overwhelmed. Facing the street is a circular glass wall and one floor had eight Christmas trees standing in front of the glass. One had just lighted bulbs of food, animals, clothes, modes of transportation. No other adornment. I've never seen strings of lights like this. Another tree had a volcano at the top and big rocks were tumbling down. There were prehistoric animals on this too. Another tree was sitting on a cutwork circular linen table cloth and it was adorned with angels made from napkins. The napkins were tied with ribbon and they really did look like angels. Another tree had lights in the shape of icicles. One tree had a toboggan slide encircling the tree. One had gyroscopes and balls with heat-light panels in glass balls. Slinkies too fell down this tree. Very modern. Another tree was decorated by a Boys school and it had paper ornaments that looked like wood. Another had tin ornaments, similar, only nicer than Mexican ones. What a sight. The symphony hall itself is very pretty but for Christmas the background for the chorus of fifty four was eleven Christmas trees with white lights. Simple songs in foreign languages. The chorus is taught the correct pronunciation by a native of that country. Five different languages for this performance. A San Francisco composer's new work was done for the first time last night and the composer was there. Then came the Christmas carols. I've never heard the carols sung as they were last night. The director said IT CAME UPON THE MIDNIGHT CLEAR should be sung with awe. He directed it thus. How impressive!

I've been busy with Christmas activities, shopping, wrapping presents, mailing cards and baking cookies. But it was only with this soothing, inspiring performance that Christmas came alive to me. Gene was as thrilled as I.

DECEMBER 8, 1992

It is 2:30 and I've just finished my eighteenth batch of cookies. I started two weeks ago. My plan was to make twenty batches but I've had it. No more cookies this year.

Mother dies
Balloons at California memorial service

JANUARY 9, 1993

Dear Vi and Bill,

1992 wasn't the best year for Norma, Gene and Norma's mother.

My mother was failing all of 1992 but she would not admit it. Every visit to the doctor she told him she had not an ache or pain. She used to go out in the car with me each day but this year she rarely wanted to go. She was slower to get around in the house. Her attention span was lessened. She used to assemble a five hundred piece jig saw puzzle in less than a day and a thousand one took only two or three days. In the last couple months a five hundred jig saw took a week or more and a one thousand was impossible. She took morning and afternoon naps and formerly she only had an afternoon nap. So Gene and I were well aware that my mother's health was failing. In the last couple months eating became a problem. We knew she had cancer of the colon but she didn't. She didn't want to know the results of her hospital stay in April. I think she suspected, though. She had all the symptoms but she never admitted them to the doctor.

On December 31st we took my mother to the emergency room of the hospital. She was there from eight till three and then transferred to a convalescent hospital. We left her there at four. Her hearing aid wasn't working so that night Gene fixed it and early New Year's day he went to the hospital with it. Sometime during the night she lapsed into a coma and on January 3rd at 10:05 PM she died. Death was due to heart failure.

He body has been shipped to Geneva, N.Y. and we shall go there in April and have services and burial. My mother told me a few days before she died that she wanted to die. We are glad she had such an easy death and that she was only in the hospital three days. She was 43 days less than ninety nine years old.

Since January 3rd, Gene and I have been busy. We have completely redecorated her bedroom and sitting room. Paint, new mattress, bedspread, sheets, pillows, blankets. We have sorted and thrown away and given things to Goodwill. The legal steps have been taken.

I am getting along pretty well but sympathy cards break me up. I read them and cry. I'm putting them aside and in a few months, I'll reread them and then throw them away.

Death at 98 is not really sad. My mother had a long, and aside from polio at age six., healthy life. A good marriage. What else can you want?

Gene and I are adjusting. We find it strange to do things on the spur of the moment. We have eaten out twice. I hope we can go out much more than we previously have.

JANUARY 13, 1993

Dear Helen and Herb.

We still aren't back to normal but we are making progress. Yesterday I found a flowered quilt with a white background that will go well with the colonial furniture of my mother's bedroom. The walls of this room are white and the sun shines in most of the day. I have a rocker there and this is where I'll do hand sewing.

We were astonished to see the bill for the emergency room for my mother. She was there about 6 hours and the cost was $1400

Gene had his three months check up today and everything was o.k

On the way back from the doctor's, we stopped to pick up the motorized drapery machinery. Gene can't work on this till the two rooms and bathroom are finished.

Last year I saw a yellow slicker type raincoat in Nordstrom's which I wanted but it was too expensive. In June they had their half yearly sale and it was reduced 50% so I bought it. The nurse in the doctor's office admired my raincoat and as we were leaving the urologist also commented upon it. Gene was impressed and said he was going to have to have a yellow raincoat because nobody said anything about his black one.

JANUARY 22, 1993

What a weekend this has been for Gene and me. Maryann and Dick dropped Molly off at about 7 Friday evening and thereafter every minute was occupied. We took this four year old to the park twice. I read books till my voice was hoarse. We borrowed nine books from the library. I had three of my own and Molly brought five. I read Peter Pan again and again. Jennie's hat, I believe I read 15 times. It isn't that good but Molly liked it.

Molly brought a musical jewel box and in it she had her allowance,three quarters. She said if I wanted an allowance, she would ask her daddy and he would give me one.

On Saturday she cuddled up to Gene on the love seat as he watched a game. He switched to a cartoon and all was quiet till it finished. Then

Molly began tickling Gene and Gene tickled back. Such commotion and laughter. Sunday as I was doing the dishes Molly went in the living room and sat on Gene's lap and instigated more lovemaking. I'm amazed at Gene's actions with Molly. He forgets his dignity and reserve. At one point Molly said Gene was a cute little fellow.

Maryann called at 8:30 Saturday morning and asked how Molly was. This is the third time Molly has stayed with us and Maryann has never called to check. It seems Dick came down with a bad virus, and the bathroom was his best friend. Maryann was worried that Molly might also have this. I told Molly that her father had a "bug" and was sick. Molly wanted to know what bug had made her father sick. I tried to explain it was an invisible germ. She wanted to know if you ate it. I said you probably breathed it in. She told me a fly was a bug. When they came for Molly today, Molly asked her daddy why he let the fly go up his nose. Dave didn't know what she was talking about.

Friday I bought some daffodil buds. One flowered during the night and three others on Saturday. Sunday morning Molly came in our bedroom, took my hand and showed me all the buds were now flowers. She was extremely interested to watch the tight buds become flowers.

With Kate and Molly, Gene and I have had a good taste of what it is like to be grandparents. We may not be called grandma and grandpa but we function like them when we take care of either these little girls.

I had ten little presents for Molly and I said she could open five on Saturday and five on Sunday. She opened five and begged for the rest. I resisted for awhile and then gave in and let her open three more. Gene hid the last two. Today Gene produced these. Molly can manipulate us more than her parents. She didn't succeed at the park today. A foreign mother allowed her little boy to go barefoot. It was 48 degrees. Molly told us her feet were hot and she wanted to go barefoot. No way, Jose!

We have had the care of the old and the young and the young are more interesting. Molly occupied our every minute.

FEBRUARY 8, 1993

Dear Connie and Herb,

Today I received a letter from the minister in Geneva who was so wonderful to my parents during the four years my father was sick. Dr. Hart wrote :

"I have long admired how you and Gene looked after your mother".............. and ended with " Praise be for her loving daughter, and hallelujah for her devoted son-in-law."

It was a full page letter and I left out part of the paragraph. The letter had me in tears. Gene and I did get to know Dr. Hart during those years.

I didn't realize how much Dr. Hart knew about us but his letter shows that he didn't miss a thing. Dr. Hart is now retired so he won't do the service. Rev. Gerling is new and I don't know him but he has written two lovely letters.

This morning I called someone who buys old jewelry and also costume jewelry. This lady is coming tomorrow morning.

For years my mother has collected stamps. She has two suitcases full and lots of albums. It will take more than a day or two to work on those stamps. We can count up the value of the unused stamps but the others we'll have to research. Then we'll have to find somebody to buy then.

We return to Geneva on April 18th and on the 21st there will be a memorial service in the chapel of First Presbyterian Church. I don't expect more than ten people. My mother outlived friends and relatives. I'll have a dinner in a restaurant afterwards for my close friends and few relatives.

FEBRUARY 13, 1993

Dear Jennie,

Everyone thinks I'm crazy. My actions are not understood but really I'm quite sane. Let me explain.

I had no services here for my mother because she had no friends here. She did make some 20 years ago when we first moved here but they are all dead now.

When we moved to California, my mother made me promise to bury her with my father in the family plot in Geneva. This is where Gene and I also will be buried.

Why did we wait till April? Two reasons. Twenty years ago people who died in the winter were not buried till spring because the ground was frozen and they couldn't dig the grave. I have since learned that they now have equipment to dig graves, something like they use to dig up concrete on roads. The second reason is that we had no winter clothes. I talked to Phyllis today and it was six below zero last night in Geneva and this afternoon it got warm, just zero. Where would I get a winter coat and galoshes?

The cemetery has a chapel where coffins are stored.

I've registered the reaction of my friends when they hear about the delayed burial. I believe they think I'm queer and maybe I am but the delayed service and burial seems logical to me. So be it.

We did make one mistake. I thought it would be better to make one trip east. We plan a vacation in Holland so I decided we would stop on the way for the burial. This was a bad idea. It would have been cheaper to have a round trip from San Francisco to Holland and we could have gone non-stop. With the stop over in Geneva, the fare was higher and we can't have a non stop flight either way.

Tonight we went out to dinner. This is the 29th anniversary of the day Gene proposed. Another couple went with us to the BRIDGES, the restaurant where part of Mrs. Doubtfire was filmed.

The food is excellent but expensive. I had curried butternut squash soup with fried apples. Their specialty is fried spinach. You would never know it was fried. It is like tissue paper and has a wonderful flavor. Lamb is served in many ways but Gene and I had chicken breast coated with pecans. For us eating there is a once in a lifetime experience but for Danville residents with high incomes, it is just a regular eating spot. Only dinner is served and you must reserve days in advance.

I had a hard time selecting a valentine for Gene. Finally I found one that said simply, "I insist on only the best. That's why I married you." Gene read it and said he absolutely agreed with the card. No modesty there, eh?

I hope you had a happy Valentine's Day.

P.S. FEBRUARY 18, 1993

Today Pat called and invited us to visit them Grass Valley on March 10th. I miss Pat since she moved away so I'll be delighted to go.

Gene finished this second week of working on my mother's stamps. He works all day and part of each evening. Mostly now he is checking the value of each stamp. With all those stamps, it could take months.

Sympathy notes are not arriving daily any more and life is returning to normal. I'm getting along fine.

FEBRUARY 24, 1993

Dear Annette and Claude,

I'm trying to decide what clothes to take on our trip. What I'll need in Geneva, I won't need in Holland and Austria. We have decided to pack the Geneva things on top and the last day, we'll pack them in a box and send them back here to a neighbor. We are warned that it may be cold in Holland and Austria, colder than winter here. I was talking with Jacqui recently and she offered to lend me her mink jacket. I surely don't want that but it was a lovely gesture on her part.

Jacqui has been very ill since last September and the only place she has been is to and from the hospital for stays and chemotherapy. Yesterday she had her second outing in six months. She went to a luncheon at the home of someone in Blackhawk. There were thirty at the luncheon, four tables, and the dining room wasn't even crowded. This is one of those luxury homes but it pales next to the Behring home in Blackhawk where a trunk show was the entertainment. Behring is WEALTHY. His home is only 33,000 square feet. One room was 10,000 square feet. The bathroom was bigger than our whole house. It had trees growing in it. There were his and her areas.Other than the Jacuzzi, I can't remember all Jacqui described. Blackhawk has a security gate and is surrounded by high iron fences. The most expensive houses have more iron fences and gates, so there is double protection. Behring's house is nestled among the hills and cannot be seen but it has a wonderful view. Jacqui said that in this exclusive area there are many houses for sale because the original owners have lost money or gone broke.

Today I noticed Mt. Diablo was covered with snow down to the 1600 foot level. This is the most snow I've ever seen on Mt. Diablo. The road to the top was closed today.

Lois called this afternoon with the news that her daughter, Midge. had given birth to twins on Feb 25th. The due date was March 17th. Jan called her sister that day and Midge said she wasn't having labor pains but she didn't feel good. Jan rushed to her parent's house and told them they should be off. In an hour they were packed and on their way from Geneva, N.Y. to Winchester, Virginia. They arrived a little after 10 PM and the twins were born just before midnight. One little girl weighed 6 lb 4 oz and they named her Amy Marie and the other one weighed 4 lbs 13 oz and they named her Abigail Lee. They test babies immediately after birth now and the little one had a 10-10 and the bigger one had a 7-9. 10-10 is excellent and 7-9 is not bad. Midge and the twins will be home on Sunday the 28th. Lois and Fred rushed down so they could take care of Aaron who will be four in June. They plan to stay six weeks because the doctor said Midge would need help for that period of time. They will probably be back in Geneva for my mother's service.

My mother had one living relative of her generation, a cousin, aged 97. Mary called me after my mother's death and was fine. Recently she had a perforated appendix. They operated and the operation was successful but she had a stroke and died of that.

Maryann called tonight and reported that they had taken Molly up on Skyline Drive tonight to play in the snow. I don't think Molly has ever seen snow. The TV stations took pictures of people playing in the snow. One woman skipped work to take her family to the snow and she was embarrassed when photographed,

All the letters from N.Y. state report that the weather has been cold and snow hasn't melted so there are banks of snow along streets and road. These people are all saying the delayed burial of my mother was wise.

Gene is still working on my mother's stamps, every day and evenings. He has the non used U.S. stamps done but not the non used foreign ones. He is working on foreign canceled stamps. Gene has a few more weeks work.

MARCH 5, 1993

Dear Lois and Fred,

About a month ago I hit my hand on the edge of the car door. It hurt but I didn't pay too much attention at the time. I decided I would wrap it in an ace bandage. It only hurt when I moved my hand in a certain way. It was much better with the ace bandage. Monday I decided I better have my hand looked at because I knew I couldn't help with suitcases on the trip if it still hurt. I called and got a 9 AM appointment this morning with the orthopedist. He was a little late because he had been called to the hospital at 2:30 AM this morning.His assistant had already had my hand x-rayed and thought I had a crack in the navicular bone. The orthopedist ordered two more X-rays and a decided fracture was found. I was sitting on the examining table when the orthopedist, still in his operating clothes, sat down close beside me. He probably was tired. The orthopedist said the fracture had healed slightly and there was no displacement. He said had he seen me immediately he would have put me in a cast. Now he had a choice but he felt a cast was better because this bone doesn't heal well due to lack of blood. He said if it didn't heal an operation would be necessary and he felt the cast was the lesser of the two evils. So now my right hand and arm to the elbow are in a cast. My thumb sticks straight out and there is only an air hole at the end of my thumb. I can't get my thumb and first finger together. Can't hold a fork. Can't turn the key in the ignition of the car. I just tried to drive the car but my right hand can't grip the wheel so I guess my driving is over for a month. I go back April 2nd and, if all is well, he will take the cast oft.

Gene and I made bread but now Gene has to mix the dough as well as knead. I just chose the recipe.

I didn't know if I could use the word processor but I can use my fingers. It is awkward but I'm getting along.

MARCH 7, 1993

Friday night my hand was very painful. I went to bed at 10:30 but not to sleep. I got up at 2 AM. At 4:45 we went to the emergency room. My poor doctor was awakened at home and he said to loosen the cast by cutting the sides of the cast. I was to call him at 10 if I was still in pain. The doctor talked to Gene and told him if cutting the cast in the hospital wasn't enough to ease the pain, then Gene was to cut the cast off completely on each side and use only half of it as a cradle. He was scheduled to give a lecture in San Francisco so couldn't see me that day. My hand was too swollen to fit the half cast so I discarded it and used an ace bandage. I had pain pills and I took them. I soaked my hand when I took a bath and you are supposed to use ice for swelling but the hot water felt wonderful.

MONDAY THE 8TH

I have just returned home after having a new cast put on by the doctor. The assistant who put on the first cast puts on twenty two casts a day and hasn't had a tight one in six months. I had a pressure spot where a bone sticks out and this was causing the pain.

Tuesday I had my hair washed and set and came home with my hair in pin curls. Wednesday morning we were at the beauty parlor at 9 AM to have my hair combed. We left at 9:17 for Grass Valley to visit Pat and Bob.

First Pat and Bob bought a house in Grass Valley and the lot next door with a pond. They planted fruit trees and flowering shrubs and fixed the house to suit them. One thing bothered them about the house and that was it sat on a hill and the garage was on a lower level and there were twenty six steps to the main level of the house. They decided to sell and build a house. The architect builder found them a lot overlooking the golf course. They told the architect they wanted two master bedrooms, a living room, dining room, kitchen, breakfast room and a mud room with bath. They showed the architect Pat's oriental artifacts and said the house must accommodate them. Pat's grandfather was a sea captain in the clipper ship days and he brought back from China things that today are priceless. We had breakfast on Imari plates that Pat put in the dishwasher.

This house could only fit on this piece of land. The back and one side are ground level. The front and other side have a forty foot drop. There is a wide deck on two sides where you could entertain a hundred people, I think. You can see one hundred miles away to Donner Summit and the snow capped Sierras. Gorgeous. The house is more window than wall.

It is a two and half hour drive from our house to theirs in the foothills of the Sierras. We are nine feet above sea level and they are two thousand feet above sea level. The land between the road and their house is a forest with no undergrowth and they have planted thousands of daffodils which were at the peak of bloom while we were there. That is the only flowering thing they can have because the deer eat everything else. One day last month Pat was entertaining and heard a noise. Everyone looked out the window and there on the deck was a deer. He climbed the steps so they put a gate there. A couple weeks later another deer was on the deck so they put a gate at the other end.

After lunch they took us to the Empire Mine which was famous in the gold rush days, but which no longer is in operation. Another couple joined us for dinner at a restaurant in Grass Valley. It was a unique place because you could grill your own steak, chicken, ribs or fish if you wished. We returned to Pat and Bob's and had a second dessert.

Thursday Bob drove two hundred miles thru the mountains and up seven thousand feet to see the snow and scenery. Although it was warm and sunny, the snow was taller in height that we are. There was a grocery store with a lunch counter where we had lunch. Pat and I each had a hamburger which was 1/3 of a pound. Had I known this, I would have shared one hamburger with Pat. It was just too much.

Because the roads are so winding and twisty, Bob could never go more than thirty miles an hour. He must have been exhausted from all this driving. Fortunately we hardly met eight cars the whole time. That night we went to the country club for dinner and I had scampi which I love.

We left after breakfast and got home at noon. Going was pretty because it was a clear day and California is green right now. Today it was slightly overcast and it wasn't as pretty.

Gene didn't have to cook for three days and he enjoyed that.

Since my right hand is in a cast, I can't cut or carry anything that requires two hands. I can't write my name or write checks but with my left hand I do use this word processor.

MARCH 27, 1993

Dear Marge and Roy,

Rain again today. Will it never end this year? After six years of drought we are having a super abundance of rain. ENOUGH!

Emme and Ken took us to lunch at a Chinese restaurant in Lafayette today. Uncle Yu's. Excellent, especially the Chinese chicken salad with the tasty light dressing. You may remember that Emme and Ken were in that eight car crash in Maine last September. They were hospitalized in Maine and then came home but they still aren't well yet. Ken has to use a crutch. Emme can hardly walk. Before the accident Emme had a youthful walk. We haven't seen them since the accident because they have only been driving about a month. We feel so sorry for them.

They came to our house afterwards and I decided to be a showoff and operate our motorized drapes. They were agog as they watched the living room drapes close. Then I opened them and they were almost completely open when down crashed the rod and drapes. Emme was sitting near the window but she didn't get conked on the head. She surely was surprised, as were Gene and I. That will teach me to be a show off, won't it? One end came loose from the wall. Gene has now repaired it and he is again hanging the drapes.

APRIL 3, 1993

From necessity I've become very interested in the architecture of houses on South Main Street in Geneva. From the time of the memorial service for my mother to the time of the dinner there is a void and I'm planning to fill this with a walking tour of South Main Street which I think we may enjoy.

APRIL 8, 1993

Dear Raedina and Milton,

I now have the use of my thumb but my wrist is another matter. It really hurts when I try to move my wrist.

Leta called this week and said several people living in the same retirement home as she had died suddenly since Christmas. Usually they become ill and move to a medical facility and weeks or months later they die. So they aren't missed. However when you see a person and then a few hours later, learn that person has died, they are missed. The management of the retirement home, at the request of some residents, arranged a brief service in memory of these people. Leta didn't want to go alone and asked if Gene and I would go with her to the service and then stay for lunch. I said yes.

The little service was held in the rose garden. Everyone was given a balloon. The minister said a few words and mentioned the names of all nine persons who died suddenly since January. I cannot remember the minister's exact words but he told everyone to release their balloons at a specified time. Everyone did but two caught on trees and made a bang. Did two bangs mean two went to hell and the other seven to heaven? it was a novel, unique service and those old people were all saying how nice this service was. It doesn't take much to please those old persons.

To me balloons are for parties. The grocery stores and florists do a big business in balloons for birthdays and wedding parties. I consider this minister a bit far out. Am I in a rut? Too old fashioned? Should I provide balloons for my mother's memorial service? Are they doing this in staid Geneva? Or is this a kooky California trend?

Gene wants to use senior coupons of United Airlines in the future and today he had me call to ask about them. The man I talked to on the phone said my voice was young sounding. He suggested that we bring some proof of age for the senior coupons. THAT GUY MADE MY DAY.

Today I had reason to talk to the undertaker in Concord who was hired to do the necessary things at this end. It was discovered that a California tax was added to the bill and since the merchandise was being shipped out of state, the tax didn't apply and had to be subtractred. When he referred to my mother as merchandise, laughter overpowered the tears. MERCHANDISE! So that is what we eventually become. To me merchandise is something that can be sold.

The mail just arrived and my mother got a jury summons for June 7th. I don't think she will be able to serve, do you

I don't need to tell you about the weather back East, I know. The monument dealer in Geneva reported that he hasn't been able to get in the cemetery to see my father's headstone. I ordered the same headstone for my mother that my father has. He finally resorted to researching his records and now knows what is needed. Letters from Geneva report that the snow is melting but the piles made by the snowplows are so big that they haven't melted. I hope the snow is gone by the 21st.

Yesterday the cast came off my hand. My hand and wrist are stiff and sore but the bone has healed nicely. I'm to wash lots of dishes and do anything to keep my hand in hot water. This certainly helps because my hand is not as sore today but I still cannot move my thumb. If I'm not better in two weeks, the doctor suggested physical therapy.

I recently had a letter from Lois and she said the first weekend the twins were home, they wanted to take pictures of them. All the baby clothes they had were too big so they sent a SOS to an older granddaughter to send her doll's clothes and they took pictures of the newborn twins in the doll's clothes.

JUNE 11, 1993

Dear Isabel,

Today I decided to inquire at the library about my reservation for THE BRIDGES OF MADISON COUNTY which has been on the best seller list for forty four weeks. Today I was told I was 300 on the list and that they have thirty four copies. It will be a few months, I think, before I read that book.

I picked up LIVING WITH THE QUEEN, BEHIND THE SCENES AT BUCKINGHAM PALACE and I'm half way thru it. I always thought the Queen's establishments ran smoothly but this book disapproves that idea. It is sometimes sordid and very funny. I won't go to sleep tonight till I finish this book.

It is now 8:30 PM and I finished the book. At the end the authors told of the trouble getting the book published. It is banned in England. In Canada it is titled COURTING DISASTER and with the epilogue its title is what I mentioned in the U.S. The authors have been on most of the popular TV shows. The book has been translated into several foreign languages. It is easy to read and I guarantee you won't go to sleep reading it.

Wednesday night Gene was flossing and he thought he lost a filling on the upper right. He had an appointment today and he had lost a filling on the lower left. Wrong twice! Is he slipping?

JUNE 12, 1993

Tonight I decided to have a Chinese crab salad for dinner. The recipe called for roasted sesame seeds. It said to heat up a frying pan, no oil, and put the sesame seeds in and stir till golden brown. I put my porcelain coated frying pan on the burner, dumped in the sesame seeds and they all flew up in the air. Not many landed back in the frying pan but those that did jumped again. There were sesame seeds all over. I added some more sesame seeds and by this time the pan had cooled down enough so I could stir gently and they did become a golden brown. The dressing was a healthful one and tasty but Gene said it had an odd flavor. He isn't used to the taste of sesame oil. 2155 is a jumping place these days!

JUNE 14, 1993

Gene started LIVING WITH THE QUEEN yesterday and he can't put it down. Gene can't believe the shenanigans that go on in the palace. They need somebody to oversee the running of the palaces and to throw out the no-goods.

JULY 4, 1993

Dear Pat and Bob,

We ran out of bread this morning so I started to make bread right after breakfast. I hoped to be finished before it got hot outside. I found a recipe for potato, onion, bacon bread last week and this is what I wanted to make. I asked Gene to get the instant mashed potato box down from the top shelf. I measured out my cup and found an extra ingredient, little black bugs. I called Gene, showed him the bugs and told him to go to the store and get another box of mashed potatoes. While he was gone, I poured the mashed potato flakes down the disposal and turned on the water. WOE IS ME. The water caused the potatoes to expand and both sinks began to fill up with water. I tried everything I knew and nothing helped. When Gene came back, I showed him what I had done. He got the plunger and used that. No success. Then he crawled under the sink and tried to loosen the pipes. There are two 90 degree bends in the pipes and he assumed the pipes were plugged at those spots. His wrench wasn't big enough to loosen the bolts. He worked and worked. Finally he got one loose and some water spilled over but he couldn't get at the plugged part. He used a snake and that didn't help. Finally he went outdoors and used the snake there. The plug was not under the sink but outdoors under the house. He put the hose in the pipe and turned on the water full force and it became unplugged. By the time everything was back together, it was 1 PM. I expected Gene to get really mad at me but he didn't. However, let me do some little bad thing and he will get mad. After this I made the bread. It was after three and I had expected to be finished by 9 AM.

JULY 10, 1993

Dear Lois and Fred,

Today I went to the library before lunch and got books for the weekend. We had lunch. At 1:30 the mail came and there was a notice that THE BRIDGES OF MADISON COUNTY was waiting for me. I hopped into the car rushed off to get it. I started reading at 2 PM and I finished it at 4:45 PM. What a love story. I said love story, not sex chronicle. Sex is implied and not described, breath by breath, movement by movement. The exact opposite of what Danielle Steele writes. I cannot stomach Steele books but others like them and she is making a lot of money.

In 1970 Gene and I visited all the covered bridges of Madison County and we have pictures of all them. I can see why this book has been on the best seller list for a year, lacking four weeks. It is only 170 pages. The build up to the climax at the end is tantalizing. It brought tears to my eyes. In spite of that, I thought it had a correct ending. Lots of trashy best sellers have a price tag of $25 and this books sells for $15. The short length of the book, ease of reading and low price probably contributed to its success but more important is the fact that an ordinary woman, with a good, but unromantic, taken for granted marriage found a brief interval of romance which she didn't allow to ruin her marriage and disrupt her chldren's lives. It isn't a great book but it satisfied a hidden want all women have who are in a comfortable but unstimulating marriage. Love is like a fire. It needs fuel to keep burning brightly, otherwise it smolders. Smoldering is all right when you are aged but a few sparks in mid life add zest. Even a husband can provide the sparks.

Are you concerned as I as by the Jessica De Beer case? August 2nd will be a sad day for the De Beers. I think Jessica should have stayed with the people who love her.

AUGUST 4, 1993

Dear Jacqui,

Monday was a busy day for me because I was giving a book review luncheon on Tuesday. Shopping, preparing food, rearranging furniture, cleaning, getting out good china, setting the table occupied every moment from 5:45 AM till 8:30 PM. I was exhausted when I finally sat down that evening. I invited seventeen but two had to cancel at the last moment.

I reviewed three books by Niall Williams and Christine Breen.

Niall is Irish and was studying for his MA in American and English Literature at the University College, Dublin. Christine is American and was studying for her MA in Irish Literature, UCD. They married in New York City in 1981 and worked there for four years. Each had good jobs in the publishing field but in 1985 they chucked their jobs, sold their belongings and moved to County Clare and set up housekeeping in a cottage in which Christine's grandfather had been born and which was two hundred years old. It was a primitive existence and nothing either had ever before experienced. So that is the setting of the story for the first book, O COME YE BACK TO IRELAND. In the second book, WHEN SUMMER'S IN THE MEADOW, they adopt a little girl and this account brought tears to my eyes. THE PIPES ARE CALLING tells of their travels in Ireland. It makes me want to go back to Ireland and stay in the places they visited. It sounds so scenic and unspoiled. Another book will be published in November of this year. They have adopted a little boy and I assume this coming book will tell about that. I had seen this couple interviewed by Jane Pauley on the TODAY show a few years back.

How did my guests receive my review? Well, the majority listened intently. Two went to sleep but they go to sleep any time, even when talking with you. One glared at me most of the time. She is a talker and I gave her no chance to interrupt with a silly question. I've never known this one to read a book. When I read a book I empathize with the characters and their problems and I cry and laugh with them. Some people can't do this, especially people who are wrapped up in themselves.

Yesterday I empathized with Sposato, the lawyer in San Francisco whose wife was killed by that gunman who killed all those people in the law office a couple weeks back. Sposato, with his ten months old daughter on his back, testified in Congress. My heart went out to him. That adorable baby with no mother. My admiration for Sposato is extremely high. We must have that gun control law passed. The TV camera did pick out one Congressman who had tears. He wasn't somebody I knew. Maybe a first termer.

Monday and Tuesday I empathized with the De Beers. The De Beers had tears when on TV and so did I. Some people should never be parents and some who should be parents can't be.

We have one problem as a result of the luncheon. Lots of left overs. We are eating oriental turkey salad and layered vegetable salad. We haven't touched the seafood aspic. Only two pieces of cake were left and they didn't last long.

Kay does a Mary Poppins
Hing to Kaiser, Best compliment

AUGUST 9, 1993

Dear Phyllis,

Saturday night we substituted at bridge at Ginnie and Ed's. As usual, we first had dessert at the dining room table. We adjourned to the living room where Ginne had two card tables set up. An organ, extra long sofa, tables and chairs are on one wall. Bookcases and windows on the end wall and chairs and tables and chest on the other wall. There is no fourth wall. Because the room is more rectangular than square, there is room to walk around the card tables but not much room between them.

When we changed partners and tables, Hank and Kay who were back to back at different tables touched behinds very gently and this threw Hank off balance. Hank says he is 5 feet 18 inches tall and he is a big man but not fat. Kay is tiny. Hank, feeling himself falling, grabbed for anything and apparently got Kay. Hank went face forward toward the organ and between the card table chairs and Kay went flying up in the air as Hank went down. Like a see saw. For a time Kay was suspended three feet above the sofa in a parallel position. She came down face first on the sofa. Such a graceful Mary Poppins she made. She rolled over and not a hair was out of place, nor was her dress in any way disturbed. Hank crashed down like a falling tree and his head just missed the corner of a wooden chair and the organ bench corner. He was wedged between the two. Gene felt the air as Hank passed by on his way down. Hank needed to get over on his bottom and this was almost impossible for such a big man in such a small space. The wind was knocked out of Hank. He didn't seem to be hurt.

Ginnie and Ed were in the kitchen and this scene greeted them as they returned. Ginnie and Ed each took a hand of Hank. Hank brought his knees up to his chest and they PULLED. Neither Kay nor Hank seemed to have any bones broken but Hank was pretty shaken up and had to rest once he was pulled to his feet. After a few minutes we resumed playing bridge.

When we were back home, Gene and I discussed this and I got a fit of laughing. I kept seeing this episode in my head. It happened so suddenly and the funny part was Kay sailing in the air. During the night I woke and started to laugh again. Since Gene and I sleep with bodies entwined, Gene woke because of my shaking body. I'm still laughing. I talked to Kay today and she said she didn't know what happened. All she knew is that she was taking an ariel trip without her consent or intent. All we thought was going to happen Saturday night was a bridge game. We didn't count on this acrobatic performance. I still see in my mind Kay about three feet above the sofa in that parallel position. She was Peter Pan.

Gene showed me his lower right arm last night as we prepared for bed. It had a round red spot about two inches in diameter and a streak about three inches long extending to the elbow. I thought it was an infection and Gene should see a doctor. Gene got an appointment and the doctor thinks Gene was bitten by a bug whose stinger carried bacteria. He outlined the area with a ball point pen. If it exceeded that area in two days, he was to come back for another appointment. He gave him an antibiotic. It is better today. If it isn't one thing, it is another.

SEPTEMBER 15, 1993

Dear Catherine and Larry.

Maryann reports that Molly is thrilled with kindergarten. One day they made a gingerbread man, a big one. They put it in the oven and went off to the playground. When they came back, the gingerbread man was gone. The teacher took the kids on a tour of the building, looking for the gingerbread man. When they got back to the room, the gingerbread man had returned and he had raisins for buttons. One afternoon at home Molly took a nap and when she woke, she told Maryann that the gingerbread man had run right across her room. One night they passed her door after putting her to bed and she was murmuring "Kindergarten, kindergarten. kindergarten." School certainly stimulated her imagination. She has so much to tell Maryann every day. This community spends money on education and the quality of education is pretty high. Parents with children in the upper grades seem quite satisfied.

SEPTEMBER 17, 1993

I had dental surgery on September 7th for a lump, large and white, on my upper right gum. First I consulted the internist who sent me to the periodontist. He operated within a few minutes of seeing it and sent the lump to a lab in Berkeley. After a week I went back to have the stitches removed and another lump had formed under the stitches. He said it could be a root canal gone wrong or a cracked tooth. He took the x-rays next door to the endodontist who said it wasn't a cracked tooth. Both said there was chronic and acute infection and both said it wasn't magligant. I have another appointment for next week. In the meantime we wait for the pathology report and to see what else happens.

OCTOBER 18, 1993

Dear Marguerite and Ed,

Sunday at 3:10 PM our telephone rang and it was Sue, our Chinese neighbor, who said they were in real trouble. Hing became ill at 7 AM. She had an appointment at Kaiser for him at 3:40. Hing was vomiting and so dizzy he couldn't drive and she doesn't drive. She asked if we would take them to the hospital and, of course, we said yes. They wanted us to drive their car because the front seat reclined and Hing could lie down for the ride. With pans, bags and tissues, we loaded Hing in the front seat next to Gene.

Kaiser is the biggest HMO in the U.S. and notoriously known here for six to eight hour waits till you see a doctor. We are unacquainted with Kaiser and Gene drove into Emergency because we didn't know where Urgent Care was. I ran in and asked for a wheel chair. We almost had Hing loaded when an aide came out. She wasn't much help. Although we thought this was the worst attack of an inner ear problem Hing had ever had, I decided to mention that Hing had had a triple bypass last year and perhaps this was a heart attack. Things speeded up and Hing was taken to an examination room instead of the waiting room.

Gene and I found a seat in the crowded waiting room and waited. At intervals a nurse would call a name and often the person didn't respond. After a few hours, they would get discouraged and leave. At 5 Sue came to us and said it was an inner ear problem and they were going to keep Hing for two more hours. She suggested we go home and return at 7.

We came home and had a bite to eat. We were slated for bridge at 8 PM. At 7 we returned. Hing was still vomiting. He was taking Dramamine. With Hing lying on the reclining seat, Sue and I had to squeeze on half the back seat. There were people walking around and cars backing out and I attempted to help Gene by warning him of people and cars in that small space. I twisted my head right and left and felt a sharp pain.

During bridge my neck pained, but I said nothing to Gene. At 1 AM we returned home and I put the heating pad on my pillow, hoping this would ease the pain. It didn't. At 5:30 AM I took a hot shower and let the hot water run on my neck. No relief, so at 6 AM we went to the emergency room at John Muir. The doctor said I had either pinched a nerve or strained a muscle. They gave me a relaxant and a pain killer and I've been on the sofa all day, awake only for meals, which Gene prepared.

Sue called today and said Hing could sit up for brief periods and the vomiting had lessened. She said they had never had such swift service at Kaiser as they had yesterday. They didn't know I mentioned heart attack. Hing also helped by vomiting three times in less than five minutes in the lobby.

Just a few minutes ago Gene was saying he is glad we aren't connected with Kaiser. In a few hours, we used both an HMO and a private hospital, and the difference is like black and white. I'm afraid this is the wave of the future if we have national health care based on HMOs. In the past we have been very pleased with the care both my mother, Gene and I had at John Muir Hospital, a private not for profit hospital.

I had an appointment with the endodonist Monday morning and the emergency room doctor said I could go to it. I wore a foam collar. The endodonist looked at me, asked what the problem was and if I wanted him to work on me or postpone it. I couldn't have canceled this appointment on Sunday and I was the first patient on Monday so I felt I had to go thru with it. In addition I was so sedated, I didn't care what was done to me. I wasn't even nervous. The endodonist went in and removed some infection, and syringed it out. He took several x-rays. I'm to go back in a week and he will remove the packing and see if more infection has formed and check to see if the lump on my gum has disappeared.

Sometime after five that day Gene answered the phone and a man asked to speak to Norma. I rose from the sofa and went to the phone and it was the endodonist who wanted to know if I had any problems. I said it was beginning to throb a bit because the Novocain was wearing off. He said if any problem developed, I was to call him immediately. Wasn't this nice of him?

I don't think the new health plan will give such service. Gene and I have been very pleased with the doctors we have. The gastroenterologist, urologist and my internist have all called after procedures. On the day Gene was told he had cancer, I saw the internist in the morning for a routine check up and I was my usual self. In the afternoon the nurse called me for some reason. When she heard my crying, she told the doctor and he called me to see why I was so upset. I told him of Gene's cancer and he tried to reassure me. I'll never forget this. Will we get this kind of care with a national health plan? I don't think s

.NOVEMBER 11, 1993

Dear Ingrid and Jan,

Last Saturday I borrowed from the library James Mitchener's THE WORLD IS MY HOME, A MEMOIR. I just finished the last page, 512. Long ago I read TALES OF THE SOUTH PACIFIC but I have to confess I've never read completely any of his other books. Some I've scanned and that is all. I read every word of this autobiography and found it fascinating. Because Mitchener doesn't know who his mother and father were, heredity cannot account for his success. His environment certainly was the opposite of privileged and you can truly say he was a self made man. The book isn't just an account of what he did but his thoughts and reasons for his thoughts are described. Once when he wanted to join the navy and another time when he wanted a passport, he had to have a birth certificate. All that was known is that his foster mother got him when he was two weeks old. He had to hire a lawyer and the lawyer made up a story that he was the son of Edwin Mitchener and his lawfully wedded wife, Mabel, and that he was born February 3. 1907. Everyone in the town knew that Edwin had died five years previously but the government accepted this.

Last night we had bridge at our house and I made cream puffs and filled them, not with whipped cream, but rather an orange sauce. This was to cut down on fat. There still was cholesterol but we had watched our cholesterol intake all day and could afford a cream puff.

The Wongs had been in San Francisco for a few days and during bridge when I was dummy, I called them and said I would bring over their mail. They said they would prefer to come to our house and they did and brought us a chiffon cake, a lobster and some peppers from their daughter's garden. We always have dessert before we start playing and nothing at the end. I told our guests that we would have a second dessert when we finished. So at I AM when they were eating the second dessert, they suggested that they play some more bridge and go home after breakfast.

NOVEMBER 22, 1993

It is the Monday before Thanksgiving and I'm starting preparations for our feast. I've spent hours looking at recipes and deciding what to serve and enjoying every minute. Some of our friends buy a cooked turkey dinner at the grocery store and they think I'm crazy to go to all this work but to me theirs is the lazy way. I recently learned to use sherry instead of water in the dressing. I tried it and Gene said the dressing was the best he ever had. He didn't know I did this. I'll sneak sherry in the turkey dressing too. In an oven bag the sherry permeated the turkey. My mouth waters just thinking of all this good food.

1993 HOLIDAY SEASON

Dear Fran,

On our Georgia Elderhostel we heard much about Eugenia Price who has written thirty four books and lives on St. Simons Island. Our history course peaked my interest in the region and since we have returned home, I've been reading her historical novels and I really like them

In October the N.T. Times reported that Proctor and Gamble, who sell products around the globe, had a learning lesson. This company introduced Pamper diapers to Japan in 1980. At first they sold but soon they found there was a cultural difference. Japanese mothers change diapers on the average of fourteen times a day and American mothers seven. Japanese mothers wanted thin diapers and not the bulky kind we have. Japanese manufacturers realized this and made thin disposable diapers and stole the market from P & G.

In the U.S. diapers are made in pink and blue and they didn't sell in Korea, China and other Asian countries. Why? Pink diapers advertise a daughter and male children are the desired sex there. So they had to switch to white diapers so no mother was embarrassed when she bought them.

P & G also failed with detergents. They advertised whiter shirts and socks with their brand and they were outlawed because the Japanese like politeness in business dealings. All temperature Cheer also didn't go over because the Japanese do their laundry in tap water and left over bath water and different temperatures for different clothes meant nothing to them.

In Poland P & G sent samples of shampoo. The people were delighted to receive something free. P & G had to abandon this because thieves ransacked mailboxes and P & G had to pay huge repair bills for damaged mail boxes.

It was a most interesting article and I've only scratched the surface.

This Christmas letter is being written in the first week of October. The reason? One copying store is have a .02 sale for a week and since I send lots of letters with our Christmas cards I'm taking advantage of this. I don't have any personal news to tell you but I want this letter to be personal so I'm going way back and resurrecting some memories.

A month after Gene and I were married, we had a dinner party. As one couple thanked us, the husband said "In this house I would eat the garbage." What a compliment. My head sure did swell but it was deflated about an hour later when, as we were preparing for bed, Gene critiqued the meal. He found something wrong with every dish I served. Trust Gene to take me off cloud nine and get my feet firmly back on earth.

The next day I had time to think this over. I had learned in that month that Gene liked about ten foods, all plainly prepared. I decided right then and there that I wasn't going to go by his likes and dislikes. I like everything, except liver. So I continued to serve a great variety of food and to experiment with recipes. That first year was hard for both of us.

Gene and Toby both attended a SIRS meeting one day and when Gene came home, he said the lunch wasn't very good. Later in the afternoon Toby dropped by and asked Gene what he thought of the lunch and Gene repeated what he had told me. Toby said "They should hire Norma to prepare our lunch." I liked this unexpected, low key compliment.

This past Monday night we had a dinner party before we had our vacation slide show. I served heavenly sole which used to be a favorite of Gene and my mother. When my mother got cancer of the colon, she rejected food and, like a child, Gene joined her in some things. So I stopped serving heavenly sole. I decided to serve it again, even though Gene said he no longer liked it. The guests were enthusiastic and Gene ate his whole piece. The next day he told me the fish was really good last night. First Gene was influenced by my mother and this time by guests. Hurrah! Heavenly sole will again grace our table.

Recently I made a "pig eating good cake" which is made with a mix. I used a mix we had had a long time and apparently the mix had lost its rising ability. It turned out heavy and soggy.

I sent Gene to the store for a new box of cake mix and redid the cake and it was wonderful, just as it has been in the past. I was about to throw out the failure when Gene said he would eat it. What does this say about Gene's standards when he will eat a failure? He is loyal. I thought I had Gene trained to know what is good and what isn't. What does this say about me? Almost any moron can make a cake from a mix. I'm going to attribute this failure to baking powder that has lost its umph. It can't be my fault! Or can it?

As I write this, Christmas is not in the air. It will be 73 today, October 7th. The sun is shining brightly. Flowers are still in bloom. In spite of that, I'm saying MERRY CHRISTMAS.

JANUARY 1, 1994

Dear Jennie,

My friend, Connie in Boston, called a couple days ago. She reported that her daughter saw a set of Dickens' Christmas Carol stamps for sale in Boston for $50. This story was first published in 1843 so this is a 150th anniversary. England published a series of 5 stamps based on the story. I received one on a Christmas card, one of Bob Cratchit and Tiny Tim. It sells in England for 19 pence which is about 30 cents so the 5 sold for about $1.50. Andrea thought $50 was too much to pay for 5 uncancelled stamps. She called her friend in England and had them buy the same thing for $1.50

The one I got wasn't canceled so in time it could be valuable.

Boy, stamp dealers who know their stuff can make a bundle. All they had to do was send to the post office in England and buy 5 stamps for $1.50 and resell them here for $50. I bet it works in the reverse too. English stamp dealers could buy special U.S.stamps at cost and resell them for a lot more. I doubt that any of our Christmas stamps would be so valuable but some of the others might.

JANUARY 23, 1994

Dear Helen and Herb,

Last night the Wongs took us to dinner at the China Station in Berkeley. They ordered a special meal which the restaurant will only prepare for ten or more. A special meal it was. First came a Chinese chicken salad, the like of which I've never had. Everything was cut so finely that each item was hardly thicker than a string. There was a delicate, sweet taste to this salad. I remarked about it and Darren said it was papaya, dried and sugared.

About a year ago other friends took us to a Chinese restaurant for lunch and ordered chicken salad. That salad had a predominate sesame taste. I researched my 15 plus Chinese cookbooks and found a recipe that closely resembles that salad but I don't remember any recipe that had papaya in it. I think Gene and I will have to go back to this restaurant some day and order this salad. I'll eat each ingredient separately and try to identify the ingredients. I probably won't be able to figure out the dressing, though. This was a wonderful starter to a delicious meal.

Next came a sizzling rice soup. My first time to have a soup that sizzled. We've had other sizzling dishes. Even without the sizzling rice, the soup would have been good.

The piece de resistance was lobster with a black bean sauce. Yummy.

After that three platters were placed on the table, cashew prawns, mushroom chicken and beef with broccoli. All very good. The main course ended with red snapper, I think, with macadamia nuts and some vegetables. The fillet was in the middle of the platter and at one end was the head of the fish which had been coated with a batter and deep fried. The tail and the fins had been prepared the same way and were in appropriate positions. I've seen fish baked and served and always I'm offended to see the eye of the fish but this fish had a half of a maraschino cherry for an eye. Such a pretty dish. Dessert was almond pudding, sort of like jello, but not really. Gene and I love Chinese food, American style, so this was a real treat.

It wasn't just the food, however, that was pleasing. We ten were five of Chinese descent and five Caucasians. Our hosts, their son, mother and a girl married into the family were the experts on Chinese food. They know their cultural food and anyone is lucky to partake of the food they select. Darren tells me that one of the things I love, prawns with fried walnuts, is nouvelle cuisine. I think nouvelle cuisine originated in California but it sure has spread. I understand even the French are starting to prepare some of their traditional dishes with less cream and fat and are making slight inroads into nouvelle cuisine.

Gene and I will never forget the wedding dinner for Diane, their daughter, that we ate in March of 91. Nor will we forget this dinner. When we left the restaurant, my tummy suggested a budding pregnancy,. False alarm. It was the wonderful food.

Gene and I like cruises, so when I saw the ad for Seabourn, I sent for the brochure. On this ship, there are no cabins, just 500 sq feet suites. Tux and evening gowns are de rigueur. The cost is just a little under $1000 per day, per person with no discounts for early booking. However, you would save money because tipping is absolutely prohibited. Even so, in order to afford a Seabourn cruise we would need to win the sweepstakes or have a rich uncle and neither is on the horizon.

The newspapers today reported a new stamp which is supposed to come out in March in Bend, Oregon. Four stamps were sold before it was discovered that the man on the Bill Pickett stamp was not Bill, but his brother. The post office recalled the two hundred fifty million stamps but three are still missing. Why couldn't Gene and I find one of these stamps'? Maybe then we could take a Seabourn cruise.

JANUARY 28, 1994

Dear Millie and Jim,

I don't think I have an accent but at least once a week someone asks where I'm from. Yesterday I called a tourist office in Oregon and at the conclusion of business the woman asked if she could detect a New England accent. She said she knew I wasn't a westerner because I said Or-e-gon and westerners say Ore-gun. I listen closely to the local and national anchormen on TV and I think I pronounce words as they do. So how come everybody in California thinks I m a foreigner?

We are having a busy weekend. Gene invited Hal for lunch on the 27th and Leon for dinner on the 28th. Let me tell you, it you want to feel good about your cooking, invite a widower who lives alone and does most of his own cooking, with an occasional meal out. He will eat heartily and compliment you.

Sunday we are having nine for dessert after the von Polen slide show. Don von Polen is a super photographer and every year he and his wife travel the country with his three screen show. This time he will cover 12 countries and give the background of 12 songs of faith originating in these countries. All are well known hymns sung in Protestant churches. All his programs are given in churches and no fee is charged. There is no advertising. A notice appears in the church bulletin the week before. They do have a free will offering that goes to von Polen. Our neighbor has been informing us of his visits for the past five to eight years. He travels all over Canada and the US. and is always here in January. He stays in the warm part of the U.S. in the winter months and goes to the snowy regions in the spring, fall, and summer. We'll have to be there a half hour early to get a seat.

Monday is Gene's birthday. We invited Madeline and Lee to have dinner with us at Pacific Fresh and then will return here for birthday cake.

I spent the morning looking for a new book case. We have a book case in the living room, three in the family room and one in the kitchen and one beside the word processor. Now I want another on the other side of the word processor. We should be throwing stuff away but I can't part with my books. I came home with sizes and prices and tomorrow Gene and I will make the purchase.

I want to look at a book about Minton china, published in 1993. It cost $128. The library doesn't have it but they could get it for me if I wanted to pay $5. I'll pass on that. This is a coffee table book, I think. I would guess the pictures would be superb and probably the two hundred year history is interesting. Maybe some day I'll be at the Library of Congress and then I'll look at it.

FEBRUARY 1, 1994

Gene's birthday was a red letter day. As usual, we exchanged the number of kisses Gene is old and this year he kept giving a bonus so I think I ended up with more than one hundred. I'm not complaining.

Everyday we look for sprouts from the tulip bulbs we bought in Holland. Not yet. Maybe Gene planted them too deeply because other bulbs are up. Spring is on the way so it won't be long.

Betty Beale's book
Red Eggs and Ginger party

FEBRUARY 6, 1994

Dear Isabel,

Friday at the library I borrowed POWER AT PLAY by Betty Beale. Betty Beale wrote a syndicated column for years and it was all about life in Washington, D.C. At one social event in Texas, Foreign Minister Romulo of the Philippines, who was a short man, was asked how he felt among all those tall Texans. He replied, "Just like a dime among nickels." What wit!

Maybe I knew, but if I did I forgot, that Nixon chose Willard Marriott of the Marriott Hotels to run his inaugural. He is a high ranking Mormon. People wondered if there would be any dances but Marriott said Mormons are the greatest dancers in America. I didn't know this.

Another thing I learned from this book is that cheese isn't the word to say when you are having your picture taken. Julia Child says souffle makes your lips look better, but an English duchess says bitch is even better. I just had Gene saying these words and I think Gene has the most pleasing expression with souffle. Try it, looking in a mirror, and see which you think gives the most pleasing expression.

Betty Beale says that she and Julia Child lived in the same house at the same time when they both attended Smith and that it was no secret that Julia couldn't even boil water! Boy, has she come a long way.

The last chapter describes dinner parties Betty Beale gave for three presidents and the preparations for them. It was supposed to be a big secret for security reasons but neighbors homes and gardens had to be inspected by the Secret Service who told then not to breathe a word about the party. So the neighbors, important and well known people, gave spectator parties at the same time and their guests watched the procession of six motorcycle policeman, nine car entourage, fire department truck, ambulance and hovering helicopter. Now that is giving a party.

Today I learned from the N.Y. Times that Japan prohibits handguns. Period. As a result Tokyo had a total of 8 gun related murders in 1992. NY city has eight every two days. Japanese can own as many rifles and shotguns as they please but licensing requirements are stiff. Firearms must be stored in a locked cabinet. If not, they get jail sentences and they don't get out early for good behavior. If Japan can do it, why can't we?

Reading all about Washington, D.C. entertaining reminds me of our coming entertainment- As you know, I like to cook and have company at home. I wanted to invite a couple in for Gene's birthday dinner but Gene said we should take them out. We did and came back here for birthday cake. We need to entertain two other couples who have recently entertained us in a restaurant. I wanted to invite then for dinner here at our hone but Gene says these people entertained us in a restaurant and we should return in kind. We investigated restaurants near the Civic Arts theatre and decided upon one but I'd rather buy some really good fish or meat and have dinner at home. It is more work but more intimate. To me a dinner invitation at our home is just as good a return as a dinner we host in a restaurant.

When Pat's mother and my mother were alive we four and the nurse went out to lunch occasionally. I always invited them here for lunch, but the others always took us to a restaurant. It was never anybody's turn. It was an easy relationship. I remember once having a shell fish entree, hot olive bread just out of the oven and fresh strawberry pie. What else I don't remember. They ate a whole loaf of bread. Pat said she never before had eaten so much. I think they enjoyed my lunches at home because almost every day they had lunch at a restaurant. I'm going to have to change Gene's mind. Never before has he thought a restaurant invitation couldn't be returned by a home meal. Just where did he get this new idea?

A couple weeks ago Ginnie called and said her sixth grade granddaughter was assigned a report on the foods of Greece for her social studies class. Ginnie knew I had more than 500 cookbooks. She asked if I had any information. At first I thought I didn't. I have Chinese, Italian and Scandinavian cook books. When I looked, I found I did have chapters on foods in foreign countries, explanations and recipes. I sent Gene off to xerox eight pages. We found lemon soup, moussaka and kouranbiethes were very popular. A few days ago Ginnie was visiting Michele and Michele was working on her report. She said she was going to write me a thank you but not till she got her report back with a mark because she wanted me to know what mark she got. I hope she gets an A+.

I make moussaka with beef but usually in Greece it is made from lamb. I've never made kouranbiethes but I've eaten some a friend makes. They are so rich they melt in your mouth.

FEBRUARY 11, 1994

After dinner last night we four walked across the street to the Civic Arts Theatre and saw the MERRY WIDOW. Ken had reserved our seats by phone on Sunday. He went to pick then up yesterday afternoon and they couldn't find them. Apparently they had sent then and they will probably arrive today. Fortunately the theatre wasn't filled, so they gave us other seats.

All of us enjoyed the performance. The elaborate set was rented from a company in N.Y. city and it was beautiful. So were the costumes. I guess you would call the actors and actresses semi-profesional. They are constantly working but only in the bay area. Afterwards Ken and Emme came in our house for hot chocolate. In the winter, about every six weeks, Gene and I treat ourselves to hot chocolate in the evening. We had Chinese cookies too. Ken and Emme said it was good, not something they often have.

Our social life in 1994 has started off with a bang. Tomorrow night we play bridge and Monday we go out to dinner again.

We heard on TV that N.Y. city got another foot of snow today. Here the sun is shining brightly and it will get up in the mid 60's. You need sun glasses today.

MARCH 8, 1994

Dear Bertha and Eleanor,

Last year we bought tulip bulbs in Holland for us and our neighbors who took care of our mail and house. They had to be sent because immigration doesn't allow you to bring agricultural products into the country. We planted ours and they are now in bloom and have been for a week. The neighbors had leaves poking thru before we did but when our leaves poked thru there were also buds. They opened when the stems were only six inches tall. We were disappointed because the tulips in Holland had long stems. Next time we looked we decided the stem was taller and Gene measured it with a yard stick and it was eight and a half inches tall. Next day he measured it again and it was eleven. Sunday it took a day of rest and didn't grow at all. Monday it was thirteen inches tall and today it is fourteen inches. We learned something new. I always thought the stem grew to full height before the bud opened but that isn't true with these tulips. When the Wongs saw Gene with a yard stick, they came over to see what he was doing and they are getting a laugh about Gene and his measuring.

I talked to Betty, our other neighbor. She said her sister who lives in Antioch, recently received a notice that her new Visa card would arrive soon. Hers didn't and she read in the paper that others on her street reported theirs had been stolen. The sister checked on her new Visa card and found that already four thousand dollars had been charged. In one case there were five charges of one hundred dollars each on the same day at the same store. She asked about this and found that these were gift certificates. There were gasoline charges, and grocery store charges. The police have arrested two men. There has to be a woman because a women would have had to sign the Visa slips. We try each day to pick up our mail as soon as the mailman leaves it, but sometimes you are away and can't. Our mail right now is delivered anytime from noon till 6 PM.

Service is terrible. Our regular mailman is o.k. but his days off are unpredictable.

MARCH 22, 1994

Dear Mary and Dave,

Saturday we went to the Ikebana Show in San Francisco. I didn't enter an arrangement this year. There were some lovely arrangements but also this year there were some arts and craft arrangements which are no part of ikebana. Whoever entered these knew nothing of the principles of ikebana.

After viewing the show we went to a Greek restaurant near Golden Gate Park where the food is wonderful. I had lemon soup and it was delicious. Don drove us around San Francisco. He used to live there and we saw much that we have never before seen.

We recently made a cheese bread and it was so good we made it three consecutive times. Next we made a Mediterranean bread with olives and oregano and we ate this fast so we had to remake it. Tuesday we made hot cross buns. I thought I had dried fruit for the buns but I had used it up. I asked Gene if he would go for the dried fruit and he was so anxious for the hot cross buns that he wanted to go before the store opened. Gene likes hot cross buns and these were the best I've ever eaten. New recipe.

APRIL 16, 1994

Dear Gertrude,

It is Saturday afternoon and I've just finished reading ABBY ALDRICH ROCKEFELLER of Bernice Kert, a 1993 book. It is an excellent book because the subject was a strong woman whose strength was so gracefully and lovingly given that it didn't appear strident. She ruled but didn't appear to. She had a tense life because her husband wanted all her attention and felt the children competed with him for it. John 2nd was brought up sternly and didn't know how to relax. Abby's family life was very different. So she really had a total of seven children, six she gave birth to and one she married. She could mold the six but to erase the strict upbringing of her most intelligent husband wasn't possible. That John 2nd loved her comes across firmly. He just couldn't relax and enjoy family life.

John wanted his children to be frugal. When the oldest was ten, she got a dollar a week and the next oldest seventy cents. Father said one third should be spent, one third saved and one third went to the church. Each child had an account book and at the end of each week before more money was given., the account book had to be submitted and it had to balance. Each amount had to be defended. Abby was the one who helped balance the books each week. John didn't want his children's life wrecked by money so he always gave less than the children needed. They could earn more if they needed it and some of the ways they earned it was if they caught one hundred flies on the porch, they got ten cents. If they trapped mice in the attic,they got five cents per mouse.

Things were more relaxed when John 2nd was away from home. The children begged to sleep with their mother and once she reported to her husband that Nelson, eight, slept with her five nights. It was John 3rd, ten, next and then came Laurance, six. I guess Winthrop and David were just too small at this time.

A few years before this, Babs, the oldest, wanted her mother to sleep with her when the father was home. Abby asked who would take care of papa and the child said the nurse could sleep with papa and take care of him.

When Babs was at the age for a coming out party, the Rockefellers did not have the big dances the Astors, Whitneys, and Vanderbilts had. They had a musical at Pocantico with dancing afterwards, at which five different kinds of WATER were served. NO ALCOHOL.

The six kids invited friends to their home and Abby took an interest in each. Sometimes they stayed overnight and if they did, the guests had to appear at breakfast. A servant served BIBLES on a tray and each had to take one. John 2nd choose the chapter and every one read a verse. After this breakfast was served.

When the older boys were teenagers, they took a poll which asked if the boys could chose their mother from any the group had, which one would they choose. Abby won unanimously. This says something for Abby.

I'm so enthusiastic about this book, I just had to write you about it while it is fresh in my mind.

APRIL 20, 1994

Dear Connie,

Life gets complicated but the alternative is no choice. Right now I'm seeing doctors and dentists and I'm not enjoying it at all.

While on our recent trip, I found something hard in my baby greens salad. It turned out to be half of my tooth. Upon returning home, I saw the dentist who put a temporary cap on till he could get the old filling out and see if a root canal was needed. At another appointment he determined that a root canal wasn't possible so he sent me to an endodonist who also said a root canal wasn't possible but he could do something to save the tooth. He put another temporary cap on while a crown is being made and after that the endodonist will do some surgery.

That isn't all. For some years I've had a mouth problem, not tooth. The dentist, periodonist and my doctor have all had a fling at it. Nothing solved the problem. The doctor sent me to an ENT man. He identified it as lichen planus and said I should see a specialist at UC SF Medical Center. In a little while Gene and I take off for San Francisco and this appointment at 1:30.

How to get to San Francisco? You must be at the BART parking lot at 10 AM if you are to get a place to park, too early for my appointment. Parking at the Medical Center is almost impossible to find, even in the parking garage. The solution was accidental.

The Wong's daughter gave birth last week and Sue and Hing have been staying with the daughter. Sue does the cooking and cleaning and Diane takes care of the baby. Hing came home last night and was going back today. We asked if he could drop us off at BART. He could either go to Belmont thru San Francisco or San Mateo, so he said he would go thru San Francisco and drop us off at the hospital. It was out of his way, we know, but did we appreciate it. You bet.

APRIL 22, 1994

We saw not the doctor with whom I had an appointment but her assistant and two medical students. Nine actual pictures, not x-rays, were taken of my mouth. I was given two prescriptions to take for 2 weeks and an appointment. This doctor doesn't think it is lichen planus but rather a reaction to some medicine I'm taking, but in any case the treatment is the same. The biopsy did not confirm lichen planus.

UC SF Medical Center extends blocks and blocks on the side of a hill. We finally located the right block and the right building. I want to be transferred back here. It wastes a whole day going in for this.

My appointment for surgery was May 11th. Yesterday at 9 AM I had a phone call and was told there was a cancellation for 10 that morning and could I come in for the surgery. I had plans for that morning but nothing I couldn't cancel. I had to go alone because Gene was bowling. Actually I'm glad this happened because I didn't have three weeks to anticipate it. I came home with an ice pack on my cheek and a sheet of instructions, Do nothing the rest of the day. No trying to see the incision because opening my mouth might break the six stitches. Cold liquids for a week and only yogurt, milk, eggs, ice cream and juice for a week. No toothbrush is to go in my mouth for a week. Nothing warm because the blood clots might bleed. No food because it could collect around the stitches and cause an infection. I'm taking an antibiotic so I won't get an infection.

Gene bowled yesterday and he is bowling again today. I had to sleep sitting up last night. Today I'm not taking a pain killer so I'm not groggy. I cleaned two bathrooms and I then I rested.

With everything quiet, I started thinking about our vacation in September. We had a pile of brochures about Greece and Italy, so I concentrated on them. We had been considering two cruises but I came upon a land and sea trip by Central Holidays. I had never heard of this tour company so called our travel agent and asked if they were reliable. She said this company was connected with Alitalia Airlines. She called to get some answers to my questions and found only eight spaces were left. When Gene came home, I told him and we decided to book immediately. The travel agent just called and said we are booked. I'm glad this is decided. Indecision is trying. Now we'll settle down to reading about Greece, Italy and Turkey because we see one of the seven wonders of the world in Turkey.

Summer is here. The ice plant is in full bloom and is making quite a show.

We hope all is well with you.

APRIL 29, 1994

Dear Dorothy and Lars,

What's been happening to Norma? Here is a run down.

Yesterday was the first day I could have solid food. For a week, I've existed upon yogurt, ice cream. baked custard, juice, as per the endodontist written instructions. Gene snuck in two cans of Ensure because I was supposed to take vitamins too. I got along fine and lost two pounds. My mouth seems to be healed but some of the stitches are still there and hang down and I keep playing with them with my tongue. They are supposed to disappear by themselves but if they don't, they will be taken out at my next visit.

One day last week Gene said he wanted to invite his pal, Hal, for lunch and asked what day I wanted to do this. I said I would think about this because I wasn't going to cook when I couldn't eat. My idea was to take Hal to a Chinese restaurant on the first day I could eat. Chinese food is usually soft and I thought that would be a good introduction to food for me. They had a buffet with soup, three entrees, rice, won tons, egg rolls, fruit and tossed salad. I took very small helpings of a few things. This was the first day I could have warm food or a hot drink so I ate the warm food first and saved the salad and fruit till last. Upon finishing the warm food, I was so stuffed I couldn't eat the salad and fruit. Since you can't have a doggy bag at a buffet, Gene ate what I couldn't.

At dinner time Gene asked what we were having. I had planned a dinner but I wasn't in the least hungry so I told Gene I would prepare his dinner but I wasn't eating. Gene said in that case he would prepare a salad for himself and he did. I've never done this before. I consider it my duty to prepare meals. At bedtime I still wasn't hungry but I knew it would be twenty hours before I had breakfast so I had a thin slice of bread. I wasn't hungry at breakfast. Can it be that a week of not eating shrank my stomach? Never before have I eaten so little and felt so full.

Gene also wanted to invite Leon to dinner. We decided to also invite his girl friend. They are coming tonight for dinner. A few years back the girlfriend wrote a cookbook and Leon bought a copy and gave it to me. I'm a bit hesitant about my dinner tonight. I'm having two standbys which are usually well received. Heavenly sole with sea bass substituted for the sole and strawberry pie. The appetizer and two salads are first time ventures. The appetizer is a shrimp cheese cup. One salad is sweet and sour zucchini and the other greens, topped with fruit and a honey-lemon-cinnamon dressing. I sampled the dressing and it is tasty. The vegetable is asparagus. I saw in the NY Times an asparagus dish where the asparagus was arranged like the spokes of a wheel around fish so that is what I'm doing. Will I measure up to the girlfriends standards? Last time Leon was here he said this lady asked Leon to bring home a recipe from me. I m all a dither. I've never cooked for somebody who wrote a cookbook.

We always enjoy Leon. He always has such interesting things to tell. One son has been married four times and divorced three and he is friendly with the first three wives. The children of his third wife, by a former husband, all work for the son. Even the third wife works for her former husband. This is so unusual. I think the son should patent his secret for staying friendly with former wives.

I'm working on a little cookbook of recipes that have California as the first word of the title. One copy place has a special of two cents a page so I'll xerox my little cookbook today.

While Gene was bowling, I prepared the pie and fixed four flower arrangements. Gene just came home and his team lost four games. The opposing team was good. However, Gene's team is now number one. I hope they can stay in this position for this season.

Our hot days disappeared and it is more like spring. The flowers are lovely and the front of our house never looked so pretty. I'm concentrating on blue and purple flowers in front because I think these colors go well with our pale green house. Roses are in full bloom.

How was your day?

APRIL 30, 1994

The girlfriend was a real lady, classy, friendly, down to earth. She asked for two recipes. We got along famously. Both of us really liked her.

MAY 12, 1994

Dear Raedina and Milton,

I just finished reading Kristin Clark Taylor's THE FIRST TO SPEAK, A WOMAN OF COLOR IN THE WHITE HOUSE. I thought it was an excellent book. A couple of things are worth mentioning. Kristin believed that the way you acted at an introduction spoke of character and self confidence. She was brought up to meet people head on, eye to eye, man to man, with self confidence and energy and she and her lawyer husband started early training their children. Lonnie Jr. was just one and a half when the family was invited to the VP residence for a picnic. For weeks before hand, they practiced shaking hands with Lonnie. The husband would get down on the floor and say to his son, "Well, hello there, young man. What is your name?" The child thought this was play and he would laugh and say "Lonnie, Pa." and then put out his hand for shaking. They finally got him to firmly shake hands. Hugs and kisses for a job well done. The day came for the picnic. The child had his first hot dog, lots of potato chips and lots of Hawaiian punch. Kristin didn't know how he could eat so much. Bush spied Lonnie and came over. Now would come the proof of the pudding. Kristin introduced Lonnie to Bush and waited but nothing happened. Then Bush bent down and said, "What's your name, son?" Automatically Lonnie looked Bush directly in the eye and said, "Lonnie, Pa." and put out his hand for shaking. Bush was pleased and picked up Lonnie and put him on his shoulders and started to give him a horse ride by jouncing him up and down. Kristin saw Lonnie having difficulty and asked Bush to put him down but Bush was having fun and continued. Kristin got out a diaper but before she could get it in place, there was Lonnie upchucking all over Bush's head. Kristin tried to mop up Bush as Bush lowered Lonnie to the ground. Bush took the diaper and wiped himself off and said, "I didn't realize I had such a profound effect on people." Kristin worked for Bush when he was president also. She had very nice things to say about him. She admired him as a person.

She mentioned, not by name, some others in the White house that she didn't think were nice.

I liked her description of Reagan. She said Reagan was soft spoken and appeared sincere but he reminded her of an onion. No matter how many layers you peeled away, another always remained. Like an onion, the man could bring tears to your eyes. She said he was graceful, classy and eloquent with a quiet EVERYMAN sincerity. However it was impossible to discover any layer difference from the one that came before.

I couldn't put this book down till I had read all three hundred two pages. It isn't a kiss and tell book. It isn't an as told to book either. The words are her own.

Tonight we took the Wongs out for dinner. They are always bringing us things or doing things for us. We appreciate this. Hing thought this must be some occasion but we said we took them out because they are nice people.

We went to a tiny French restaurant, La Tour. The food was excellent. I don't think I've ever had better

Wednesday I had my second visit to UC SF Medical Center. I was given another prescription which we had filled last night. I should have purchased smelling salts with it because the bill for thirty pills was $196.17. This is about $6.50 a pill. I will go one more time but after that no more.

Today is cold. A couple days ago I asked Gene to turn on the air conditioning. Today I had him turn on the heat. This is a queer May.

Connie and Andrea from Boston arrive in San Francisco today. Tomorrow we are going into San Francisco and have lunch with then. They came for a Victorian house tour program which lasts several days. I invited them to stay with us but they want to go to Carmel too so they will pass on that this time.

People are different. The Wong's daughter had a baby and they went to their daughters the day after it was born and are staying for two weeks to help out.

Another friend's daughter had her second child and these parents visited the daughter in the hospital and the day she came home and other wise helped in no way.

My cousin and wife went from New York State to Virginia and stayed six weeks to help take care of a three year old grandson, their daughter and her newly born twins.

Grand parents are different as the above show. The ones that live the closest see the grandchildren the least.

I'm glad I had the paternal grandparents I did. They were superior. I knew I was loved and special to them. When my mother was annoyed with me and told my grandparents, my grandfather would soothingly say. "Norma is a GOOD girl." How can you be bad when somebody thinks you are good?

MAY 20, 1994

Dear Isabel,

This week I have only one doctor's appointment, at UC SF Medical Center. Last week I saw a dentist, an endodonist, dermatologist and ENT specialist. The week before it was an orthopedic surgeon and a dentist. Frankly I'm getting sick and tired of all these medical appointments, even though each has helped me.

The arthritis in my wrist is about five percent better. This new medicine, Relafen, has reduced the swelling and I can bend my wrist slightly. An evaluation will be made after a month. I really don't want the bones in my wrist fused because the wrist will be rigid for the rest of my life. I think of the people who have arthritis in many places in their bodies. How do they stand the daily pain?

I like letters.Need I say more,

JUNE 4, 1994

Dear Kathryn,

Always something new! We are invited to a RED EGG AND GINGER PARTY. We have never been to one of these. They are held when Chinese babies are born. The Wong's grandson was born April 14th and immediately Sue and Hing decided to have this party. I don't know if it is usual for the grandparents to give the party or the parents. The party will be held in a Chinese restaurant in San Francisco on Market Street. Because so many are invited, it will be buffet. Hing says the Empress of China in Chinatown is often used but they serve only 5 dishes and one is chow mein. This one will have 20 dishes, all selected by the Wongs, and no chow mein because that isn't Chinese. The usual time for this kind of party is Sunday and it is a come and go party with nobody staying the whole time. I asked Hing the significance of red eggs and ginger. He didn't know but hard boiled, dyed red eggs are always served. The invitation was designed by the parents and has a baseball theme because Jay is enthusiastic about baseball. He not only watches but plays on a team. The banner says OUR LITTLE SLUGGER and the bat has ALL STAR RYAN MICHAEL ANTHONY on it. The baseball is unmarked. Weddings and baby parties are one of the main social activities of the Chinese. Some months every weekend has one or the other for the Wongs to attend. A couple of years ago it was weddings of children of family and friends and now it is baby parties.

SUNDAY JUNE 5, 1994

When I do my daily stint on my exercycle, I look at TV. Today a doctor from Stanford University Hospital was talking about bran and cancer. He said that no one bran is better then another, but all brans are important because they cause food to go thru at a quicker rate and so there is less time for carcinogens to be absorbed, so less chance of developing cancer. He also said our bodies have cancer cells all the time and only when our immune system breaks down can cancer get a toehold. The advice was to eat all kinds of foods. The large variety of foods is very good. Eliminating any food is bad. Some foods are carcinogens and some are cancer inhibitors so you need to eat every food to balance one against the other. It was a good program and the half hour went fast because I was so interested.

Today Gene had a skin cancer removed from his cheek. It took eight stitches to close the incision. He can't shave for a week. Gene looks funny with black threads hanging down his cheek. It is a vertical incision and maybe it will look like a smile wrinkle.

This week we received a brochure from Holland American and they have an 82 day cruise around the world for $63, 466. You could go economy for $27,680, though. This is on the SS Rotterdam. The only thing keeping us from going is having another couple to accompany us! So how about it? Want to go? We'll wait with bated breath to hear from you.

P.S.

Well, maybe not having somebody so accompany us is not the only thing that keeps us from going. Another thing could be, WE AREN'T RICH.

JULY 11, 1994

Dear Shizuko, Kaoru, Sohoko and Tae,

Yesterday was the RED EGG AND GINGER PARTY in San Francisco. We drove to Bart in our car and Hing and Sue followed and picked us up and we went into San Francisco with them. The Empire Restaurant had a very small amount of parking and where the 160 people parked, I don't know.

Sue and Diane had covered tiny little baskets with lace and a blue ribbon surrounded the top of the baskets and said Ryan Anthony, April 14, 1994. Attached to the handle was a tiny blue pacifier. Inside was some candy. Each woman got one of these.

The restaurant was well organized with two sides having buffet areas so there was never a waiting line. One area was hot food, another

Japanese, another noodles and soup, another salad, another dessert. The food was very good, but Hing said it was high cholesterol and some was deep fried. I especially liked the deep fried zucchini. I was about to take something when Hing said not to because it was deep fried chicken feet. I took only one piece of any dish and lots of dishes I never touched. There was just too much.

Diane is back to her normal size, either a 4 or 6. Ryan was dressed in a baby tuxedo and he had on black patent leather shoes. The time before when I saw him, he had on a baseball outfit, even the cap. Ryan's features and coloring are Chinese but he has blond hair.

So many presents have already been given this baby and lots more were given yesterday. I watched Diane opening envelopes and thought they contained checks but instead they contained gold chains which Diane put around Ryan's neck. I don't know the significance of this. It is customary for grandparents, great grandparents and other close relatives to give gold chains. Sue and Hing decided to omit the chain and give stock but Sue's mother said they HAD to give a gold chain. Afterwards these gold chains just go into a safety deposit box.

I did find a book that said in ancient times in China the infant mortality rate was extremely high and a sumptuous feast for relatives and friends was given at the end of the first year of life. Dyed red eggs and ginger were given to express thanks and joy at the survival of a male child. Today this is done for females, too. Nobody in either Hing or Sue's family knew why a red egg and ginger party is held. They only know all their Chinese friends and relatives have them. Now Hing wants to know why eggs, why dyed red eggs and why ginger? I couldn't find this in the library so I wrote a letter to the Chinese consulate and asked them. I hope they respond.

Ryan is a very much desired baby. The father is so attentive. I remarked that his life was probably greatly changed and he agreed and said that even with all the work Ryan caused, he felt his life was better than it had ever been. Ryan didn't spend much time in the baby carrier because so many arms were carrying him around, great grandmother, uncle, father. As hosts Sue and Hing circulated. Their turn to hold him would cone at home where the immediate family gathered after the party.

We too watched the O.J. legal proceedings. I think he is guilty and deserves the death penalty but I wouldn't be surprised if he receives no punishment. Race and popularity will make it hard to convict him.

We have just finished dinner. I made a big chicken salad and served it with fresh peas and fresh fruit. I'm trying to make up for the fried food yesterday.

It is hot today and I'm glad our air conditioning is working.

HALLOWEEN 1994

Dear Emma and John,

When we first moved to California, one of the first persons I met was Pat. I had contacted Ikebana International and asked if anyone in this area went to San Francisco meetings and I was given her name and number. I called her and she took me the first time and ever after that we and others went together. We learned immediately that we had much in common. We were only children, each had a widowed mother we were responsible for, each had a silent, quiet, no small talk husband who neither smoked or drank. Our religious, political and social thoughts were similar. We were two peas from the same pod who ended up in different pans.

The first time Pat came to our house, she exclaimed that we had Heywood Wakefield furniture. She had furnished one of her houses with it and had always liked it. Hers was wheat color and ours is champagne. She still has one bedroom of Heywood Wakefield, Another bedroom she gave to a granddaughter. Pat's house now is oriental.

When Pat came yesterday, she said she had read an article this past week that stated Heywood Wakefield furniture is now a collector's item. When I bought the dining room furniture, I had no choice as to table. My table could only seat six. We really needed a bigger table and I tried to contact the company in Gardner, Massachusetts to see if I could buy a bigger table from them. To reduce production costs, the company had moved to one of the Carolinas, after over 100 years in Gardner.

I did a lot of research and finally located the name of the town. I wrote and my letter was returned as undeliverable. I then wrote the postmaster and he replied with the news that the company had gone out of business. Too bad because this was good quality, solid birch furniture with clean lines. I liked the furniture when I bought it in the 50s and I like it just as much today.

Yesterday Pat and Bob came to visit and we went to Boundary Oaks Country Club for their bounteous, good brunch. We returned home and showed our slides of Holland because Pat and Bob are most interested in spring bulbs. Their home in Grass Valley sits four hundred feet back from the road with lots of tall trees under which they have planted thousands of daffodil bulbs. It is a sight to see in the spring. Before they left. I prepared a small supper. I wanted then to stay overnight but they were having guests tomorrow.

When Pat moved to Grass Valley, she got rid of lots of things, some of which were her Ikebana containers. She gave me quite a few. I got out one big one and bought sun flowers and made an arrangement, which I had on the coffee table. Pat recognized the container. She thought the sun flowers looked artificial so she touched them to see if I was cheating.

We bought the sunflowers at the market. I only needed three but they came in a bunch of six so I had two arrangements. I always thought sun flowers wilted fast but they really last about a week and they're spectacular in an arrangement.

Betty, our neighbor, came over for a few minutes on Saturday and before she left she said she had been staring at the sun flower arrangement because it was so striking. I hope I can get some plants next year for the garden.

Last week I read Peter Mayle's HOTEL PASTIS. I like his books. This is a novel instead of an account of his life in Provence.

Tonight is Halloween and Gene is ready. He buys the candy and carves the pumpkin. We don't have as many kids as we used to and those we do have come with parents. People are afraid to let their kids out at night.

Neva and children in Italy
Molly and tooth fairy, Gene a father??

NOVEMBER 18, 1994

Dear Phyllis,

Our bank statement came today and I tried to balance our check book. We are two cents off and Gene is trying to find the mistake.

Today I went to my monthly meeting of ikebana in San Francisco. The demonstrator was good but he took one and a half hours and we found it hard sitting on steel bottom chairs for that length of time. I have lots of natural padding but even my bones rebelled. One of my riders displayed an arrangement so we had to delay our departure till everyone finished viewing the arrangements. Then we made a stop in Japantown. We didn't get on the freeway till after 3:30 and we didn't get home till after 4:30. Gene was walking the floor. Traffic was heavy and stop and go near the tunnel.

Neva was a passenger today. She and her husband were born in Italy and came to the U.S. in their teens. She went to nursing school and her husband studied to be a doctor. They have four children. Three girls are nurses and the boy is in medical school. Neva said that when the oldest was thirteen they decided to take their children back to Italy to meet grandparents and other relatives and show them their childhood homes. In addition to the visits, they took an American Express tour. The first free day on the tour Neva and her husband were approached by couples on the tour who wanted to borrow a child for the day. Each couple said they would take good care of the child and give it lunch and in return they wanted the child to be an interpreter for them. They had observed that the children spoke fluent Italian and the tour people spoke no Italian. Neva says the kids don't read and write well but they are proficient vocally. Neva and her husband were surprised at these requests and we were amused by her tale.

Tomorrow we are driving to Albany to have some books autographed. Elisa Kleven's new book, THE PAPER PRINCESS, just came out for Book Week and I'm giving two copies away and keeping one for myself. I wanted them autographed.

We had an unveiling today. Just before vacation I started a plastic net cover for a child's ice cream chair that was given to me shortly after I was born. My mother had painted it white. It was chipped and a mess. Gene took it all apart and took all the paint off and sprayed it with gold paint. The he reassembled it with my new seat cover. Gene did a beautiful job. Color wise, it fits right into our decor. Period wise, no. We don't have antiques in our house. When Pat and Bob visited us, Pat said a relative had just sold four adult ice cream chairs for quite a profit. We aren't selling this chair.

JANUARY 5, 1995

Dear Linda, Bob and Kate,

From 11 AM on December 31st our quiet lives changed and we learned much we didn't know about the tooth fairy. Halfway between our two houses, we met Maryann, Dick, Molly and Phyllis. At a designated small plaza Molly and her grandmother, Phyllis, transferred to our car and came home with us while Maryann and Dick went to San Francisco where they spent New Year's eve and the night at the Hyatt on the Square. As soon as Molly saw us, she showed me her loose tooth and it really was loose, just hanging by a thread. When we unpacked her things, she showed us an enlarged felt tooth with one end open. Inside was some cotton. Nowadays a child just doesn't put a tooth under his or her pillow. They put the tooth in the felt tooth and then insert the cotton so the tooth can't fall out and this is what goes under the pillow.

When Molly was showing her tooth, I said, "Oh boy, oh boy, oh boy!" Maryann, Molly and Phyllis laughed. It seems Grandma says, "Oh my gosh" when she is surprised and Molly picked up on this and told Phyllis everytime she said it. Phyllis asked what Norma said and Molly replied, "Oh boy, oh boy, oh boy". When I did exactly what Molly said I would do, they all thought it was funny. Several times while Molly was with us,

I said this. Gene says I never say this when we are alone. Guess he either doesn't surprise me or he doesn't have any loose teeth.

We had a mini Christmas after we got home. Presents were exchanged in front of our Christmas tree. We read some stories and then I suggested Molly make a butterfly salad for dinner. Molly isn't a salad eater but I thought if she had a hand in the making, maybe she would eat it. She was enthusiastic about arranging six big spinach leaves on the plates, cutting a slice of pineapple in two and placing the two slices with the curved sides facing and a date between. I had some pieces of pepper for the antenna. We sliced ripe and green olives and placed them on the pineapple and it really looked like a butterfly, if you have a good imagination. Some honey mustard dressing was placed on the spinach. At dinner Molly ate all but part of one piece of spinach. Hurrah! I sent all the ingredients home with Molly so she could make the salad for her parents. Maryann reported she made the salad but didn't eat any of it at home. Why?

After dinner we took down our Christmas tree. This year we had a magic Christmas tree. We bought one tree and put it in the corner of the living room. There was a reflection in the living room window and this reflection was repeated outside the dining room window and we had a total of five reflections and the real Christmas tree. We invited neighbors in to see our six trees.

When she was put to bed, Molly was too keyed up to go to sleep immediately. She listened to tapes on her Sony for a long time.

Sunday Phyllis went to church and Gene and I took Molly to the park. She wanted to go there but it was too wet and we knew it. She was only satisfied when nobody was around. I told Molly I had an anytime present she could have after dinner so she ate pretty well for her. The present was an autographed copy of THE PAPER PRINCESS by Elisa Kleven, dedicated to Molly, a special princess. We read more books. Molly sat on Gene's lap. She likes Gene. Phyllis played GO FISH with her. Three people were kept busy entertaining this child. At the transfer Dick kept muttering, "48 hours." No Molly for 48 hours! Oh boy, oh boy, on boy.

Molly went quietly to bed this night but about an hour later, she appeared in the living room. with a bloody kleenex in one hand and her tooth in the other. It had just come out. So we got the felt tooth holder and Molly put the tooth in it and then it went under her pillow. I called Maryann and asked the going rate of tooth fairies. Maryann said the tooth fairy always leaves four quarters and takes the tooth. I thought the tooth should be left on the bedside stand so it would be easy for the tooth fairy to find it but Molly said the tooth fairy always finds it under her pillow. And she did because the next morning there were four quarters and the tooth. Seems the tooth fairy got confused and forgot to take the tooth. Guess the tooth fairy must be getting old and forgetful.

Monday Phyllis. Molly, Gene and I went by BART into San Francisco.

We got off at Embarcadero and walked to Market and after a long wait rode a bus to Pier 39 where the sea lions are. Phyllis had wanted Molly to see the sea lions who are so playful and make a lot of noise, arc, arc. arc. We looked till Maryann and Dave appeared and then we went upstairs to a restaurant and had lunch. We gave Molly a window seat but by this time sea lions no longer interested her and she just wanted to draw on the paper tablecloth.

After lunch Dick showed us his new office in the financial district and then Phyllis, Gene and I came home by BART and Molly went home with her parents. Molly had school the next day. That night we showed our slides of the Columbia-Snake River trip to Phyllis. Tuesday we three had lunch at Spruzzi's in Lafayette. Afterwards we came back to Walnut Creek and walked the renovated Broadway Mall, stopped in one store to see the music box selling for $11,800 and the crystal aquarium with crystal fish for $10,500. We'll put these on our note to Santa next year! Then home to prepare dinner for eight, after which we showed our slides of the Italy- Greece trip.

Wednesday we went to Blackhawk to see the Behring Museum of antique classic cars. To say we were impressed is putting it mildly. We spent an hour and a half, had lunch and went back for another hour. One car was one of two made. One was made in 1897. The cars gleamed. I never heard of some of the makes of cars. Our ticket was also for another museum but we decided to see the movie, LITTLE WOMEN, so we had to pass this up.

After dinner we showed Phyllis our slides of Kentucky. Kentucky is really beautiful in June. Everything is so green.

Tuesday we left at 9:15 to take Phyllis back to Maryann's where she will spend the night and tomorrow will fly home. We were at Maryann's just long enough to have lunch and then we headed home. Maryann was taking her mother to SUNSET MAGAZINE for the tour this afternoon.

We had a most interesting five days.

P.S.

Our neighbor's son and his family stopped to show us the children. Andrew who isn't quite two is a lively one.I had some hanging reindeer and Andy asked what reindeer say. I don't know and I doubt that I'll find this in the encyclopedia. Do you know what reindeer say. Tell me if you do.

Vacation back East
Hospital stay in California, O.J. verdict

FEBRUARY 23, 1995

Dear Jennie,

In November arrangements were made by telephone for Helen and Herb to visit us in February when they came to an Elderhostel. It ended Friday the 17th and that night they would spend with their daughter, Margaret, and family at Vandenburg Air Force Base. The next day they would arrive at our house. Since Santa Barbara is about 350 miles away, we expected them late in the afternoon. They arrived mid morning because they had received a message that the daughter and family had been called to Beale Air Force Base due to a medical emergency of Tom's sister, Barbara. So instead of leaving Saturday morning they left at noon on Friday and stayed the night south of San Francisco. Thus the early arrival.

We all wondered what the medical emergency was and that night Margaret called and reported what had happened. Each day she called and each day the news was like a soap opera. Tune in tomorrow to find out what happened to Barbara? Did she recover quickly? Did Helen and Herb see Margaret? Did Helen and Herb's grandchildren remain well?

What a vacation! Nothing worked out as planned. Neither Helen nor Herb saw their daughter and this was the whole point of the vacation. The Elderhostel and the visit to us were extras.

After dinner each evening we looked at slides of our trips and slides we took years ago when all four of us were single and dating. Our friendship goes back at least to 1955 for the four of us and Helen and I go back a year or two more. We all met at the Young Professionals Club of the YWCA in Niagara Falls. This club no longer exists but at one time it thrived and many are the couples who first met there and later married.

Helen and Herb are a relaxed, but responsible couple and there has never been a cross word or misunderstanding between us in all these years. Since we have been in California these twenty years, Helen and Herb have visited us three times. It is so good to be with them again. I had some tears when they left this morning. Buffalo is so far away from California. Old friends are a treasure.

Linens and towels have been washed and the bed remade. Tomorrow we'll clean the guest room and it will be ready for the next visitors. Could that be you?

SATURDAY MARCH 11,1995

Dear Halys,

For several years I wrote you about the drought here in California. Today I'm going to write about the flooding. We aren't having it near our house but it isn't too far away.

Thursday we woke to terrible winds. The TV said they were seventy five mile an hour winds. They swayed the trees. Rain was coming down in sheets. It was dark and we had to have the lights on. I was looking at the Today show when the TV went black. No electricity. I decided right then and there that I was going shopping because there wouldn't be any traffic, there would be parking spaces near the stores I wanted to go to and there wouldn't be many customers. So I left Gene home and off I went to Walnut Creek. I found nothing I wanted. I came home and we had a salad and then I went to Concord. I found a real buy, a long sleeved top for $5.99, reduced from $30. It will be just right for our October cruise.

I got home about 3 PM and we decided to take the Wongs out to dinner. The electricity still wasn't on and our house was cold and there was no way we could cook dinner. At first, they said no when I called at 1 PM. I told them to think about it and I would call later. When I got home I went over and they still said no but after a little persuading, they changed their minds and we went to a Chinese restaurant that is quite new. We were most pleasantly surprised. Every Chinese restaurant we go to I order prawns with fried walnuts. These were the best yet. In fact, everything was excellent. The appetizer was pickled Chinese turnips and I could have eat the whole dish. Dessert was a peanut soup sort of thing but not the peanut soup we serve as a soup. We'll go back there again and even the Wongs said this was excellent Chinese food. We also ordered lemon chicken. Was that wonderful! We got home about 8 PM and the electricity was on. Ten hours we didn't have it.

Friday morning Gene went bowling and right after he left I began to get cold and by the time he got home at 12:30 I was freezing. The electricity was on but the furnace just kept going on and off with just a minute in between. Gene said probably the pilot light was out and it was. He lit it and pretty soon we had heat.

This morning was dark and dreary and raining again or still. I went out again. I found a top to match some pants that aren't wine or plum or lavender. I don't know what color they are. I've been looking for a top to match and have found nothing. This $42, top was $9.99. It matches perfectly and I grabbed it. I also got dressy black pants that I can wear with my gold sweater. Again $9.99, reduced from $54. I wasn't looking for this but I certainly wasn't going to pass up such a bargain.

I still don't have what I started out for so on Monday when Gene goes to SIRS I'll go again with two pairs of pants I want to match tops to. Gene says one suitcase and so I need more than one top with these two pairs of pants. I got home at 12:30 and we had lunch and then I made hot cross buns. They have just come out of the over and we have just eaten one. They are good. In fact, I guess I'll have another.

So much for letter writing.

MARCH 15, 1995

Dear Jacqui and Will,

February 23rd when I passed thru the living room on my way to the kitchen to get breakfast, I saw the garbage man dumping our neighbor's garbage in the truck. I rushed to the garage and opened the door and the garbage man waited till I got it to the curb. Gene was still in the bathroom.

Usually the garbage man comes late in the morning so Gene always put the garbage out after breakfast. We decided if the garbage man was changing his route, we better get it out the night before. So on March 1st I reminded Gene a couple times about the garbage. As I was doing the dinner dishes, Gene attempted to pick me up, put me down and then said that I was too heavy. Because I had reminded him twice about putting out the garbage, he had decided to include me in the garbage.

Last Wednesday night Gene told me I better hide. Hide! Why? He said he just might put me in the garbage. So I made myself scarce. Marriage is a dangerous business.

Tonight is garbage night again. If you don't get another letter, you will know what has happened to me.

Yesterday I went to Rossmoor to a luncheon. Today I went for Book Review. The book was KREMLIN WIVES by a Russian whose first name was Larissa and translated by somebody named Post. An excellent book.

My reading at the moment is about Charleston. S.C. and I'm typing up notes about places we want to visit when we go for an Elderhostel on the 29th.

MARCH 16. 1995

In the March 20th issue of Time on Pg 40. I quote the last paragraph.

EVEN IN THE SIMPSON TRIAL, THERE IS A DOUBLE STANDARD. NO ONE SEEMS CONCERNED THAT ROBERT SHAPIRO, WHO HAS YOUNG CHILDREN, IS OUT MANY NIGHTS AT THE ECLIPSE, THE BEVERLY HILLS RESTAURANT OF THE MOMENT, AND NO ONE DWELLS ON JOHNNIE COCHRAN'S TROUBLED

RECORD AS A HUSBAND. THE DOUBLE STANDARD MEANS A
WORKING MOTHER NOT ONLY HAS TO WORRY THAT SOMEONE
ELSE WILL SEE HER CHILD TAKE HIS FIRST STEP WHILE SHE IS
READING A BRIEF BUT ALSO THAT IF SHE ACHIEVES SUCCESS IN
A MAN'S WORLD, HER CHILD WON'T BE THERE WHEN SHE GETS
HOME.

Shapiro, Cochran and Bailey want to appear so Godlike but they
have plenty of warts. Marcia Clark has been put down because she has
child care problems. I admire her for taking care of her children. The
defense aim is to win, no matter what dirty tricks they use. I always
thought it was how you played the game that was important, not win-
ning, especially when the defendant is almost certainly guilty. I don't
think justice will be served in this O.J. case.

Last week the Elderhostel sent a letter stating that afternoons would
be free so we can do some sightseeing. Thursday I called the Elderhostel
in Charleston to ask what the tours would be. We didn't want to overlap.
I got an answering machine that said my call would be returned. It was-
n't, so Tuesday I called again and stated this was my second call. This
morning before 7 AM the phone woke us and it was the person at
Elderhostel. They are going to send us the program of the tours they
offer. We are really looking forward to this trip to Charleston. There is so
much history connected with the place and this is ordinarily the perfect
season when flowering shrubs and flowers are in bloom.

It is now 1 PM and Gene has gone to the bank. The phone just rang
and a nice woman's voice asked if she could speak to Eugene Davidson. I
said he wasn't here right now but I was his wife and maybe I could help.
She said she had the wrong number because she was looking for her
father and he was going thru a divorce right now.

For the past week we have been getting calls around dinner time and
when we answered, nobody spoke. Has this girl called and then lost her
courage?

I'm beginning to wonder about these Eugene Davidsons. A couple
years ago Gene got a letter from a young fellow in Seattle who was looking for his father. His mother and father met at a motorcycle event in this
area and apparently he was the result of the meeting. He gave the year
and Gene had never set foot in California at that time. What kind of guys
are these Eugene Davidsons?

With that, I'll sign off.

MARCH 21, 1995

Dear Raedina,

This morning I packed my clothes for our trip to Charleston. Gene did the same. We want to see if we can take just one suitcase. Maybe.

I had to go to the library so I decided to look up Du Bose Heyward. He wrote that wonderful book, COUNTRY BUNNY AND THE LITTLE GOLD SHOES which is to Easter what THE NIGHT BEFORE CHRIST-MAS is to Christmas. Was this the same man who wrote Porgy and Bess? I checked the encyclopedias and biographical dictionaries and found all about Du Bose Heyward of PORGY AND BESS fame but there wasn't a mention of this book. So I went to the children's department and asked to see their biographical dictionaries of children's authors. Sure enough he is one and the same person. The librarian said she never connected the two. Gershwin made the opera from Heyward's story and later his play. This man comes from a distinguished family. One ancestor was a signer of the Declaration of Independence.

When I returned home, I asked Gene if he had ever heard of THE COUNTRY BUNNY AND THE LITTLE GOLD SHOES. He hadn't. It wasn't published when he was a child. It is bedtime now and after Gene and I are in bed, I'm reading THE COUNTRY BUNNY to him., so when he sees the Heyward house in Charleston, he can associate it with this book, as well as with PORGY AND BESS.

MAY 5, 1995

Dear Lois and Fred,

The alarm went off at 5 AM this morning and at 5:50 Gene and I were on our way to John Muir Hospital where Gene checked in for cataract surgery on his left eye. We had a little wait in the waiting room and then Gene was taken for preparation. After half an hour or so, I was called and told I could sit with him for awhile. Then came the anesthesiologist who explained the proceedure. As soon as he finished, the ophthalmologist arrived and I had to leave. We had been told Gene would be ready to go home about 9:30. So I took along a book. QUEEN ELIZABETH, A WOMAN WHO IS NOT AMUSED.

While I was reading, suddenly a man sat down beside me and it was the ophthalmologist who said the surgery was picture book perfect and they could have photographed it. He said they had Gene up and walking and in a short time he could go home. He said Gene's kit contained his home phone number and we could call if any questions, no matter how silly we thought they might be. He wanted us to make no guesses.

At 8:50 a nurse came to me and told me to get the car to the curb. They were dressing Gene and he would be ready very soon. I got the car and waited a few minutes and then Gene was wheeled out and brought to the car and we were home at 9AM.

I gave Gene breakfast and he decided to look at the O.J. case but he is very sleepy. I checked a few minutes after he sat down and he was sleeping sitting up, I've done the dishes and Gene is lying down now and he is asleep with the TV on. He probably will be sleepy all day.

Gene wasn't completely out. They don't want this because if he were completely out, his body might twitch while the operation was going on. The doctor's last words to Gene were that he was not to make any jokes while the operation was going on because laughter would cause his body to jiggle and it was absolutely essential that he be still. Gene's hands were tied to the gurney upon which he was operated. This was so he couldn't scratch his nose or rub his other eye.

I'm glad this is over. He will have to have his other eye done but we don't know when. Depends on the healing. This eye was the worst so he should see a bit better. Gene was near sighted but the new implanted lens will change that and make his eye normal. The doctor said Gene could do anything he wanted, except drive or strain.

Becky, the daughter of our next door neighbor, is being married in Sacramento and we received an invitation today but we shall have to decline. I keep checking on Gene. He is sleeping soundly. No matter how much noise I make, he isn't disturbed. One down, one to go.

Gene had a 9 AM appointment with the ophthalmologist this morning. He removed the metal cone that was over Gene's eye. He cleaned the eye. It is blood shot but that is to be expected. Gene will have to wear the cone only at night. Gene can't see well because the eye with the new lens doesn't fit his old glass. The doctor showed us the cataract he removed. It is quite thick and a deep amber color. It had dried up a little from yesterday. This doctor goes over things thoroughly, not once but several times. He said he was going out of town in about an hour but would be back by 4 PM tomorrow. If we needed any assistance, we were to call his office and another doctor would see Gene this weekend. He gives you confidence because you know you can always get help. I like this. Gene has another appointment Wednesday afternoon but we can call anytime if we need to, office or home.

We want the other done as soon as possible and it will be when this eye has healed. The doctor said occasionally he does both close together. Once when a Japanese woman had to return to Japan because her visa was expiring. Another time a truck driver had his two done close together. He had no income when not working, so wanted to get back to work as soon as possible. I'll be glad when the other operation is over.

As you can guess, we aren't doing much this weekend. The sun is too bright for Gene to go outdoors. He must wear special glasses for this.

Gene says the sky is so blue.
So goes our life!

JUNE 13, 1995

Dear Bonna and Wayne,

This week promises to be busy.

Sunday we drove to Maryann's for dinner. I was hesitant about going because last Friday Gene got a new lens in his glasses for his eye that has the lens replacement. He can see straight ahead very well but up or down or either side, he gets double vision. We understand this is normal because the operated eye is so different from the one which won't be operated upon till July 11th. I wanted to drive but Gene wouldn't let me. I told him to stay in the right lane and to put the car on cruise at fifty five. It all went well but I was relieved when we got home. This coming Friday Gene sees the ophthalmologist again.

Monday SIRS had their ladies luncheon and we went to that. The food was good but the entertainment just so-so. I wore a dress and that is something I seldom do.

This morning Gene had his 3rd year exam after his prostate operation. Everything was normal, thank goodness. As we walked into the urologist office., we saw him leaving an exam room and coming to the secretarial office and he saw us. He looked at us and said, "Ah. my favorite couple." I was pleased to have such a greeting.

Medical care is changing and the doctor said now people are going to have to be referred to him because of the managed care program that is being created. He had previously had an independent office. All but he and another urologist have formed a group urology office. He doesn't like to be part of such a group because the personal contact is gone. So he and another urologist share a waiting room but maintain their own staff. They also have agreed to cover for each other. We know this doctor very well and he knows us well and we could talk socially if we had enough time.

I did have a question that has nothing to do with Gene's visit. Our Chinese neighbor had a triple bypass in a Kaiser hospital the same time Gene had his cancer operation at John Muir. Last week Hing was outdoors on a warm day and he was wearing shorts and a tank top. From his neck down to the top of the tank top was this ugly red, raised incision. The raised part was about the size of my little finger. It looked terrible. It has been three years and I asked Hing if he had questioned the doctor about this incision.

He said yes and that the doctor said it was like that because he was Chinese. I didn't say anything but I never heard that Chinese people heal differently from Caucasian and I never saw any medical books stating this. So today I asked the doctor if I could ask an unrelated question to Gene's appointment. When he said go ahead, I asked. He said some people heal like this and explained about this upraised skin and how it is formed but it has nothing to do with being Chinese. So how come the Kaiser doctor told Hing this? My opinion of Kaiser was never high and it bottomed out after I heard this.

The trouble with HMOs and managed care is that they offer cut rate service in the effort to make a profit. You are on an assembly line and there is no time or inclination for a doctor to know a patient. Neither Gene nor I want that kind of care and we haven't had that kind of care. We don't belong to an HMO.

Awhile back, I read that the salary of a CEO of an HMO was two million a year. Recently I was astounded to read it was sometimes five or seven million. Seems to me a business man with no medical knowledge is reaping all the profit. Doctors aren't getting this. If I were in charge the doctors would get the millions and the CEOs the thousands the doctors get. Managed care isn't reducing costs when CEOs get salaries like this.

JUNE 14, 1995

We woke to a dark day today and before we had breakfast, it started to rain and it has rained off and on since. We NEVER have rain in June, July and August. TV news said we might have rain tomorrow too.

Before lunch, as I was going out the front door to put some letters in the mailbox for the mailman to take, a big bird flew over my head and right in the house. I called Gene and we searched the house but didn't find the bird. Gene said it probably veered off and didn't come in. After lunch I started across the living room and the bird flew just inches over my head. I was so startled, I screamed. Gene came running and was just in time to see the bird hit the ceiling in the corner of the living room and then go down behind the sofa. Gene moved the sofa but didn't find the bird.He got down on the floor and looked under the sofa. The bird flew up and then down behind a chair near the window. Gene got some plastic and leaned over the back of the chair and captured the bird. I opened the door and Gene released the bird on the porch. It was a dove. Gene said I might have been scared but my screams petrified him.

JULY 10, 1995

Dear Marge and Roy,

Today everything that could go wrong went wrong!

I arranged to pick up Connie and her granddaughter, Kate, after my 11:30 AM appointment with the podiatrist. He was only going to check on my ingrown toenail operation. I said I would be at Connie's at noon.

Upon my arrival the receptionist said I could leave and come back in half an hour because the doctor had had an emergency at the hospital and that operation had been delayed one hour and twenty minutes so he was going to be late. A waiting woman would be taken first. When the doctor returned, I was taken into an examining room where I removed my stocking. I hadn't put a bandage on the toe and it had bled all over the stocking. The doctor said it looked good but should be kept bandaged two more weeks and probably wouldn't be normal for a year. The doctor said he wanted me to put some fat on my feet! The orthopedist wants me to put fat on my hands. Both are just skin and bones and they need fat as cushions. I have more than enough cushions every place else in my body. Why can't I have fat where I need it?

As I backed out of the parking space at the medical building, I went about twenty feet and a man in an incoming car waved his arms and stopped me. He said my right front tire was very low on air and I should get to a service station as soon as possible. I had to go a whole mile before I came to a station. I parked at the air gauge and looked at the tire before I went for a service man. I saw a nail right on the top of the tire. The service man pulled out the nail and then injected some stuff to fill the hole. He ran water over it and put in air and said it was fixed. I misunderstood him and handed him $1.50. He said it was $11.50

Connie wondered where I was when I didn't show up on time but she was still waiting. On hearing my story, she decided to follow me in her car to the restaurant. Connie and I had a good lunch but Kate ate little She is a tiny eater yet she is normal size for her age. From observation I note that most children today eat very differently from my generation. I used to be amazed at what was thrown away in the school lunch rooms when I was a librarian and drew lunch room duty.

I don't give Kate birthday or Christmas presents because she gets lots at both those times. I give anytime presents, so we went to a children's book store and I had Kate pick out three books. Her grandmother decided to buy her two so she ended up with five books.

Upon arriving home, I went shopping with Gene. As we backed out of the drive the gas gauge began signaling. Gene drove to a station and the tank took 15.5 gallons and it is a 16 gallon tank. I could have run out of gas. I never check the gas gauge because that is Gene's job. From now on I will.

It is now two hours later and the phone just rang. Connie said if we had a flat tire tomorrow morning I was to call her and she would come and take us to the hospital. Gene has to be there at 6 AM for his second cataract operation. Gene is checking the tire every two hours to see if air is escaping. At that hour it would be impossible to get a cab. This is real friendship. I am so relieved. I won't worry all night about getting Gene to the hospital on time.

JULY, 11, 1995.

Gene was in pre op from 6–7 AM. The operation was over and we were on our way home a few minutes after 9. Gene is now sleeping and probably will most of the day because it take that long for the anesthesia to wear off. In ninety days Gene should be seeing well again. Hurrah!

FRIDAY, AUGUST 11, 1995

Dear Marilyn and Dave,

For two months I've badly needed a permanent but I put off having it till July 31st because I wanted my hair nice for the wedding and I wanted the permanent to still be good for the Oct. 7th cruise in Puget Sound and the British Columbia coast.

August 1st Gene and I took the Wongs on a tour of Rossmoor, ending up with a really good lunch at a Chinese restaurant. I was late in reading the newspaper and we didn't know till 10:30 that Gene's eighty six year old bowling pal, Leon, had died while on vacation in Mexico. The service was in San Francisco at noon. We couldn't cancel with the Wongs and get into San Francisco in time for the service. Everyone wondered what happened to Leon.

Wednesday, the 2nd, Gene and I had to reinvest some money from a CD. We had visited several banks but interest rates have fallen greatly and we were going to lose 2.5 % or over $200 a month and since this is part of our monthly income, we wanted to shop around and get the most we could. Each bank would offer 5 -10 more points but still we would lose $200 a month. We passed a Bank of the West which we had never been inside and decided to stop. It is on Treat Blvd. where there is no parking. So we drove into this business complex and found a place to park and started looking for the back door to the bank. There were several unmarked doors with no windows. I wasn't paying attention to the sidewalk which was a large one running the length of the building.

Suddenly my foot hit a raised corner of a cement slab and down I went. Gene had a hold of my hand but I fell anyway and I knew immediately that a bone in my hip was broken. I told Gene to get 911 and while he was in the building, people gathered around me. I was taken to John Muir. My doctor was vacationing at his home in France but one of his partners was available. After it was determined that the right femur was broken, I was taken to a room in the orthopedic wing. I had an intertrochonteric fracture of the right femur.

The doctor visited me between operations. He had just finished one and would start another. Then there was a short one and after that came my turn. I was taken to the operating room at 4:40 and arrived back in my room at 9:30 PM, after having a pin and plate inserted. The next day the doctor said I was unusual for my age. My bones are hard and firm and it took all his strength to get the pins thru the bones. He also said that my thighs have firm tissue, not the kind a person my age has. I think this is do to my exercycle. He said diet plays a large part and he assumed I ate lots of vegetables, fruit and milk. We do.

Wednesday till Monday I was in the orthopedic unit. Monday I was taken to TCU which gives a little less care. Monday night I had a roommate who also had a broken hip. She was very old and very disoriented and a diaper case. At 1 AM that night she had a bowel movement and it took almost an hour to clean her up. They had just turned out the light when she had a second B. M. at 2 AM. It wasn't till 3:30 AM before I could settle down but then she talked. Her babbling kept me awake till 6:15 AM and and then I slept till 7, forty five minutes. I was fit to be tied and said I wanted to go home, physical therapy or not. Somebody left and so a private room was available and I was moved to that after lunch. This was much better. When the doctor came Wednesday morning, I asked to go home and he said I could but I would need physical therapy home and he would arrange for that. It was very tiring just getting home, but oh, so much better. I'm not in pain unless I do the exercises I must do. I think the nerves get disturbed and that is what causes the pain. Just lying still is fine.

Recovery will be at least 12 weeks and then I hope to be able to walk again. The cruise in October had to be canceled. The doctor said I would not be up to it. Maybe not even walking.

Gene had everything ready for me. He had the wheel chair, walker, toilet seat stand that fits over the toilet and a cordless phone so I can talk on the phone anyplace in the house. Friends have sent in dessert, vegetables, a ham and flowers and plants. So I'm being treated VERY well.

Wednesday afternoon I used the cordless phone to call the daughter-in-law of Leon whom I did not know. I wasn't going to call his son at work. Leon had decided to take a week's vacation every month beginning with July. The first vacation was to Mexico where he stayed at a Club Med. He decided to go snorkeling and apparently had a heart attack and drowned. He was a good swimmer. He was found by an eleven year old boy. We'll miss Leon. He was on Gene's bowling team and they always went to the SIRS meetings together. He was a member of an athletic club and enjoyed working out. Because he was so active, everyone was surprised at his sudden death. We had Leon to dinner often and enjoyed his conversation.

I really am embarrassed. When we were married we were given a wool blanket and it has been on our bed for thirty-one years. Twice I've replaced the satin on the top and bottom but about a year ago I took it all off and didn't replace it. In the summertime we have two very light summer blankets on our bed and they are old. I meant to replace them but didn't. Now when the physical therapist comes and I have to do the exercises on the bed, those darn blankets are in view. Gene tried to cover them with the sheet today. When I'm walking again, I'll buy new summer blankets. We have plenty of good winter wool blankets for all our beds so I'm not embarrassed about blankets our guests see.

Our Chinese neighbors always have something interesting to tell. While they were visiting me in the hospital, I noticed Sue had a large bump on her forehead. They went to a Chinese wedding on Sunday. The reception was in a restaurant that had a balcony around the edge of the large room. The photographer took the bride and groom up there and took pictures. He placed a 120 roll of film in a can on the ledge and it fell off. Thirty feet below it landed right in the center of Sue's head. Sue was startled and asked who was throwing things at her. A lawyer rushed up to Sue and gave her his card. Another person said they should lay Sue on the floor and pour catsup on her forehead. Wasn't this a freak accident? She still has the bump and it is sore.

Hing was reminded of Halloween when he visited. He said on Halloween all the office employees dressed up and one woman came in a hospital gown. As she did her work, he noticed that her behind was really showing. She was a demure person so he was surprised. Then he found she had on flesh colored panty hose and so her behind really was covered. Hing said this woman got the prize that year.

Gene and I have a little game we play. Each day we mention where we were supposed to be and make some comment about the surroundings or food. Our vacation never materialized and Gene didn't get to take the wedding pictures of his great-nephew's wedding. He did take a picture of my nine inch incision that is stapled together with thirty-one metal staples. It won't take long to show these vacation pictures!

I'm so sorry spoiled our plans.

AUGUST 27, 1995

Dear Colette,

Since I'm housebound because I'm getting physical therapy at home thru Medicare, we had bridge at our house last night. I told Dawn, the physical therapist, that I would have to buy a dessert but I really wanted to make a raspberry walnut cheese cake. Dawn suggested we go to the kitchen, see the layout and figure out a way this could be done. Dawn determined that I could stand on one foot with the wheel chair back of my knees and use the mixer. If I fell, my bottom would land on the seat of the wheel chair. Gene could get out the ingredients, pour the mixture in the pan and carry it to the oven and remove it from the oven. It worked fine and what a dessert! The bottom crust was walnuts, about an inch thick. Then the cheesecake. After it was baked you put on a raspberry sauce and covered this with fresh raspberries. The recipe said it would serve 16 but eight people finished every crumb. I even sat in the wheel chair and did the dishes after they left.

Today Dawn taught me how to go up and down steps with the walker. We practiced on the one step to the front porch. Going down is fine, coming back up is hard. I also wanted to use my exercycle. Dawn helped me to do this. The seat is high and that poses a bit of a problem but now I'm allowed to use the exercycle five minutes at a time., with Gene standing beside me and helping me on and off.

I'm shedding. After the staples were removed from the incision, tape was put on. Since the incision is about 9 inches long, I have lots of tapes and these little tapes get all over the bathroom rug.

Thank you for the birthday card and get well card. The get well cards are all attached to the iron railing in the living room and the birthday cards are in the dining room on the two chests. As I lie on the sofa, I can see both.

Gene is about ready to do some errands. He will mail this after he picks up books at the library for me. I read at least one book a day. What else can I do?

OCTOBER 3, 1995

Dear Pat and Bob,

I am just devastated!

It is about an hour after the verdict of the O.J. Simpson trial was announced. We and all our friends expected a guilty verdict because we think he killed his wife and Ron Goldman. Instead a not guilty verdict.

Why? My opinion follows:

The jury was made up of 9 blacks, 2 Hispanics and 1 white, none of whom were educated enough to understand the DNA evidence which proved he was the murderer. RACE WAS THE BIG FACTOR. The jury majority was black and they held together and did not convict one of their own, even though guilty. Is this justice? I THINK NOT. From the very beginning I said there should be 6 blacks and 6 whites on the jury. Then the TWO VICTIMS WOULD HAVE BEEN REPRESENTED. As it is, the victims were NOT represented.

MONEY TALKS and Simpson had the money to hire sleazy lawyers who ignored the facts and just tried to confuse the jury and they did a good job. The fact that smooth, oily talking Cochran was the main attorney and he was black made a bond between the jurors and the attorney and was in Simpson's favor.

What does this verdict tell us? In the U.S. you can commit murder and go free provided you have money and notoriety. THE LAW IS NOT JUSTICE in the U.S. It is sickening,

Any thinking person felt Simpson was guilty. The polls showed that the majority of whites thought him guilty and some blacks but lots of blacks didn't look at the facts. All they saw was a black person being accused and they got back at the whites by declaring him not guilty. Cochran told the jury to send a message. They did and it was don't convict one of your own race, even if he is really guilty. WHAT A TERRIBLE MISCARRIAGE OF JUSTICE! I'm ashamed for the whole world to have seen how the courts in the U.S. work

Connie and Andrea from Boston are in San Francisco and tomorrow will come to see us and we'll take them to lunch. There are here for a quilt convention. At least I have something to look forward to. I'm really depressed as a result of this farce of a trial.

Oh, dear! I cannot dwell on this unfairness. Tears come and go. I keep thinking RIGHT IS RIGHT and I'm disillusioned because it didn't turn out that way.

OCTOBER 21, 1995

Dear Jacqui and Claude,

Yesterday I felt like the pre-hip fracture Norma. I went into San Francisco with Barbara to an ikebana meeting, which I have done the third Friday of each month for the last twenty years. Shig missed the meeting because her husband's funeral service was that morning. A month ago Virginia had the same hip fracture as I did when she was on vacation in Colorado so she could not go. Usually I drive but today Barbara did.

We took along my handicapped sign and found a handicapped place on Lincoln Street. I only had to walk about one hundred fifty feet.

Ponchon, my former teacher, was the demonstrator and she made six gorgeous arrangements and three huge structures. It would take pages to describe them but the most unusual I will tell you about. She took a day old baguette of French bread and hollowed it out. She inserted a small plastic dish filled with oasis. Into this she arranged yellow and orange lilies, small sunflowers and goldenrod. It was a monochromatic theme but so very pleasing. Usually ikebana arrangements are one sided and need a wall as background but this one could be used as a table center-piece.

When Barbara and I returned to her car, we found a citation on the car. We didn't understand because we had the handicapped sign and were parked in a handicapped place. It seems Friday is street sweeping day and you can't park on Lincoln in the morning. We parked at 11:45 AM. At noon you can park. I doubt that they cleaned the street in those fifteen minutes. So we have a twenty five dollar fine! Ugh! What good is a handicapped sign or parking spot if on some days it is not honored. I'm just as handicapped on Friday as any other day of the week.

Virginia and I are being treated very differently. Both Virginia and I were hospitalized for a week. Virginia was in a nursing home for a week. I could have been in TCU at the hospital for a week but after one day I asked to come home. I shared a room with a woman who was confused. I mean CONFUSED! I just couldn't take that. Virginia called the nursing home she was in a loony bin. My room with that woman was a loony bin. For the first six weeks I was housebound and had to lie with my foot ele-vated. The first week Virginia was allowed to walk with fifty percent of her weight on her foot. I wasn't allowed to do this till the 7th week. I had to use a wheel chair. Virginia was told to use a walker. I had physical ther-apy for seven weeks, Virginia only those two weeks she was hospitalized. Virginia was given a muscle relaxant. I was not. Virginia was woosey all the time, probably due to the relaxant. I wasn't. My thirty-one staples were removed at the end of the 4th week. Virginia's at the end of the first week. I was allowed a shower after the fourth week. Virginia after the sec-ond week. I was told my recovery would be 12 weeks, Virginia was told 3 months. Same difference. My eight days of hospitalization cost almost $26,000.Virginia's seven days in Colorado, $12,000. Now that is a differ-ence. I had no swelling in my leg or ankle. Virginia did. I think this is because she was allowed to put weight on her foot too soon.

Virginia and Don had tickets to JESUS CHRIST, SUPERSTAR pro-duced by the college. They gave them to Gene and me. This was the first rock opera for us and I think it will be the last. Costumes were colorful. Staging good. However the loud, ear splitting noise that was supposed to be music drowned out the vocal parts and nothing was comprehensible. There was little applause and no encores. People left before the curtain call.

NOVEMBER 2, 1995

We asked Maryann, who works at Apple, to buy us a computer and it arrived today. Now I must learn to use it. Gene is at bridge but when he comes home, he will unpack it and then we'll have to play around with it till we are proficient. That will take awhile. A computer isn't simple, like my word processor. I slit the top of the box and there was the manual. I'm signing off so I can study the manual.

CHRISTMAS SEASON 1995

Dear Andrea,

For quite some time Gene and I have realized we aren't of the 20th century. We knew of computers but we had never touched one. This is the computer age and we thought we should join the crowd.

I've had a word processor for several years but a word processor is a glorified typewriter. It is much better than a typewriter but the printing still looks like typewriter printing and computer printing looks like real printing. My Word processor hasn't been made for several years and it was hard to get ribbons. I was afraid it would break down and since parts aren't available, I'd be back to a typewriter so we decided to buy a 638 CD Macintosh Apple computer with a laser printer. A whole new world opened up to us. In the summer we took a computer course, taught on IBM machines, and we missed two important sessions because of Gene's cataract operations. The course was mostly theory and not much hands on and it covered not only word processing but database and spreadsheets. I was so dumb I didn't know what database and spreadsheets were. Now I know what they are but not how to make them.

UPS delivered the two boxes Nov 2nd and Gene put the computer, monitor and keyboard together. Then came the experimenting. I tried to make the computer do what I wanted but it wasn't simple. You do what the computer says and we have learned that our command of the English language is not the same as a computer's. I had some letters I wanted to print so on Nov. 3rd Gene attached the printer. He worked all day trying to get it to print. No soap. He was still working when we went to bed. He would read the instructions and check each thing and everything seemed to be O.K. Sunday he called the Apple hot line and told them his problem and outlined everything he had done. The Apple person listened and at the end asked Gene if he had clicked customize. He hadn't. He didn't know what customize meant. So he came and did that and I clicked printer and lo and behold a letter popped out of the printer. So we learned a new meaning for customize

A few letters I did not want to save so we looked in the instructions to see how to delete these letters. It made no sense to us. After a day or so we studied the instructions enough so that we knew we had to "throw in the trash" and then "empty the trash "in order to delete, eliminate or erase a letter. I now get a kick out of tossing Isabel, Phyllis, Jennie or whomever into the trash. You could be next to be tossed into the trash! I don't write letters to myself so I won't get tossed into the trash.

Another problem I had was with the right margin. On the word processor you set it on justification if you want a straight margin on the right. No justification in the computer manual. Our neighbors came over and tried to help us. They use an IBM at work. After a day or so we discovered it is alignment. To me margin or border would best describe what I want. I never did understand why justification was used on the word processor because justification as defined in the dictionary says nothing about margins.

All this is very confusing to a librarian. We were taught that you classify under the exact thing and you make cross references. So a librarian would have—Eliminate document see throw in the trash or erase see throw in the trash but this manual has no cross references and somehow you have to figure out what they title a subject.

Then there is the paging of the manual. Chapters are paged with two numbers. For instance chapter 3 is paged 3-20 and chapter 4 goes from 4-17. Why not just straight paging 1–300 or whatever the last page is.

Somehow maybe Gene and I will get with the 20th century but it isn't easy.

Both of us found it extremely difficult to justify the O.J. Simpson verdict.We think he killed two persons and yet he went free, not on the evidence, but because a slick lawyer advised the jury to "send a message". They did and it was a racial message and not justice. If this is justice in the 20th century, we definitely are not with it. Maybe we can attempt to get with the 20th century as far as technology is concerned but certainly not as justice is concerned.

Finally I get to the reason for this letter and that is to hope that your 1995 was a good one and that 1996 will be an excellent year for you. In addition, Gene and I say —
MERRY CHRISTMAS,

DECEMBER 26, 1995

Dear Connie and Herb,

After we retired Christmas eve, Gene asked me if I heard something. I replied that it was only a little after ten and I assumed that Santa would start on the East coast where it was then 1 AM. I assured Gene he could go to sleep because I was sure Santa would come. We saw on TV where Santa got Joe Montana out of bed to help him by throwing packages down chimneys. We don't know whether Santa came down our chimney or whether Joe threw the packages down, but they all got here.

We had a quiet Christmas with just Leta and Hal. Hal had bronchitis and couldn't talk but I made up for that by doing a lot of talking.

Our friend, Lee, is in intensive care at John Muir and Madeline was spending five hours each day at the hospital, seeing him for five minutes at a time. His future is iffy and there was talk of withdrawing the support system but his children don't want that yet. We four attended a concert in San Francisco on Sunday the 10th. Lee was found to have pneumonia on the 12th and on the 16th and 17th the doctors said he could expire on either day. His kidneys have shut down and he is conscious only minutes at a time. We can hardly believe this happened two days after we all had such a good time at the concert.

My cousin, Fred, sent a program of a play put on by the children of his church. His granddaughter, Marcy, was co-lead, being the ANGEL OF THE LORD whose name was Norma Gene. How do you like that? Gene and I did not know there was such an angel! Needless to say, neither Norma nor Gene are angels.

We had two items for Christmas dinner that everybody loved, scalloped onions and praline pumpkin pie. I've had scalloped onions before but nothing as good as these and so easy to make. A combination of pearl onion, green onions, whipping cream and Parmesan cheese is baked. This is a new recipe to me but one I'm going to use again. Not often because of the whipping cream, but definitely for special occasions The praline pumpkin pie was chosen this year because it should be made the day before. Over the crust is sprinkled praline chips. Then the pumpkin mixture and more pralines on the top. The recipe said you could decorate with whipped cream but it was pretty enough without the whipped cream. And simply delicious.

As I was writing this the phone rang and we learned that Lee just died. Two weeks ago we had no hint of this happening. How quickly things change. We are sad.

After nine days of no solid food, the stitches were removed from my mouth and on December 19th Gene and I celebrated by going out for lunch. On the square across from the restaurant was a farmer's market. We strolled thru and saw some lily blossoms, ten stalks for $4. Usually they are $1.98 a stalk. The farmer would not divide the bunch. We bought one and I made two arrangements for Betty, two for us and one for another neighbor. They weren't Christmasy but with tall bird of paradise and short lilies the arrangements were effective and eye catching. Wonderful ikebana!

JANUARY 3, 1996

Dear Emme and Ken,

We haven't made any specific New Year resolutions but the events of 1995 have reinforced the idea Gene and I had at the beginning of our marriage. At that time we decided not to wait till retirement to travel, but to live life each year as fully as possible on the means we had.

This past year, due to my fall, we missed Eric's wedding and our August vacation back East. Our October vacation to the British Columbia area had to be canceled because the doctor said I wouldn't be up to it at that date.

With 1996 we have turned the page to a new leaf on which we immediately inked in a trip to Arizona, beginning January 13th. We have also booked a Puget Sound cruise in October, similar to the one we had to cancel. Our bags are out and mine is packed except for cosmetics. We are really looking forward to Arizona and the night at the Grand Canyon. We spent our honeymoon there. This time we'll have an afternoon and a night instead of a whole week. It will be different because the honeymoon was in June and this will be winter. I hope we'll see snow at Grand Canyon. This time we know we won't take the mule trip to the bottom of the Canyon. Too many years have intervened for that.

Now that both of us are back to normal, Gene and I plan to live each day to the best of our abilities and to make plans with the expectation that these plans will materialize.

In his RAINY DAY Longfellow wrote INTO EACH LIFE SOME RAIN MUST FALL. We experienced that rain in 1995 but this is 1996 and we are living in California and sunny days are ahead, we hope.

HAPPY NEW YEAR TO YOU!

SOMETIME IN 1997

Dear Reader,

Shakespeare said in JULIUS CAESAR "There is a tide in the affairs of men, which taken at the flood, leads on to fortunes."

When I think back on my life, I see some tides which shaped my life and future.

One came in 1950 when I was offered a position as school librarian in two different places, Jamestown, N.Y. and Niagara Falls, N.Y. I had a decision to make. Jamestown offered a bigger salary but was further away from my home in Geneva, N.Y. and I thought the drive in the winter might be worse. I mulled over the pros and cons and finally decided to take the lesser salary, with perhaps an easier drive. That was one of the best decisions I ever made because it put me in the same city with an Iowa man whom I otherwise never would have met.

Another tide came when I decided to join the Young Professionals Club of the YMCA in Niagara Falls, N.Y. This club was for young, unmarried, professional people and weekly meetings were held at the Y. Lectures, discussion, field trips, camping, square dancing were some of the activities the club sponsored. I heard about this club but didn't join when I first arrived in Niagara Falls. Unmarried, out of town, intelligent young men were looking for male and female companionship not connected with bars and drinking and unattached female professionals were interested in the same. This club was a success and many couples who met at Young Pros eventually married. It was at one of these meetings I met my future husband.

The initial courtship was most satisfying. However, the course of true love never runs smoothly. Gene's reticence caused me to misunderstand his actions and thereby resulted in a nine year hiatus. Other boy friends came and went.

Sometimes I wished for the married state. To my surprise I found that some married women envied my freedom. At a certain age, I decided my fate was a single life and I adjusted and enjoyed my life style.

Another tide came along when I innocently decided to cut my Christmas card list and Gene and I got back together and married.

Both of us were satisfied with life in a suburb of Buffalo, N.Y. I liked our home so much I never wanted to move from it but a job moved us from Buffalo to Ann Arbor, Michigan, where we lived two and a half years. Again I liked our new house and I thought Ann Arbor was a wonderful city.

The tide that brought us to Ann Arbor, also transferred us to San Francisco and we settled twenty five miles away in Concord. Never did we hope, plan or expect to live in California but we have been happy here. We knew not a soul in California. Friends and relatives were all far away. With time on my hands, I wrote letters. Some of them I saved and some were lost in moving. Those saved, except for the accounts of our vacation trips which will apear in my next book, WE AREN'T RICH, comprise this book.

About the Author

NORMA LERKINS was born and lived in Geneva, New York throughout her school years, including attending William Smith College, which is a coordinate institution with Hobart College. Upon graduation, she taught junior high history for a year in Waverly, New York. After a second summer session at the School of Library Science, Syracuse University, she was qualified to serve as a provisional school librarian and moved into her chosen field.

After two more summer sessions, she received her library degree but a fifth summer session was necessary to get a New York State certificate as a school librarian. As a part history teacher, part school librarian one year was spent in Holland. New York and two years in Palymra, New York. For four years she was full time librarian at an elementary school in Poughkeepsie, New York. Upstate New York was still home, so in 1950 she went to Niagara Falls, New York, one hundred twenty five miles from Geneva. Here she stayed, serving as elementary school librarian through June 1964 when she married Eugene Davidson, an electrical engineer . For eight years they lived in Clarence, New York while Gene worked for Westinghouse in Buffalo. and Norma became a homemaker with leisure time for hobbies and reading. The next two and a half years they lived in Ann Arbor, Michigan while Gene worked for Bechtel. In January, 1975 her husband was transferred to San Francisco, California and Norma followed in March 1975 after the sale of their house. Here they presently reside.